# THE BARBARISM OF REASON

Max Weber and the Twilight of Enlightenment

The recent renewal of interest in Max Weber evidences an attempt to enlist his thought in the service of a renewed dream of Enlightenment individualism. Yet he was the first twentieth-century thinker to fully appreciate the pervasiveness and ambiguity of rationalization which threatened to undermine the hopes of the Enlightenment.

Asher Horowitz and Terry Maley present a collection of essays tracing the contemporary significance of Weber's work for the tradition of Enlightenment political thought and its critiques. In its critical inquiry into Weber's thought, *The Barbarism of Reason* continues the exploration of the limits and prospects of politics in a rationalizing society.

The first section comprises a set of both historical and philosophical reflections on the political implications of Weber's central concepts. The second section examines the institutional and historical context that framed Weber's inquiries into structures of the modern mode of domination, as well as his understanding of the nature of the modern state. Among the topics examined are Weber's strategic intervention in the development of the liberal theory of the state, the theoretical and pre-theoretical roots of his construction of the subject, and the schizophrenic structure of modern subjectivity. The third and last section attempts to trace the vicissitudes of Weber's problematic assumptions concerning rationalization, power, and disenchantment through some of the most important responses to his work in the twentieth century.

ASHER HOROWITZ is an associate professor in the Department of Political Science at York University. He is the author of *Rousseau, Nature, and History* and, with G. Horowitz, *Everywhere They Are in Chains: Political Thought from Rousseau to Marx.*

TERRY MALEY is a PhD candidate in the Department of Political Science at the University of Toronto.

ASHER HOROWITZ AND TERRY MALEY, EDITORS

# The Barbarism of Reason: Max Weber and the Twilight of Enlightenment

UNIVERSITY OF TORONTO PRESS
Toronto Buffalo London

© University of Toronto Press Incorporated 1994
Toronto Buffalo London
Reprinted in paperback 2015

ISBN 978-0-8020-0558-8 (cloth)
ISBN 978-0-8020-6980-1 (paper)

☻

Printed on acid-free paper

**Canadian Cataloguing in Publication Data**

Main entry under title:

The Barbarism of reason : Max Weber and the twilight of
enlightenment

Includes index.

ISBN 978-0-8020-0558-8 (bound)  ISBN 978-0-8020-6980-1 (pbk.)

I. Weber, Max, 1864–1920.  I. Horowitz, Asher,
1950–     . II. Maley, Terry.

B3361.Z7 B37 1994        301′.092        C94-931820-5

University of Toronto Press acknowledges the financial assistance to its publishing
program of the Canada Council and the Ontario Arts Council.

# Contents

## Part III   The Dilemmas of Rationalization

# Acknowledgments

The editors would like to thank the Social Sciences and Humanities Research Council of Canada and York University for their generous support of this project in its earlier stages. We are also grateful to Alkis Kontos for his spirited encouragement of this endeavour and for his lucid counsel. Finally, we would like to thank our editors at the University of Toronto Press, Virgil Duff and Anne Forte, for their patience and care in shepherding the manuscript through to completion.

# THE BARBARISM OF REASON

# 1

# Introduction

ASHER HOROWITZ and TERRY MALEY

I

Max Weber's work is exemplary in expressing and at least partially articulating the moment at which the Enlightenment becomes irreversibly reflective concerning its own reason. In the period of its innocence up to Nietzsche, the historical enlightenment in the European West was supremely confident that it had grasped the meaning of rationality and was also entirely sanguine about the effects of rationalization. In the contemporary world the rationality that once fought to fill the vacuum left by a *deus absconditus* increasingly appears in the guise of a malicious spirit. The empire of reason has cast off its cloak of benevolence: one need look no further than the spectre of irreversible ecosystemic damage; one need read no more than Foucault's meticulous dissection of the physiology of power.

In the tradition of Enlightenment the modern world was to be one refashioned by universal reason as a fitting habitat for its natural masters. For Kant, seeing in enlightenment the courage to call into question all that appeared to be given, the moments of reason still retained a substantial unity that preserved the hope of a concrete mediation of the actual and the ideal. In the nineteenth century, liberal thinkers such as J.S. Mill still assumed reason's power to correct and heal distortions inherited from the past. More critical thinkers such as Marx retained a persistent confidence not only in the rationalization of production, but also in the rationality of the dialectical movement of history to reveal the irrationality of modernity in its capitalist incarnation. For all of them, subjects remained, either a priori or potentially, agents of rational progress. None of them, however, had Rousseau or Nietzsche's sense, inherited by Freud, that 'the liberty of the individual is no gift of civilization.'

In Weber's work the modern world, characterized by the virtually self-propelled rationalization of every sphere of life, becomes one in which the promise of rational autonomy has fallen apart into heteronomous moments. The possibility of autonomy, for the individual and the polity, now hinges on extrarational forces. The bureaucratization of politics, together with the positivization of law, heralds 'leader democracy with a machine.' An inexorable rationalization at the very least runs perpetually ahead of its subjects' collective capacity to make sense of or to will their ends. The subjectivization of ends in the wake of the irrepressible advance of scientific culture splits political ethics into, on the one hand, the calculation of effects and, on the other, the privatization of affect. The disenchantment of the world leaves its masters in a state of dazed omnipotence.

The recent revival of Weber scholarship since roughly 1980, a revival initiated largely by social theorists and historians such as Wolfgang Mommsen, Friedrich Tennbruck, Wolfgang Schluchter, and Guenther Roth and taken up in the current work of Jürgen Habermas, has succeeded in shifting attention from Weber as either a value-neutral social scientist or a prophet of the 'iron cage' to Weber as a theorist of universal history. The careful reconstructions of the unity of Weber's works on the part of several of these scholars, as the logic of development of religious world-views, have served to distance Weber from the uses to which he was put in earlier debates over positivism. Separate from but corresponding to those earlier discussions in sociology, political theorists such as Leo Strauss and Eric Voegelin had assimilated Weber's value pluralism to a reading of the trajectory of Enlightenment political thought ending in modern nihilism. In the 1950s Strauss elaborated a critique of Weber as a value-relativist. Yet this was simply an occasion for Strauss, the traditionalist and objectivist, to return to an older pessimism, the unhappy consciousness of his version of classical political philosophy. Beginning with Parsons in the 1940s and continuing through the 1960s, many liberals, in contrast, were too often content to see Weber as a value-pluralist and a defender of the fact/value dichotomy. His name was added to those moderns who argued against *any* substantive theory of the good.

The recent renewal of interest in Weber evidences an attempt to rescue his thought from either fate and to enlist it in the service of a renewed dream of Enlightenment individualism, a dream of cognitive and emotional equipoise in which advancing capitalism celebrates itself on the eve of its third industrial/technological revolution. This renewal has focused on a Weber who is certainly no positivist, who is not simply a theorist of instrumental rationality, and who does have an idea of substantive rationality that can be reconstructed to affirm the central pillars of modern social life: the irreversibility of disenchantment, the irreducible plurality of value spheres, and the possibility of a non-foundationalist recovery of meaning in committed choice. It has, with good reason, been suggested that contemporary interpretations of Weber are internally related to current debates on the limits and grounding of liberal moral and political philosophy.[1] For Schluchter's Weber, for example, the deep structure of the modern is an immanent dualism of fact and value, the dialectical outcome of the transcendent dualisms of the era of salvation religions, the progeny of the process of disenchantment, in which an ethic of responsibility becomes truly possible for the first time. 'Only the ethic of responsibility endeavours to keep both appropriateness and efficiency in a precarious balance by a strategy of optimization ...'[2]

Yet this revival of Weber scholarship tends no longer to see Weber in terms of his critical ambivalence towards modernity. The reconstructions impute an underlying logic to Weber's comparative historical studies, a logic that, whatever its interpretive merits, quickly overshadows his concern with the discontents and contradictions inherent in the predicament of the modern individual and the modern polity. The reconstructions, wishing to affirm an ethic of responsibility, tend also to counsel adaptation to the modern world as the only rational course of action. In doing so – in revealing a practical significance in Weber's most abstract theoretical dimension, in his theory of disenchantment as rationalization – they have reaffirmed for us his central place for the political understanding of modernity. This does not mean that critics of modernity must grasp Weber's relation to enlightenment as a stage in the unfolding of nihilism. But it does indicate that Weber's questions about living in the modern world have to be repoliticized.

*The Barbarism of Reason* traces the contemporary significance of Max Weber's work for the tradition of Enlightenment political thought and critiques. It takes up the problems Weber inherited from Enlightenment political discourse, his attempts to face the disintegration of the Enlightenment project, and engages and advances the debates with Weber's ghosts that have helped shape political thought up to the present debates over post-modernism. Weber's thought is itself a dialogue with earlier figures from Kant to Nietzsche. Yet most of the interpretive commentary on Weber does not locate his thinking extensively within the traditions of political thought since the Renaissance. Reading Weber outside of this theoretical context is, to some extent, like approaching Marx while ignoring his Hegelian lineage. Conversely, practising political theory in the late twentieth century requires coming to terms with the problems Weber delineated.

The essays in this collection aim at contributing to this two-sided process – understanding Weber in the light of modern political thought and practising political theory in the light of Weber's problems – by locating elements of Weber's work within a series of critical reflections that attempt to problematize Enlightenment's identification of freedom with the subjective rationality of autonomous individuals. Political theory has, on the whole, overlooked the critical dimension inherent in Weber's historicization of the problem of rationality. *The Barbarism of Reason* takes up, once more, the exploration of the prospects and limits of politics in a rationalizing society.

Two central themes emerge in this collection. The first involves an elaboration of Weber's efforts to respond to the growing crisis of the tradition of Enlightenment. These efforts led in one direction to the impasse Wolfgang Mommsen has succinctly described as 'the maximum possible freedom through the maximum possible domination.' The second involves an attempt to go beyond Weber's impasse, still rooted in liberal individualism, in order to imagine the possibility of a post-liberal polity. Weber's historical and critical reassessment of the axiological limits of reason not only posed a problem for his own historical sociology, but it attempted to restore certain Enlightenment ideals whose philosophical bases had been radically cast into doubt. His social theory confronts the problem of the survival of individuality in an age in which the historical conditions from which it emerged were fast disappearing. Weber is the first twentieth-century thinker to appreciate fully the pervasiveness and ambiguity of the rationalization which threatened to undermine the hopes of the Enlightenment.

In redefining the nature and tasks of liberalism to correspond to a new stage in the development of capitalist rationalization, Weber inaugurates the political discourse of disenchantment. Moving, in his own estimation, beyond secularizations of religious/metaphysical world-views, no longer sharing J.S. Mill's implicit reliance upon an Aristotelian teleology, Weber's political thinking threatens to precipitate a collapse of the utopian dimension in liberal thought about the prospects for optimizing the fulfilment of individuality. This development, spreading quickly beyond liberalism, has also affected subsequent attempts to theorize the possibilities of post-liberal politics.

II

The first part of the book is an attempt to begin the contextualization of Weber's thought within the development of political thinking since the eighteenth century and up to Nietzsche. These three chapters seek to grasp Weber's significance for modern political thought by relating important aspects of his work to a series of crucial thinkers who, even when they did not influence his thinking directly or positively, did play the part of 'switchmen' who guided the development of enlightenment in the directions that laid the intellectual foundations of the world within which Weber was working. Accordingly, part one begins with a juxtaposition of Weber to central aspects of the Kantian legacy.

For Christian Lenhardt the fundamental thrust of Weber's work cannot be fully understood apart from his relation to the tradition of German Idealism. It is, specifically, Kant's critical idealism that sets the agenda for Weber's understanding of the program of enlightenment. Not only does Weber's theory of rationalization find its roots there, but it shares with Kantian critical idealism a starting-point in the subject and a rank-ordering of the sciences that privileges natural science. Perhaps most importantly, however, Kant and Weber accept a dichotomy between consequentialist and intentionalist conceptions of moral action.

Kant's critique of speculative metaphysics makes possible Weber's sociology of religion along with his intense concern for religion's 'operative conditions.' The sociology of religion together with the theory of rationalization can be seen as a continuation by other means of the Kantian program that understands enlightenment to be a negative movement in the emancipation of human beings by detaching reason from the absolute. As for Kant, for Weber also, the impossibility of a rational metaphysics poses a problem for moral theory. But Weber's moral theory departs significantly from the Kantian in its meta-ethical relativism, while Weber misunderstood the extent to which Kant's deontological ethic could after all be reconciled with a consequentialist point of view. On the basis of this misunderstanding, Weber goes far beyond even neo-Kantian philosophers such as Rickert in conflating moral theory with value theory. When this is combined with the questionable assumption that rationalization means an antagonism of values, Weber's actualization of the Kantian program of enlightenment ends up in a moral decisionism that apologetic Weber scholars cannot easily reconstruct as antifoundationalist and liberal. A comparison of Weber's value theory with Rickert's, which recognized both the necessity of a transcendental analysis of value and that values enjoy an objectivity of sorts in being shared collectively, displays the former's debt to positivism, a debt at least recognized by an earlier generation of political theorists of both the left and the right, by both Marcuse and Strauss.

The *locus classicus* in modern political thinking for a dialectical integration of public and private is to be found in Hegel's conception of ethical life in the state. For Fred Dallmayr it is Hegel's conception of *Sittlichkeit*, a conception that is not radically at odds with the Enlightenment, but a supplement to the Kantian focus on moral autonomy, that poses the central question for modern Western society and politics. For Hegel, the state must be conceived as the culmination of a will that understands and wills itself to be free. This will manifests itself in law and knows the law as its own manifestation. The *Rechtstaat* as the ethical life of the free modern individual does not stand over and against the will, but rather achieves the unification of universality with substantial individuality. At the modern antipode of this conception of the state stands Weber's value-neutral definition of the state based upon a 'legitimate' monopoly of force. Weber's modern state, which identifies rationality with effective control, is Hegel's state dissolved into its *disjecta membra*; it is the ethical state in ruins. The legitimacy attaching to Weber's conception of the state is not, as for Hegel, its ethical essence or rational core in which freedom is realized; legitimacy is simply a subjective factor added on to an effective instrumentally rational organization. Exemplified in the dialectic of bureaucracy is the split between a formal and empty rationality of rules that inevitably calls up the non-rationality of decision or power as its supplement.

Whereas for Hegel the state, as the realization of the idea of freedom, had been the embodiment of Spirit, the advance of disenchantment has rendered Weber's state in the form of a 'frozen spirit' or 'living machine.' The other side of bureaucratic rationalization is a subjectivization of beliefs divorced from public bonds. The problem for contemporary political thought is how this apparatus may be unfrozen to approximate Hegel's *Sittlichkeit*. One influential avenue has been pursued by Habermas who, although rejecting decisionism and non-cognitivism in ethics and critical of the decay of the public sphere, is unable to recover public ethical bonds because his model of a normative communications community still reflects the dilemmas of formalization emphasized by Weber. Dallmayr himself, although attentive to Hegel, but pursuing a direction that is post-metaphysical and non-essentialist, suggests a different course, one that does not privilege the model of testable cognitive claims but requires a more poetic mode of thinking capable of thematizing the life-world as a field of 'co-being' and revealing a '*minima moralia* predicated on the intrinsic mutual inherence of otherness and self-hood.'

If Weber's work cannot be appreciated in abstraction from German Idealism, it is also clear that it is informed by the dissolution of that idealism as represented by Friedrich Nietzsche, especially by Nietzsche's break with epistemology. In Mark Warren's estimation, Weber's departure from Kant draws heavily on Nietzsche's insistence that the thinking subject is constructed in culturally codified power relations. Where Kant and the Enlightenment in general had understood reason and power to be antithetical, both Nietzsche and, following him, Weber are now centrally concerned with the reasons why power does not or cannot recede as rationality becomes institutionalized. Both suggest a dialectic of enlightenment and trace its historical course in sometimes overlapping but somewhat different domains. Thus their analysis of the ways in which reason and power come to be joined supplement each other. Weber, in extending the relationship between reason and power into his analyses of the market and bureaucracy, recasts Nietzsche's insights in institutional terms, thus lending them a public and political import that is found wanting in Nietzsche himself. Yet Nietzsche and Weber both, in their understandings of reason, fail at crucial times to differentiate a 'thin' sense of rationality that stresses instrumentality and consistency from reason in its 'broad' sense – as including a reflective autonomy incompatible with domination. That they neglect this task, despite the fact that their heroic idealizations depend upon a notion of broad rationality, leads in both cases to an impasse. In Nietzsche the impasse takes the form of a one-sided prioritization of culture and the culture-hero; in Weber it leads to the pessimistic truncation of modern politics and especially to his view of liberal-democratic constitutional law as merely an institutionalization of thin rationality. For Warren a way out of both impasses is suggested by the fact that even conflicts over constitutional law presuppose a commitment to rational agency and that therefore thin rationality must always live on the broad promises that make its institutionalization possible.

III

Where the first part of the book involves discussions of Weber's dialogue with the history of enlightenment and its vicissitudes immediately behind him, the second explores the implications of the politics of disenchantment and the status of political thinking in Weber's thought directly. Weber never did produce political theory in the traditional senses of the term. The implications of this omission concern all the contributors to these three chapters, for Weber's political impulse did find expression not only directly but also by other means. His professed value-neutrality as a social scientist is actually implicated in a dense web of prior commitments, inner experience and intersubjective contexts that reach into the most abstract regions of his thought. Paradoxically, important aspects of Weber's thought – what it means to be a person in a modern world created by the Enlightenment; the relation between science and politics – may have a quite different meaning than he could have easily or fully anticipated.

David Beetham examines Weber's contribution to liberalism in the socio-political context of the turn of the century, at a critical moment in the development of that tradition. There have been two broad positions regarding Weber's relation to liberalism. Weber has been seen either as a problem for liberalism or as an analyst of the problems of liberalism. According to the former view, Weber's rejection of the tradition of natural right entailed a

rejection of the egalitarianism of classical liberalism. A liberal lacking fundamental liberal values, Weber is simply part of the broader challenge to the values
of earlier liberalism that was prevalent at the end of the nineteenth century. In
the latter view, as analyst of the problems liberalism comes to face, Weber
provides the definitive examination of the erosion of its social basis. In his
hands, liberalism comes to be reformulated as the competition of leaders in a
capitalist democracy. Beetham, however, rejects both positions as inadequate,
preferring to ask instead why Weber redefined liberalism in precisely the manner
he chose. This entails raising questions fundamental to liberalism: why is
freedom of value and for whom?

Weber's illiberal liberalism emerges more clearly in a contrast with the British
social liberals who were his contemporaries, and also with J.S. Mill, whose latent
Aristotelianism best embodies the tension identified by Macpherson between
its developmental strain and market commitments. The difference is ultimately
traceable to Weber's conception of the individual, a conception based now upon
a sociological rather than natural rights account. Weber's individualism is a
highly unnatural affair, the product of quite special historical circumstances,
the expression of an extremely confined social milieu marked by a high level of
psychic repression. In the bureaucratic age it has helped produce, individualism
has two possibilities. One is rejection of the world; the other places exemplary
individuals at the head of bureaucratic organizations. By the latter option,
democracy is justified by the scope it gives to leadership. The generalized
individualism of the heroic age of entrepreneurial capitalism now becomes the
specialized quality of the heroic leaders of an age of bureaucratic, machine
politics. In this regard, Weber's originality lies in his insight into how mass
democracy may facilitate the formation of leaders. But the space that the
bureaucratization of politics leaves to individual leaders has the consequence
of depoliticizing the masses. For Beetham, then, Weber is both a problem for
liberalism and problematic in the solutions he offers. Plebiscitary leadership
without general freedom means that Weber does not resolve Mill's dilemma.

Tracy Strong places the problem of what it means to be a person in modernity
at the centre of a discussion of the meaning of Weber's social science and its
relation to politics. North American social science has portrayed Weber as
value-neutral, but Strong notes that Weber's repeated emphasis on what it
means to be a person in a world where domination has been effectively
bureaucratized has been neglected.

The premise of Weber's social science is that it deals with objects that have
meaning for human beings. But in conferring meaning on the world, people
give it limits. Those limits are not freely chosen by us; they are, rather, given to
us by the world as it is. That world defines us as cultural beings. The fact that

we are cultural beings who confer significance on the world is, in an echo of Kant, the 'transcendental presupposition' of our existence. For Weber, this also means that we are historical beings. To engage in social science is thus to ask who and what we are, what kind of historical beings we are.

Weber's answer is that we are beings who live in a world in which domination, *Herrschaft*, has been bureaucratized and bureaucratic domination means obedience to rules without regard for persons. This is the opposite of politics, which, for Weber, consists of conflict between people. The discharge of business without regard for persons is also, Strong notes, the watchword of the market. Bureaucratization tends to encourage the domination of the market over politics. It is thus not simply a neutral or purely instrumental process. It entails the rationalization and acceptance of the division of labour, which has become the precondition of modern life.

Strong then returns to the question of what kind of person one has to be in order to make claims about knowledge in such a world. Weber recognized that in order to make claims regarding the validity of knowledge in the modern world, one must accept science as a valid pursuit. Accepting the assumption that the kind of knowledge produced by scientific inquiry is valuable means that one also has to accept the position of the professional classes within the division of labour. In other words, to do social science, one has to accept the position of the professional, middle classes; one has to accept oneself as a member of the bourgeois class. Strong argues that for Weber, this is the limit which both the scientist and the mature politician must accept if their work is to be meaningful, and not simply an empty gesture.

Terry Maley's contribution continues the inquiry into the presuppositions behind Weber's conception of the political. In one of his late essays Weber posed the problem of politics in an era of post-Enlightenment in this way: 'Given the basic fact of the irresistible advance of bureaucratization, the question about future forms of political organization can only be asked in the following way: How can one possibly save any remnants of individual freedom?'

The possibilities Weber did see, however, were conditioned by proto-Hobbesian assumptions he made about history and politics. The political assumptions are liberal; but there are also assumptions about temporality embedded in the liberalism. This interest in Weber's conception of history does not lead Maley to search for a theory of evolutionary history which implicitly resurrects the universalism of the subjectivity of the Enlightenment, in the recent fashion of Schluchter or Habermas. Instead, Maley argues that assumptions about temporality embedded in Weber's liberalism reflect, presuppose and struggle with a fragmented, even schizophrenic, experience of historical time.

In his politics, as in the methodological writings, Weber struggles to come to terms with the spatialization of historical time and the devaluation of persons characteristic of the highly bureaucratized, disenchanted liberal-democratic polities emerging in Europe at the turn of the century. It is that historical moment in which the conditions which had produced the bourgeois hero of the *Protestant Ethic* were being undermined by the very world that hero had created, and it represents the disintegration of the imaginary of modernity.

The relentless obliteration of the sphere of individual autonomy by the 'irresistible advance of bureaucratization' leads Weber to engage in a process of historical recovery, first in the *Protestant Ethic*. There, Weber recreates the mythical Puritan of the heroic age of the bourgeoisie. This fictional, nostalgic re-creation of the past represents the utopian impulse in Weber's later conception of the political actor.

In the later political reflections, Weber locates the mature political virtuoso in a foreboding, dystopian image of the future – the future as more of the present but worse. In Weber's vision of the future, historical time is not open as a horizon of possibility. Yet there is a different conception of history, open-ended, perpetually in flux, which we find in the methodology essays. Weber's own 'schizophrenic' separation of social science from politics prevents him from importing the open notion of history into his more closed 'illiberal liberalism.' It is this open, fluid conception of history which must be recovered from Weber now, in a time of momentous, world-historical change which challenges us to move beyond the politics of disenchantment.

## IV

The six chapters in the third part of the book examine the ways in which various currents of twentieth-century political thought have been exercised by Weber's dilemmas, by the problems that emerge from his richly suggestive analyses and his problematic assumptions. The first two chapters focus on the appropriation of Weber's thought by German writers during the twentieth century. Lukács, Mannheim, the Frankfurt School and Habermas all took up aspects of Weber's thought in elaborating their own critiques of the politics of disenchantment. Weber's formulations were crucial as boundaries against which critical thought sought to come to terms with the twilight of the Enlightenment's visions of modernity, its science and its politics.

In an era when Weber's conceptions of both science and liberal politics have been subjected to radical scrutiny and when, at the same moment, communism in Eastern Europe has suddenly collapsed, the fact that thinking through his work can provoke such varied and impassioned responses indicates the depth of his current significance. The last section raises the question of whether and how, in the apparent age of post-enlightenment, it is possible or indeed desirable to resuscitate the ideals of the Enlightenment project.

For Raymond Morrow, the development of left post-Weberian social theory has been dominated by the confrontation between Marx and Weber. The first fully developed version of a Marx-Weber debate took place in the very different appropriations undertaken by Karl Mannheim and by the Frankfurt School. Despite the mistaken judgment of some that Mannheim was a Weberian, and despite some similarities in his scepticism regarding proletarian revolution and rejection of a dogmatic theory of ideology, Mannheim was actually a sympathetic critic of Weber, attempting to achieve a synthesis of Weber with Marx. His later writings especially can be read as a prolonged critique of Weber's theory of bureaucracy and rationalization ending in an optimistic, three-stage model of development leading towards a politics of democratic planning in which the war of ideologies can be transcended. Methodologically, Weber's principal shortcoming versus Marx rests in his failure to advance to a structural level of sociological theory. Philosophically, Mannheim retains a counterfactual dimension rooted in a substantive understanding of reason. But the weaknesses of Mannheim's 'Marxisant Weberianism' become the starting-point for the later Frankfurt School's attempt to rethink historical materialism. Rejecting Mannheim's claim that the sociology of knowledge can transcend the materialist/idealist dichotomy, Horkheimer and Adorno, in particular, begin to look to Weber above all for an understanding of rationalization in which it is traced not to capitalism but to 'the Enlightenment conception of reason underlying modern science.' The radical but abstract negativism of Horkheimer and Adorno, although it retains a critical edge lacking in Mannheim, cannot point to the conditions of realization of the objective reason their approach shares with him over against the subjectivism of Weber. In the contemporary context it is Habermas's revival of the Marx-Weber debate that represents an attempt to heal the rivalry between the two classic exponents of post-Weberian critical sociology. Although Habermas remains largely rooted in critical theory, he converges with Mannheim in attempting to refound historical materialism via an anti-foundational theory of knowledge, in hoping to reconcile formal and substantive rationality and in pleading for participatory democracy and democratic planning.

The most extensive effort thus far to resuscitate Weber as a universal historian and in defence of modernism is to be found, as various contributors will have already alluded to, in Habermas's *Theory of Communicative Action*. Asher Horowitz looks critically at Habermas's tortuous effort to go beyond both Weber and the Frankfurt School in providing an alternative theory of the development of modern, decentred rationality in its relation to reification. According to Habermas, Weber in his account of disenchantment blurred the distinction between rationalization which, from a reworked systems-theory perspective, is taken to be the logic of development, and the reification the Frankfurt thinkers took up from Lukács's Hegelian treatment. Habermas seeks to detach the phenomena of reification, as the empirical dynamics of development, from the logic of rationalization. Disenchantment, as we have experienced it so far, may then be understood as selective. Other possibilities lie dormant in the logic of rationalization, possibilities for a communicative ethic which for Habermas are the potential achievement of all subjects of an advanced capitalist society. Yet Habermas's attempt to revive a 'utopia of reason' is ultimately premised on a slender and questionable formal unity among the value spheres Weber thought to be antagonistic. Moreover, Habermas provides no argument in the end to rule out the possibility of a selective rationalization overdetermined by both capitalism and disenchantment itself.

For Horowitz, Habermas's attempt to excise reification in thought from the history of rationalization gets itself caught not only in new forms of aporia; Habermas must simultaneously idealize the morality of the bourgeois subject, accepting it as the model of social individuality. Paradoxically, it is Weber's ambivalence regarding modernity that can serve as a reminder against a premature conflation of utopia with the logic of development and its achievements. To distinguish properly between the two moments of rationalization, between basic and surplus rationalization, Horowitz appeals both to Marcuse's theoretical strategy in *Eros and Civilization*, a strategy also aimed at an account of selective rationalization, and to his project for a libidinal rationality. In doing so, he argues for a return to a moment beyond both Weber and Habermas, for the recognition of the erotic as the basis of subjectivity and intersubjectivity.

One thing that serves to distinguish Weber from many who following in their analyses of contemporary social life is, for Gilbert Germain, his ability to retain a guarded optimism about the possibilities for some form of freedom under modern conditions. For Germain, it is the work of Jacques Ellul that reveals a potential theoretical weakness of the first order underlying Weber's optimistic moments. Weber refrains from drawing the conclusion that disenchantment is immediately and necessarily a re-enchantment. His emphasis upon the role of charisma even in the liberal-democratic state is evidence of this. Yet for Ellul, the Durkheimian and systems-theorist, modernity in the form of the technological phenomenon is immanently re-enchanted. Unlike other systems, the technological system, responding only to the call of efficiency, is no longer guided by a feedback mechanism; it has lost all 'sense' that nature is an autonomous power that can limit collective technological will. Modern society has therefore lost the capacity for self-steering and is now out of control. In these circumstances, the function of human beings is maintenance of the system and our role becomes 'custodial.' Weber was able to avoid such a conclusion not simply because of methodological differences but because he saw the technological superstructure of disenchantment resting upon the shifting grounds of conflicting valuations. For Weber, modernity retains, if not realizes, the potential for a truly heterogeneous mix of ends; the determination of ends is strictly incommensurable with the determination of means, and therefore the determination of ends remains insulated from the homogenizing effects of the technological ethos. It is this assumption that is challenged by Ellul, for whom technique fills the void created by the erasure of substantive ends. For Weber, technique can never be anything more than a mere means. Firmly in the tradition of enlightenment, Weber does not suspect that technique 'can evade its own demystifying gaze.'

In his discussion of the dialectics of disenchantment in Weber, Alkis Kontos argues for the normative significance of disenchantment as the concept upon which Weber's philosophy of history and ontological postulates rest. The latter lead Weber to look beyond the iron cage and, in an echo of Machiavelli, to see politics again as the art of the possible. But this rests on Weber's claims regarding the possibilities of re-enchantment.

The originally enchanted world was a place of mystery and wonder, where human knowledge was not a prevailing over the world or an attempt to conquer it. Yet the world of the primitive is not an adequate model for Weber's idea of enchantment. Without disenchantment there can be no moral complexity, and the full meaning of enchantment cannot be clearly seen. In Kontos's interpretation, enchantment is both a historical condition *and* a metaphor whose meaning is revealed only by looking back on the confrontation between nature and culture.

Weber's normative and ontological idea of enchantment takes its bearings from the 'imperative he assigns to the ethical choice making which promotes character formation.' The agonizing, but exhilarating, process of recreating the 'polytheistic firmament of vying ultimate claims which cannot be ... fully resolved' provides the humanizing context in which the passionate, thinking self creates meaning in a world where it may no longer be discovered. For Weber, disenchantment does not simply provoke threnodies; it also heralds new modes of being. The critique of disenchantment becomes the affirmation of a specifically human heroism for which authenticity is possible. For Kontos, the newly enchanted world liberated by disenchantment is austere, not a garden but a desert; but it is a desert in which people may now being to create their once-again-enchanted beings.

If Weber's ambivalent relationship to the Enlightenment is evident in his possible underestimation of the mystifying potential of technique or in his ambivalence with regard to the meaning and possibilities of disenchantment, it is equally traceable in his methodological and metatheoretical reflections. For Susan Hekman, although Weber embodies many themes that have dominated the post-positivist approach to social science and has, as a result, been enrolled as an ally by anti-positivists, he remains within the Enlightenment tradition in attempting to redefine the positivist program in such a way as to allow the social sciences their particular place, their own claims to objectivity and their consequent legitimacy. This effort entailed for Weber a defence of the objectivity of the 'ideal type,' and a search for a middle ground between positivists and subjectivists on the questions of objectivity and causality. But Weber's efforts to retain the subjective elements of both the objects and methods of social-science analysis end not in a relativization of the universal truth of scientific method but in a claim for equality between the natural and the social sciences. Weber, although realizing that the value of scientific truth can be no more than a transcendental presupposition, maintains that it is a value we must presuppose. He thus 'effectively returns scientific rationalism to its universal status.' From a post-modern perspective such as that of Foucault, Weber's heroic effort to challenge the Enlightenment estimation of scientific rationality is insufficiently radical. He cannot in the end fit the social sciences to the epistemological plane of the modern episteme, yet he cannot move on to the position that every discourse identifies its own criteria of truth. Weber had, in effect, deconstructed only one side of the subject/object dichotomy that post-moderns reject altogether. Rooted in the subject/object dichotomy is a second dichotomy that Weber retains: that of fact and value. It is this, construed as the silence of science on the question of values, that gives Weber his answer to the nihilism implicit in the failure of the Enlightenment project: the ethic of responsibility. Accepting the constituting subject as given, Weber could not agree with Foucault's critique of the inherently repressive humanism of the Enlightenment. He cannot see in his positivistic separation of fact and value the very creation of the iron cage.

Sheldon Wolin's seminal chapter brings together and extends issues raised by a number of previous essays. Identifying Weber as a profoundly political thinker, and thus debunking the still prevalent notion that he was a value-free sociologist, Wolin sees him instead as the founder of the post-modern form of political theory, social science. In the Western tradition of political thought, founding is the supreme political act. Theoretical founding, by contrast, has both a politics as well as a political dimension. The political dimension concerns ontological principles; the politics consists in the struggle to legitimate the ontological truths against rival theoretical claims.

Where ancient political thought had sought ultimate truths in its search for a solution to the riddle of politics, the riddle of combining perfect right with supreme power, the Enlightenment based its claim to a solution on science. But by the late nineteenth century, even as it displaced earlier forms of theorizing, it could offer no such panacea. Increasingly, vast power without right became the order of the day. It was in this context that Weber politicized social science. For Wolin, Weber's politics and social science are inseparable. In the disenchanted world where capitalism and bureaucracy restricted the theorist's ability to engage in politics, Weber's powerful political sensibility finds expression in his methodology. Politics becomes allegory; methodology becomes the new, but inadequate, form of political theory. The paradox from which Weber cannot extricate himself is that his social science can, in the end, only supply the legitimacy of fact.

## NOTES

1 Sam Whimster and Scott Lasch, eds, 'Introduction,' in *Max Weber: Rationality and Modernity* (London: Allen & Unwin 1987), 12.
2 W. Schluchter, 'The Paradox of Rationalization,' in G. Roth and W. Schluchter, *Max Weber's Vision of History* (Berkeley: University of California Press 1979), 57.

**PART I**  REASON AND DISENCHANTMENT

# 2

# Max Weber and the Legacy of Critical Idealism

## CHRISTIAN LENHARDT

Max Weber was not a philosopher, yet much of his thought cannot be understood except in relation to modern philosophy, more narrowly German idealism.[1] While his formal training in this discipline was limited to Kant's *Critique of Pure Reason*, selections of which he read in high school, and two philosophy courses audited at the University of Heidelberg during his first year of study, he had an intense interest in some of the philosophical debates of his time, appropriating them for his own purposes. I will argue in this chapter that these appropriations were not always successful. Substantively, I will look at three areas: the impact on Weber of Kant's critique of speculative reason (section II), their differing conceptualizations of the moral (section III), and Weber's value theory as it relates to Kant and the neo-Kantians (section IV). These more systematic comparisons are preceded by a short introductory discussion of alternative versions of idealism in an effort to understand why Weber was attracted to one and repelled by others (section I).

I

German Idealism after Kant splits into two strands, absolute and critical idealism. By absolute idealism what is referred to are the philosophical systems of Fichte, Hegel, and Schelling; critical idealism, on the other hand, refers to Kant after the so-called critical turn and neo-Kantianism in the nineteenth and early twentieth centuries.[2] We can isolate three distinct features of absolute idealism, features that generally occur together, forming a syndrome: (a) the absolute as the unity of being and thinking; (b) the absolute as the unity of truth, goodness, and beauty; and (c) the absolute as a philosophical system. Historically, speculative idealism went into decline after the deaths of Hegel and Schelling, boasting few adherents by the year 1900. Weber was not among them.[3] Indeed it is unlikely that he knew much about absolute idealism, except at second hand.

Kantian idealism, by contrast, is not a philosophy of the absolute. Of course Kant antedates the absolute idealists, which makes it difficult, though not impossible, to guess what his response to them might have been. That he would have rejected absolute idealism, especially in its Hegelian form, cannot be doubted. Philosophy for Kant cannot be grounded in the absolute. In an attempt to lay some distance between himself and the rationalists of his day, Wolff in particular, Kant came to consider their reliance on reason to be naive. Not that Kant was an out-and-out sceptic; he was sceptical only in comparison with the seventeenth- and eighteenth-century rationalists. One can assume he would have been no less critical of Hegel and Schelling. For Kant, our rational faculties can be relied upon, but only after a rigorous investigation during which all dogmatic uses of reason are discarded as illegitimate. Critical idealism, then, believed it had strengthened reason by cutting away what is considered to be false claims to an absolute ground.

Why was absolute idealism so unpopular after the death of its founders? Why was Hegel, whose singular importance only dawned on academic philosophy in the twentieth century, so quickly forgotten in the nineteenth? Three reasons are usually cited for this decline: Hegel's political stance was viewed as reactionary at a time of incipient liberalism and anti-monarchist leanings; Hegel sold out reason to theology, or so it seemed; and Hegel reduced all philosophers after him to intellectual lackeys. Among German academic philosophers in the nineteenth century, apolitical as they were, the second and third motives for being against Hegel seemed to prevail. Among neo-Kantians, hostility to Hegel revolved on the second reason. Most of them saw in him a force of religious counter-Enlightenment, someone who turned back the clock of progress.

Apart from the biographical fact that Weber, both as a student and professor, was associated with the neo-Kantians at Heidelberg, his ideas share some powerful structural affinities with Kantianism. Weber's theory of rationalization makes more sense within a Kantian philosophical paradigm of idealism than in any other. A case in point is the differentiation into spheres of rationality, which are not *aufgehoben* in some higher medium of oneness. The reader of Weber is unlikely to find, here or elsewhere, the typically Hegelian movement from undifferentiatedness to diremption and back to unity (on a presumably higher level). Dialectical progress of this sort is absent from Weber's thought. At least on the face of it, he presents a linear framework for a discussion of progress (which is not to say he is uncritical of it; far from it). The important point to make here is that, while rationalization proceeds within spheres (economic life, science, art, law, and so on), there is a greater tolerance of differentiation. Where Hegel's synthetic reflex twitches in every movement of thought, Weber is content with stylistic gestures such as compiling, assembling, laying rationalization patterns alongside one another – without asserting their unity. Difficult as it may be, it is possible to relate Weber's tolerance of differentiation to Kant's equally relaxed conceptualization of philosophy as a system. Both forms of tolerance are compatible.[4]

There is an element in Weber's conception of social theory which puts him even more unambiguously in the neo-Kantian camp. That element is his subjectivistic starting point. To presuppose an instrumentally rational actor is something a Kantian might do, whereas an absolute idealist would not. Individuals have values, experience the need for meanings and articulate interests. Groups do not. Subjects are also the only agents to have the ability to calculate, which makes them superior to groups. Of course Weber is careful to flesh out his concept of man in several directions and it would be wrong to label it idealist. Quite the contrary; Weber's empirical subject is a healthy mixture of value orientations and material interests. Psychologically, this subject is anything but 'idealistic.' What is idealist is the fact that he grounded his social theory on subjective premises.[5]

If one investigates Weber's idea of the moral, wondering what philosophical origin it might have, one is sent back once again to Kant rather than Hegel. Conceptually, Weber's juxtaposition of intentionalist versus consequentialist moral theories is rooted in Kant's practical philosophy, not Hegel's *Sittlichkeit*, which posits the dialectical unity of the two. Conventional wisdom has it that Kant promulgated an unmitigated *Gesinnungsethik* and that Weber departed from that by defending an ethic of responsibility. In section III, I will take a critical look at both wisdoms.

Least contested among the indebtedness to the Kantians is Weber's concept of a science of culture, which he derives from Rickert. Since scholarship on this filiation is relatively plentiful, and since interpretive disagreements are hard to find, I have decided to omit this subject except to mention its existence in passing.[6] Less explored and probably more controversial is the parallel one can draw between their conceptions of natural science. Kant and Weber, I think, agree that in terms of cognitive objectivity and certainty there is only one true science, the science of external nature. In comparison with it, the cultural sciences are poor cousins that tend to have a much lower coefficient of objectivity. Weber takes over this rank-order including the idea of privileging natural science from Kantianism. Kant himself did not have an idea of cultural science, but if he had, it would probably have taken the form Rickert gives to it. One gets the impression that a science of culture under Kantian auspices will never cease to rest on shaky foundations. Again this rank-order differs from absolute idealism where the state, history, and art all rank higher than natural science because culture is more spiritual. This affinity between Kant and positivist philosophies of science may be one of the more dubious legacies that came into its own in the twentieth century. Kantianism and positivism both take it for granted that natural science is a privileged form of cognition in comparison to which other forms of knowledge are inferior. The only difference between them – and I dare not say this is a negligible difference – is positivism's belief in the unity of science and the notion that the science of man has no choice but to try to catch up to its rich cousin. Neo-Kantians, by contrast, were prepared to live with the dualism, accepting in effect the inferiority of cultural science on a long-term basis.

Along with the methodology of the cultural sciences, what constitutes perhaps the only claim to originality on the part of the Southwest German school was its attempt to develop a theory of value. Culture and value are intimately linked. Culture represents a manifold of values. It is only natural to ask what value, in the singular, is, what the being of value is, whether it is something objective or merely a subjective whim. This was to become the central focus of the work of Windelband and, more particularly, Rickert. Although there were some non-Kantian value theories during the second half of the nineteenth century, for instance Nietzsche's, the majority were neo-Kantian in orientation.

I shall end these introductory remarks by considering if and why Weber was an idealist *tout court* and not a materialist. T.E. Willey sums up his intellectual history of the neo-Kantian movements by saying that if one compares degrees of idealism they were more idealistic than Kant himself: 'By overvaluing the power of the mind, the [neo-Kantians] consistently undervalued the force of circumstances. Their faith in noumenal freedom, always tempered in Kant by his awareness of human frailty, soared beyond their understanding of the phenomenal obstacles in their path.'[7] I doubt this is an accurate gloss on Weber, let alone the whole school, although it puts the emphasis on a potentially disabling weakness. The phrase 'power of the mind' suggests a foreshortened understanding of what idealism in the twentieth century is all about. There are at least two distinct debates between idealists and materialists, of which only one is hinted at in the passage quoted above. The first one concerns the question of whether ideas are effective or ineffective as causes of socio-political change. The second focuses on the question of how human beings, individually or collectively, constitute symbolic meanings or interpretations of their/our world and their/our place in it, and how autonomous these interpretations are.

Weber had links to both sorts of discussions but was embroiled mainly in the first, ceding the second to phenomenology. His position on the first debate is far from simple-minded. Can he be said to have 'underrated the force of circumstances' and overrated the 'power of the mind'? At the most general level, the basic drift of his historical sociology is to assess the force of circumstances so as to be able to say why specific developments occur in their spatio-temporal settings and not in others. In 'Critical Studies on the Logic of the Cultural Sciences'[8] this rump idealism, if one may call it that, manifests itself most clearly. If I understand the debate with E. Meyer and others, it was not couched in terms of freedom versus determinism, or idealism versus materialism. Rather, Weber concedes materialism's advantage but reserves the right to participate in the debate over the meaning of determinism. Let me quote Weber's 'idealist' emendation of Eduard Meyer: ' "Developmental tendency," "driving force," "obstacles" to development – all these are perfectly acceptable terms provided you keep in mind that they are conceptual in nature ... Causes constitute abstractions ... from the actual chain of causation.'[9]

In uncharacteristically dialectical fashion, Weber takes this occasion to argue that there is an irreducibly idealistic component in the conception of cause, a fact that is generally ignored by determinists. He also makes the point that causal explanation need only be adequate, which adequacy varies from discipline to discipline, the implication being that the materialist position unnecessarily projects the stringent requirements of causal analysis in the natural sciences on to the social sciences. If this is idealism, it does not strike me as offensive from a materialistic perspective, although it may be naive in other respects, especially the notion of adequacy of causal explanation.

This discussion throws light on a rarely perceived continuity between idealism and materialism: the latter, by its stress on causation, makes itself the heir and victim of some of the former's problems.[10] One has to wonder if causal analysis in the social sciences is not an anachronism in late capitalist society. Perhaps the socio-economic and cultural formations that were the subject of Weber's and Marx's investigations lent themselves to the kind of causal analysis these two thinkers were promoting, or perhaps to yet others. But complex late capitalist societies are different. In them the totality militates against causal explanation of either kind, for everything is 'equidistant from the centre' (Adorno); everything is both cause and effect.

II

Undoubtedly Weber is being idealistic because he accords such a prominent role to religion in his analysis of the transition to capitalism. Certainly on first inspection, there is a vast amount of idealism in a work like the *Protestant Ethic*. But such first impressions cannot be seriously upheld in view of Weber's claim that there is a world of difference between himself – a contemporary scholar who studies the this-worldly asceticism of a Calvinist in the late sixteenth or seventeenth century – and that person himself. In order to emphasize this difference we shall for a moment go directly to Kant for clarification.

When the post-critical Kant talked about God, immortality of the soul, and so on, he referred to these as 'ideas of reason.' By that he meant that their noumenal character was unknowable; hence only their phenomenal character can have any significance for the rational person. A rational science of nature is possible; a metaphysics as it had been traditionally understood is not. Kant's objective in the *Critique of Pure Reason* was not to affirm an idealist metaphysics, but to ground natural science by refuting scepticism. He disagreed with Hume on whether empirical knowledge of objects is necessarily subjective and idio-syncratic, or whether such knowledge can be systematically organized in accor-dance with concepts of the understanding. Kant believed such knowledge to be objective (although he initially held a different view). For him, no genuine knowledge of objects is possible except within the limits of science, which in turn rests on the twin pillars of sense perception and understanding, and only these.[11]

Speculative metaphysics or theology survives in Kant's system in an oddly curtailed form: As a query, theology will always be with us. But this query has no rational answer. Kant's thought opens a sharp cleavage between the realm of cognitive certainty, of which phenomena of perception are solely constitu-tive, and metaphysics, which gropes in the dark. Kant does believe, however, that questions about God and the soul's immortality are privileged at least in the sense that human beings keep posing them. Reason does not engage in this substitute metaphysical speculation out of proneness to error or playfulness, but because doing so fulfils a deep human need.

The ideas of reason in Kant are modelled on the concepts of the under-standing, but they have no basis in experience. God, the universe, the soul – these all have in common that they are not phenomena, but things in themselves which are unknowable while at the same time having a 'regulative' character; they 'point to' the noumenal world without being able to prove its existence. The Transcendental Dialectic of the first critique, then, is an anti-idealistic exercise in theology bashing, in keeping with the general tendency towards secularization with which the Enlightenment has since become synonymous. Marx's approving statement from the *Preface to the Critique of Hegel's Philosophy of Right* that 'the critique of religion is the premise of all criticism'[12] puts this fact in the proper perspective. I am quoting Marx to emphasize the point that he, the Hegelianizing anti-idealist, was appreciative of Kant's crucial contribution to the project of Enlightenment. So was Weber. His sociology of religion takes off from this premise. What is Weber's sociology of religion if not a continuation by different means of the Kantian programme of 'critical idealism'? What is it if not a factual inquiry into the operative conditions of religion? It is certainly not an analysis of the claims to validity raised by religion. Those who criticize Weber from a materialistic point of view for his idealism forget all that.

Those who had some familiarity with Kant in the late eighteenth and early nineteenth centuries tended to judge him by the powerful refutation of received religion and speculative metaphysics. At the time, Book II, chapter 3 of the 'Transcendental Dialectic' served as the most powerful leaven of Enlightenment thought, unmistakably influencing those who were looking for some measure of philosophical support for their vaguely irreligious feelings. No less impressive did Kant's achievement appear to counter-Enlightenment thinkers, if only because they realized that philosophy of religion would never be the same again. Hegel was among the latter. His attempt to resuscitate religion – an attempt he began with *Glaube and Wissen* (1803) and on which he never stopped working – is marked by the awareness that Kant's refutation of the three proofs of God was a turning-point in metaphysics. He realized that if he wanted to work towards a restitution of speculative theology, he had to sink his grappling-hook into this mountainous structure which was Kant's rational theology. On the face of it, Hegel does seem to go back behind Kant, notably because of the august station he was to accord religion in his later system. (Hegel's philosophy of religion is, of course, more complex than that, but here is not the place to examine it.)

In the Kantian perspective, the attempts by medieval and early modern philosophers to develop conceptions of God and immortality that are strictly rational appear misguided. In the *Critique of Pure Reason*, Kant is centrally concerned to take stock of these arguments of speculative metaphysics. He finds them wanting in the same sense that they overrate the reach of the 'speculative employment of reason.' In the context of a general critique of mind's cognitive faculties Kant examines three, namely sense experience, understanding, and reason, and finds the first two in combination adequate to their task, which consists in showing that knowledge of objects is possible through these 'two strands (*Stämme*) of human knowledge, (sense experience and understanding). By means of the first, objects are given to us; by means of the second, they are thought by us.'[13] It is otherwise with reason in its speculative use. Should we be interested in applying reason to the question of the *ens realissimum*, we find ourselves surrounded by a host of complexities. For example, what do we mean by 'most real'? What by 'being'? Is reality a predicate of God? Is being a predicate of God? Is God an object or merely an intellectual construct? None of these questions which form the staple of speculative metaphysics down to Kant's day can be satisfactorily answered by reason. Reason is equally impotent in the face of another question that has been raised in one form or another by philosophical theology since Aristotle: Must we not accept a notion of an *ens necessarium* if we pursue causal regress beyond finite, natural causes? Kant insists that our faculty of reason cannot give answers to this question either. Oddly enough, Kant's depiction of speculative reason entails the view that the human species has no learning capacity. Every individual can and must learn (that his or her speculative reason cannot know the ultimate foundation of things) and can do so only for himself or herself. I, having made this discovery, cannot pass it on to you. Rather, the rational faculty of every individual is disposed to ask the same questions about the ideas of God, immortality, and freedom, over and over again. One might be inclined to call this disposition compulsive stupidity. For Kant, however, it is typical of speculative reason to raise problems for which it has no answers to recognize that this process is part of what it means to be human. It is in this sense, then, that the ideas of God and the immortality of the soul are 'regulative' (rather than constitutive), for we come away from speculation holding nothing in our hands. There is nothing out there but the verbal confusion of traditional metaphysics and we are better off without it. The torso of metaphysics in Kant's *oeuvre* is called rational theology or rational metaphysics. As I noted above, the species cannot learn rational metaphysics; the latter cannot be handed down like a compendium on how to grow roses or make textiles with the aid of eighteenth-century steam engines. In Kant, this part of enlightenment is an ontogenetic struggle for emancipation that repeats itself in every individual as he or she reaches maturity. On the basis of the Kantian rational metaphysics, the choice in favour of religion is still possible but it can now be seen more clearly for what it is – a leap of faith.

As is well known, Kant himself made such a leap – some would even call it a *sacrificium intellectus* – in his *Critique of Practical Reason*. In his reflections on the so-called postulates of practical reason,[14] he reintroduces the idea of God that he had seemingly refuted in the first *Critique*. His justification for such an about-face? Man who intends to follow the dictates of the moral law is unable to realize them by himself. Realization presupposes the existence of God. Therefore, anybody who wishes to live a fulfilled life must assume the existence of an ultimate intelligence which is moral and which has created the world that it now controls. Its properties, according to Kant, are understanding, will, and power. These divine qualities, and only these, a moral agent must presuppose; he need not hold anything about God's essence or ontological constitution. In this manner, Kant hoped to preserve the basic theorems of his rational theology while at the same time making God a necessary component of moral action. Did he delude himself?

The incompatibilities between the rational metaphysics and the moral theology are too obvious to vanish in the face of Kant's apologetic paste-over. The tendency in Kant scholarship has always been, instead of trying to harmonize the two, to sort out just how important they are relative to each other; in other words, just how expendable one is and how inexpendable the other. Opinion on this point is sharply divided. Allan Wood, who has written books on both aspects of Kant's theology, comes to the conclusion that 'the moral side of religion is more important for Kant. He takes the moral standpoint on God and other theological issues to be the only one capable of yielding any positive results.'[5] What Wood calls importance may be the result of a word count; if so, I have no quarrel with it. More, however, is claimed here for moral theology. While Wood's assessment may well be within the letter of Kant's corpus, it is not in its spirit. Conceptually, it strikes me as spurious to distinguish between negative and positive results on the basis that Kant's rational theology leaves one empty-handed whereas moral theology does not, and then proceed to value the positive results more highly simply because they are positive. The distinction is of course correct but the valuation does not follow from it. Logically, I see nothing wrong with conceiving of growth in learning/knowledge/enlighten-ment as a movement away from errors held previously; logically, intellectual growth towards a more self-reliant, complete individual need not always be a 'positive' process where blanks and blind spots are filled with content. The precisely limited and 'lucid' place of indifference that on the Kantian view our speculative reason should occupy, the state of rest that it should enjoy, is a valuable result in my view. Is not this what the enlightenment is all about? Anyway, is not this what Kant contributed to the intellectual movement called Enlightenment?

During the first half of the nineteenth century the typical response to Kant was that while people applauded his move away from rationalist metaphysics, they were unhappy with the concession he had made in his ethics to moral theology. Many thought this step was an inconsistency. Hegel did, although he bit his tongue when articulating such criticisms, for they were not in his best considered interest. So did Heinrich Heine, who was definitely sincere when he charged Kant with selling critical idealism short. 'In general, if there was one weak link in Kant's *oeuvre*, it was this. And this remains the case even today. Hegel was only the first to put his finger on Kant's inconsistency.'[6] Despite his lack of decisiveness on this score, Kant was much more in the mainstream of the Enlightenment than his critic Hegel, whose retrograde position on religion caused him to become a 'dead dog' – one that Kautsky and Lenin would, ironically, resuscitate. Certainly for the neo-Kantians, including Weber, there was no question to whom they would look for guidance. Weber stood *outside* of religion, and analysed its workings. As well, his position is external in a temporal sense: by looking *back* at religion, he analysed its past historical shapes. Both standpoints together define Weber's distance to the subject of his science of culture. That distance is vastly greater than it ever was in Kant, and it is that distance that marks Weber's modernity (and Kant's traditionalism).

## III

What is singular about Kant's position in ethics is the fact that he combines the most rigorous conception of the ought as universal law with the idea of subjective freedom. This amalgamation is unlike anything one finds in classical Greek philosophy, utilitarianism, or rationalism, although there are of course links with some of these. Kant's is an ethic of conviction (*Gesinnungsethik*), to use Weber's terminology, insofar as it enables the moral agent to hold moral norms unconditionally. In addition – and this I suppose requires a separate train of reasoning – Kantian ethics is hostile to hedonistic and eudaemonistic moral systems alike. For Kant, only the morally good will is truly free, whereas motives like pleasure, happiness, or utility are heteronomous. In terms of moral psychology, Kant reduces legitimate moral motives to one: respect for the moral law. To adduce the often discussed example of the rich man who donates millions to sundry charities to save taxes: utilitarians would think his actions to be morally good; not Kant. If the person were motivated by love of duty, Kant would have said the generous act is morally good. Whether one or the other of the two possibilities obtains depends on the inner state (*Gesinnung*) of the agent.

In technical terms, since the Kantian prescriptive norms obligate unconditionally, his moral philosophy is called absolutistic. The individual, it seems, can become moral only by succumbing to the rule of some pre-existing law. Anticipating criticism, Kant goes out of his way to explain why that is not the case, arguing that the moral law is both self-legislated and grounded objectively in reason. This feat is accomplished mainly by Kant's famous categorical imperative, which states that an act is morally right if (a) the actor determines it freely but in such a way that (b) it can be readily/rationally adopted by others, thus (c) becoming a universal law. Colloquially, universalization obtains when an actor is convinced other people in the same situation would and ought to act as he or she would and ought to act. Kant implies that it is this universality principle that inhibits the taking or offering of bribes, stealing, and – Kant's favourite example – lying. If I engage in any form of these immoral actions, I actively contribute to the destruction of society, for I cannot wish my action to be universally accepted and emulated. To so wish would be against my particular interests as a social being, and hence irrational. Kant here presupposes a universal interest in the continuance of society or civil life that serves as a backdrop against which individual acts can be judged morally. Moral wrong is produced by the particular will going haywire, forgetting that foremost among the ends of man as a species is the maintenance of civil society; moral right in contrast is the general will that chooses in conformity with those ends.[17]

In terms of the broad but useful dichotomy between teleological and deontological conceptions of ethics, Kant subscribes to the latter. The teleological view judges the moral rightness of an action in terms of the good that ensues from it, in other words, in terms of consequences. This might be a good for the agent, for others, or for both. Utilitarianism and moral egotism are examples of teleological theories of obligation. The deontologist, by contrast, denies that the consequences of an act determine its moral rightness; rather, he believes that an action is morally right if it is based on conscience or good will. In Kant this idea takes the form of rule deontology where the criterion of rightness of an act is its conformity with a maxim or imperative. Kant, at least on a superficial reading, is a deontological monist enjoining moral agents to follow one rule, and one rule only, this rule being called categorical imperative: 'Act according to that maxim by which you can at the same time will that it should become universal law.'[18]

What underlies this dense formulation are several presuppositions that Kant spells out in greater detail. First, moral maxims must be self-legislated rather than heteronomous so that will is 'a law to itself independent of any property of the objects of volition.'[19] Second, moral agents are capable of acting according to maxims or moral principles. Third, maxims are right, if they are universalizable.

On this view, the moral rightness of an act lies not in the act itself (nor of course in its consequences), but in the maxim or rule from which the actor acts or intends to act. Hence the designation 'rule deontologist' for Kant. Some rules will meet the universality postulate, others will not. Only the first are right maxims. As far as the categorical imperative itself is concerned, it differs from other moral rules in that it is a procedure whereby the universalizability and hence the moral rightness of other maxims can be tested. It is not itself a maxim from which to act. Rather, whenever the free will intends to act on a substantive maxim, the categorical imperative is called upon to determine whether the maxim can become universal law. If the maxim passes that test, it is a valid moral rule from which to act.

A thumbnail sketch, then, of Kant's moral agent includes at a minimum the following features: He has a free will; he acts from rules (such as 'promises must be kept') rather than from impulse, irrational choice, or similar motives; he has more than a basic understanding of human nature and culture, which enables him to say with certainty whether others (to a man) can will the adoption of his maxim; he empathizes with the rest of mankind and has no trouble treating others as ends in themselves; in practical reason, he possesses an unfailing mechanism for weeding out particularistic, non-universal moral rules; and he can ignore pleasure, happiness, and other non-moral goods when exercising his moral will. Kant knew only too well how tall an order this is for some real-life moral agents, but he did not think the average person had trouble acting like his transcendental ideal-type. Moral philosophy after Kant has criticized everything from his formalism to the concept of duty, everything from his moral psychology (sympathy) to his idea of universalizability.[20]

Difficulties with this moral theory abound, and the absolute idealists were quick to jump on them. Already Hegel's early *Natural Law* essay of 1802 punctures the obnoxious formalism that characterizes Kant's doctrine of duty, and similar critical remarks can be found throughout Hegel's mature works. Kant to him is inadequate because he leaves us guessing as to what might be the content of the moral law, about which we know nothing except that it is apodictical and has a few other formal characteristics. Moreover, since Hegel's time readers have tended to question the absolutism in Kantian ethics: There seems to be an insufficient sensitivity to exceptions, mitigating circumstances, or what the ancients called prudence, which had seen a considerable resurgence in the Scottish Enlightenment. The absence of moral common sense is all the more damaging because Kant's moral universal is conceived on analogy with legislation. Judging from the first part of the *Metaphysics of Morals*, Kant knew full well that what stands between a general rule and its application in the sphere of law is a process called interpretation or legal construction. Its analogue in the moral sphere is known as prudence or moral common sense. This analogue is missing in Kant, who can therefore be said to show little sensitivity to the prudential problems of moral judgment.[21] That criticism is frequently found among assorted neo-Aristotelians; Hegel uses it only sparingly.

A third weakness, exposed first in Hegel's *Phenomenology* and *Philosophy of Right* and regurgitated time and again since, concerns the danger of self-righteousness to which Kant's principled moral agents are more prone than others. Since they are so convinced of the moral rightness of the inner law to which they are beholden, they tend to follow it blindly. Occasionally they commit acts of political foolishness, Hegel thinks. More likely than not, the moral forces that are personified by the revolutionary 'fury of destruction' are provided philosophical sustenance by Kant's moral theory. Despite his presumed Kantianism, Max Weber shared this alarmist criticism, unaware of its Hegelian origin. Weber too thought that *Gesinnungsethik* has an essentially uncontrollable inner tendency to give rise to self-righteous and destructive actions in politics. To follow moral conviction is to be blind to the unintended consequences of one's action, which blindness to Weber was a sign of moral weakness. Moral strength, especially in the political actor, consists in giving up the ethic of conviction. Modern man, whether in a position of importance or not, has to act as if he were important – as if his action did have consequences for many others – or else modern life will be threatened by rebarbarization. Unlike Kant and the philosophically sophisticated neo-Kantians of his time, Weber discussed ethics from the elitist point of view of someone whose intellectual identity is threatened by the reckless conviction of left-wing radical. In so doing, he joined the conservative *Internationale der Staatsphilosophen* founded by Hegel. Contrariwise, Kant to his undying credit has no truck with elitism of this sort.

I shall end my review of the infirmities of Kant's moral theory with some comments on his universalism and why it is perceived as a weakness. Universalism is the notion that moral practices – both at the motivational-behavioural and at the definitional-legislative level – are the same everywhere, irrespective of social context and historical time. The vantage from which this criticism is launched is that of ethical relativism. Potentially, ethical relativism is the most cancerous form of criticism: If one accepts it, it will undermine Kant's position more thoroughly than all three other weaknesses combined. Eventually nothing will be left of it. Since ethical relativism is a feature of Weber's world view, there is every reason to clarify what the term denotes.

W. Frankena provides a useful tripartite classification of ethical relativism. The first is descriptive relativism, which holds that the fundamental ethical convictions of different societies or groups within the same society differ. The second form is meta-ethical relativism, which denies that there is any 'objectively valid, rational way of justifying one ethical judgment against another.' The third is called normative relativism; it postulates that relativism should be established as a normative principle: 'What is right or good for one individual or society is not good or right for another.'[22] The third type is quite uncommon and can be ignored here. Evidence for the first kind of relativism seems so easy to come by – one need only think of cross-cultural studies on moral judgment the majority of which seem to support descriptive relativism – that it is very difficult for universalists not to be stumped by it. Once one is a descriptive relativist, the progression to meta-ethical relativism, though not a necessary corollary, is difficult to escape. Descriptive and meta-ethical relativism are roughly coeval; their origin can be traced to the beginning of ethnography and the resurgence of sceptical philosophy in the eighteenth century. Later, in the nineteenth and twentieth centuries, meta-ethical relativism became an integral part of positivist thought. Though not a dyed-in-the-wool positivist, Max Weber shared its ethical relativism. He was a descriptive as well as a meta-ethical relativist, whereas Kant was universalistic on both counts.

In view of the potentially destructive impact these two forms of relativism have on moral theory in general, they have attracted a lot of criticism from several quarters, not just philosophy. These studies, to the extent to which I understand them, converge in a critique of relativism that suggests that differences of moral judgment at the descriptive level tend to be erased by ontogenetic growth in understanding or enlightenment. From this consideration and others, Frankena concludes 'metaethical relativism has not been proved and, hence, that we need not, in our ethical judgments, give up the claim that they are objectively valid in the sense that they will be sustained by a review by all those who are free, clear-headed, fully informed ...'[23] Note the twofold nature the complementary idea of universalism has in Frankena's formulation: Not only are moral judgments universal (empirical universalism), they can also be shown to be universally valid (meta-ethical universalism). The second claim implies the possibility of an affinity between moral argumentation and other rational discourses in which knowledge is produced. This strong definition of universalism is of course compatible with Kant's position.

Since I may have misrepresented Hegel to a considerable extent by casting him in the role of the antagonist of Kant in ethical matters, I must try to qualify what I have said so far and talk about the other side of the story, namely, the continuities between them. For despite the serious reservations Hegel harboured against Kant's theory of the moral point of view, Hegel was also positively impressed by it. To the extent to which Kantian ethics effected a fusion of freedom of the will and action under a rational principle or law, Kant had achieved something that, in Hegel's judgment, was light-years ahead of the ancient Greek conceptions of ethics, and the contemporary teleological ones such as utilitarianism. In comparison with them, Kant's moral philosophy was the only game in town. If any discrete chunk of the Kantian system was sublated in Hegel's own systematic philosophy, it was neither the epistemology of critical idealism nor its aesthetics, but its practical philosophy. As I said, Hegel was intrigued by Kant's breathtaking *tour de poche* which demonstrated the dialectical unity-in-difference of moral freedom and objective constraint; he ungrudgingly acknowledged the fact that Kant epitomizes the spirit of modernity like no other ethical philosopher before him. Hence his own program of a renascence of *Sittlichkeit* was conceivable only with Kant as an ally rather than an enemy.

Critical idealism is such a towering presence in the history of German Enlightenment that one ignores it at one's peril. Hegel was far from ignoring it. In ethics, he and Kant agreed on many things but nothing as central as this: that the moral point of view is anchored in and flows from a rational faculty of the mind. Reason, they thought, helps discover what is morally right and makes the individual responsible for his action. By the same token, moral norms can be known to be right or wrong, thus constituting an object of rational cognition. In short, they share a position of meta-ethical universalism.

Before turning to Weber's thoughts on ethics, I want to take a closer look at my initial characterization of Kant as an exponent of a deonotological ethics. Of course such a portrayal is seriously in need of modification. Much has been written, especially in the last fifteen or twenty years, on the consequentialist or teleological nature of Kant's principle of universalization, as it is found in his moral doctrine.[24] Since Kant believed that the universal principles underlying right action presuppose a procedure for general adoption, he is setting up *teleological boundary conditions* within which the moral agent must act. Consequences, it can be argued, far from being unessential, are constitutive of the definition of moral rightness. 'The universalization of a maxim amounts to an imaginative projection of the consequences of a type of behaviour for the purpose one has in mind, and a right action is one whose consequences as a universal practice would not destroy the purpose that prompted the proposing of the action.'[25] What this reinterpretation does is emphasize, correctly I think, the somewhat hidden teleological import of Kant's universality postulate, enabling us to appreciate the fact that rule deontology is not as absolute as it seemed to Hegel and Weber.

Weber still construed Kant's ethic to be deontological throughout; in so doing he was merely following the *communis opinio* of Kant scholarship of his time. In that context, Weber intended his own preference for *Verantwortungsethik* to be a departure from the Kantian foundation. Only in retrospect do we realize that this departure was less incisive than Weber thought. The convergence of the two ethical theories in Kant and their divergence in Weber opens up a major contrast. Weber's unsystematic, almost casual ruminations in the essays on science and politics as vocations, as well as 'The Meaning of Ethical Neutrality,' testify to the fact that he held some views that can be called ethical; but nowhere does he develop a sustained argument for those views. The 'Ethical Neutrality' essay is replete with disclaimers to the effect that the author does not plan to defend either particular ends and values or particular ethical theories. Rather, as he expressly says, he wants to limit discussion to what he calls a 'realistic science of ethics,' focusing on the impact ethical evaluations have on non-ethical spheres such as economic life.[26] Weber is quite conscious of the fact that in this manner he will not be able to say anything about which values ought to be followed, Such abstinence comes with the scientistic territory.

So far, so good. All this is in harmony with Weber's legitimate interest in pursuing causal strategies in the analysis of modernization that had been overlooked by others or to which others were blind by design. Several 'territorial' or 'jurisdictional' problems trouble Weber's conceptualization of a science of culture. Perhaps more disabling than anything else is the shifting boundary between moral theory and value theory. In Weber, and this also is a more general trademark of neo-Kantianism as a whole, value theory tends to crowd out moral theory, of which only fragmentary notions like the split between consequentialism and deontology remain. By contrast, while Weber displays an abbreviated, if not clichéd, understanding of the problems of ethical theory, he was more familiar with value theory as it had sprung up in many philosophical quarters in Germany, that is, Nietzsche, *Lebensphilosophie*, phenomenology, and neo-Kantianism.

IV

Unlike an 'ought,' which in Kantian ethics is an unalloyed rule of right action, a value in the neo-Kantian canon is a mixture of 'is' and 'ought.' Rickert's negative definition of value is vague enough to qualify as a general neo-Kantian working definition, one that Weber certainly would have accepted: 'Values ... are neither objects nor subjects ..., neither part of the external world, nor part of the internal world, neither nature nor spirit.'[27] There is a general tendency among neo-Kantians to avoid positive definitions. Even so, it is possible to arrive at an adequate understanding of what they mean by value, if we encircle it. As a concept it is 'underivable.' When we say that value is both real and unreal we are using ordinary, non-philosophical language.[28] As a philosopher Rickert is able to distinguish the moral ends and means of an action from values – a distinction that tends to get fudged in Weber. Neo-Kantians in various degrees, and Weber more than most, stress the subjectivity of values. Objective notions of value are foreign to them. Value tends to be seen as a *value for somebody* rather than a value for a totality, or value in itself. As I said, Weber is particularly prone to this tendency, even more so than his philosophical mentor Heinrich Rickert. Valuing is more important than value itself. From the subjectivity of valuing as a process, Weber concludes – and here we come to the most exposed part of his value theory – that values cannot be grounded in reason and are therefore irrational. This gratuitous inference has prompted much shaking of heads. That this position is more than a small logical lapse is clear, for the consequences of accepting it are momentous. On this view, anybody who ever thought he could, through reasoning – that is, an appeal to a rational ground common to all human beings – make a case against tyranny or for justice or for equality before the law or for any value whatever simply falls victim to delusion. According to Weber, all these attempts to use reason as an instrument to make choices among alternative values are misguided since there is no such faculty of the mind that would correspond to that. Value rationality does not exist: Weber is adamant about this claim. It would be hard to find anyone outside the positivist camp similarly sceptical. Certainly most fellow neo-Kantians did not share Weber's view that because of their subjectivity, values were irrational.

Let us look at this position more closely. Weber's scepticism comprises some propositions that are not strictly speaking reducible to ethical relativism in its descriptive and meta-ethical forms. It would in any case be more appropriate to see his value theory as the context in which the Weberian scepticism is played out. Weber believes values always occur as a manifold and that the organization of this plurality of values is contingent at best, warlike at worst. There is no value rationality (apart from the rational assessment of the consistency of partial values and the rational anticipation of consequences). Nor is there a sense of hierarchy governing this universe of values. And yet Weber's values do *interact, forming a dynamic whole* over and above the mere manifold. I think one can capture the dynamic properties of this totality by stating that (a) values are on a footing of equality in terms of their validity (value relativism); (b) values are in conflict with each other (value antagonism); and (c) since choices have to be made between values and since we have no rational grounds for making them, the basis for choice is irrational decision (decisionism).

I should point out that in speaking of value 'antagonism' I have made a silent correction. Weber himself speaks of value 'antinomies.' Now, in the Kantian canon, antinomies are pairs of antithetical trains of reasoning, each of which is equally plausible to our rational faculty. By contrast, what Weber refers to by the term value antinomies is almost the opposite: the fact that values are equally irrational such as 'God' and 'devil' and that they fight each other to the death because it is of the nature of values to fight one another. By rejecting Weber's term and replacing it by another, I want to avert the misunderstanding that Weber theorizes in the tradition of critical idealism. He does not. It strikes me that 'antagonism' is a more descriptive term for what Weber believes exists in the realm of values. It may well be the term he might have chosen upon reflection.

It goes without saying that on this subject the gulf that separates Kant and Weber is immeasurable: Where Kant is a rationalist (of sorts), Weber is the opposite – an irrationalist (of sorts). What surprises the reader more than anything is that the sceptical-irrational turn in Weber's value theory comes about unreflectively, without forewarning, certainly without awareness on his part of the import of what he is doing. A more elaborate case can undoubtedly be made for the positions he is taking (that is, value relativism, value antagonism, and decisionism); only Weber fails to make it. Is it conceivable he thought he was reiterating received neo-Kantian opinion? If he did, he deluded himself, as I will show below in my analysis of Rickert's very different theory of value.

Again, I cannot insist strongly enough that the above propositions on value dynamics have no resemblance to Kant at all. They represent a hodgepodge of value relativism, antagonism, and decisionism. Leo Strauss rightly remarked many years ago that *proving* these sceptical assumptions would require 'an effort of the magnitude of that which went into the conception and elaboration of the *Critique of Pure Reason*; it would require a comprehensive critique of evaluating reason. What we find in fact are sketchy observations that intend to prove that this or that specific value conflict is insoluble.'[29]

There has been considerable debate on whether Weber's value theory is sceptical in all three respects or only in some of them. More particularly, the disagreement focused on the question whether Weber was a decisionist. The stakes in this debate are high: If Weber's value theory is decisionistic, it would not be possible for him, or for someone sharing his view, to identify a rational basis of one's preference for parliamentary democracy. Rather he/we would have had to have chosen his/our form of government 'for no good reason.' Conversely, if Weber's stand is not decisionistic, we could take more seriously those protoliberal leanings that he has in abundance but which he never gathers up into a coherent statement or argument. In North America opinion was about evenly divided after the Second World War between those who discerned decisionism in Weber and those who did not. Roughly, the dividing line coincided with that between sociologists (Parsons, Bendix, Roth) and assorted others. The sociologists tended to be more forgiving, excepting Weber from the charge of decisionism. The assorted others were unimpressed. It should be noted that this group spanned a wide ideological gamut, from Strauss and Voegelin on the right to Marcuse on the left.

By contrast the postwar appropriation of Weber in Germany was both simpler and more ideologically charged. Weimar sociology had drawn a sharp line between Carl Schmitt and Max Weber. This delimitation was extrapolated by most middle-of-the-road sociologists after the Second World War. Since Schmitt had collaborated with the Nazis, they felt they were even more justified than during the Weimar period in exculpating Weber, defending him against charges of irrationalism and decisionism. The only sizable contingent of scholars who refused to go along was the extreme left: the Frankfurt School, Habermas, Lukács, and many others. Habermas, on the occasion of the Heidelberg centenary of 1964, ably articulated the collective astonishment of the postwar German left in the following remarks.

I cannot help envying our American colleagues for the fact that they come from a political tradition that allows them to interpret Weber so generously, so liberally (in the two senses that this word has). As Germans on the lookout for excuses, we are only too ready to follow in their footsteps. But we mustn't. Weber's political thought has had a different history in this country. During the First World War he promoted caesarism and leader democracy, and he sided with imperialism at the time. What resulted from this during the Weimar period is the misguided liberalism of that time, a liberalism that was militant. Weber is not responsible for it ... But any attempt to come to terms with Weber in Germany in 1964 should not ignore the fact that Carl Schmitt was Weber's legitimate student (if someone proposed to call him Weber's illegitimate son, I have no objection).[30]

Habermas is absolutely correct in suggesting that Germany is a special case demanding a special response to Weber. Ironically twenty-five years later these cautionary tales are forgotten as Weber scholars everywhere, including Habermas himself, extend the same measure of largesse that was once the prerogative of the Americans. Only the Straussians have stayed the same. For a while Weber stayed a decisionistic *bête noire* in the eyes of critical theory but not forever.[31]

Leaving the problem of decisionism behind, I want to address briefly the presumed antagonism of values. Actually, Weber gave a more temporal cast to this proposition than I have indicated so far. Correctly stated, he held the view that values have grown more antagonistic under the aegis of rationalization and that they would continue to do so as rationalism advances in the future. Correspondingly, the farther we travel back in the history of Western rationalization, the more imposed harmony among values do we find – until we reach a point in our backward journey where polytheism comes into view. As modern unbelievers we find polytheism very familiar because of its high incidence of value conflict. In the West, Judeo-Christian monotheism was the great pacifier of value antagonism, but this achievement did not last forever. It was only an interlude. And now we are back to square one. Without the monotheistic religions we are in a no-man's-land, as far as the possibility of value consensus is concerned. These religions are dead.

So goes Weber's story in 'Intermediate Reflections' and 'The Meaning of Ethical Neutrality.' While it may be a suggestive story, it is dubious social science. Apologetic Weber scholars – W. Schluchter is an example here – tend to distinguish between Weber's contribution to historical sociology and his *Zeitdiagnose*. The latter is not synonymous with the genre of occasional writings, but refers more broadly to a diagnosis of the problems of the present time. As is well known, Weber interspersed such diagnostic statements in scholarly works such as *Economy and Society* and *Protestant Ethic*, rather than devoting separate pieces to the subject. Anyway, the presupposition behind the above distinction is that what Weber says, for example, about the twentieth-century crisis of values, since it is not part of his science of reality, is not subject to scholarly standards of criticism. In what follows I do not adhere to this stricture. Someone who has studied values in a historical context all his life must be able to understand how they interact in the present.

Putting the best (that is, a probabilistic) construction on Weber's idea of value antagonism, I would paraphrase him as saying that we can describe the statistical population of relations between values in any rationalized, contemporary society better by employing predicates like conflictual and hard to reconcile than by using their opposites (consensual, harmonious, etc.). Even this reformulation, which I consider an improvement over what we find in 'The Meaning of Ethical Neutrality' and 'Intermediate Reflections,' is full of holes. Is not the notion of value antagonism, however carefully recast, simply counterfactual? Does it not fail at the rudimentary level of description? 'One might describe the situation differently by suggesting that our daily affairs rest on a great many largely unspoken ideas of fair play and obligation. One might point out that when these break down there are serious and visible consequences. Indeed, one might say, were all morals to break down into dramatic, "rationally irreconcilable conflicts" ... little of what we know as modern life would continue.'[32]

Objections to the effect that somebody has his facts wrong are always more disconcerting than those that nibble at the consistency of a theoretical framework. This one against Weber strikes me as potentially deadly. Possible rejoinders are of the 'yes but' variety. While Weber would have to agree with a good part of the criticism, he might defend himself by stating that the above argument is an American argument applicable to American society (which is in all other respects, except value antagonism, a *modern* society). If the question of the antagonism or non-antagonism of values were transposed into the hypothetical form that is requisite for it to be empirically treated, presumably Weber and the argument from consensus would likely accept all of the following: A war between values and peaceful, harmonious value dynamics are opposite poles of a spectrum; most real-life cultures probably find themselves at neither end of the spectrum but somewhere in the middle; we have no terminology that maps out the middle ground; such a descriptive terminology would be desirable; what kind of dynamics between values exists can only be ascertained *a posteriori* and in the framework of a comparative analysis of concrete cultures; longitudinal data might be important if Weber's thesis about secular change – from consensus in traditional society to antagonism in rationalized society – is to be tested; finally, while we are at it, we might try to validate Weber's thesis that values in post-religious societies cannot be consensual. What gets in the way, and this is my polemical point, is the apodicticity of the claims on either side of the issue. Weber's obiter dicta on a resurgence of polytheism and on the irreconcilable nature of plural values are no less tenable than the American view that 'modern life as we know it' would cease to exist without fair play and consensus.

Weber's attempt to grapple with the dynamics of value pluralism is so grotesquely inferior to anything that you and I would come up with on the fly, as it were, that one wonders what devil – it cannot have been a god – possessed him, making him say the things he did. As I indicated, the crutch called *Zeitdiagnose* that people have generously handed to Weber to enable these ghostly ideas to walk at all is a cover-up. Weber had studied values all his life in a historical perspective, especially as they bore on religious institutions, the state, and the economy. It is not that he was new to the subject of values. Is it therefore unfair to expect him to assess how values interact in the present age more accurately or at least to suggest, as I did, a way to study value dynamics more systemically and hypothetically?

Before concluding my remarks on Weber's theory of value, I will take a brief look at Rickert's, in the hope that some of the obscurity in the former will be dispelled. Though not exclusively the product of the Southwest German School, neo-Kantian value theory is primarily associated with the names of Windelband and Rickert. In discussing Rickert's theory of value, I want to see if it generally supports Weber's at a philosophical level and if it can throw light on any or all of the following: The presumed subjectivity of values, why it is that they cannot be rationally grounded, and why there is struggle between them.[33]

Unlike Weber, Rickert began by setting himself off decisively from what he takes to be a widely accepted view on values. Although he does not affix a label to it, this view can be identified with positivism.

> The conventional view on values is that they are nontheoretical (*atheoretisch*) and incompatible with a scientific search for truth. This view is based on the presupposition that values are the product of a valuing subject, whereas truth is conceived as objective. According to this view every individual has his or her values and they are as particular as his or her inner life.[34]

Rickert's antipositivistic theory program by contrast entails the view that knowing and valuing are not strictly separable, at least at an empirical level of life.

> People who do science *strive* to understand true constructs of meaning, just as they *want* to stay clear of error. Or, which is the same, in science we *seek* the truth and *avoid* falsehood ... It follows that our conduct is an alternative taking of perspectives. When we seek something it is because the looked-for

thing has a *value* for us. It would never occur to us to look for something that has no value.[35]

Clearly, Rickert's position has a certain affinity to the view that values are subjective, but this is rather different from the positivistic usage of the term. Values for Rickert do 'exist' out there (in a specific sense that I will define presently) but without the subject they would not be experienced or known. The subject has a motivational constitution such that it is always attracted to or repelled by a specific value. Let there be no mistake: Rickert is talking about the level of empirical subjectivity, as he repeatedly reminds the reader (at 111 and 117, for example, and passim). Then there is the matter of value pairs:

> For a scientific person true and false are a *value pair* or value contrast, just as pleasure and pain, good and bad, beautiful and ugly are value pairs for human beings that are differently disposed. What is common in all these cases is that one side represents what ought to be because it is positively valuable, whereas the other side represents what ought not to be because it is negatively valued.[36]

While Rickert criticizes the positivist concept of the subjectivity of values, he cannot assert their objectivity either except if he moves in the direction of a transcendental theory. This he does. The need for a transcendental concept of value arises when we ask ourselves what sort of objectivity or reality values have. After all, values are different from nature. Rickert knows, and this he takes from Kant, that concepts like 'world,' 'reality,' or 'objectivity' cannot be applied to nature and value at the same time. If we have reserved reality for nature, we create confusion by applying it to values. This is where transcendental analysis comes in. The postulate of value reality makes sense only if we grant that it is a reality that 'we cannot experience because it is not "given." And yet the presupposition of such a value reality is inescapable. Thus we reach the idea that reality and value must be connected in an "otherworldly unity." Carried to its logical conclusion, the examination of value reality points to a new ontology or metaphysics.'[37]

In this way Rickert hoped to mitigate the much-criticized formalism of Kant's practical philosophy, giving it content. His critics were not impressed, however. Scheler, for one, pointed out that you do not leave formalism behind if you move from one level of apriorism to another. Variants of this criticism were very popular in the 1910s and '20s. Rickert himself must have realized how exposed the move to a value ontology was. In response he constructed a relational concept of value as a second line of defence. Here value is considered to be a relation between value as object and the valuing subject where both poles are equally constitutive of value as is their relation to each other. No relativity is implied, Rickert insists, in this construct, only relationality. Again relation raises a host of other logical and methodological problems which Rickert tended to brush aside.[38] The point I want to emphasize again is that Rickert developed a complex theory of values which has no analogue in Weber. The confusion Weber creates results precisely from his tendency to adopt some of the Rickertian terminology while neither being aware of its subtleties nor trying to avoid its pitfalls.

If a synopsis of Rickert's entire position on value can be made without violating its complexity, it would read something like this. (a) The pursuit of knowledge is not value-free, nor is value non-cognitive or irrelevant to knowledge. (b) Values come in antithetical pairs or logical opposites. (c) Valuing is a behavioural-attitudinal faculty of empirical subjects. (d) Expressions like reality of value, objectivity of value, and the like, point to the need for a non-scientific, non-empirical aspect of value theory called transcendental analysis.

If we now compare those points to Weber's conception of value, we see few parallels. There are echoes of point (a) in *The Methodology of the Social Sciences*, 'Science as a Vocation,' and Roscher and Knies, but Weber's position here is far from clear. Let us quote for comparative purposes a typical passage from Weber's ' "Objectivity" in the Social Sciences':

> Without the investigator's value ideas there would be no principle for selecting a subject-matter and no meaningful knowledge of concrete reality. Without *faith* in the *importance* of some specific cultural content his work would be ... utterly pointless. In short, personal beliefs of the researcher will always refract values as in a prism ...[39]

Superficially this passage is not unlike something Rickert might have written. It shows Weber echoing Rickert's notion that in the day-to-day activity of doing social (or natural) science, the researcher need not keep values at bay when selecting a field of inquiry. So far, so good. What makes Weber's value theory unsatisfactory, if not untenable, is the fact that he ignores the extent to which values are shared collectively, thus enjoying an objectivity of sorts. The social scientist does not generate them, nor are they his. Clearly, Weber's awareness that values are 'our' values rather than 'my' values is underdeveloped. It is this one-sidedness which gives the Weberian value theory its overly subjectivist cast, even when viewed from a neo-Kantian perspective.[40]

There is no evidence that Weber would have accepted point (b) about value pairs. For Rickert value pairs are logical opposites; for Weber value pairs are antagonistic opposites. Could Weber have misread Rickert so grossly on this score as to believe the latter's concept of opposites supported what he himself postulated about value antagonism? Possible, but not very likely. Whatever the case may be, Weber finds no neo-Kantian benediction when he seems to need it most badly: As a neo-Kantian, Weber is very much alone in defending the concept of values-in-struggle, and as I have argued before, he is doing a lousy job of it.

As far as points (c) and (d) are concerned, I again discern huge differences. In terms of the relativity and irrationality of values, Weber's perspective has less in common with Rickert than with the positivist conception from which Rickert separates himself. Relativity and irrationality of values are absent from the Rickertian formulation; they are not from that of Weber. What Weber holds to be the case empirically, Rickert considers to be true transcendentally: For Rickert, the subjective constitution of values does not 'cheapen' them because there is the other side of a pre-existing value reality. If one gives Rickert the proverbial benefit of the doubt, a big concession indeed, his values do not undergo 'de-objectification' or loss of reality because of the *a priori*, transcendental status of object and subject. By contrast, for Weber de-objectification is an ever-present threat in his conception of an objective science of cultural reality. Pointedly, the dilemma for Weber is how values which are defined as (necessary and legitimate) determinants of the scientist's research design can lead to knowledge of culture as the other of the subject. Does not 'the strict adherence to the principle of value freedom [entail] the logical disintegration' of the concept of being?[41] I would agree it does. To the extent to which a culture is an objective reality, the simultaneous assertion by him of free value selection is contradictory. True to form, Weber shirks this problem of what objectivity in the cultural or value sciences might be, as opposed to its meaning in, say, the natural sciences.

All things considered, Weber had a rough-and-ready value theory which found only scant philosophical backing in Rickert.[42] It would hardly distort the truth to state that Weber owed a large, unacknowledged debt to positivist value theory and a rather small one to his neo-Kantian friends.

Weber scholarship has always been marked by a search for Weber's own value position. These values are perhaps less difficult to find and reach agreement upon than is the identity of a guiding value. Did Weber subscribe to a *valeur maîtresse* which gave organization to his values, subordinating them in some hierarchy? Leo Strauss contends that war is the only candidate for this distinction.

Nothing is more revealing than the fact that Weber ... when speaking of conflict and peace, put 'peace' in quotation marks, whereas he did not take this precautionary measure when speaking of conflict. Conflict was for Weber an unambiguous thing, but peace was not: peace was phony, war is real.[43]

According to Strauss, this was the ultimate value perspective from which Weber understood politics and human life in general, reducing it in essence to ineluctable conflict. The moral corollary of such a world view is what Strauss calls a 'warrior ethic.' Hardly anyone who has read Weber and is familiar with the surrounding neo-Kantian context of Weber agrees with this interpretation. The evidence for the supposition that Weber not only positively valued war but made war his supreme value from which the manifold of life fell into place is too scant to support such a sweeping thesis. So consistent, for example, is Weber's hostility to evolutionary theory and social Darwinism that he can hardly be said to have elevated conflict above all other values.

The search for a supreme value – and war is of course not the only possible candidate – represents a sizable, complicated chapter in Weber scholarship. Certainly, today the prevailing trend is to view Weber as someone whose work is free of foundational values, value hierarchies, rank orders. His 'refusal to ground a science of social reality in any substantive predicate is today referred to as antifoundationalism.'[44] Time was when such a gloss sufficed to put Weber in the nihilist camp or in the company of self-appointed irrational anti-nihilists such as Nietzsche. Is there a way of rescuing Weber from this predicament? Or is the predicament only a pseudo-problem? My own interpretation has stressed the fact that Weber's anti-foundationalism is one possible outcome, or legitimate actualization, of the Kantian theory program. Throughout his life, Weber remained committed to the project of Enlightenment, especially its secularism, reaffirming the drift of Kant's first critique which, biographically and intellectually, was the catalyst of the young Weber's initiation to the world of thought. A century earlier this commitment might have prompted him, after a thorough analysis of the faculties of the mind, to make foundational claims for human reason, as critical idealism did. Such a philosophical strategy is no longer timely. If enlightenment, for Weber, is not a supreme value, but a more exalted one than other values – and I stress the conditional nature of the statement – then philosophy cannot ground it. As I have said before, enlightenment is a negative value, one that posits the absence of something. This something is the unity of rationalism and speculative metaphysics; colloquially, enlightenment posits the freedom of man from the absolute. Beyond that, enlightenment in its philosophical shape, that is, as critical idealism, cannot help us.

NOTES

1  As a non-philosopher, I gratefully acknowledge the assistance of the Kant scholar Claude Piché, whose eagle-eyed perusal of an earlier draft helped me correct some of the errors and ambiguities in it.

2  In this historical overview I shall follow the very able books by H. Schnädelbach, *Philosophy in Germany 1831–1933* (Cambridge 1984), T.E. Willey, *Back to Kant* (Detroit 1975), and to a smaller extent F.J. von Rintelen, *Twentieth Century Philosophy and Its Background* (Bonn 1973).

3  However, Kuno Fischer, Weber's philosophy teacher at the University of Heidelberg, had the rare distinction of being a Hegelian.

4  I have neither the intention nor the space to dwell on such a comparison here. Suffice it to point to a different interpretation by J. Habermas in his essay 'Philosophy as a Stand-in,' in K. Baynes et al., eds, *After Philosophy* (Cambridge, MA, 1987), in which Habermas argues (pp. 310–15) that Kant is just as foundationalist as Hegel. I have some doubts about that.

5  For a critique of Weber along post-Marxist, to wit, rational-choice, lines, see B. Hindess, 'Actors and Social Relations,' in S.P. Turner and M. Wardell, eds, *Sociological Theory in Transition* (London 1985).

6  Two titles must suffice: A. von Schelting, *Max Weber's Wissenschaftslehre: Logische Probleme der Kulturerkenntnis* (Tübingen 1924); P. Winch, *The Idea of a Social Science* (Cambridge 1972). See also the excellent survey by J. Habermas, 'Der Dualismus von Natur- and Geisteswissenschaften,' in Habermas, *Zur Logik der Sozialwissenschaften*, 5th ed. (Frankfurt 1982), 89–143.

7  T.E. Willey, note 2 above, 181.

8  M. Weber, *The Methodology of the Social Sciences* (Glencoe 1949), 113–88.

9  Ibid., 188 (translation changed).

10  See T.W. Adorno, 'World Spirit and Natural History,' in *Negative Dialectics* (New York 1973), 300–60.

11  A third pillar, termed 'theoretical reason' by Kant, is assigned a clearly subordinate role, that of providing a means for an economic presentation of our findings. Whether our explanatory models are 'elegant' and 'parsimonious' or simply clumsy and loquacious is of secondary importance to him.

12  R. Tucker, ed., *The Marx-Engels Reader*, 2d ed. (New York 1978), 53.

13  I. Kant, *Kritik der reinen Vernunft* (Felix Meiner Verlag 1956), 58–9 (B 30).

14  Book II, chapter 2, sections 4–6.

15  A. Wood, *Rational Theology* (Ithaca 1978), 9.

16  R. Malter, 'Neue Bücher zu Kants Rationaltheologie und Philosophie der Religion,' in *Akten des 4*. Internationalen Kant-Kongresses, special issue of *Kant-Studien* (Berlin 1974), 165.

17  The basic structure of Rousseau's *l'homme moral* is of course quite similar, as Kant acknowledges and as Ernst Cassirer documented in detail.

18  *Foundations of a Metaphysics of Morals*, trans. L.W. Beck (Indianapolis 1969), 44.

19  Ibid., 67.

20  Today, if there is one objection that is more widespread among philosophers than any other, it is that Kant, while ostensibly concerned to validate norms, employs the wrong means – rational rather than linguistic ones – to achieve this end. That, I agree, is a major liability.

21  It would be erroneous to think that Kant has no conception of common sense. He does. It is called judgment and occupies a lower station in his hierarchy of the faculties of the mind. More important in our context, Kant 'eliminates the idea of common sense entirely from his ethics ... The basically moral connotations that this concept has traditionally had are forgotten; moral common sense plays no part in Kant's system.' H.G. Gadamer, *Wahrheit und Methode*, 3d ed. (Tübingen 1972), 29. Contrary interpretations, such as that by Hannah Arendt, remain essentially unconvincing.

22  W. Frankena, *Ethics*, 2d ed. (Englewood Cliffs 1973), 109.

23  Generally, relativism had a wider following in Weber's time than today, which may be a function of the fact that developmental psychology did not exist, whereas anthropology did, and it, somewhat naively, supported relativism. Ibid., 110.

24  Cf. M.G. Singer, *Generalization in Ethics* (New York 1971), and T. Auxter, *Kant's Moral Teleology* (Chapel Hill 1982).

25  Auxter, 3.

26  M. Weber, 'The Meaning of Ethical Neutrality,' *The Methodology of the Social Sciences*, note 8 above, 13.

27  H. Rickert, *System der Philosophie* (Tübingen 1921), 11.

28  Ibid., 113–14.

29  L. Strauss, *What Is Political Philosophy?* (New York 1959), 22. For a more elaborate discussion of these points by Strauss, see his *Natural Right and History* (Chicago 1953), chap. 2.

30  J. Habermas, 'Eine Diskussionsbemerkung' (1964), in Habermas, *Zur Logik der Sozialwissenschaften*, 5th ed. (Frankfurt 1982), 84–5.

31  Habermas is an interesting case in this respect because the above interpretation of Weber as a decisionist (which he had first developed in the late 1950s in 'Scientization of Politics and Public Opinion' and to which he had held firm until the seventies) has undergone a change by 180 degrees. Along with a generally more positive assessment of Weber as an empirical theorist of rationalization, Habermas's *Theory of Communicative Action* also puts to rest the old lament about Weber's ties with political irrationalism. All of a sudden Habermas credits Weber with the insight that factual acceptance of values is deficient and must be based on what Weber calls 'ideal validity.' Questions concerning 'ideal validity' feed into social rationalization, making

it more self-conscious and problematic. Weber, says Habermas, saw the need for norms to be supported by reasons. The focus of this interpretation is Weber's debate with Rudolph Stammler and bits and pieces of the Weberian sociology of domination, especially the concept of legitimacy therein: a rather narrow textual basis, if I may say so, for a sweeping revision of one's original reading. Anyway, my general point would be that in the eighties the 'liberalization' of Weber in the eyes of his interpreters has proceeded apace with the result that hardly anyone takes pot-shots at him anymore for being a value-relativist and decisionist.

32  R. Factor and S. Turner, *Max Weber and the Dispute over Reason: A Study in Philosophy, Ethics and Politics* (London 1984), 260.

33  I am using one of Rickert's last works, titled *Grundprobleme der Philosophie*, to make this comparison, even though it came out after Weber's death. The fact is there was not all that much of an internal development; to a large degree Rickert's position on values did not change substantially after 1902.

34  H. Rickert, *Grundprobleme der Philosophie* (Tübingen 1934), 87.

35  Ibid., 86.

36  Ibid.

37  Ibid., 138–9.

38  Just how problematic the idea of value as relation is has been pointed out by numerous critics. See H. Höffding, *Der Relationsbegriff: Eine erkenntnistheoretische Untersuchung* (Leipzig 1922); O. Kraus, *Die Werttheorien: Geschichte and Kritik* (Brünn 1937); J. Salomaa, *The Category of Relation* (Helsinki 1929); S. Pepper, *The Sources of Value* (Berkeley 1958).

39  Translation modified; italics in the original but not in the English edition by E. Shils. Compare M. Weber, *Gesammelte Aufsätze zur Wissenschaftslehre* (Tübingen 1951), 182.

40  For an analysis of this problem, but one that reaches a different conclusion, see H. Brunn, *Science, Values and Politics in Max Weber's Methodology* (Copenhagen 1972), 120–44.

41  Ibid., 133.

42  The conception of a science of culture is a different matter. Here the impact of Rickert's *Grenzen der Naturwissenschaftlichen Begriffsbildung* (1902) is more directly traceable.

43  *Natural Right and History*, 64–5.

44  S. Whimster and S. Lash, eds, *Max Weber, Rationality and Modernity* (London 1987), editors' introduction, 12.

# 3

# Max Weber and the Modern State

## FRED DALLMAYR

We are today the heirs – the reluctant heirs – of Max Weber. In bold and penetrating strokes, his sprawling opus pinpointed the sinews of our restless strivings as well as our frustrations. It was Max Weber who, in the opening decades of this century, captured the path of Western society as a process of relentless rationalization geared towards growing efficiency – a process of which we are both the beneficiaries and the targets or victims. With his notion of 'disenchantment,' Weber laid bare the motor or inner dynamism of Western progress seen as man's ascendancy over nature and the world – a dynamism which undergirds both the West's technological triumphs and our growing sense of alienation and 'anomie.' In the political arena, his theory of bureaucracy or rational-administrative control has been largely predictive of twentieth-century developments, quite independently of the excesses of totalitarianism. Bureaucratic control, in Weber's view, was coupled with or buttressed by individual subjectivism, that is, by the steady atomization of society and the privatization of beliefs and preferences. In the latter respect, his work supplemented, and drew the lessons from, the Nietzschean 'twilight of the idols' construed as the erosion or demise of publicly binding standards and absolute principles in favour of private choices and willful decisions. As he observed in his 'Science as a Vocation,' elaborating on the notion of disenchantment: 'Precisely the ultimate and most sublime values have retreated from public life either into the transcendental realm of mystic life or into the brotherliness of direct personal relationships – in either case into the realm of privacy divorced from public bonds.'[1]

It cannot be my ambition here to review the broad spectrum of Weber's teachings, despite their close interconnectedness. For present purposes I want to focus instead on his conception of the modern state, that is, on the state characterized by effective bureaucratic management. As it seems to me, Weber's formulations in this domain have acquired for us nearly canonical status or the status of truisms. In an effort to unsettle these truisms or their seeming self-evidence, I shall initially approach my topic indirectly or through (what may appear as) a lengthy detour: namely, through a return to Hegel. In his *Philosophy of Right*, Hegel had articulated a conception of the state and public life which – perhaps for the last time – paid tribute to the classical tradition of Western rationalism and thus to those 'ultimate and most sublime values' which, according to 'Science as a Vocation,' later retreated from the public scene. Following a condensed synopsis of the core themes of Hegel's treatise, I shall profile against this backdrop Weber's view of the modern state as a mode of rational domination, particularly legal and bureaucratic domination, and his construal of public legitimation as an expression of subjective beliefs or sentiments. A major issue which will emerge at this point is the contrast or conflict between formal-bureaucratic reason and political unreason or between procedural rationality and substantive-ethical whim. By way of conclusion I shall explore various paths pointing beyond Weberian dilemmas or antinomies – paths which, without being merely restorative or retrospective, promise a recovery of public reason and of public ethical bonds. Attention will be given at this juncture to Habermas's ambivalent position or response: that is, his endorsement of Weber's theory of rationalization (including the division of modern 'value spheres') and his simultaneous rejection of ethical 'decisionism' (or non-cognitivism). My own reflections in this field lead me to a reconsideration of the 'life-world' and its relation to politics and ethics.

I

As presented in the *Philosophy of Right,* Hegel's conception of the state has a captivating though alien ring to contemporary ears: the notion of the state as embodiment of ethics or 'ethical life' (*Sittlichkeit*) seems alluring but far removed from experience. The distance is compounded by Hegel's affirmative style. 'The state,' he writes, 'is the actuality (or reality) of the ethical idea (*sittliche Idee*); it is the ethical spirit qua substantial will manifest and transparent to itself, a will knowing and thinking itself and accomplishing what it knows and insofar as it knows it.' Clearly a formidable and daunting sentence – one containing *in nuce* all the distinct premises and complex insights of Hegelian philosophy (and of German idealism in general). Packed into the sentence is a view of reason or rationality as human self-consciousness and moral autonomy (actualized through human will) and, as a corollary, a theory of modernity or modernization according to which consciousness, extricated from nature and blind habits, finds free expression and concrete embodiment in the structures of the modern state. Moreover, as formulated by Hegel, moral autonomy and human will are by no means divorced from consciousness or reason; instead, ethical life is precisely the medium where reason and will are joined, that is, where knowing and doing, theory and praxis, are intimately combined. These notions – and particularly the linkage of the state with rational autonomy and freedom – are underscored by Hegel in the paragraph which follows immediately the preceding sentence: 'The state is absolutely rational inasmuch as it is the actuality of the substantial will which consists in particular self-consciousness as it is raised to consciousness of its universality. This substantial unity is an absolute unmoved end in itself in which freedom comes to its supreme right.'[2]

It is not my goal in this context to disentangle the dense thicket of Hegelian thought; however, a few clarifying comments seem in order. How does the modern state come to represent rationality (even 'absolute' rationality) and simultaneously the 'substantive will' and the 'supreme right' of freedom? What is the place or status of the state in the *Philosophy of Right*? This place emerges in the course of a complex web of arguments (of which I can only provide some hints). Basically, for Hegel, the state is the culmination of reason or the idea of the 'rational will,' that is, of a free will which does not simply factually exist but rather wills itself as free. The expression or manifestation of rational free will is '*Recht*' in the broad sense – which can be variously translated as 'law' or 'right.' In Hegel's words: 'A being or *Dasein* of any sort embodying the free will, this is what right (*Recht*) is. Right therefore is by definition freedom as idea.' In his *Philosophy of Right* Hegel traces the unfolding of rational will over three main stages. The first is the stage of rational will in its immediacy or pure givenness – which finds expression in abstract or formal law (*abstraktes Recht*) with its focus on property and contractual relationships. The second stage is that of rational will as internally self-reflected or subjectively conscious of itself; hence, this is the level of subjective will thematized under the heading of 'morality' (*Moralität*) and focused on conscience, intentionality, and guilt. The third and final stage mediates and unifies abstract law and morality while preserving their respective 'truths.' This is the stage of ethical life or *Sittlichkeit*, of rational free will 'in and for itself' or willing itself as free. Ethical life in turn is subdivided into the three dimensions of family, civil society, and 'state' – dimensions which reveal a further development of rational freedom. As Hegel writes, stressing the ascending path of reason: 'Morality and formal law are two abstract moments whose truth is *Sittlichkeit* alone. Hence ethical life is the unity of the will in its (abstract) concept with the will of the individual or subject.' Similarly, he notes the ascendancy from family over civil society to state: 'The state, however, is the third stage, the stage of *Sittlichkeit* and spirit where the prodigious unification of self-subsistent individuality with universal substantiality has been achieved.'[3]

In stressing the primacy of *Sittlichkeit* over morality and formal law Hegel's

*Philosophy of Right* clearly deviates from and amends Kant's practical philosophy; yet the discrepancy is not radical. Looked at from the vantage of modernity or modernization, Hegel's system does not so much cancel as rather supplement and complete the Kantian focus – and that of the Enlightenment in general – on critical rationality and moral autonomy. Instead of construing the legal order merely as a boundary or external limitation of individual autonomy, Hegel's approach treats *Sittlichkeit* as the fulfilment and inner essence of reason and subjective will (or subjectivity). As the *Philosophy of Right* states: 'The crucial point in both the Kantian and the more broadly accepted definition of *Recht* ... is "the *restriction* (*Beschränkung*) which makes it possible for my freedom or self-will to co-exist with the self-will or caprice of each and all according to a universal law." ' This definition, Hegel elaborates, has basically a 'negative or restrictive' character, while the positive element – the reference to universality or the so-called law of reason (*Vernunftgesetz*) – amounts to no more than 'the principle of non-contradiction' and the 'familiar notion of abstract identity.' The entire conception, he adds, derives from the view 'popularized since Rousseau' according to which 'what is primary, substantive and fundamental is not the rational will in and for itself, not spirit as *true* spirit' but rather 'the will of a particular individual, the will of the single person in his or her idiosyncratic caprice.' Once this outlook is adopted, reason or the rational can come on the scene 'only as a restriction of this individual freedom and thus not as something immanently rational' but only as 'an external, abstractly formal universality.' This critique of Enlightenment rationalism is continued in the next paragraph, which asserts dramatically: '*Recht* is something *sacred as such* because it represents the being (*Dasein*) of the absolute concept and of self-conscious freedom.'[4]

As indicated, the modern state for Hegel is the culmination of *Sittlichkeit* or the ethical idea which, in turn, is the embodiment of rational autonomy and moral freedom. Some of the distinct accents of this view deserve brief comment. In articulating his conception, Hegel opposes a number of alternative formulations – in particular the conflation of the state with 'civil society,' that is, its reduction to the arena of competing individual wills or the competitive pursuit of self-interest. In this context, Hegel also criticizes the contractarian tradition which derives the state from the agreement of isolated individuals (a legacy still operative in Rousseau's 'general will'). More importantly, *Philosophy of Right* sharply challenges empiricist or historicist construals according to which the state is simply a contingent historical entity with given resources and empirical capabilities. In particularly vehement language, the treatise attacks the identification of the state with a mode of power or domination – the notion that the state reflects the social struggle for survival where the big fish eat the little fish or (in Hegel's terms) where 'the mightier or more powerful rules, must rule and always will rule.' It is clear, Hegel observes at this point, 'in which sense "might" is taken here: it is not the might of justice and *Sittlichkeit*, but only the irrational power of brute force.' This observation is amplified in one of Hegel's most celebrated (and most controversial) textual additions: 'The state is in and by itself the ethical whole, the actualization of freedom; and it is an absolute end of reason that freedom should be actual. The state is spirit standing in the world and consciously realizing itself there ... It is the march of God in the world which makes the state what it is; its ground is the power of reason actualizing itself as will.'[5]

II

The point of the above was not to offer a full-fledged exegesis but only to recall some Hegelian themes. Let me now shift swiftly and without transition to Max Weber and his conception of the modern state. We find this conception succinctly profiled in his *Economy and Society* in the introductory chapter, 'Basic Sociological Concepts.' 'A ruling or dominating organization (*Herrschaftsverband*),' Weber states, 'will be called "political" insofar as its existence and order are continuously safeguarded within a given territorial area by the threat and application of physical force on the part of the administrative staff. A compulsory political organization with continuous administrative operations (*politischer Anstaltsbetrieb*) will be called a "state" insofar as its administrative staff successfully upholds the claim to have the monopoly of the legitimate use of physical force in the enforcement of its order.'[6] Read immediately after the cited passages from *Philosophy of Right*, Weber's statements seem like a cold shower. In these statements and elsewhere, Weber looks at the state not as a philosopher – and certainly not as a moral philosopher – but rather as a sociologist, that is, as a 'value-neutral' social scientist analysing or describing an empirical object domain (in this case the administrative organization called 'state'). With its focus on the monopoly of physical force and its identification of rationality with effective control, Weber's conception (we might say) presents the Hegelian idea of the state 'in ruins' or dissolved into its *disjecta membra*. As it happens, contemporary readers are so accustomed or habituated to ruins that Weber's outlook appears to us as completely 'natural' when compared with Hegel's far-fetched or stilted-speculative approach. What is at issue, however, is more than merely a speculative view of the state – for the latter is intimately connected with modern notions of reason and moral autonomy.

Let us look more closely at Weber's definitions. As indicated, the state for Weber is a compulsory administrative organization or '*Anstaltsbetrieb*' where *Betrieb* means an enterprise engaged in a 'continuous purposive-rational activity

(*Zweckhandeln*) of a particular kind,' and where *Anstalt* means an organization whose statutory order, within specified parameters, can be imposed successfully on every member or inhabitant. As an *Anstaltsbetrieb*, the state is thus basically a purposive-rational (or instrumental-rational) enterprise endowed with a monopoly of physical compulsion or with the capacity to monopolize successfully the (legitimate) use of force in a given territory. Moreover, according to Weber, the state is also a type of a ruling or 'dominating organization' or '*Herrschaftsverband*'; and here we have to take into account his definitions of power (*Macht*) and domination (*Herrschaft*). In the terms of the same introductory chapter, power (*Macht*) is 'the probability that one actor within a social relationship will be in a position to carry out his own will despite resistance (irrespective of the basis on which this probability rests)'; more specifically, domination (*Herrschaft*) is 'the probability that a command with a given content will be obeyed by a given group of people.' This amounts to saying that the state's monopoly of physical compulsion ultimately rests on a command or an imperative (rather than a Hegelian 'idea') – despite the fact that the state's internal operation has the character of an *Anstaltsverband*, that is, of an orderly enterprise with a statutory order geared towards rational efficiency and general predictability of behaviour.'[7]

To be sure, my account so far has neglected an important element in Weber's conception. *Economy and Society* does not merely say that the state has a monopoly of physical power, but that it has a *legitimate* monopoly or a monopoly of the *legitimate* use of such power. This requires attention to Weber's theory of legitimacy or legitimation. One thing, however, should be noted right away: despite his stress on legitimacy, Weber does not treat the latter as the rational core or the ethical 'essence' of the state but rather as a 'subjective' factor or evaluation added on to the state seen as a compulsory *Anstaltsbetrieb*. In other words: legitimacy is viewed as a set of subjective beliefs or a psychological state of mind – a set which can be studied by the sociologist in the same value-neutral manner as the organizational structure of the state itself. This conclusion is evident already from the manner in which Weber introduces the topic of legitimacy, namely, in his discussion of social action. 'Action, especially social action which involves a social relationship, may be guided by the belief (*Vorstellung*) in the existence of a legitimate order. The probability that action will actually be so guided will be called the validity (*Geltung*) of the order in question.' From here Weber moves on to his famous classification of types of legitimate order – types which in every case are predicated or premised on subjective beliefs, emotions, values, or states of mind. The legitimacy of a public order, he says, may be secured or guaranteed in two basic ways. On the one hand, the warrant may be of a 'purely internal (*innerlich*)' character, being either 'affectual' (or emotional) or 'value-rational' (that is, prompted by 'belief in the absolute validity' of the order) or else 'religious' (linking obedience with divine salvation). On the other hand, the order may be secured externally, that is, by the 'expectation of specific effects' which, in turn, are assessed in terms of interest situations.[8] The distinction between internal and external warrants should not mislead us at this point because both affects or beliefs and expectations are subjective dispositions or states of mind. No doubt, Weber would have ranked Hegel's notion of the state as ethical idea under the 'value-rational' category; but, of course, for Hegel the state's *Sittlichkeit* was not simply a subjective belief but the core of its definition. Clearly, something important or dramatic had happened in the interval between Hegel and Weber (something which provisionally may be described as an advance or 'progress' of disenchantment).

Based on the preceding classification of legitimating warrants, Weber proceeds to his formulation of different modes of public legitimacy or legitimation – each mode being assigned or attributed by participants to the order in question. The actors or participants, we read, may 'ascribe' legitimacy to a social order by virtue of 'tradition' (which validates what 'has always been'), or of 'affectual belief' (devoted to the revealed or exemplary), or of 'value-rational belief' (a deduction from absolute premises), or finally by virtue of 'positive enactment' (which is assumed to be legal or to have the force of 'legality'). For Weber, the most important or relevant type of legitimacy in the modern age is the one premised on positive enactment or legality. Just as his action theory treats purposive-rational (*zweckrational*) action as the standard case from which other action types are seen as deviations, so his theory of legitimate order takes as prototypical (at least in modernity) the model of a deliberately constructed legal order governed by positive enactments or formal law. The origins of this legal order are traced either to an explicit social contract or agreement among participants or else to an act of imposition by a dominating power, with the dividing line between the two alternatives being fluid. As he writes: 'Today the most common form of legitimacy is the belief in legality, the compliance with enactments which are *formally* correct and which have been made in the accustomed manner; in this respect, the distinction between an order derived from voluntary agreement and one imposed from above is only relative.' Legality obviously refers to a rule- or law-governed social order – which brings into view Weber's notion of 'law' or 'right' (*Recht*). In terms of rule-governance, *Economy and Society* distinguishes between convention and law in the strict sense. While convention is an informal fabric of norms whose violation occasions disapproval, positive law is said to be externally sanctioned 'by the probability that physical or psychological coercion will be applied by a specially appointed staff of people in order to bring about compliance or punish violation.' Thus, far from embodying the idea of freedom (in Hegel's sense), law or *Recht* for Weber denotes a framework of formal (and not substantively rational) rules maintained or enforced by a legal and administrative apparatus. In his words: 'For our purposes the concept "law" will be made to turn on the presence of a staff engaged in the enforcement (of rules).'9

Weber's conception of legal order or *'legale Herrschaft'* – which is closely joined with his view of the modern state – is spelled out more fully in a later chapter of *Economy and Society* headed 'Types of Legitimate Domination.' The chapter initially repeats the earlier definition of domination (*Herrschaft*) to the effect that the latter signifies 'the probability that specific commands (or all commands) will be obeyed by a given group of people.' Compliance with commands may be based on diverse motives; in ordinary life, these motives may range from habit, to calculation of material advantages, to broader speculative grounds. Yet, Weber notes: 'Custom, personal advantage, purely affectual or ideal (value-rational) motives of solidarity do not form a sufficiently viable basis for a given domination; a further element is normally added: the belief in legitimacy (*Legitimitätsglaube*).' At this point, the chapter offers a new and streamlined classification of legitimate orders and modes of legitimation focused on three pure or 'ideal types.' Viewed ideal-typically, Weber observes, the legitimacy of a social order may be based on 'traditional,' 'charismatic,' or 'rational' grounds, giving rise respectively to traditional, charismatic, or legal forms of rule or domination. While the first type rests on 'everyday belief in the sanctity of immemorial traditions,' and whereas charismatic leadership depends on 'the exceptional sanctity, heroism or exemplary character of a person and of the normative order revealed or ordained by him,' legal rule reflects the 'belief in the legality of the enacted rules and the right of those elevated to authority under such rules to issue commands.' In terms of the earlier scheme, charis-matic order seems to rely on affectual sentiments (or else a combination of affective, religious, and value-rational motives). As in the previous context, Weber portrays legal rule or domination as the standard case in the modern age or as the crucial emblem of the modern state; in his own words: 'The specifically modern type of administration is deliberately taken here as point of departure, in order to make it possible later to contrast it with the others.' Established on 'rational' grounds, legal order or rule coincides basically with rational order or formally rational authority (in the sense that reason demands a formally consistent system of rules). At this juncture, the chapter offers a detailed list of the constitutive ingredients of rational or legal order – among which these factors stand out: a 'continuous rule-bound conduct' of official business; a specified 'sphere of competence'; a hierarchical structure of organization; and a specially trained administrative staff.10

The last item brings into view the central feature of the modern state seen as a rational-legal order: the role of bureaucracy. According to *Economy and Society*, modern bureaucracy with its statutory rules and clearly defined modes of competence is the prototype of rational organization – in the sense that non-rational elements are marginalized or pushed to the boundary of the system (namely, to the level of executive fiat). 'Experience shows universally,' Weber asserts, 'that the purely bureaucratic type of administrative organization – that is, the monocratic variety of bureaucracy – is, from a purely technical point of view, capable of attaining the highest degree of efficiency and is in this sense formally the most rational known means of exercising authority over human beings.' Bureaucracy's superiority over other forms of rule resides in its greater precision, the rigour of its discipline, and particularly in the 'high degree of calculability of results for the heads of the organization.' In Weber's view, modernization or the rise of modern social structures coincides basically with 'the development and continual spread of bureaucratic administration'; in fact, this development is said to be 'at the root of the modern Western state.' The primary source of bureaucracy's ascendancy and sway in modernity is its reliance on expertise or on technical-professional knowledge, in lieu of habit, guesswork, or caprice; to this extent, bureaucratic organization means rule or 'domination through knowledge (*Herrschaft kraft Wissen*)' – a formula capturing and bringing up to date Bacon's equation of knowledge and power. Knowledge in this context does not mean essential insight (in line with Hegelian 'spirit' and *Sittlichkeit*) but rather 'technical' knowledge, that is, a knowledge geared towards efficiency of goal attainment and predictability of results. By virtue of its consistent structure of tightly meshing rules, bureaucratic organization is the epitome of formal-legal rationality; simultaneously, being geared towards efficiency of performance and outcomes, the same organization obeys the dictates of purposive-technical or instrumental rationality and, more broadly, of utilitarian calculations of benefits. The congruence of these standards is underscored by Weber when he depicts the 'spirit of rational bureaucracy' as exhibiting two main traits: first, "formalism" deriving from interest in predictability and the "security of individual life chances"; and second, utility calculation or the tendency of officials to treat their function from a basically "utilitarian vantage." [11]

Epitomized by the modern state, rational-legal rule or *legale Herrschaft* is distinguished in the following from other types of social order which are comparatively non-rational or irrational in character (where non-rational and irrational are not simply synonyms). The chief type of a non- or pre-rational (but not a counter- or irrational) order is 'traditional' rule or domination. In traditional rule, Weber observes, the ruler is not a manager or a 'superior' in an administrative sense but rather a personal lord or master; obedience in this case is owed not to general and anonymous rules or principles but to the person of the lord with whom subjects are linked through direct bonds of fealty or loyalty. Legitimacy accrues to the lord's commands mainly on the basis of traditions which specify substantive content, and subsidiarily on the basis of free decision – a discretionary sphere situated at the margins of traditions. In the latter sphere, the master can display grace or favour in line with personal (or kinship-related) preferences. In every case, his commands or actions are guided by substantive considerations of equity, common sense, and loyalty, not by 'formal principles as in the case of legal authority.' The range of discretionary power is vastly expanded and actually unrestricted in 'charismatic' orders or modes of domination. According to Weber, there are no rational rules or yardsticks governing charisma; what is alone important is the intense bond generated between leader and disciples. To this extent, shamans, maniacs, and berserk people properly exemplify the model: 'Value-free sociological analysis will treat all these on the same level as it does the charisma of men who are the "greatest" heroes, prophets, and saviors according to conventional judgments.' Like traditional order, charismatic rule is basically a non-rational system – not, however, in being tied to custom, but in being dependent on sovereign will or discretion; 'non-rational' here has the meaning of extra- or counter-rational (or extra-legal, *hors la loi*) which shades over into irrational caprice. Since it is 'extra-ordinary,' Weber writes, charismatic rule is opposed to traditional as well as to rational-legal authority – both of which are ordinary or rule-governed types of systems. In terms of rationality, however, the basic contrast is with modern bureaucracy: 'Bureaucratic authority is *specifically rational* in the sense of being bound to intellectually analyzable rules, while charismatic authority is *specifically irrational* in the sense of being foreign to all rules.'[12]

On an ideal-typical level, rational-legal authority and charisma, formal reason and non-reason are thus sharply segregated in *Economy and Society*. Among the followers of Weber or in the wake of his work, this division has sometimes been erected into full-fledged and radically opposed legal or political doctrines. Thus, in his 'pure theory of law,' Hans Kelsen developed legal rationality into a self-contained system of formal rules, a system ultimately premised on a 'basic norm' or rational precept (from which all traces of political will are exiled). On the other end of the spectrum, Carl Schmitt extolled political sovereignty as a purely extraordinary and extra-rational power – namely, as the power to decide on the 'state of exception,' that is, the situation when formal legal rules are suspended or inoperative.[13] In Weber's own treatment, the opposition was never quite pushed to this point – except on the plane of ideal types which, as mental constructs, were not expected to match social reality. As Weber recognized, legal-rational authority necessarily makes room at its margins for executive discretion, that is, for the intervention of political decision-making in the rule-mechanism of bureaucracy. More sharply phrased: the formal rationality of rules (which can never be fully stipulated or defined) inevitably conjures up as its supplement the non-rationality of decision and power. This tensional correlation or intertwining is dramatically depicted in Weber's sociology of the state in terms of the conflict between bureaucracy and politics or between technical expert and politician. While the bureaucrat or expert, he writes, is supposed to 'stand above' the fray of politics and political parties, politics means the struggle for power and for influence in the shaping of collective life; this struggle for power and for the 'autonomous advancement of one's cause' is the very 'life-element of the politician.' As is well known, Weber was not complacent about the conflict of roles (between expert and politician); nor was he sanguine about legal rationality and the modern state. At one point, *Economy and Society* portrays the modern bureaucratic state as a congealed or 'frozen spirit' (*geronnener Geist*) or as a 'living machine' (*lebende Maschine*). 'Together with the dead machine (in the factories),' we read, 'this machine is in the process of erecting the scaffolding of that future subjection or enslavement (*Hörigkeit*) to which someday perhaps human beings, like the fellahs of ancient Egypt, have to surrender helplessly – if, that is, they assign the final and highest value in the conduct of their affairs to a technically correct administration and that means: rational bureaucratic administration and management.' These comments are amplified by the somber assessments in 'Science as a Vocation' and 'Politics as a Vocation': 'The fate of our time is characterized by rationalization and intellectualization and, above all, by the "disenchantment of the world" ... No summer's bloom lies ahead of us, but rather a polar night of icy darkness and hardness, no matter which group may externally triumph now.'[14]

III

Let me recall again briefly the contrast from which I started: that between Hegel's and Weber's conceptions of the modern state. While in the *Philosophy of Right* the modern state is the embodiment of 'spirit' or the idea (of freedom), the same state in Weber's treatment appears as a 'frozen spirit' or a machine-like apparatus. The question which emerges here is how this apparatus can be 'unfrozen' so that it begins to approximate again the public bond thematized in Hegel's *Sittlichkeit*. This I take to be a crucial, if not the central, question of contemporary Western society and politics. One of the most intriguing and influential remedies proposed in our time is Habermas's theory of communicative rationality and interaction – which deserves attention here both because of its strengths and its instructive drawbacks. Significantly, Habermas's proposal takes its point of departure from the predicaments and dilemmas highlighted in Weber's work; over long stretches, his own reconstructive endeavours explicitly build upon and extend further the lines of inquiry inaugurated in *Economy and Society*. This is particularly true of his more recent writings, which, in large measure, underwrite or endorse Weber's conception of the modern state as a formal-legal structure, as well as his notion of modernization as progressive rationalization and disenchantment. In line with Weber (and Lask), the same writings depict rationalization as the growing separation and specialization of distinct 'value spheres,' that is, of the spheres of science, ethics, and art, which increasingly tend to divide modern culture and reason among them. Yet, as is well known, Habermas's proposal exceeds the confines of value-neutral sociological description; taking a critical stance, he deplores the decay of the 'public sphere' and the rampant sway of subjectivism and strategic modes of interaction. In strongly engaged and engaging language, his publications plead for the restoration of public life via communication and for the advancement of modern rationality (as a continuation of the 'Enlightenment project'). While impressed by the verve and scope of Habermas's pleas, I have doubts or qualms about the viability and direction of his remedy (qualms which I can express here only in very summary fashion).

Basically, my doubts have to do with Habermas's ambivalent appropriation of Weber's work: that is, with his attempt to correct and transcend Weberian dilemmas while simultaneously endorsing key Weberian concepts and propositions (including the conception of the modern state). As it happens, this ambivalent appropriation is not of recent date but can be traced back at least to *Legitimation Crisis* (of 1973). In that study, Habermas differentiated between 'system' and 'life-world,' where system designates an objectively analysable, formally (or instrumentally) rational structure geared to efficiency of performance, while life-world denotes the realm of subjective (or intersubjectively shared) beliefs, values, or states of mind. The two concepts were said to correspond to the distinction between two types of societal functions, namely, 'system integration' and 'social integration' respectively. 'We speak of social integration,' Habermas wrote, 'in relation to systems of institutions in which speaking and acting subjects are socially related; social systems are seen here as *life-worlds* which are symbolically structured. By contrast, we speak of system integration with a view to the specific steering performances of a self-regulated *system*; social systems are considered here from the vantage of their capacity to maintain their boundaries and their continued existence by mastering the complexity of an inconstant environment.' As the study indicated, the notion of 'system' had been developed and refined by functional systems theory and social cybernetics. By contrast, the term life-world was borrowed from phenomenology, particularly the version articulated by Alfred Schutz – a perspective marked by its focus on the subjective intentions of 'speaking and acting subjects' in their social correlation (or else on intersubjectively shared beliefs on the level of everyday social life). 'Both paradigms, system and life-world,' Habermas added, 'are important and legitimate; the problem is how to construe their connection.' A main task or ambition of *Legitimation Crisis* was precisely to forge this kind of interconnection (an effort inspired at least in part by the precedent of Parsonian functionalism).[15]

My intent here is not to pursue the broader argument of Habermas's study. At this point I simply want to alert the reader to notable parallels with the Weberian legacy – a legacy, to be sure, filtered through a number of accretions (especially functionalism and phenomenology). A major parallel resides in the theoretical separation of systems and life-world – that is, in the opposition of formal-rational structure, on the one hand, and the domain of subjective or intersubjectively held beliefs or evaluations, on the other. In Habermas's words: 'If we conceive a social system as a life-world, then the steering aspect is bracketed or blended out; if, on the other hand, we understand society as a system, then the fact that social reality shows the presence of recognized, often counterfactual, validity claims is left out of consideration.' This opposition replicates in large measure Weber's distinction between objective structures or organizations and modes of legitimation seen as supplemental features rooted in values or states of mind. The parallel is even more pronounced in Habermas's construal of the 'state' as a political-administrative structure located – like the economy – on the level of system integration and geared towards systemic efficiency. While the economic subsystem revolves around the 'distribution of economic power and available forces of production,' the state is said to be concerned with the advancement of 'system autonomy' (that is, power or structural force) and to be endowed with a distinctive 'organizational rationality.' As in the case of Weber, the state for Habermas is not a perennial institution, but rather the outgrowth of social development and especially of modern (class-divided) society. 'With the rise of a bureaucratic apparatus of authority (*Herrschaft*),' the study notes, 'a steering center is differentiated out of the kinship system, thus allowing the transfer of the production and distribution of social wealth from familial settings to ownership of the means of production. No longer serving as institutional nucleus of the entire system, kinship surrenders the central functions of power and control to the state.' By contrast with economy and the state, the dimension of normative legitimation is thematized under the heading of 'socio-cultural' subsystem – a domain which embraces traditional cultural beliefs as well as the generation and critical assessment of social norms. As discussed in the study, the main 'crises' or crisis potentials in modern society are specifically traced to normative and motivational factors, that is, to legitimation deficits arising in the socio-cultural life-world.[16]

While patterning itself in these and other respects on Weber's legacy, *Legitimation Crisis* at the same time sounded a strongly discordant note: turning from appropriation to critique, the study took sharp exception to Weber's limited notion of legitimation, namely, his assumption that legitimacy (at least in modernity) is based simply on subjective beliefs in the sense of arbitrary preferences not amenable to further validation. As Habermas states in the concluding chapter of the study: 'In contemporary sociology the usefulness of the concept of legitimacy, which permits a demarcation of types of legitimate rule (in Weber's sense) according to the forms and contents of legitimation, is undisputed; what is controversial is the *relation of legitimation to truth*.' This relation to truth, he adds, must be presumed to exist 'if one regards as possible a motivation crisis resulting from a systematic scarcity of social "meaning." ' The controversy was basically triggered by Weber's notion of legal or rational authority (*legale* or *rationale Herrschaft*) seen as a rule- or law-governed and procedurally regulated mode of domination characteristic of modern society. From a purely sociological perspective – the one adopted by Weber – legitimacy in this context has the status of an empirical-psychological belief devoid of intrinsic truth content; the extent to which such belief is sufficient for securing stable legitimation depends simply on 'institutionalized prejudices and observable behavior dispositions.' In sociological (Weberian) terms, the study notes, a rational-legal order (that is, the modern state) is legitimate insofar as the order is 'positively enacted or established' and insofar as legal subjects 'believe in its legality,' specifically in the formal correctness of procedures for the creation and application of laws. From Habermas's vantage, these criteria are plainly insufficient for purposes of legitimation; legality or the correctness of the rational-legal order in his view is itself in need of normative justification. To satisfy this need, he states, at least one further condition must be fulfilled: valid 'grounds' for the legitimacy of enacted rules and procedures must be adduced. This point is connected with the broader claim of the cognitive status or truth-relation of legitimation. The moral rightness or validity of rules, the chapter continues, cannot be established 'without recourse to a rationally motivated agreement or at least to the conviction that consensus on the adoption of norms could be secured *with reasons*.' This means that the primacy of individual decisions has to be replaced by a consensual or communicative model of ethical legitimation: 'The appropriate model is the communication community (*Kommunikationsgemeinschaft*) of those affected who, as participants in a practical discourse, test the validity claims of norms and, to the extent that they accept them with reasons, arrive at the conviction that in the given circumstances the proposed norms are "right." "[7]

Although eloquently stated and backed up by impressive arguments, the conclusion of *Legitimation Crisis* remains elusive and problematical – mainly because it militates against the study's beginnings. As it seems to me, Habermas's proposal pursues the valuable aim of restoring the 'public sphere' – but does so on premises scarcely congruent with this aim. Differently and more sharply phrased: the model of 'communication community' seeks to recapture elements of Hegelian *Sittlichkeit* – while simultaneously endorsing Weberian conceptions which undermine or nullify the Hegelian legacy. A case in point is the status of legitimacy. How, one may ask, can the usefulness of the Weberian notion be presented as 'undisputed' – and only its 'truth-relation' be chided as inadequate or controversial? As previously indicated, legitimacy in Weber's treatment functions basically as a subjective-internal supplement to a given public order; given this treatment, Habermas's proposed 'truth-relation' of legitimacy partakes necessarily of the same supplemental or corollary status – which is squarely at odds with Hegel's teachings. The same supplemental (or inner-outer) relation is evident in the opposition of 'system' and 'life-world' – where system means an objective, formally rational structure and life-world an arsenal of subjective or intersubjectively shared values and meanings. In conformity with Weber, the state itself is seen as a formal-rational 'system' geared towards efficient control of public life. Moreover, in Weber's view, formal rationality is not only a feature of the state, but a general trademark of modernity or modernization affecting the (increasingly rationalized) 'value spheres' of science, ethics, and art – a trend not really disputed by Habermas. As *Legitimation Crisis* states at one point: 'To the extent that (traditional) world-views are impoverished or depleted, morality too is detached from substantive meanings and progressively formalized.' Although transcending 'bourgeois' law and ethics in the direction of universal principles, Habermas's communicative remedy still reflects or instantiates the dilemmas of internalization and formalization (or abstraction from substantive content). To this extent, his model accentuates inner *Moralität* over public *Sittlichkeit*.[18]

The noted quandaries persist or are aggravated in Habermas's more recent writings. As is well known, Habermas has developed and further refined his notion of communication and linguistic interaction in the direction of a theory of 'universal pragmatics' thematizing the rational validity claims implicit in different modes of linguistic interaction. However, apart from its preferred reliance on speech acts and thus on speaking subjects, universal pragmatics is basically a framework of 'formal analysis' abstracting from the multivocal density of language (as Habermas recognizes in differentiating his theory from hermeneutical as well as empirical-linguistic approaches). Elaboration on the validity claim of 'rightness' has led to the formulation of an ambitious and complex theory of 'communicative' or 'discourse ethics' focused on the argumentative redemption of moral norms or rules. Again, however, discursive testing is orientated towards the validation of universal principles of formal justice in preference to substantive conceptions of the 'good life'; moreover, the proposed standard of the 'ideal speech situation' has itself chiefly procedural character (by assigning equal roles to participants in discourses). The most explicit critical appropriation of Weber can be found in Habermas's magnum opus, *The Theory of Communicative Action*, which offers a detailed discussion of rationalization and disenchantment – without, however, departing radically from the premises of *Legitimation Crisis*. The division between system and life-world is now amplified by the distinction between 'instrumental' and 'communicative' rationality – but both types exhibit the momentum of rationalization (and its corollaries) noted by Weber. This momentum is present not only in systemic structures (exemplified again by the state) but also in the progressive segregation and formalization of modern 'value spheres' seen as formalized domains of culture. By comparison with the earlier study, the life-world is assigned a larger role, serving basically as a reservoir of traditional meanings and beliefs. Yet, *The Theory of Communicative Action* also portrays modernization as a progressive 'uncoupling' not only of system from life-world but also of formalized culture spheres from substantive content. Against this background, the proposed antidote to modern ills – communicative ethics and interaction – remains at best precarious. Wedged between modern rational structures and the traditional life-world, it is unclear how communicative action is supposed to gain a foothold and unfold its potential. In Hegelian terms, communicative bonds either pertain to the traditional life-world – in which case they are pre-rational or pre-ethical; or else they are generated by participants in modern discourses – in which case they fall prey to the divisions of modern culture and thus lose their remedial capacity.[19]

My own theoretical inclinations lead me in a somewhat different direction – a direction attentive to the spirit, but by no means the letter of Hegel's teachings. As I fully recognize, there is no way of rehabilitating in our time Hegel's emphatic and 'essentialist' conception of the state – given the serious erosion of its underpinnings (including subjectivity and univocal reason) in our postmetaphysical context. In lieu of his focus on the state as embodiment of freedom, I prefer to accentuate the dimension of the life-world – the latter term taken not so much in an ontic (descriptive) as in a loosely ontological sense, where life-world also means 'death-world' or the intersection of presence and absence, of finitude and infinity. Instead of being a synonym for traditional behaviour or else for intentional projects (of speaking-acting subjects), life-world here points to the open arena which undergirds tradition and future designs and in which cultural meaning is simultaneously disclosed and suffused or covered over. Attentiveness to this dimension requires a stepping back from the glare or self-sufficiency of knowledge in the direction of (what Heidegger has called) a recollective or 'poetic' mode of thinking – which is not simply a denial or antithesis of reason. From the vantage of recollective attention, the life-world shows itself to be an always already shared world or a field of 'co-being' – but a field eluding homogeneity or streamlined synthesis. In ethical terms, co-being reflects a concrete *Sittlichkeit* or primary bonding – a bonding which yields not so much universal principles or norms as rather an ethics of concrete, everyday engagement, a *minima moralia* predicated on the intrinsic mutual inherence of otherness and selfhood. Seen from this subdued perspective, the late-modern state in Weber's sense does not simply vanish but is reduced to limited house-keeping or protective functions (akin to Hegel's *Not- und Verstandesstaat*), leaving ethics to more amorphous cross-cultural institutions or contacts. Regarding the latter I find support in one of Derrida's recent writings where he says that the antecedence of language to discursive reasoning is 'a kind of primary pledge or bonding to which we have already consented, which we have already affirmed, to which we have already pledged ourselves' regardless of the character of subsequent discourses.[20]

## NOTES

1 See Max Weber, 'Science as a Vocation,' in H.H. Gerth and C. Wright Mills, eds, *From Max Weber: Essays in Sociology* (New York: Oxford University Press 1958), 155.

2 See *Hegel's Philosophy of Right*, trans. T.M. Knox (London: Oxford University Press 1967), paras. 257 and 258, pp. 155–6 (in this and subsequent quotations I have slightly altered the translation for clarity). For an insightful discussion (written from a Nietzschean, post-modern perspective) of Hegel's conception of the state as the actualization of rational freedom see William E. Connolly, *Political Theory and Modernity* (Oxford: Blackwell 1988), 116–21. Compare also my 'Rethinking the Hegelian State,' in *Margins of Political Discourse* (Albany, NY: SUNY Press 1989), 137–57.

3 *Hegel's Philosophy of Right*, paras. 29 and 33 (addition), pp. 33, 234.

4 Ibid., paras. 29 and 30, p. 33. As the latter paragraph elaborates further (pp. 33–4): 'The pure formalism of law (and also of duty) emerges as a distinct stage in the development of the concept of freedom. By contrast with this stage of *Recht*, which is comparatively formal, that is, abstract and so comparatively restricted, a higher

right belongs to the sphere or stage of spirit in which spirit has determined and actualized the further moments contained in its idea – a sphere which is more concrete, intrinsically richer, and more genuinely universal.'

5 Ibid., para. 258, pp. 156–8, 279.

6 Max Weber, *Economy and Society: An Outline of Interpretive Sociology*, ed. Guenther Roth and Claus Wittich, 2d printing (Berkeley: University of California Press 1978), vol. 1, part 1, ch. 1, para. 17, p. 54. (In the above and subsequent citations I have slightly altered the translation for purposes of clarity.)

7 Ibid., paras. 15 and 16, pp. 52–4.

8 Ibid., paras. 5 and 6, pp. 31–3.

9 Ibid., paras. 6 and 7, pp. 34–7.

10 Ibid., chap. 3, paras. 1, 2, 3, pp. 212–19.

11 Ibid., para. 5, pp. 223–6.

12 Ibid., paras. 6 and 10, pp. 226–7, 241–4 (emphasis added). Because of its extraordinary or not-rule-governed character, charismatic order is marked by a restless dynamism – which can manifest itself in revolutionary or counter-revolutionary movements. Weber distinguishes here between the 'revolutionary force' of charisma and of (technical) reason: while reason operates objectively or 'from without,' charisma possesses an inner or subjective élan. The revolutionary force of reason, he states, 'works from without, by altering the situations of life and hence its problems, finally in this way changing men's attitudes toward them; or it intellectualizes the individual. Charisma, on the other hand, may effect a subjective or internal reorientation born out of suffering, conflicts or enthusiasm. It may then result in a radical alteration of the central attitudes and directions of action with a completely new orientation of all attitudes toward the different problems of the world.' Ibid., vol. 1, part 1, chap. 3, para. 10(5), p. 245.

13 See Hans Kelsen, *The Pure Theory of Law*, trans. Max Knight (Berkeley: University of California Press 1967); Carl Schmitt, *Political Theology*, trans. George Schwab (Cambridge, MA: MIT Press 1985).

14 See Weber, *Wirtschaft und Gesellschaft, Grundriss der verstehenden Sociologie*, ed. Johannes Winkelmann (Studienausgabe; Cologne: Kiepenhauer & Witsch 1964), vol. 2, 1043, 1060–2; also 'Science as a Vocation' and 'Politics as a Vocation,' in Gerth and Mills, eds, *From Max Weber*, 128, 155.

15 See Jürgen Habermas, *Legitimation Crisis*, trans. Thomas McCarthy (Boston: Beacon Press 1975), 4, 148 (note 13).

16 Ibid., 5–6, 18–19; for a fuller discussion of 'legitimation crisis' and 'motivation crisis' see 68–92.

17 Ibid., 97–8, 105.

18 Ibid., 120. Regarding internalization and formalization compare also these comments (pp. 87–8): 'Since morality based on principles (*prinzipielle Moral*) is sanctioned only

through the inner authority of conscience, its claim to universality stands in conflict with a public morality still tied to the concrete citizen (as subject of the state): the conflict is between "humanist" cosmopolitanism and the loyalties of the citizen . . . I draw the distinction between norm and principle (that is, metanorm from which norm can be generated) by applying the operation of generalization itself. Moreover, universal validity is the only formal point of view which allows the selection of one principle from among other (contingent) principles.'

19  See Habermas, 'What Is Universal Pragmatics?' (1976) in *Communication and the Evolution of Society*, trans. Thomas McCarthy (Boston: Beacon Press 1979), 1–68, especially 5–25; *Moralbewusstsein und kommunikatives Handeln* (Frankfurt-Main: Surhkamp 1983), especially 53–125; *The Theory of Communicative Action*, trans. Thomas McCarthy, vol. 1: *Reason and the Rationalization of Society* (Boston: Beacon Press 1984), vol. 2: *Lifeworld and System: A Critique of Functionalist Reason* (Boston: Beacon Press 1988). The dilemma can also be formulated in these terms: either communicative action participates in the formalization and progressive specialization of value spheres, in which case it cannot be an antidote to modern divisions, or else it is part of the life-world, in which case the latter cannot simply be traditional (in Weber's sense) or a pliant backdrop to modernization. (Habermas, one might add, consistently reduces Hegel's *Sittlichkeit* to empirical-historical conventions.)

20  Jacques Derrida, *De l'esprit: Heidegger et la question* (Paris: Editions Galilée 1987), 148 (note). Regarding the life-world see my 'Life-World: Variations on a Theme,' in Stephen K. White, ed., *Life-World and Politics: Between Modernity and Postmodernity* (Notre Dame: University of Notre Dame Press 1989), 25–65; for a critique of Habermas's notion compare my 'Life-World and Communicative Action,' in *Critical Encounters* (Notre Dame: University of Notre Dame Press 1987), 73–100. Regarding ethics compare also Theodor W. Adorno, *Minima Moralia: Reflections from Damaged Life*, trans. E.F.N. Jephcott (New York: Schocken 1978); and Drucilla Cornell, 'The Ethical Message of Negative Dialectics,' *Social Concept* (1987), 3–37.

## 4

# Nietzsche and Weber: When Does Reason Become Power?

MARK E. WARREN

The question 'When does reason become power?' is not one that Nietzsche or Weber would have put quite in this way. Reason, they would argue, is always a kind of power. To ask when reason becomes power gestures towards this possibility, but also presupposes that in some fundamental way reason and power are separable and even opposed kinds of interaction. The question supposes that there is some merit to the more optimistic side of the liberal view of reason – not the Hobbesian one, where reasons of utility reduce to a calculus of power, but the Kantian one, in which relations of power may, progressively and over time, be transformed into relations of mutual recognition between rational beings who are ends in themselves. Reason, on this view, can replace power as the medium of political interaction. As Foucault has pointed out, Kant philosophically transformed enlightenment into a political problem by defining it in terms of a relationship between reason, will, and authority.[1] Immaturity, the opposite of enlightenment, is not a lack of understanding, but the inability to use it 'without the guidance of another.'[2] Kant demanded not private freedom, but freedom for a public space, constituted by argument, a space that would change the nature of political interactions. As reason extends into the public realm, politics is less characterized by coercive power, paternalistic benevolence, utility, and instrumental reciprocity, and more by agreements between free, rational subjects.

When we look back on Kant's elegant formulations, we cannot but do so through the prism of Nietzsche and Weber. Because Kant's world is no longer ours, we are struck by a simplicity that borders on naivety. Today what are called 'rational' social organizations involve the least autonomy, the most discipline, the most immaturity. Rationality often seems to demand a Puritanical suppression, even denial, of internal and external nature. Apparent autonomy of judgment often legitimates submission. Attributions of responsibilities and duties tie individuals to hierarchies in which they have little effective voice. Thus it seems quite possible to extend reason into the public sphere while increasing domination rather than producing rational autonomy.[3] No doubt this is why, at least since de Sade, we have witnessed rhetorical and sometimes politically influential reversals of the Enlightenment expectation that reason and freedom reinforce one another. These reversals indicate that formulations such as Kant's obscure as much as they illuminate.

It is not that Kant would have failed to recognized modern institutionalizations of reason for what they are. Rather, the difficulty is that his account of reason is not sufficient to his problematic. His assumption – common to much of our political tradition – that reason and power are opposed in principle leaves us unable to understand how reason can become a kind of power. I shall assume here that the Kantian ideal of a community of individuals who have managed to develop a politics that relies on reasoned argumentation rather than coercion remains valid. But the terms in which the ideal is cast – power receding as reason is progressively institutionalized – has often made it possible to use reason ideologically, to justify domination in the name of reason. The question, as Foucault has put it, is 'How can the growth of capabilities' associated with enlightenment 'be disconnected from the intensification of power relations?'[4]

Nietzsche's and Weber's challenges are important because they help us understand why power does not necessarily recede as reason becomes institutionalized, but may organize and legitimate new kinds of domination. The two men are, as often noted, the first non-theological thinkers to suggest a 'dialectic of enlightenment' – the argument that enlightenment has a dark side related to the insufficiency of reason to comprehend the totality of existence.[5]

By suggesting this comparison between Nietzsche and Weber I am not suggesting that their responses to enlightenment were identical, but only that there is an instructive affinity of perspectives.[6] This is not to deny the differences, most of which are well known. For example, Weber's responses were measured, if not optimistic. Nietzsche's were often apocalyptic. Weber was more optimistic than Nietzsche about science as a meaningful enterprise, and he spelled out an epistemology. Nietzsche's epistemology, reflecting a less optimistic view of science, must be reconstructed from his 'perspectivalism.'

But if we were to focus on these differences alone, we would fail to see how Weber incorporates key aspects of Nietzsche's views of reason and religion in Western history. We would miss the extent to which Weber transforms Nietzsche's views into a more extensive and methodical template for his own account of rationalization. This affinity of perspectives is especially important for this chapter, because it is only when we look at Weber in the light of his Nietzschean heritage that his compelling analysis of the relationship between reason and power comes into focus.

I proceed as follows. First, I specify 'reason' or 'rationality' (terms I use interchangeably) more closely, distinguishing between 'thin' and 'broad' conceptions, between consistency and instrumental correctness on the one hand, and rational autonomy on the other.[7] Second, I examine Weber's concept of rational domination to show how he conceives thin reason as a kind of power, so much so that the problematic of reason and power penetrates the core of his sociology. Third, I compare Nietzsche's and Weber's critiques of Enlightenment views of reason. Reason is never simply a cognitive capacity, nor are its products neutral and disinterested. Rational capacities are always closely allied with conflicting interests and institutional forms, and this causes different dimensions of reason to develop in contradictory ways. Fourth, I examine Nietzsche's critique of thin forms of reason in terms of the kinds of subjective identities they provide and the power relations they sustain. Fifth, I turn to Weber to examine his extension of Nietzsche's general critique to three institutional spheres of rationalization – bureaucracy, economy, and constitutional law. Here, I am interested in the relative ease with which reason can be allied with domination in bureaucracy and economy, as compared with the more ambiguous and promising case of constitutional law. Finally, I criticize Weber and Nietzsche for missing the bases of rational autonomy in social relations, and thus for their view that all institutionalizations of reason must lead to domination. For the most part, Nietzsche failed to analyse public life at all. Weber, by contrast, simply identified public life with thin rationality. I agree with Habermas's criticism of Weber, that he mistook a selective institutionalization of reason for intrinsic paradoxes of rationalization.[8] The same could be said of Nietzsche. The problem, I suggest, is that we need to understand reason as a distinctive set of capacities cultivated by certain kinds of social relations. This would allow us to distinguish between social relations that cultivate broadly rational capacities from those that do not. Presumably, a politics oriented towards the maturity of its citizens would select for, cultivate, and protect the social relations that make maturity possible.

KINDS OF REASON

With Nietzsche and Weber we lose the Enlightenment confidence that the world may be fully comprehended and mastered according to laws of nature that, in principle, are (a) consistent, (b) instrumentally manipulable, and (c) good in the sense that mastering them increases human freedom and autonomy. For Nietzsche and Weber, these assumptions fall into separate, potentially conflicting, domains, according to how they are embedded within (i) thought/culture, (ii) actions, and (iii) institutions. Our ability to answer the question 'When does reason become power?' depends on distinguishing these domains of reason along both axes, in this way identifying the kinds of partiality that permit reason to become power. Reason as consistency and instrumentality, when institutionalized by themselves, can underwrite domination. But reason interpreted as a kind of agency – rational autonomy – is incompatible with domination in any form.[9] The schema I use to compare Nietzsche and Weber on reason and power, as well as to portray the limits of their analyses, is summarized below.

Nietzsche and Weber: Comparative Fields of Analysis

|  | *Mode of reason* | | |
|---|---|---|---|
| *Expression* | Consistency | Instrumentality | Autonomy |
| Thought | Rationalized religion | Natural science Behavioural science | Critical analysis and judgment |
| Action | Intentionalist ethics Action expressing divine will | Engineering Market exchanges | Ethics of responsibility Positive freedom Autonomy |
| Institution | Church Rationalized domination: the legal dimension of bureaucracy | Rationalized domination: market allocation and the instrumental dimension of bureaucracy Technocracy | 'Kingdom of ends' Mutual recognition Diversity Democracy |

Compatible with domination      Incompatible with domination

━━━━━  Field of Weber's analysis
------------  Field of Nietzsche's analysis

*Reason as consistency.* To the extent that reason means consistency, it can refer to internally coherent systems of thought, to actions that stem from a consistent set of intentions, or to institutions that assimilate concrete situations to a uniform mode of treatment. I distinguish consistency on the grounds of its purely internal qualities and potential for disconnection from worldly contingencies of action. This means that consistency alone is 'thin': it is never sufficient to exemplify rational autonomy, nor to insure rational outcomes, nor is it necessarily opposed to domination. With respect to consistency of *thought*, both Nietzsche and Weber note that the internal structure of Christian thought is highly consistent. But in most cases it remains 'otherworldly' with respect to action, while reinforcing the worldly authority of the church, an example I develop below.

*Actions* that are motivated purely by internally consistent intentions may produce results that are quite irrational measured by these same intentions. This is why in 'Politics as a Vocation' Weber argues that the 'ethics of ultimate ends' – that is, ethics that measure the goodness of an action according to a consistent set of ethical intentions – will often produce results that are inconsistent with ultimate ends.

Finally, *institutions* exhibit a rational consistency if they formalize rules of conduct, treat cases equally and impersonally, or discipline members to exhibit a uniform mode of behaviour.

These senses of consistency ought not to be confused with Weber's dichotomy of formal and substantive rationality. For Weber, formal rationality refers to applications of formal rules without regard to substantial values or individual cases. Thus, on the one hand, while formality always implies consistency, it may also include instrumental rationality.[10] On the other hand, 'substantive' rationality – which Weber often uses to refer to conscious consideration of values – may also exhibit internal consistency together with an indifference to worldly consequences of actions. Thus, both formal and substantive rationality may be thin in ways that make them compatible with domination. Yet, as I shall argue, both may also have broad manifestations that underwrite rational autonomy.

*Reason as instrumentality.* One of Weber's most famous distinctions is between instrumentally rational and value-rational action, a distinction he uses to emphasize an increasing predominance of ways of thinking oriented towards means alone. Instrumentally rational *thought* is oriented towards practical mastery of the world and involves an increasing knowledge of empirical conditions of action. Natural science typifies this mode of thinking. For both Nietzsche and Weber, the advances of science produce a progressive disenchantment of the world. Beliefs in other-worldly forces and causes, intimately connected to value-rational systems of meaning, are progressively eroded by increasing empirical knowledge of the world. But science cannot, as Weber puts it in 'Science as a Vocation,' tell us how we ought to live, or what meaning our life might have. Science may be a condition of rational autonomy, but it is not sufficient.

Weber spoke of *actions* as instrumentally rational when they involve calculated applications of technically adequate knowledge. Rationality in this sense is indifferent to rational autonomy, primarily because it is indifferent to whether humans or natural objects are used as means to a given end.

Thus instrumentally rational *institutions* involve instrumental and strategic social relations in which individuals become means to ends that are not their own. For this reason, economic and bureaucratic organizations involving command hierarchies organized for instrumental purposes alone are founded upon domination. Individuals are treated as costs of production; they become means to organizational goals that are not their own. Domination is necessary if individuals are to be used in instrumentally rational ways, and this is why Weber could argue that increasing rationalization involves increasing discipline and domination.

*Reason as rational autonomy.* But reason has always evoked something more than consistency and instrumental mastery. For the Greeks, reason meant release from mere convention, allowing considered choice of a good life. For the moderns of the early Enlightenment, reason meant freedom from determination by external powers – powers of nature as well as those of feudal hierarchies. For the later Enlightenment – from Kant through Marx and J.S. Mill – reason came to imply rational autonomy: considered choice of futures. Reason implied a mode of agency, or maturity – as Kant put it, the capacity to use one's understanding for the guidance of self and society towards considered ends. In each of these cases, 'rational' refers to processes of reflexive examination and justification of beliefs about the world such that the practices they affect sustain an integration of personality and a capacity to achieve worldly values. 'Autonomy' refers to the resulting capacities for self-determination.

Nietzsche and Weber rely on these broadly rational ideals, and it is only because they hold broad conceptions that they can identify certain forms of rationality as partial and pernicious. They present their broad conceptions as 'types' of personalities, emphasizing the integration of rationality with capacities for agency. We can extrapolate Nietzsche's model of rational autonomy from his 'sovereign individual.' In two well-known sections of the *Genealogy*, Nietzsche describes the sovereign individual as the 'ripest fruit' of the 'tremendous process' of forging human nature into something 'regular, calculable, necessary, even in his own image of himself.'[11] Two distinct qualities are present in the sovereign individual: he represents a self-overcoming (*Selbstaufhebung*) of the morality of convention (*der Sittlichkeit der Sitte*) into moral responsibility. And he represents the kind of individual who has the capacity to practise this morality by virtue of a fully developed agency, a capacity that gives him the 'right to make promises.'[12] For a morality to be responsible, one must be able to anticipate the consequences of one's actions, and in this way to 'stand in security' of the future. Nietzsche calls this capacity 'a real *memory of the will*: so that between the original "I will," "I shall do this," and the actual discharge of the will, its *act*, a world of strange new things, circumstances, even acts of will may be interposed without breaking this long chain of will.'[13] Agency in this sense presupposes, Nietzsche argues, that humans in fact are able to anticipate the future, to think in causal terms, to understand necessities, to choose means and ends, and to calculate and compute. These thin rationalities take on broad functions with which they are integrated into a self with capacities for direction.

In 'Politics as a Vocation,' Weber politicizes Nietzsche's emphasis on responsibility by arguing for an 'ethics of responsibility,' an ethics that describes the rationality of an ideal political actor. This kind of rationality, he argues elsewhere, requires a personality focused on the 'consistency of its inner relationship to certain ultimate values and meanings of life, which are turned into purposes and thus into teleologically rational action.'[14] In this way Weber equates meaningful action with what is potentially rational, in the sense that one who is living a meaningful life can, in principle, provide a consistent account of his or her actions in relation to values as well as circumstances, in this way combining instrumental and value rationality in practices.[15] Weber's concept of rational autonomy requires not only that individuals make conscious choices between the demands of conflicting value spheres, but also have a clear understanding of the means and contingencies of action.[16]

These broad conceptions of rationality – rather than the two thin conceptions – are antithetical to domination in the sense that they cannot coexist with domination. Both Nietzsche and Weber, however, limit their broad conceptions of rational autonomy to *thought* and *action*, since in institutions they see an alliance between thin rationality and domination to be more or less inevitable. For the same reason, both were pessimistic about the extent to which broadly rational individuals could become historical possibilities. Just because neither can locate institutional conditions of broad rationality, they portray these individuals as heroes who rise above modern conditions. Nonetheless, we can imagine such institutions, if only as ideals. Institutionalized rational autonomy would require self-examination occasioned by social interaction, conflict, and common projects. Capacities for self-examination are in part developed by dialogues through which one examines one's own interests in relation to constraints and possibilities of the social world. These developmental processes can only be institutionalized where dialogue is protected from coercion in such a way that dialogue-induced decisions can become principles of collective action. By their very nature broadly rational institutions would be incompatible with domination because their goal is to foster the self-governance of their members. Thus we can also describe such institutions as strongly democratic.[17]

## RATIONAL DOMINATION: REASON AND POWER AT THE CORE OF WEBER'S SOCIOLOGY

We still need to specify the concept of power more closely in order to see why it is not logically incompatible with reason. It is common to distinguish power as a social relationship, as in 'power over,' from power as a capacity, as in 'power to.' On the face of it, if power is a capacity, then there is no necessary conflict between rational autonomy and power. Indeed, one could reformulate Kant's ideal of maturity in this way: politics becomes more desirable as decision-making moves from 'power over' and towards 'power to.' The assumption would still be that 'power over' recedes as 'power to,' the power of rational agency, gains, building a public sphere to replace the politics of unquestioned authority.[18]

Nonetheless, a central concept of Weber's sociology challenges or at least complicates this dichotomy – the concept of *rational domination*, which Weber uses to denote the most important kind of organization-building power in the modern age.[19] At the same time, this concept illustrates the extent to which the reason/power problem penetrates the core of Weber's sociology.

Rational domination is a subcategory of power ('power over'), which Weber defines as 'the probability that one actor within a social relationship will be in a position to carry out his own will despite resistance, regardless of the basis on which this probability rests.'[20] 'Power over' in *institutional* relations Weber more narrowly specifies as *domination*, which he defines as 'the situation in which the manifested will (*command*) of the *ruler* or rulers is meant to influence the conduct of one or more others (*the ruled*) and actually does influence it in such a way that their conduct to a socially relevant degree occurs as if the ruled had made the content of the command the maxim of their conduct for its very own sake.'[21] The 'as if' is important in Weber's definition, since individuals may act according to the will of the ruler either because it is in their interests to do so under the circumstances structured by the ruler (that is, they are coerced), or because they hold the ruler's will to be right.[22] In this latter case, domination is *legitimate*. If legitimacy rests on value-rational faith, or on the perceived rightness of a process of selection, then legitimate domination is also (thinly) *rational*.[23]

In such cases, a belief in the rationality of order causes individuals to define their wills through their role in the larger whole. Because they do so, the rationality of their actions cannot be the rationality of autonomy. In the limiting case, individuals' cognitive capacities of self-direction become indistinguishable from the rationality of the organization. This is not, of course, a situation in which an individual's cognizance of their interests is in conflict with the organization: the rationality of the organization forms individual wills in such a way that their capacities are integrated into rationalized subsystems.

In this way Weber inserts the problematic of reason and power into his sociologies of action and organization, a problematic we might call anachronistically his 'Foucaultian dimension.' Still, it is more apparent in Weber than Foucault that this problematic depends on an attachment to the Enlightenment ideal of rational autonomy. *Rational domination* describes situations in which the rationality of institutions conflicts with the rational autonomy of individuals. Reason becomes power where institutionalized reason conflicts with, or stunts, the formation of rational autonomy.

### NIETZSCHE'S AND WEBER'S BREAK WITH THE ENLIGHTENMENT VIEW OF REASON

Weber's analysis of the 'deep' relations between reason and institutional forms is possible largely because of his departure from the Enlightenment view, typified by Kant, that reason can be analysed as something distinct and apart from modes of power. For Kant, reason is disinterested, universal, and rooted in a rational, transcendental subject, even if this subject is, ultimately, simply a regulative assumption necessary to the possibility of reason. The *telos* of reason is distorted by considerations of interest rooted in the phenomenal realm of experience, but in itself it is unconditioned and unconditional. Power may keep reason from expressing itself in the phenomenal world; it may be the cause of political immaturity. But reason and power remain distinct in principle, qualities of differing realms of existence. Rational domination, either as a concept or as a fact of political life, is simply unintelligible in Kant's universe.

Weber's departure from Kant draws heavily on Nietzsche. Kant hoped to show that it is rational to believe that the political world will one day assimilate itself to a reason that, in important ways, is not of this world. This is the focus of Nietzsche's critique not only of Kant (with whom he had similarities with respect to critical thinking about the limits of reason),[24] but of the entire rationalist tradition. Rationalism sought the authority of reason in its universal, disinterested representation of a morally good nature (Plato); in representations of empirical laws of nature (Locke); or in comprehensiveness and consistency (Hegel).[25] For Nietzsche, reason is thoroughly interested and contingent, rooted in experiences of all sorts, from the personal to the social: this is what he means by calling reason (or truth, the *telos* of reason) 'perspectival.' Reason consists in culturally codified and transmitted articulations of experience. It is rooted in history and structured by necessities of communication. Its different forms (Heraclitan, Platonic, Christian, Utilitarian, etc.) express the conditions of life of different peoples – not in any reductive sense, but as distinctive ways of articulating the meaning of existence, where conditions of existence vary widely, not only between peoples and times, but also between different classes drawing from the same pool of interpretive possibilities. Truth, Nietzsche wrote in a famous fragment, is a 'mobile army of metaphors, metonyms, and anthropomorphisms – in short, a sum of human relations' which have come to seem 'firm, canonical, and obligatory to a people ...'[26] Truth becomes 'worn out' when we forget these contingent origins of our rational capacities. We misunderstand how to renew these capacities, because we think of them in terms of their products (representations) rather than as contingent processes. Nihilism involves, among other things, the failure of expectations levelled at seemingly solid symbolic representations whose situated conditions of meaning no longer exist.

Nietzsche's hope, of course, was that nihilism would 'bring us back to ourselves.' We need to understand the conditioned and conditional nature of our rational capacities if we are to continue to assert them in meaningful ways. For Nietzsche, rational autonomy requires an understanding of the conditional nature of cognitive processes.[27] 'Coming to know,' he writes, means 'to place oneself in a conditional relationship to something; to feel oneself conditioned by something and oneself to condition it – it is therefore under all circumstances an establishing, denoting, and making-conscious of conditions ...'[28] Existence involves an 'otherness' – the otherness of situated social relations and nature – that is, 'conditions.' Experiences of these conditions are 'thick' in the sense that they are always something more than what can be conceived and articulated. The ideals of Western rationalism – diverse as they are – tend to involve a suppression of this otherness. Reason is never self-sufficient or detached from these experiences and the values that express them; pretensions of disinterestedness and self-sufficiency only mask these origins. Experiences can be more or less conflicting, more or less painful; but they remain the root of all living values. Nietzsche's account of the history of reason is far from systematic, but its logic is clear: universalist pretensions tend to dissociate individual capacities for agency from their experiential conditions of possibility. In the process, reason assumes thin forms that can comfortably coexist with domination.

Weber is an heir to these dimensions of Nietzsche's critique. Weber's account of Western rationalization presupposes that reason is not, and cannot be, any one consistent group of orientations or attributes. His sociological method, for example, is insistent on the difference between intellectual constructs and the more complex and multifaceted reality.[29] It is not, for Weber, simply that intellectual constructs always simplify a more complex reality, but rather that different interests produce perspectives that are inherently contradictory. The norms and inner consistencies of different spheres of value – the spheres of science, economics, spirituality, eroticism, military valour, aesthetics, and morality – are inherently conflictive, simply because the world is not the kind of place in which one can pursue diverse values simultaneously and yet consistently. Indeed, much of the development of Western rationalism is driven by conflicts between its formal and substantive dimensions.[30] Western rationalism, far from being universal, is unique and historically contingent. Its increasing universality is not propelled by a *telos* of reason, but rather by its active character, by the fact that its inner logic combined with historical accidents in ways that drove it from the realm of thought into the world.

Weber's account of rationalization is not simply a sociology of ideas, but also a sociological demonstration of the way cognitive processes depend on cultural 'templates,' experiences, and configurations of interest. The point could be argued philosophically. Some, like Adorno and Derrida, have done so. Weber chose a sociological genre to display rationalities so diverse that they cannot, without doing violence to the texture of human practices, be assimilated to a single set of criteria. In *Religious Rejections of the World and Their Directions*, Weber shows that different configurations of reason are unique to specific cultures, propelled along culturally available trajectories by tensions between different spheres of value, according to how these values are served, blocked, or transformed by the experiences associated with different life-situations.

## NIETZSCHE'S BREAK WITH EPISTEMOLOGY

Weber's Nietzschean point is that the modes of reason that become dominant in a culture result from interactions between interests and power relations.[31] Weber's ability to show this, however, depended not only on a break with rationalist universalism, but also on a break with the rationalist's way of posing the problem of 'reason.' In this respect Nietzsche's critique of rationalist questions is decisive. The central questions of rationalism are epistemological, having to do with the authority of mental representations of the world – whether the world is conceived as made up of natural laws accessible through contemplation, or as states of affairs accessible through perception. Even at its most sceptical, as in Descartes's minimalist supposition that 'I think, therefore I am,' rationalist questioning presupposes a thinking subject confronted with a world it seeks to know. Power can be conceived *only* externally to this relation,

simply because the criteria of reason are different from those of social convention or coercion, the two primary modes in which rationalists conceive social
relations. If rational agency is given in the form of a knowing subject, power
relations can threaten rationality only from the outside but never operate in and
through reason itself. In this way, an epistemological definition of the problematic conceptually polarizes reason and power.

Nietzsche's questions go 'behind' epistemology: he wished to know how
thinking subjects are possible at all, and this is why he could originate a critical
stance toward the question of reason and power. A close reading of the first
sections of *Beyond Good and Evil* reveals the care with which Nietzsche introduces
his new orientation. Practical and intellectual interactions with the world are
primary. The development of thinking subjects and rational agents must be
explained as a contingent result of these interactions. These interactions are
structured by internal and external experiences, as well as by cultural and
linguistic structuring of cognitive processes. Thinking subjects (and the epistemological questions that follow) are contingent outcomes of such processes.
Nietzsche argued, for example, that the idea of a 'neutral subject' was, historically, a result of interpretive attempts to guarantee the existence and dignity of
the individual against greater powers by dissociating the existence of the
'subject' from its situations and actions.[32] It goes without saying that the result
is not a guaranteed subjectivity, but an ideological subject – Nietzsche would
say an 'imaginary' subject, a 'lie.' For Nietzsche, the thinking subject of the
rationalist tradition is an outcome of culturally codified power relations. But it
is an outcome that masks its own origins in power relations, and rationalism is
thus not capable of deciphering relations between thin reason and power, nor
of grasping the conditions of 'sovereign individuality.' Weber draws the consequences of Nietzsche's break with epistemology even in his sociological method:
his ideal types of reason describe culturally contingent action-orientations
rather than possible epistemological stances.

## CONSISTENT REASON AS POWER: NIETZSCHE'S AND WEBER'S
## CRITIQUE OF CHRISTIAN REASON

Nietzsche's critique of the thin kinds of reason associated with domination are
not as varied or careful as Weber's, but they are more striking, and underscore
the magnitude of Weber's own intellectual shifts. At the same time, they show
that Nietzsche's critiques are not reductions of reason to irrationality (as
Nietzsche's interpreters often hold), but rather elucidations of the conditions of
rational agency that are not conceived within the rationalist tradition itself.
What Weber and Nietzsche understand is that configurations of interests and

rationally structured culture may enter into the constitution of agency in ways that tie the individual's sense of self to systems of domination.

One example is Christian reason (that is, its theology, as opposed to its institutions, rituals, myths, and miracles) – the carrier of highly idealized rationalist thought from the Middle Ages through to the Renaissance. Nietzsche's most sustained critique is in *On the Genealogy of Morals* and continued in *The Antichrist*. It is a critique that seems to have provided Weber with the theoretical core of his sociology of religion, notwithstanding his somewhat disingenuous critique of Nietzsche.[33] Nietzsche's focus here is the origin of Christian morality, with its ascetic condemnation of worldly concerns, its promises of salvation, and its supporting, intellectually rationalized, theology. He portrays a kind of reason that, by virtue of its mere consistency, permits and justifies the domination of the church, while defining individual agents in such a way that meaningful action violates rational agency. The example is interesting not because Nietzsche gives a full account of the sociology of Christian reason (Weber is much more sensitive to its historical variations), but because it provides the model of analysis upon which Weber relies, and which he refines and elaborates.

Nietzsche's account is well known: he looks for the origins of 'the Christian-moral hypothesis' and other ascetic ideals in the existential interest situation of those who suffer, especially at the hands of others.[34] Suffering is not, in Nietzsche's view, problematic in itself. Rather, it is problematic when it is senseless, without meaning.[35] For Nietzsche, the requirements of meaning are key elements of human motivation which deepen with every fragmentation of worldly goals and practices. Meaning is not given by true representation or signification, but rather by individuals' abilities to interpret their situation such that they can form a 'will' – an orientation towards conditions of self-reproduction. Meaning becomes estranged from practices and is idealized as the problem of 'truth,' however, when, for reasons of experience or cultural mapping, practices become so disjoined that individuals can no longer plausibly interpret them as effects of their 'will.' It is not that humans always connect meaning to will-formation. Rather, suffering produces the problem of meaning because the 'will' that one would form through traditional orientations, habitually and without thinking ('instinctively,' in Nietzsche's terminology), is no longer possible. This is why humans 'would rather will nothingness than not will.'[36]

Suffering at the hands of others produces a problem of meaning because it violates an existential need for will-formation – a point that Nietzsche seems to have loosely borrowed from Hegel, and bequeathed directly to Weber. The key to both Nietzsche's and Weber's analyses is that *suffering structures interest situations that are inducements to, and require, interpretation.*[37] Christianity addresses these interest situations by imposing a relatively rationalized image of the world. The Christian narrative about sin, punishment, the need for obedience, and behavioural conditions of salvation draws much of its strength from its internal coherence, an internal coherence that makes contact with the world only with respect to a few crucial experiences. In fact, the narrative serves those who subscribe to the story precisely because it inverts the world: oppressors will be punished rather than saved, the 'will' that is lacking in practice is restored to individuals as children of God, the community lacking on earth will exist in an afterlife, and the suffering that one experiences is nonetheless a just consequence of human sin.[38] The interpretation depends on the projection of another world, a world of spiritual causalities and happenings. Because the projection is 'imaginary,' it must be preserved in large part by intellectual means. In this way, internal coherence comes to be vested with the existential interests violated in everyday life.

For Nietzsche and Weber, the powers of internal consistency do not spread without a strata of practitioners who institutionalize them as a way of life in the church.[39] It is here that a merely consistent universe, one that nonetheless provides salvation and thereby defines the 'wills' of its adherents, becomes a form of power. Three aspects of Nietzsche's account of the 'priestly power' of the church are especially noteworthy in this context. First, the basis of the church is a power relation between priests and followers: priests exercise an interpretive monopoly over the means of will-formation for followers. In exchange for obedience, the church provides access to means of salvation – or, Weber adds in discussing Protestant variants, means of legitimating good fortune.[40] Second, a church is an example of the integration of reason and power. The church embodied, in Weber's terms, a value-rational form of legitimate domination, at least when and where it was called upon to justify itself through appeals to reason.[41] Third, if Christian reason is ultimately irrational on Nietzsche's and Weber's account, this is not because it must ultimately resort to faith, but rather because it is a thin form of reason, a form particularly exploitable for purposes of power. According to Nietzsche, the priestly rulers of the church do not simply minister to the sufferings of their followers. They exploit suffering in such a way that they gain control over the capacities of sufferers to sustain their sense of subjectivity. The priest entices his followers to interpret experiences they find psychologically overpowering though a Christian schematic. They become dependent upon the priest's exegesis of the world for their self-interpretation of agency. The structure of the Christian world-view is uniquely suited to the kind of interpretive privilege that the priest claims for himself. The reason for this, Nietzsche takes care to point out, is that Christian interpretations – in contrast to earlier magical, mythical, and philosophical modes of thought – remove all criteria of truth from the sensible world of everyday experience, with the exception of experiences of hardship and bad conscience that serve as evidence of guilt and sin. The other worldly structure of Christianity allows priests to create the view that all natural events are conditioned by invisible laws, causalities, and forces to which they alone have access.[42] 'When the natural causes of a deed are no longer "natural," but thought of as caused by the conceptual spectres of superstition, by "God," by "spirits," by "souls," as if they were merely "moral" consequences, as reward, punishment, hint, means of education, then the presupposition of knowledge has been destroyed.'[43] The exegesis of the world that reads all 'natural' or experienced events in terms of a shadow world of invisible actors and fictitious forces produces a conceptual incapacity to engage reality, and thus deepens whatever de facto, politically maintained incapacity already exists. This, Nietzsche claims, is the priest's 'greatest crime against humanity.'[44]

The priest's intellectual authority resides not only in his ability to locate causal agents in a non-empirical, metaphysical world but also in his interpretation of suffering and bad conscience as empirical evidence for his exegesis. Since suffering produces a hope for redemption from suffering, the priest increases the likelihood that his interpretive authority will be accepted by tying the promise of redemption to acceptance of his exegesis. Thus Nietzsche views the priest 'type' as an ideologist who employs politically produced sufferings to solidify his interpretive authority, while destroying the autonomy of his followers by disconnecting reason from worldly situations.[45] This is why he can claim, in discussing Pauline Christianity, that 'with morality it becomes easiest to lead mankind by the nose.'[46] Here a thin form of reason is fully integrated with domination, keeping humans in a 'slavish' state – Nietzsche's term for what Kant called immaturity. By constituting the 'wills' of individuals, thin reason becomes a means of social control.

We can draw three general conclusions from this analysis – conclusions that we could just as well have drawn from Weber's sociology of religion. First, individuals have an existential interest in integrating their experiences into a 'will' – which includes a demand for meaning oriented toward life-conduct. This general interest in will-formation, what Nietzsche calls 'will to power,' and what Weber calls 'ideal interests,' forms the motivational basis for the power of reason.[47] Second, at any point in time, only some internally consistent 'templates' for meaning are culturally available and socially disseminated. This is an issue of cultural hegemony: control over templates is related to the strata that bear them and that have institutional means of support. Third, ideas can become power to the extent that they are essential to will-formation, and this is why ideas with a rational structure may become resources of power. This is the way ideas may become, in Pierre Bourdieu's terms, the 'capital of symbolic power.'[48] Any thin mode of rationality can serve as this kind of power in the 'deep' sense that it enters into the formation of individual wills.

## NIETZSCHE'S CRITIQUE OF INSTRUMENTAL REASON

Nietzsche also provides a critique of the other form of 'thin' reason, instrumental reason – again parallel to Weber's, although his analysis is less developed in its institutional implications. Nietzsche, like Weber, pointed to an increasing propensity to confuse a reason of means with that of ends; to regard instrumental activities as if they were valuable in themselves. Nietzsche objected to one embodiment of this confusion, utilitarian ethics, because it consists primarily in calculating means to achieve happiness without any examination of the goods of the self – freedom, creativity, and dignity – that are, in some sense, prior to happiness. Likewise, science – a rationality of empirical means – is not equipped to examine the values it serves. Both Nietzsche and Weber were critical of the pretensions of science in this respect: the closing sections of *On the Genealogy of Morals* make precisely the point of 'Science as a Vocation.' Science disenchants other-worldly values but it cannot provide worldly ones. Both Nietzsche and Weber associate the pretensions of instrumental reason with an impoverished mode of existence, one caricatured by Nietzsche's 'last men,' who unthinkingly believe that they have 'invented happiness.' Weber evoked Nietzsche's image when he characterized his world as one of 'specialists without spirit, sensualists without heart, this nullity imagines that it has attained a level of civilization never before achieved.'[49]

It is not necessary that instrumental reason produce domination. Nietzsche and Weber value it in its own domain, as a necessary ingredient of rational autonomy. But it is quite compatible with domination, especially when it is confused with reason as such, and becomes the legitimating principle of social organization to the exclusion of other forms of reason. While Nietzsche's account of the institutionalization of instrumental reason is not extensive, his few comments are pointed, and have to do with the loss of autonomy to economic goals. For example, he viewed the capitalist work-ethic as self-destructive: what his contemporaries referred to as the 'blessing of work,' Nietzsche saw as 'mechanical activity,' resulting in 'absolute regularity, punctilious and unthinking obedience, a mode of life fixed once and for all, fully occupied time, a certain permission, indeed training [*Zucht*], for "impersonality," for self-forgetfulness, for *incuria sui* [lack of care for the self].'[50] Neither did it escape his attention that the experience of mechanized labour, justified in terms of utilitarian ideals of welfare, aided and abetted the more general logic of domination. Thus Nietzsche set himself against the prevailing 'economic optimism': 'as if the increasing expenditure of everybody must necessarily involve the increasing welfare of everybody. The opposite seems to me to be the case: the expenditure of everybody amounts to a collective loss: man is diminished – so one no longer knows what *aim* this tremendous process has served.'[51]

Nietzsche's analysis is limited – fatally, if one judges by his political conclusions – by his failure to analyse, or perhaps even to understand, the ways in which thin reason enters into modern institutions, especially the institutions of bureaucracy and the market.[52] With the exception of his analysis of the church, his account of reason remained at the levels of culture and action, and not social institutions. In this respect Weber is well beyond Nietzsche, and it is probable that Nietzsche's insights would have less significance for political thought today but for Weber's recasting of them in institutional terms.

## REASON AS POWER IN BUREAUCRACIES

Weber is perhaps best known for his analysis of bureaucracy. He is often read as equating the institutionalization of reason as such with bureaucratization.[53] Yet a careful reading shows that Weber saw bureaucratic reason as partial: bureaucracies institutionalize thin forms of reason – consistency and instrumentality – both of which can coexist with and serve as means to domination. Bureaucracies coordinate the efforts of individuals through codified rules, enforced by command. The rationality of bureaucracy is, in the first instance, the rationality of consistency. Bureaucracies treat similar cases in similar ways, they enforce consistency of behaviours with respect to organizational goals, and they practice consistency in applications of methods.

While there have been historical periods in which bureaucracies could, and did, appeal to the consistency of a set of values – that is, a kind of value rationality – Weber makes it clear that this is no longer the case. Protestant rationalization, one origin of bureaucratic reason, depended on interpreting the self as an instrument of God. That is why transforming the self into an instrument of organization could have a value-rational meaning (one of Weber's most striking examples is an account of the consequences of Puritanism for the discipline of Cromwell's forces).[54] But the universe of Christian meanings has been disenchanted, leaving only organizational discipline combined with instrumental interests external to organizations. 'The Puritan wanted to work in a calling; we are forced to do so. For when asceticism was carried out of monastic cells into everyday life, and began to dominate worldly morality, it did its part in building the tremendous cosmos of the modern economic order. This order is now bound to the technical and economic conditions of machine production which today determine the lives of all the individuals who are born into this mechanism, not only those directly concerned with economic acquisition, with irresistible force.'[55]

These points suggest one important way in which Weber is beyond Nietzsche: the collusion of reason and domination is no longer a question of the cultural formation of motives. Power and organization have taken over from culture; interests and identities are to a large extent externalized from organizations, lodged in consumer identities, ethnicity, nationality, and individualized religions.

Nonetheless, there remain two other ways of justifying bureaucratic organization such that reason as consistency retains its legitimating force. First, when consistency is of a worldly, yet formal, sort, it may be justified by its instrumental effects, and thus as an aspect of instrumental (rather than merely consistent) reason. Calculability, according to Weber, is a definitive element of bureaucracy, one involving formal consistency in the application of rules.[56] Very often this kind of consistency produces instrumentally rational effects: the efficiency of an organization will usually increase with the standardization of job descriptions, behaviours, supplies, parts, and so on, simply because this allows for coordination of diverse efforts for massive projects, increased predictability for planning, and so on.[57] Suppressing autonomous rationality, turning the self into an instrument of a command organization, is rational in this instrumental sense. This is not to say that consistency is reducible to a facet of instrumental rationality. The distinction remains important because instrumentally rational effects are essentially by-products of consistency, which remains the hallmark of bureaucracy. That this is so is demonstrated by the fact that bureaucracies usually retain consistency in structure, rules, and command even when consistency produces instrumentally irrational effects – when, for example, it produces inflexibility, dampens creativity, and causes motivational crises.

The second way in which reason as consistency justifies bureaucratic organization is more ambiguous. Weber points out that rationalization of government bureaucracy is spurred by democratization.[58] By 'democratization' he means increasing demands for equal treatment by government. Government becomes more 'impersonal,' treating individuals as instances of legal entitlements belonging to classes rather than as persons with unique situations or unique entitlements stemming from the good graces of an office. Weber classes this kind of rationalization under the instrumental interests of utilitarianism: regulation, standardization, and the like are justified as means of increasing general welfare. That is, they are justified in relation to a substantive set of interests and values. Yet Weber's analysis is not definitive on the relation between consistency and rational autonomy: I shall argue below that increasing formality and 'impersonality' may also be predicated on the recognition of political person-hood – an incipient form of rational autonomy.

Nonetheless, the central theme of Weber's analysis of bureaucracy is that reason as 'calculable rules' and instrumental efficiency is not only compatible with domination but causes it to increase. Once a 'calling' is lost, rationality for the organization (or those who command it) diverges from rationality for the individual. Bureaucratic command is merely a kind of discipline to be endured for the sake of a livelihood. Since discipline is a key element of calculability, as organizations become more calculable, more behaviours become subject to discipline.[59] As the justification for discipline is externalized from the life-worlds of individuals who make up the organization, instrumental rationality can be maintained only by combinations of coercion and appeals to interests in material well-being. In economic and state organizations, this occurs through control over means of livelihood: means of production, administration, and knowledge.[60] Today the full integration of the individual's 'will' into thinly rationalized organizations occurs, perhaps, only in the military, where the notions of duty, honour, and patriotism are cultivated and retain some sway. But the more general result is what Habermas describes as a disjunction between rationalized subsystems and the integrity of the life-world. Weber sees the split as producing a society in which technical superiority, legitimated by appeals to general welfare, coexists with the 'bondage' of increased discipline.[61]

REASON AS POWER IN MARKETS

Markets are a second way in which thin reason is institutionalized. Markets translate use-values, labour, and other resources into a single commodity, money, which can then serve as a means for calculable comparisons. Unlike bureaucracies, markets do not evoke rationality as consistency for their legitimacy, simply because coordination is not the result of planning, but rather an unintended outcome of maximizing profit. Still, market mechanisms are often said to be 'rational' in an instrumental way: price mechanisms provide a means of comparing costs, allowing an efficient use of time, effort, knowledge, and other resources. Weber refers to these mechanisms of comparison as the 'formal rationality' of the market generally, and of capitalism in particular.[62] He uses this term because markets operate 'without regard for persons,'[63] indeed, without regard to substantive rationality of any kind.

Although the phrase 'without regard to persons' is Weber's own, it tends to neutralize his analysis. On Weber's account, the instrumental rationality of markets is not simply indifferent to persons but actually hostile. Within markets, 'capital accounting in its formally most rational shape ... presupposes the *battle of man with man*.'[64] Money is 'primarily a weapon in this struggle, and prices are expressions of the struggle; they are instruments of calculation only as estimated quantifications of relative chances in this struggle of interests.'[65]

Within firms, formal rationality presupposes a 'system of domination,' that is, sufficient power on the part of owners of capital to suppress all concerns extraneous to profit maximization.[66] Bureaucratic organization is the most favourable for the formal rationality of capitalism because it allows for the highest degree of predictability and calculation both over labour and other resources. As Weber puts it, 'The fact that the maximum of *formal* rationality in capital accounting is possible only where the workers are subjected to domination by entrepreneurs, is a further specific element of *substantive* irrationality in the modern economic order.'[67] Formal rationality presupposes that owners of capital have complete freedom to maximize profit, which implies an ability to make instrumental use of labour, unconstrained by any non-economic concerns.[68] That is why, on Weber's account, capitalism is not hostile to bureaucratic domination. On the contrary, it has been the single most important impetus to bureaucratization in the contemporary world.[69]

It is well known that Weber nonetheless expressed a preference for capitalist market economies. The reason was that he believed material welfare depends on formally rational economic organization, and he held that the only other way of achieving these effects is through centralized planning – that is, hierarchical state socialism.[70] Domination, in Weber's view, is dictated not simply by considerations of power, but by technical and economic rationality.[71] Given this inevitability, the potential for autonomy remains somewhat greater in a capitalist system.

## REASON AND POWER IN POLITICS AND CONSTITUTIONAL LAW

Weber's assessments of the supportive relation between reason and power in other kinds of modern organizations are equally pessimistic. Political organizations are no exception, which Weber defines in terms of the use of coercive means to achieve organizational goals. Famously, he describes the state as a 'human community that (successfully) claims the *monopoly of the legitimate use of physical force* within a given territory.'[72] A state can claim *rational* legitimacy to the extent that coercion is governed by consistent rules.[73] This would seem to rule out, by definition, political organizations not based on domination, even as a regulative ideal such as Kant's 'kingdom of ends.' In a complementary way, Weber limits, indeed truncates, his conception of politics, defining it as 'any kind of *independent* leadership in action.'[74] The complementary emphasis on power and leadership rules out, even as a regulative ideal, a politics that might institutionalize rational autonomy.

In this section I argue that Weber's analysis of one dimension of politics, constitutional law, does not fully support the covariation of thin reason and power that sustains his analysis of other spheres of rationalization. His analysis, as Habermas has convincingly argued with respect to other examples, depends to a large extent on confusing a selective institutionalization of reason with a seemingly unsolvable paradox of rationalization.[75] This is despite the fact that, as I have suggested, Weber's analysis relies on distinctions between thin and broad reason, with his account of institutionalization showing that thin reason can legitimate domination.[76]

We can see the problem in Weber's analysis of constitutional law. He is inclined to treat contemporary liberal democratic constitutions as institutional-izations of thin reason – as merely instrumental and value-neutral mechanisms for deciding conflicts between competing interests, a position he develops most extensively in 'Parliament and Government in a Reconstructed Germany.'[77] He intended his analysis of constitutional law to parallel his analysis of rational-ization in other spheres. In some cases the analyses are parallel, but in others they are not. For example, Weber distinguishes between administrative and regulative rules.[78] The first kind of rule is the legal requisite of bureaucracy; the second sets out the parameters of social interactions without directly governing their content, as in a *laissez-faire* market.[79]

Markets are not, however, the only kind of regulative order. Constitutions fall into this class, regulating modes of decision-making rather than specifying their substance or purpose. Constitutions have a different relationship to rationaliza-tion than do markets, and this difference is important for locating alternative dimensions along which reason might be institutionalized. Constitutions are not legitimated by instrumental rationality (although they may have instrumentally rational effects), but rather by the ideal of mutual recognition by autonomous individuals.[80] This is true even when particular provisions, property rights in particular, expand the domain of instrumental rationality. Such expansions often occur only because liberal constitutions associate property ownership with personhood, ideologically dissimulating these rights from the power relations they produce. The legitimacy of constitutions depends on invoking broad rationalities even when the results combine thin rationality and power.[81] The reason is that agreements that provide regulative ideals for resolving conflicts through dialogue presuppose intersubjective recognitions of individuals as autonomous agents with capacities for considered decision-making.[82] The stra-tegic uses of constitutional mechanisms upon which Weber focuses presuppose, at least ideally, understandings that are closely related to intersubjectively sustained capacities for rational autonomy. The rationalization of constitutional law includes this broadly rational direction despite the fact that this kind of rationalization does not occur in every dimension, and despite the fact that the rationalization of some dimensions, say, freedom of contract, may increase powers of discipline.[83] These considerations suggest that Weber's account of the rationalization of law will not produce the neat relationship between thin reason and domination that it does for markets and bureaucracies, but rather an account that is contradictory and for this reason also more promising.

We can see the same problem in Weber's discussion of formal and substantive rationality in law. Law is concretely formal to the extent that it isolates distinct sets of facts and observable rituals as legally relevant. It is intellectually formal where law is rationalized according to inner logic or consistency – what Weber calls a 'gapless' legal order. 'Substantive rationality' in law, by contrast, describes the application of standards of judgment – deontological, utilitarian, and so forth – that are extrinsic to the norms of the legal process itself.[84] Thus, as Wolfgang Schluchter has pointed out, formalism in law does not imply a lack of ethical content (as it does in bureaucracy and markets), but rather the emergence of distinctive legal norms alongside the norms of other spheres of value.[85] Weber's use of the same terms to denote the rationalization of law obscures the distinctive nature of the developmental conflicts within it. Intrinsic to these conflicts is a commitment to norms of rational autonomy.

I can offer no more than a prima facie analysis here, but it is one paralleled by those of Schluchter and Habermas. In the case of law generally, Weber interprets the development of 'juridical rationalism' as a movement towards legal positivism – that is, regarding legal procedures as no more than technical procedures for adjudicating disputes. The rise of legal positivism, Weber argues, reflects an increasing disenchantment of value-rational ethical systems that might provide a normative foundation for law.[86] This is most clear in the case of natural law, but holds for any attempt to produce an ethically 'gapless' foundation for legal procedures. This is so not only for Comtean utilitarianism, but also neo-Kantian attempts to refer the law back to a 'society of free men.' Beyond the assertion that no systematic ethical system can justify rationally all legal practices that seem desirable, Weber declines to offer further analysis.[87]

Weber's analysis is implausible in part because he does not look at the normative understandings that sustain legal formalism. As Schluchter has argued, legal formalism minimally presupposes an ethic of responsibility – the same ethic Weber describes in 'Politics as a Vocation.'[88] For example, rights of due process, which sometimes produce results that are abhorrent from the perspective of non-legal values, presuppose the responsibility of the individual, and demand that the individual justify his actions. Rights of due process provide the criteria of a framework within which in the individual is empowered to take on this responsibility. That ethic is rooted in turn in a mutual recognition of rational autonomy, although the recognition is often in conflict with an individual's actual circumstances and behaviour. As Schluchter points out, this kind of recognition is genuinely ethical in Kant's sense, going beyond anything that could result from a purely instrumental contract with mechanisms of enforcement.

It is often the case, of course, that juridical attributions of responsibility increase powers of discipline. They certainly do so when they are counterfactual – that is, when individuals have never experienced social circumstances that cultivate rational autonomy. This does not reflect an ethical inconsistency, however, but rather a failure of society to underwrite the social conditions of the ethical presumptions of legal processes.[89] In this case, judicial norms function as ideology.[90]

At a political level, constitutional law embodies similar recognitions. As Weber puts it, 'Every right is ... a source of power of which even a hitherto entirely powerless person may become possessed.'[91] Rights also include protections against 'certain types of interference by third parties,' as well as 'an individual *autonomy* to *regulate* his *relations with others* by his own transactions.'[92] Interpreted ethically, *rights evoke understandings between individuals based on a symmetry of power as means of regulating common affairs.* They provide protections from coercive powers (usually interpreted in overly narrow terms as state powers) to allow these understandings to take place.

CONCLUSION

This example suggests that broad rationality is already recognized, if only implicitly, in the public life of liberal democracies. What Nietzsche and Weber provide is an analysis of the many ways that thin reason can become allied with, and justify, power. But their contributions are primarily critical rather than reconstructive: because they do not believe that broad reason can be institutionalized, they fail to identify the arenas in which institutionalization already occurs, even if in limited and contradictory ways. We can go beyond Nietzsche and Weber by noting that, whenever institutions are justified as 'rational,' a broader understanding of reason is almost always evoked, even if only ideologically. In public life, *thin rationality lives off broad promises.* Reason as mere consistency almost always locates/constitutes individuals as subjects with a meaningful order within an otherwise meaningless universe. Instrumental reason almost always evokes increased control over material circumstances of life, in this way evoking autonomy. For all of their limitations, however, Nietzsche and Weber provide critical distinctions that help clarify the problem of how broad rationality might be embodied within social and political institutions.

NOTES

1 Michel Foucault, 'What Is Enlightenment?' in *The Foucault Reader*, ed. Paul Rabinow (New York: Pantheon 1984), 37.

2 Immanuel Kant, 'An Answer to the Question: What Is Enlightenment?' in *Kant's Political Writings*, ed. Hans Reiss, trans. H.B. Nisbet (Cambridge University Press 1970), 54.

3 This case is made effectively by William Connolly, *Political Theory and Modernity* (Oxford: Basil Blackwell 1988).

4 Michel Foucault, 'What Is Enlightenment?' 48.

5 Cf. Max Horkheimer and Theodor Adorno, *Dialectic of Enlightenment*, trans. John Cumming (New York: Seabury Press 1972). On Weber, see Jürgen Habermas, *The Theory of Communicative Action*, vol. 1, trans. Thomas McCarthy (Boston: Beacon Press 1984), especially 345–65; Jeffrey Alexander, 'The Dialectic of Individuation and Domination: Weber's Rationalization Theory and Beyond,' in *Max Weber, Rationality, and Modernity*, ed. Scott Lash and Sam Whimster (London: Allen and Unwin 1987). On Nietzsche, see Heinz Röttges, *Nietzsche und die Dialektik der Aufklärung* (Berlin: Walter de Gruyter 1972), and Mark Warren, *Nietzsche and Political Thought* (Cambridge, MA: MIT Press 1988), especially chap. 1.

6 See Wilhelm Hennis, *Max Weber: Essays in Reconstruction*, trans. Keith Tribe (London: Allen & Unwin 1988), chap. 4; Ralph Schroeder, 'Nietzsche and Weber: Two "Prophets" of the Modern World,' in *Max Weber, Rationality, and Modernity*; Lawrence Scaff, 'Weber before Weberian Sociology,' *British Journal of Sociology*, 35 (June 1984), 196.

7 I borrow the terms 'thin' and 'broad' rationality from Jon Elster, *Sour Grapes: Studies in the Subversion of Rationality* (Cambridge: Cambridge University Press 1983), 15–26.

8 Habermas, *The Theory of Communicative Action*, vol. 1, 241–2.

9 In the case of Nietzsche, distinctions between these domains of reason are implicit; they must be read into his systematic, but often unelaborated and overly general critique of 'truth' and 'reason.' Weber, by contrast, makes the kinds of distinctions I suggest above, but they are not identical with his better-known distinctions between formal and substantive rationality, and between instrumental and value rationality. Weber used these later distinctions to locate the developmental consequences of the ways in which intellectual constructs diverge from the world. But he retains the distinction between consistency and instrumentality in his discussion of religion. Rationalization 'means one thing if we think of the kind of rationalization the systematic thinker performs on the image of the world: an increasing theoretical mastery of reality by means of increasingly precise and abstract concepts. Rationalism means another thing if we think of the methodical attainment of a definitely given and practical end by means of an increasingly precise calculation of adequate means.' 'The Social Psychology of World Religions,' in *From Max Weber*, trans. and

ed. Hans Gerth and C. Wright Mills (New York: Oxford University Press 1946), 293. In 'Politics as a Vocation,' in *From Max Weber*, Weber sketches a kind of rational autonomy in his portrayal of an ethic of responsibility, which he contrasts both to purely instrumental political action, as well as to that motivated simply by the internal consistency of an ethical system.

10  Cf. Habermas, *The Theory of Communicative Action*, vol. 1, 345.

11  Friedrich Nietzsche, 'On the Genealogy of Morals,' in *The Basic Writings of Nietzsche*, ed. and trans. Walter Kaufmann (New York: Random House 1966), essay II, sections 1, 2.

12  Ibid.

13  Ibid., section 1.

14  Max Weber, *Roscher and Knies: The Logical Problems of Historical Economics*, trans. Guy Oakes (New York: The Free Press 1975), 192; cf. 'Science as a Vocation,' in *From Max Weber*, 151–3; Wolfgang Schluchter, 'Value Neutrality and the Ethic of Responsibility,' in *Max Weber's Vision of History* by Guenther Roth and Wolfgang Schluchter (Berkeley: University of California Press 1979), 73–4; Karl Löwith, *Max Weber and Karl Marx*, trans. Hans Fantel (London: George Allen & Unwin 1982), 45–6; Edward Portis, 'Max Weber's Theory of Personality,' *Sociological Inquiry*, 48 (1978), 113–20.

15  See Weber's 'The Meaning of Ethical Neutrality,' in *The Methodology of the Social Sciences*, trans. and ed. Edward Shils and Henry Finch (New York: The Free Press 1949).

16  For Weber, the ethical significance of social science is its utility in clarifying conditions of rational agency. His choice of objects (social action) as well as his choice of methods (interpretive reconstruction of subjective orientations) both follow from his interest in personhood. His social science is appropriate to the study of humans insofar as they are conceived as agents, rather than, say, organisms manifesting behaviour. Wolfgang Schluchter alludes to this point when he notes that for Weber 'the *conceptually presumed* consistency of personality is a kind of transcendental precondition of interpretive sociology,' 'Value Neutrality and the Ethic of Responsibility,' 73.

17  I borrow here from Habermas, *The Theory of Communicative Action*, vols 1 and 2; Habermas, *Strukturwandel der Öffentlichkeit* (Darmstadt: Luchterhand 1962); and Elster, *Sour Grapes*, 33–42.

18  Cf. Habermas, *Strukturwandel der Öffentlichkeit*.

19  Mark Warren, 'Max Weber's Nietzschean Conception of Power,' *History of the Human Sciences* 5 (August 1992), 19–37.

20  Max Weber, *Economy and Society*, 2 vols, ed. Guenther Roth and Claus Wittich (Berkeley: University of California Press 1978), 53.

21  Ibid., vol. 2, 946.

22  Ibid., 943.

23  Ibid., vol. 1, 36.

24  See Warren, *Nietzsche and Political Thought*, 116–26.

25  Cf. Connolly, *Political Theory and Modernity*.

26  'On Truth and Lie in an Extra-Moral Sense,' in *The Portable Nietzsche*, ed. and trans. Walter Kaufmann (New York: Viking 1954), 47.

27  See, e.g., Friedrich Nietzsche, *The Gay Science*, ed. and trans. Walter Kaufmann (New York: Random House 1974), aphorism 109.

28  Nietzsche, *The Will to Power*, ed. Walter Kaufmann, trans. Walter Kaufmann and R.J. Hollingdale (New York: Random House 1967), note 555.

29  The most eloquent account of the relation between Weber's method and his critique of Western rationalism is Maurice Merleau-Ponty's, in *Adventures of the Dialectic*, trans. Joseph Bien (London: Heinemann 1974), chap. 1.

30  See especially Wolfgang Schluchter, *The Rise of Western Rationalism*, 54–5.

31  Cf. Pierre Bourdieu's illuminating comments to this effect in 'Legitimation and Structured Interests in Weber's Sociology of Religion,' in *Max Weber, Rationality and Modernity*, ed. Scott Lash and Sam Whimster (London: Allen & Unwin 1987), especially 121–6.

32  Nietzsche, *On the Genealogy of Morals*, essay I, section 13.

33  See 'The Social Psychology of World Religions,' in *From Max Weber*, 270–5; *Economy and Society*, vol. 1, 499. Weber mistakenly reduces Nietzsche's account of the origins of salvation religion to his account of *ressentiment*.

34  For an extensive account, see Warren, *Nietzsche and Political Thought*, chap. 1.

35  Nietzsche, *On the Genealogy of Morals*, essay II, section 7.

36  Ibid., essay III, section 1.

37  Compare Weber's discussion of the causality of religious ideas: 'Not ideas, but material and ideal interests, directly govern men's conduct. Yet very frequently the "world images" that have been created by "ideas" have, like switchmen, determined the tracks along which action has been pushed by the dynamics of interest. "From what" and "for what" one wished to be redeemed and, let us not forget, "could be" redeemed, depended upon one's image of the world.' 'The Social Psychology of World Religions,' 280.

38  See especially Nietzsche, *On the Genealogy of Morals*, essay I, sections 14, 15.

39  Cf. Wolfgang Schluchter's comments on Weber's methodology in *The Rise of Western Rationalism*, 23.

40  Nietzsche, *On the Genealogy of Morals*, essay III, sections 15, 16; Weber, *Economy and Society*, vol. 1, 490–2.

41  Cf. Nietzsche, *The Gay Science*, aphorism 357; Weber, *Economy and Society*, vol. 1, 490–2.

42  Nietzsche, *The Will to Power*, notes 139–41; *The Antichrist*, in *The Portable Nietzsche*, sections 47, 48.

43  Nietzsche, *The Antichrist*, section 49; cf. *Daybreak*, trans. R.J. Hollingdale (Cambridge: Cambridge University Press 1982), aphorism 58; *The Will to Power*, note 196.

44  Nietzsche, *The Antichrist*, section 49.

45  Nietzsche, *On the Genealogy of Morals*, essay III, sections 15, 16; *The Antichrist*, section 26; *Daybreak*, aphorism 79.

46  *The Antichrist* 44.

47  For an account of Nietzsche's concept of will to power, see Warren, *Nietzsche and Political Thought*, chap. 4.

48  Bourdieu, 'Legitimation and Structured Interests in Weber's Sociology of Religion,' 130.

49  Max Weber, *The Protestant Ethic and the Spirit of Capitalism*, trans. Talcott Parsons (New York: Charles Scribner's Sons 1958), 182.

50  Nietzsche, *On the Genealogy of Morals*, essay III, section 18; cf. *The Gay Science*, aphorism 329. See also Karl Löwith's excellent comments on this aspect of Nietzsche's thought in *From Hegel to Nietzsche*, trans. David Green (Garden City, NY: Doubleday 1967), especially 283–5.

51  Nietzsche, *The Will to Power*, notes 866; cf. *Daybreak*, aphorisms 175, 179, 186, 203, 204; *The Gay Science*, 40.

52  See my analysis of Nietzsche's politics in *Nietzsche and Political Thought*, chap. 7.

53  See, e.g., Herbert Marcuse, *Negations*, trans. Jeremy Shapiro (Boston: Beacon Press 1968), chap. 6.

54  Weber, *Economy and Society*, vol. 2, 1152.

55  Weber, *The Protestant Ethic and the Spirit of Capitalism*, 181.

56  Weber, *Economy and Society*, vol. 2, 975.

57  Ibid., 223–6.

58  Ibid., vol. 1, 226; vol. 2, 949, 958–6.

59  Weber sounds very much like Marx or Foucault when he writes that 'organizational discipline in the factory has a completely rational basis. With the help of suitable methods of measurement, the optimum profitability of the individual worker is calculated like that of any material means of production. On this basis, the American system of "scientific management" triumphantly proceeds with its rational conditioning and training of work performances, thus drawing the ultimate conclusions from the mechanization and discipline of the plant. The psycho-physical apparatus of man is completely adjusted to the demands of the outer world, the tools, the machines – in short, it is functionalized, and the individual is shorn of his natural rhythm through the functional specialization of the muscles and through the creation of an optimal economy of physical effort. This whole process of rationalization, in the factory as elsewhere, and especially in the bureaucratic state machine, parallels the centralization of the material implements of organization in the hands of the master. Thus, discipline inexorably takes over ever larger areas as the satisfaction of political and economic needs is increasingly rationalized.' Weber, *Economy and Society*, vol. 2, 1156. Cf. 1148–55.

60  Weber, 'Parliament and Government in Reconstructed Germany,' appendix to *Econ-*

*omy and Society*, vol. 2, 1394. Cf. *Economy and Society*, vol. 1, 219, 224–5, 253.

61 Weber, 'Parliament and Government,' 1402. Cf. Foucault's concept of 'bio-power,' which describes the shift to a society in which power is exercised not directly through coercion (power over death), but through exercising administrative control of the means of welfare. See 'The Right of Death and Power over Life,' in *The Foucault Reader*.

62 Weber, *Economy and Society*, vol. 1, 161–2.

63 Ibid., vol. 2, 975.

64 Ibid., vol. 1, 93.

65 Ibid., 108.

66 Ibid., 108; cf. 161–2.

67 Ibid., 138.

68 Where such constraints occur – in government regulations, union demands for participation in management, and so on – these represent irrationalities with respect to instrumental calculation. Still, when they do occur, it is best for the formal rationality of capitalism that they occur predictably, which means that capitalism is most comfortable with bureaucratized government and unions.

69 Interestingly, Weber was also a critic of the view – still popular today – that there is a necessary relation between market freedom and a reduction of coercion in everyday life. Weber sounds like Marx when he writes that, because there exist legally guaranteed differences in the distribution of property, 'the formal right of the worker to enter into any contract whatsoever with any employer whatsoever does not in practice represent for the employment seeker even the slightest freedom in the determination of his own conditions of work, and it does not guarantee him any influence in the process. It rather means, at least primarily, that the more powerful party in the market, i.e., normally the employer, has the possibility to set the terms, to offer the job "take it or leave it," and, given the normally more pressing economic need of the worker, to impose his terms upon him. The result of contractual freedom, then, is in the first place the opening of the opportunity to use, by the clever utilization of property ownership in the market, these resources without legal restraint as a means for the achievement of power over others.' *Economy and Society*, vol. 2, 729–30. And Weber sounds like Foucault when he draws the consequences of his analysis: the constitution of juridical subjects free to engage in contracts can produce in an increase in coercive discipline of labour. 'The more comprehensive the realm of structures whose existence depends in a specific way on "discipline" – that of capitalist commercial enterprises – the more relentlessly can authoritarian constraint be exercised within them, and the smaller will be the circle of those in whose hands the power to use this type of constraint is concentrated and who also hold the power to have such authority guaranteed to them the legal order. A legal order which contains ever so few mandatory and prohibitory norms and ever so many "freedoms" and "empower-

ments" can nonetheless in its practical effects facilitate a quantitative and qualitative increase not only of coercion in general but quite specifically of authoritarian coercion.' *Economy and Society*, vol. 2, 731.

70 Weber, 'Parliament and Government in a Reconstructed Germany,' 1454; cf. *Economy and Society*, vol. 1, 109–11; 'Socialism,' in *Max Weber: Selections in Translation*, ed. W.G. Runciman (Cambridge: Cambridge University Press 1978).

71 Weber, *Economy and Society*, vol. 1, 137–8.

72 Weber, 'Politics as a Vocation,' 78.

73 Ibid., 79.

74 Ibid., 77. On the ambiguities and possibilities of Weber's conception of politics, see Warren, 'Max Weber's Liberalism for a Nietzschean World,' *American Political Science Review* 82 (March 1988), 31–50, especially 35–7.

75 Habermas, *The Theory of Communicative Action*, vol. 1, 241–2.

76 On this issue, see Habermas's reconstruction of Weber's broad conception of rationality, *The Theory of Communicative Action*, vol. 1, especially 334–5.

77 See Warren, 'Max Weber's Liberalism for a Nietzschean World,' 32–3, 43–5.

78 Weber, *Economy and Society*, vol. 1, 51.

79 Ibid., 52.

80 See Carole Pateman's analysis of Hobbes and Locke in *The Problem of Political Obligation* (Chichester: John Wiley & Sons 1979). Pateman looks for the intersubjective understandings implicit in contractual obligations – understandings presupposed by, rather than a result of, instrumental rationality.

81 Mark Warren, 'Liberal Constitutionalism as Ideology: Marx and Habermas,' *Political Theory* 16 (November 1989), 511–34.

82 See Warren, 'Liberal Constitutionalism as Ideology: Marx and Habermas.'

83 See note 69 above.

84 Weber, *Economy and Society*, vol. 2, 656–7.

85 Schluchter, *The Rise of Western Rationalism*, 91.

86 Weber, *Economy and Society*, vol. 2, 874–5.

87 Ibid., 888.

88 Schluchter, *The Rise of Western Rationalism*, 105.

89 For an immanent critique of legal norms see Roberto Unger, *The Critical Legal Studies Movement* (Cambridge, MA: Harvard University Press 1983). Cf. Issac Balbus's framework of analysis in *The Dialectics of Legal Repression* (New York: Russell Sage Foundation 1973).

90 See Warren, 'Liberal Constitutionalism as Ideology: Marx and Habermas.'

91 Weber, *Economy and Society*, vol. 2, 667; cf. Nietzsche, *Daybreak*, 112.

92 Ibid., 668.

**PART II** POLITICS, TIME, AND BOURGEOIS
MODERNITY

# 5

# Max Weber and the Liberal Political Tradition

## DAVID BEETHAM

Anyone who writes about Weber's political thought confronts a methodological problem at the outset: whether to consider it within a German or a European context, or, if both together, what connection to make between the two. This problem applies with particular force to a consideration of Weber and the liberal political tradition. Which tradition are we talking about? As is well known, German liberalism had its own distinctive tradition, shaped by its defeat in 1848, its surrender to Bismarck and the emergence of a national liberalism in the 1870s, and its compression in the Wilhelmine Reich between the twin forces of a Marxist social democracy on one side, and a politically entrenched Junkerdom on the other. This tradition undoubtedly had its influence on the character of Weber's liberalism. I have always taken the view, however, that a sharply dichotomous treatment of Weber's work, one that accords his sociology universal significance in the history of the discipline while consigning his political thought to the category of a purely localized (and from an Anglo-Saxon viewpoint, aberrant), German history, is simply untenable.[1] This is particularly so if, as I would contend, one of the characteristics of Weber's liberalism was the restatement of its themes in sociological categories. It is within the larger canvas of European liberalism, therefore, that I propose to situate Weber's political thought: to identify the position he occupies within the wider tradition, and the distinctive contribution he made to it at a critical moment in its development.

Within this larger European canvas, then, it is possible to distinguish two contrasting positions on the question of Weber and the liberal tradition taken by commentators on Weber's work. In order to sharpen the focus of my argument I shall present these in ideal-typical terms, to coin a phrase, though

Reprinted with permission from *European Journal of Sociology* 30 (1989), 311–23.

I recognize that the positions so constructed may not represent exactly the views of any one writer.

The first position sees Weber as constituting a problem *for* liberalism.[2] This is because, although he was a self-confessed liberal in his political affiliation and his defence of liberal institutions, the terms on which he was so, and the values to which he gave priority, nonetheless diverged sharply from those of the classical liberal tradition. To begin with, Weber rejected on methodological grounds the natural rights and natural law doctrines that had provided the philosophical underpinning to classical liberalism; any idea, he argued, that the individual could be the possessor of rights or the embodiment of values independently of their social creation was 'pure fiction.' This critique, however, apparently advanced at a purely methodological or philosophical level, concealed a more substantive rejection of the egalitarian and universalistic thrust of classical liberalism, in favour of values that were anything but liberal: the primacy of the nation and national destiny, and the central importance of strong leadership to the political process. It was in terms of those values that Weber defended parliamentary institutions and open electoral competition for the leading offices of state. He was, so it could be said, a liberal without liberal values, a defender of liberal institutions without liberalism. And as such he contributed to the demise of liberalism as a political practice, which was first weakened from within before it came to be destroyed from without.

To those who thus define Weber as a problem *for* liberalism, it becomes a matter of some importance to identify the intellectual influences which contributed to his 'quasi-liberal' stance. Two candidates suggest themselves for the role. One is the tradition of legal formalism or legal positivism, which culminated in the work of Weber's contemporary, Hans Kelsen, and which found expression in Weber's radical separation between formal and substantive rationality, a separation that allowed the rules governing liberal institutions to be divorced from the normative principles that had provided their original inspiration and justification.[3] The other is the figure of Nietzsche, to whose influence can be traced Weber's conviction that ultimate values are not grounded in reason but are a matter of personal affirmation or commitment and stand in irreconcilable conflict with one another, as well as his insistence on the formative role of superior individuals in shaping the values for a whole society.[4] Insofar as Weber constitutes a problem for liberalism, then, the problem was a broader one of the respective influences of legal positivism and Nietzschean ideas on his work; or, to go one step further, a problem of a general intellectual climate at the turn of the century which was in different ways hostile to the rational basis of liberalism. At this point the problem of Weber becomes symptomatic of a wider intellectual challenge to liberal assumptions characteristic of the period.

That is the first position on Weber and liberalism to be considered. The second position, in contrast, sees Weber less as a problem *for* liberalism, than as a penetrating analyst of the problem *of* liberalism, in an age when the social conditions necessary to realize the classical liberal values had been successively undermined, and liberalism itself stood in urgent need of revision.[5] Insofar as there was a problem, in other words, it was not one of Weber and the intellectual influences to which he was exposed, but one that was intrinsic to liberalism itself. On this analysis, classical liberalism had depended upon a favourable constellation of social forces and conditions: of small-scale entrepreneurs operating in a free market, combined with the independence of self-financed activity in the professions. Together these conditions had forged an organic link between the circumstances and interests of the bourgeois class, and liberal values and institutions. By the end of the nineteenth century, however, a number of factors had conspired to erode these conditions and to break that organic link – in short, to create a 'crisis of liberalism.'

Weber's significance, according to this view, was that he provided a definitive analysis of the erosion taking place in the social basis of liberalism, and a convincing demonstration of its irreversibility. The key elements in his account will be familiar. Small-scale units of production were giving way to the large corporation, and the bourgeois class of active entrepreneurs was declining into rentiers or owners of landed property. In all areas of social life the independence of self-financed activity was being replaced by employment in a bureaucratic organization and subordination to its hierarchical authority. The admission of the working class to the suffrage brought with it an assertion of collectivist values, a new social agenda for the state, and the politics of the mass party which undermined the independence of the individual parliamentarian. Finally, abroad, the liberal optimism that free trade would create a mutual harmony of interests through the international division of labour was being shattered by protectionism and imperialist rivalry. In all these ways the conditions characteristic of liberal capitalism were being superseded, and the social basis of classical liberalism was being undermined.

What was required of liberal theory, therefore, in the face of these changes, was a reformulation of liberalism, and a redefinition of the liberal agenda, appropriate to the new circumstances. This Weber also attempted. The outlines of his reformulation are clear, even though some aspects are filled in more completely than others. It involved a redefinition of the relation between state and economy, such that the state, while guaranteeing the conditions for a competitive market, would also provide the working class with its own means of solving the 'social problem' by a legal adjustment of its relative bargaining power with capital. The case for capitalism itself had to be restated, in face of the challenge of state socialism, as part of a wider argument for a pluralism of institutional power centres as the necessary condition for freedom in the bureaucratic age. And bureaucracy itself had to be kept in check and given purposive direction by strong leaders who had proved themselves in competition with others, whether in the economic or the electoral market place, but who derived a democratic legitimacy from consumer preferences or voter choice. Leadership competition in the clearly separate spheres of economy and state, within a capitalist democracy where the working class enjoyed a rightful place – such were the terms of Weber's redefinition of liberalism, and the terms also, he believed, for the successful prosecution of a national political agenda abroad. Although these terms were worked out in the special conditions of Wilhelmine Germany, they were of equal relevance to the wider problems of liberalism in the period, to which Weber's work provided a solution rather than a contributory cause.

Weber, then, as the analyst of the problems *of* liberalism, in contrast to Weber as a problem *for* liberalism – which interpretation is the correct one? I would argue that neither of these is adequate. The first position that I have outlined (Weber as a problem *for* liberalism) presents the challenge to liberalism as occurring at a purely ideological level, as the intrusion of subversive intellectual ideas or currents, and ignores the substantial social changes that had come to undermine liberalism in its classical form by the end of the nineteenth century and were compelling its revision. The inadequacy of the second position lies in the fact that the Weberian diagnosis of, and solution to, the problems of liberalism was not the only one proposed in this period, nor the only one possible within the liberal tradition. That tradition had always been a plural, not to say a contested, one. What requires explanation, therefore, is why Weber came to redefine liberalism in the particular manner that he did. To explain his position, it is necessary to explore Weber's answer to a question that is not only fundamental to liberalism, but also importantly divisive among its adherents: why is freedom *of value*, and for whom? The answer to this question involves tracing his account of Western individualism, and identifying some of the key assumptions of his sociological perspective.

Before I do that, I should like first to underline the distinctiveness of Weber's restatement of liberalism by contrasting it with another such reformulation that was provided in this period, that of the so-called new liberals or social liberals in Britain (not to be confused, of course, with the neo-liberals of the present day). I select that group not to write another chapter in the saga of Weber and his contemporaries, but because its work offers the sharpest possible contrast to his. Theorists such as Hobson and Hobhouse were just as convinced as Weber that the changes of the late nineteenth century had engendered a 'crisis of liberalism,' as one of Hobson's most famous works was called.[6] Moreover, the features they identified as contributing to that crisis were very similar to his: the collapse of *laissez-faire*; the decline of the bourgeoisie into a passive rentier class at home; the intensification of nationalism and the struggle for empire abroad; the arrival of the working class on the political stage; and the urgency of the 'social question.' Yet the manner of their solution to the crisis, and the elements of the liberal tradition to which they appealed, were markedly different from his. For them, solving the social question and redistributing income formed the centrepiece of their agenda, and provided the necessary means to restoring both a pacific policy internationally and a properly liberal politics at home.

The political conundrum with which these 'new liberals' wrestled was one posed by the dominance of the *laissez-faire* doctrine in Britain and its automatic equation with freedom: how was it possible to support state intervention in the economy and still be a true liberal? The solution they arrived at was found in their answer to a more fundamental philosophical question: what is the *purpose* of freedom, and for whom? Simply put, their answer was as follows. The purpose of freedom, in the negative sense of absence of restraint, is to enable everyone to realize their potential for self-development unhindered by the obstacles which other people, or a paternalist or authoritarian state, might place in their way. Yet this self-realization requires more than the *absence* of restraint; it needs also the *presence* of cultural and material resources, without which freedom can have no value, because its purpose cannot be realized. A policy of *laissez-faire*, however necessary it might have been once to break down the barriers of a mercantilist regime, had created a sharp divide between the propertied, who had the means to make use of their freedom, and the unpropertied, who did not. It was now the task of the state to effect a much wider distribution of the cultural and material resources necessary to individual self-realization. Such an interventionist policy meant an enlargement of freedom – 'interfering with individuals so as to set free new and larger opportunities' – because it was directed towards the true purpose of liberty.[7]

By means of this redefinition the new liberals were able to present as authentically liberal an ambitious social agenda, including redistributive taxation, public education, and state control of key resources such as land, finance, and major utilities, so that they could be made freely available to anyone who wanted to set up in production. This agenda, they insisted, was not socialist, because its goal was individual independence, not collectivist organization. At the same time they believed that a determined redistributive policy would strike at what Hobson called the 'tap root' of imperialism: the surplus profits which, because of the limited consumer base at home, were directed overseas as capital export, involving colonial exploitation, international rivalry, and the corruption in turn of the whole character of domestic politics.[8]

The world of the 'new liberals' is thus recognizably the same world as Weber's, but their diagnosis of the 'crisis' and their redefinition of liberalism is markedly different from his. We could note their diametrically opposed attitude to nationalism and empire, or their belief in the continuing viability of small-scale production. Yet I would emphasize something more fundamental underlying the rest. Although the new liberals do not use the language of natural rights or natural law, they nevertheless retain the convictions to which that language gave powerful expression: the natural equality between people, and the potential of all for self-development. In their view this universalist principle classical liberalism had announced, but had been unable to realize, because it had been limited by a purely negative definition of liberty, and by the substantial inequalities of property associated with that definition. On a historical perspective, however, the energies unleashed by *laissez-faire* had generated the wealth to make possible a more widespread attainment of the goal of freedom, however much it had concentrated inequalities in the meantime. In other words, the new liberals saw beneath the 'crisis of liberalism' the possibility of realizing the universalist claims which the old liberalism had declared, but been unable to make good.

The contrast with the 'new liberals' exposes with particular clarity a central feature of Weber's liberalism: its rejection, not merely of the philosophical form of natural rights doctrines, but of their universalist substance also. In my view this rejection was not simply casual or contingent, but followed necessarily from the central place Weber assigned in the liberal credo to *individualism*; and judging from the characteristically sociological words, his rejection of a universalist doctrine was linked with the basic premises of his sociology.

As we know, a central theme of that sociology from the *Protestant Ethic* studies onwards was its exploration of the historically distinctive character and conditions of Western individualism. In Weber's view what was essential to Western individualism and what gave it its dynamic force was the creation of specific and localized circumstances. Far from constituting the innate characteristics or capacities of a universal human nature, a comparison with other cultures showed that Western individualism was a unique phenomenon. Of universal significance it might be, through the range and exemplary character of its achievements, but they were achievements nonetheless of a determinate and very particularized historical provenance.

At this point let me take you through the familiar terrain of Weber's studies in *The Protestant Ethic and the Spirit of Capitalism*. As is clear from his anti-critical articles, his concern in that work was not just, or even primarily, with the origins of capitalism; rather it was to define the distinctive characteristics of bourgeois individualism,[9] of which profit-maximizing behaviour was merely one, albeit a particularly effective, expression. These characteristics comprised, on the one hand, an inner isolation that came from taking responsibility for one's own salvation or destiny, without the assurance afforded by the sacraments; on the other, a relentless striving to transform the world through the organization of every aspect of life according to a methodical plan (so-called practical rationalization). As Weber indicates, the one was the product of the other; it was the inner isolation of the individual that drove him (and it was indeed 'him') 'to a relentless and systematic struggle with life,' the inner anxiety that generated an intense worldly activity as its antidote.[10] Together these qualities both defined the specific character of Western individualism and were the source of its distinctive achievements.

Now such a character was far from 'natural' in any sense of that word. To begin with, it stood in sharp contrast to the attitudes towards worldly activity typical of other cultures: the attitude which regarded work as a means to securing an acceptable or traditional level of consumption; or the passive and fatalistic adjustment to life and whatever it may bring; or the withdrawal from the world into mystical contemplation. Over against all these stood the ethic of achievement, the determination to transform the world through the discipline of work, and impose one's stamp on it. At the same time such a character was developed only by suppressing all natural and spontaneous impulses – what Weber called 'the spontaneity of the "status naturalis" ' – and by pursuing a course of life that was markedly different from those who lived in this natural state.[11] In so differentiating themselves from ordinary natures, the Calvinists, Puritans, Methodists, and others proved themselves to be the chosen, the elect, 'a spiritual aristocracy of the predestined saints within the world.'[12]

The distinctive qualities of Western individualism, therefore, and the distinctive character which was its hallmark and the source of its achievements, were on Weber's analysis the product of a unique social context. Far from embodying universal features inherent in human nature as such, which would simply flourish once the restrictions of a confined environment or an oppressive political regime were removed, individualism requires special circumstances to develop, such as the life of the Protestant sects uniquely provided. Far from being the predictable outgrowth of freedom, individualism was the product of a highly confined social milieu, and a high level of psychic repression. As Weber demonstrated particularly clearly in his article on the Protestant sects and the spirit of capitalism, it was not the doctrines of reformed Christianity on their own that developed the distinctive character of the believer, but the continuous social pressure to prove oneself within the community of the elect. In order to hold his own in the circle of believers, Weber writes, the member had to prove repeatedly that he was endowed with the appropriate qualities. 'They were constantly and continuously bred in him.'[13] Paradoxically, not only was the character of individualism a unique social creation, but its expansive dynamic was the product of a highly confined social and psychic environment.

Where, then, does freedom come in? Freedom was necessary, according to Weber, if these qualities of individualism were to have room to assert themselves and make an impression upon the world. Freedom, both as the absence of legal and political restrictions and as the personal independence associated with individual property ownership, was the historical prerequisite for the unique character of individualism to express itself in the world. If Western individualism required the social and psychic pressures of an intense and confined community for the *creation* of its distinctive human character, it also required the freedom of manoeuvre offered by small-scale capitalism operating within a free market environment for its *fulfilment*. The value of such freedom, however, was to be measured by the quality of the human characteristics that it enabled to find expression. And the crisis of liberalism, in turn, was none other than the crisis of that same individualism, brought about by the decline of the social conditions required for both its creation and its fulfilment.

Before I examine more closely the terms of Weber's resolution of that crisis, let me summarize the argument so far. I have identified two divergent tendencies within the liberal tradition. There is what can be called a universalistic or egalitarian tendency, deriving from the natural rights tradition, which emphasizes the potential inherent in everyone for self-realization. Within this perspective, the value of freedom derives from the scope it provides for all for their self-development. The 'new liberals' stood firmly within this tradition. The fault they found with the old liberalism was that the value of freedom was in practice limited by the highly unequal distribution of resources and opportunities for self-development inherent in the given system of private property ownership.

On the other side is a more exclusivist or elitist tendency, which emphasizes the differential qualities that, through a combination of inherent capacities and circumstances, come to be developed in different individuals or groups. From such a perspective freedom has value only to the extent that it provides scope for superior qualities to find expression and make their impact upon society at large. In particular, the qualities defined as superior or exemplary are those that were developed historically among the bourgeoisie in its period of ascendancy. Max Weber stands within this latter tradition. His distinctive contribution to it was to demonstrate that the qualities characteristic of bourgeois individualism were the product of a unique conjunction of social conditions; and that one unintended consequence of that same individualism was to generate processes of social change that threatened the conditions necessary to its survival.

If there is any doubt that both the tendencies I have outlined belong equally to the liberal tradition, we need look no further for confirmation than the work of John Stuart Mill. Not the least of the ambiguities and tensions in Mill's work lies in his attempt to combine the universalist principle that all have equal potential for self-development, with the insistence that the qualities developed in some are more valuable than in others and should have correspondingly greater scope for expression. Nowhere is the tension between these two principles more evidence that in his attitude towards democracy – on the one hand welcoming it as a contribution to self-development for the many, on the other fearful of it as a threat to the superior qualities of the few. The upshot is a characteristically Millite set of compromises: all should have the vote, but some should have more than others; all should have their interests protected through the representative process, but the representatives should be free to decide how those interests should best be protected and advanced.[14]

The tension between these elements is responsible for markedly divergent interpretations of Mill's work. It would be possible, for instance, to read it as an anticipation of Weber. Like Weber, Mill made the problem of the selection and development of particular character types a central one in his social theory. The crucial question about social institutions, he argued, was what human qualities they encouraged: 'the active or the passive type; that which struggles against evils, or that which endures them; that which bends to circumstances, or that which endeavours to make circumstances bend to itself.'[15] At the same time only the active types, he observed, were able to make effective use of free institutions. Notoriously, Mill chided Bentham and his own father for their failure to recognize that liberalism depended upon a particular quality of personality, and for 'claiming representative democracy for England and France by arguments that would equally have proved it the only fit form of government for Bedouins and Malays.'[16] On Representative Government provides the clearest expression of the view that the value of freedom depends upon the capacity to make use of it, and upon the distinctive qualities that it enables to find expression. And that classic statement of liberalism, On Liberty, is as much a celebration of a particular elite character – individuality or individualism – as it is of freedom itself; or rather it is a celebration of the latter because of the former.

However, Mill was no mere proto-Weberian. As Alan Ryan points out, Mill located the source of Western individualism more in the Greek than in the Christian heritage.[17] Christianity he castigated for favouring the passive rather than the active character, and he saved his special indignation for Calvinism because of its suppression of human diversity.[18] Yet the difference lies much deeper than the question of where the source of Western individualism was to be found. Mill's concept of human nature was essentially Aristotelian in its teleological assumption that there were certain capacities whose development and exercise constituted the distinctive excellence of human beings. When joined with the mid-Victorian belief in progress – in successive stages of civilization through which all societies would, and had to, travel – this Aristotelian conception delivered an expansive vision of future possibilities. If the many were not capable of realizing their distinctively human potential, this was only *not yet*; and it was possible to envisage a society in the future where the ideal of self-development would be available to all that was at present the prerogative of a superior few. It was the concept of progress that enabled Mill to square the circle, as it were, and to combine the universalizing and egalitarian with the particularistic and elitist tendencies of the liberal tradition in a single, albeit unstable, synthesis.

That synthesis could not survive the strains imposed on liberalism in the last decades of the nineteenth century, in particular by the changes in the character and circumstances of the bourgeois class. The 'new liberals' pursued the expansionist possibilities envisaged by Mill, but sought a new constituency for their support in the working class electorate. Weber, in contrast, saw only a narrowing of the opportunities for realizing the qualities that he most admired in the classical bourgeoisie.

I have said that the crisis of liberalism was for Weber a crisis of individualism. On his analysis the most serious, because irreversible, aspect of the crisis was the progressive narrowing of the scope for independent self-financed activity in all spheres of life, as the size of organizations took them beyond the range of individual ownership or financing. So the individual entrepreneur became a manager in a capitalist combine, the independent parliamentarian a member of a party machine, the individual scholar an employee of a university or a research institute, and so on. Everywhere the separation of the individual from ownership of the means of production and administration was proceeding inexorably. In the process the distinctive attributes of bourgeois individualism themselves became *institutionalized*: the impetus to practical rationalization became a function of organizational structures and technocratic systems; the achievement ethic became a matter of pursuing a predictable career within a bureaucratic hierarchy. What was lost was the possibility of making any independent and individual impact upon the world.

What room, then, was there left for individualism in the bureaucratic age? Weber considered two possibilities. One was the pursuit of individuality through a rejection of the world and its everyday demands, and the cultivation of the personality via an alternative lifestyle: that of the Bohemian, the anarchist, or the mystic.[19] This possibility he rejected precisely because it involved a retreat from the world, an individualism devoid of any public significance or of any practical impact upon society, and therefore profoundly anti-bourgeois in character.

The other possibility was the individualism writ large of those who stood at the head of organizations and whose positions provided scope for individual assertion, the exercise of personal responsibility, and the possibility of making an impact upon the world through the institutional structure they commanded and on which they were able to impress their own personal stamp. It was here that Weber saw the remaining opportunity for that practice, world-shaping individualism that had characterized the bourgeoisie in its period of ascendancy. It was an individualism, however, that had become further narrowed from an attribute shared by all among the elect, to an exceptional quality of charismatic figures who alone had the scope or opportunity to impress their individual will upon the society around them. In the *Protestant Ethic* charisma itself is a gift possessed by all believers;[20] in Weber's later sociology it becomes a special attribute of leadership. In like manner the individualism which was a general characteristic of the 'heroic age of capitalism,' as Weber terms it, becomes in the bureaucratic age a special quality of heroes.

It is these qualities of individualism writ large, however, that once more define the value and purpose of freedom for Weber. The justification he gave for the institutions of liberal democracy was in terms of their effectiveness in training and selecting political leaders, and of the scope they offered for the exercise of that leadership.[21] The advantage of a constitutionally powerful, as opposed to a merely 'token,' parliament, with its public procedures and open competition for power, lay in its development of the qualities appropriate to the highest office: a readiness to take personal responsibility for policy, the determination to see it through, and the ability to defend it in the face of public examination and criticism. Such a parliament would operate as a kind of forcing house and selection ground for these qualities.

Similarly, the justification for electoral democracy lay in the scope it provided for the individual leader.[22] Herein lay Weber's particular originality. Most liberal elitists of his time saw only the negative side of mass democracy – the surrender of independence on the part of the individual parliamentarian to the discipline of the party, and the baneful influence of the irrational masses on the political process and the quality of its elites – and they advocated the restriction of the suffrage and other measures of a reactionary kind. Weber, however, discerned the scope that the processes of mass democracy provided for individual leaders to develop and articulate a personal vision beyond the constraints of party, and the power they gave to put it into effect. But this necessitated a redefinition of democracy itself, and an understanding of the limited role that the masses could and should play within it: to elect the leader of their choice, and through that election to provide a legitimation for the leader's power, but thereafter to keep their place. In other words, the 'room for manoeuvre' of individual leaders presupposed as its necessary condition the withdrawal of the masses from any influence over the determination of policy, that is, their effective depoliticization.

Let me summarize my argument and draw to a conclusion. Weber's redefinition of liberalism in terms of competitive leadership democracy, so I would contend, demonstrates an essential continuity in his concern for the qualities of individual character that liberal institutions allowed to develop and find expression, whether that character was defined in terms of the individualism of the classical bourgeois period, or the rarer and more intensified articulation of those same qualities in the individual leader of the bureaucratic age. Such an emphasis, however, was all of a piece with that continuous preoccupation of Weber's sociological work, to understand the way in which social formations moulded and selected particular character types – a preoccupation that was evident from his earliest studies of East Elbian agriculture, his work on the Protestant ethic, his survey of industrial workers, the program of research he sketched out for the German Sociological Society, to the last comparative studies on the major world religions. With this emphasis Weber can be said to have provided a sociological foundation for the elitist tendency in the liberal tradition, to which he so clearly belongs, and according to whose conception the value of freedom is to be assessed by the quality of character that it allows to find expression. If at this point we accord a place to a Nietzschean influence in Weber's work, this is only because he was already predisposed towards it by long-standing conviction.

In the light of this conclusion it is now possible to give a clear answer to the question I posed at the outset: should we see Weber as a problem for liberalism, or as a penetrating analyst of the problems of liberalism? The answer is that he is both; he is a problem for liberalism precisely *because of* the analysis of, and the solution to, the problems of liberalism that he offered. This is to say that the problem of Weber is none other than the problem of liberalism itself, at the point when it becomes divorced from the egalitarian thrust of the natural rights tradition and its universalist justification for freedom.

What exactly is that problem? It is that a purely contingent link forged between freedom and its purposes can be the more readily broken, the narrower the group for whose qualities freedom is valued as a means. To put it simply, if it can be shown, for instance, that the qualities desired of an individual leader could emerge and develop without a general freedom, or even that they could find expression only at the expense of restricting the freedom of others, would not such a restriction then be justified? And if the chief purpose of democracy is to provide an effective legitimation for political leadership, would it not become redundant if such legitimation could be provided equally well by a revival of religious belief, or a sufficient conviction in the leader's mission, or the national destiny that the leader serves? Without a more principled defence of freedom and democratic rights they will become vulnerable to the freedom of the political leader to impose his or will upon society, a freedom whose exercise typically presupposes a corresponding diminution in the freedom of others.

We do not need the dramatic evidence from a Fascist or Nazi dictatorship to demonstrate such a tendency. We need look no further than that bastion of political liberty, in 1988 celebrating the tercentenary of its 'Glorious Revolution,' called Great Britain. No more archtypical example of the plebiscitary leader of Weberian hue exists than Margaret Thatcher. And no clearer demonstration could we have that the freedom of expression for the leader's will, when harnessed to the powers of the contemporary state, presupposes a reduction in political freedom for everyone else, not to mention an abject servility on the part of her closest supporters. A depoliticized citizenry was indeed the conscious goal of Thatcher's rule, even though the goal is itself articulated in the name of a general freedom. That freedom, however, is to be understood entirely as a freedom of choice in the consumer market, a freedom which Weber himself termed an 'iron cage,' because of the inexorable hold that he envisaged such choices would come to exercise over the whole of life. Paradoxically, however, consumer freedom is nowadays the necessary counterpart to the general depoliticization that is required if a leader is to be able to impose her will, and to assert her individual vision, upon society. And our urgent need today is not only to understand the character and implications of Weber's solution to the 'crisis of liberalism' in his time; we need also to free ourselves from the limitations of its categories, if we are seriously to confront the problems of freedom in the contemporary world.

## NOTES

1 See D. Beetham, *Max Weber and the Theory of Modern Politics*, 2d ed. (Cambridge 1985).

2 This position is mostly held by those who themselves argue from a natural rights perspective. See, e.g., Leo Strauss, *Natural Right and History* (Chicago 1953), chap. 2; J.P. Mayer, *Max Weber and German Politics* (London 1943). It is discussed in R. Bendix and G. Roth, *Scholarship and Partisanship* (Berkeley 1971), 62–7; and more recently in R. Eden, 'Doing without Liberalism,' *Political Theory* 10 (1982), 379–407.

3 For a more general argument about the effect of this tradition on German liberalism, see J.H. Hallowell, *The Decline of Liberalism as an Ideology* (London 1946).

4   For accounts of the influence of Nietzsche on Weber see E. Fleischmann, 'De Weber à Nietzsche,' in W.J. Mommsen and J. Osterhammel, eds, *Max Weber and His Contemporaries* (London 1987), 405–21.

5   This is the position advanced, e.g., by Wolfgang Mommsen in 'Max Weber und die Krise des liberalism Systems,' *Jahrbuch der Wittheit zu Bremen* (1976), 133–52; *The Age of Bureaucracy* (Oxford 1974), chap. 5. Mommsen's earlier work, *Max Weber und die deutsche Politik, 1890–1920* (Tübingen 1959), tended more towards the first position.

6   J.A. Hobson, *The Crisis of Liberalism* (London 1909), written as articles over the previous decade; see also Hobson, *Imperialism: A Study* (London 1902). For L.T. Hobhouse see in particular *Liberalism* (London 1911); *Democracy and Reaction* (London 1901).

7   J.A. Hobson, *The Crisis of Liberalism*, 94.

8   J.A. Hobson, *Imperialism*, note 6 above, especially part I, chap. 6; part II, chap. 1.

9   'The expression Individualism includes the most heterogeneous things imaginable. What is here understood by it will, I hope, be clear from the following discussion.' M. Weber, *The Protestant Ethic and the Spirit of Capitalism* (London 1930), 222 n22. See ibid., 105ff, for that 'discussion.'

10   Ibid., 105, 112, etc.

11   Ibid., 119, 127, 154, etc.

12   Ibid., 121.

13   H.H. Gerth and C.W. Mills, *From Max Weber* (London 1948), 320.

14   J.S. Mill, *On Representative Government* (London: Everyman's Library 1964).

15   Ibid., 211.

16   Ibid., 197.

17   A. Ryan, 'Mill and Weber on History, Freedom and Reason,' in W.J. Mommsen and J. Osterhammel, note 4 above, especially 117.

18   J.S. Mill, *On Liberty* (London: Everyman's Library 1964), 120.

19   For a discussion of Weber's attitude to the Stephan George circle, see Marianne Weber, *Max Weber: A Biography* (New York 1975), 455–67. For Weber and the Otto Gross circle, see W. Schwenntker, 'Passion as a Mode of Life,' in W.J. Mommsen and J. Osterhammel, note 4 above, 483–98.

20   M. Weber, note 9 above, 178.

21   D. Beetham, note 1 above, chap. 4.

22   W.J. Mommsen, *The Age of Bureaucracy*, chap. 4; D. Beetham, note 1 above, chap. 8.

# 6

# Max Weber and the Bourgeoisie

TRACY B. STRONG

> If thou will weep my fortune take mine eyes. I know thee well.
> — Lear to Gloucester in *King Lear*, Act IV

What does Max Weber mean by the words 'scientifically objective'? Only recently have scholars been able to ask that question in its proper context. This essay is an exploration of that context and, I hope, an answer to the question. Until recently, Max Weber's work has served for Anglo-American social scientists as a paradigm of detached and 'value-free' social science. That this understanding responded to needs buried deep in the collective psyche of English-language social science now seems evidence – not even the writings available in English translation supported the vision of Weber as the dispassionate social scientist the Americans sought to portray to themselves.

In great part, this seems to me to reflect the lack of a proper context in which to read Weber. No only was little attention paid to the political and cultural context in which Weber found himself,[1] but, more importantly perhaps, even less was paid to the company in which one read Weber. In the Anglo-American world, Weber was read as an opponent to Marx, and as a proto-trans-atlanticist.[2] It is with some bemusement, then, that one approaches the texts in which Weber can suggest that any honest modern scholar must admit 'he could not have accomplished crucial parts of his own work without the contributions of Marx and Nietzsche.'[3] Part of the reason for the 'new Weber' is that we have begun to read him in relation not only to Marx and Nietzsche but also to the European philosophical tradition, and with a mind educated by developments in the philosophy of language and epistemology over the last two decades.[4]

Most overlooked in the past seems to me Weber's constant and repeated focus on the changes that modern social structure is producing in what it means to be a person.[5] He writes in *Economy and Society*: 'Most generally one can say that the bureaucratization of all domination (*Herrschaft*) very strongly furthers the development of "rational matter of factness" and of "men of calling and professional expertise" (*Berufs and Fachmenschtum*).[6] This passage is about the fact that the modern world tends to produce people of a certain quality of character. In a world of such beings, all knowledge becomes instrumental and is no longer a standard for judgment. Knowledge is not 'naturally' such, only such for beings like these. For the *Fachmenschen*, the only good reason to choose one action over another is that it works, or, possibly, that it is aesthetically more pleasing. With this point in mind Weber argues that we confront a crisis in legitimacy and authority, in the sense that we no longer have (our old) criteria available by which to recognize the correctness or judge the validity of a policy choice. The question that confronts all serious thinkers, no matter of what political persuasion, says Weber,[7] has to do with the kind of justification that can be advanced for political choices in a context in which the past no longer seems to provide relevant or valid criteria.

The premise of Max Weber's social science is that it must and can deal only with those objects that have meaning for human beings. In his essay 'Objectivity in Social Science and Social Policy' Weber designates this realm as 'culture' and defines it as 'a finite segment of the meaningless infinity of the world process, given meaning and significance from the standpoint of human beings.'[8] Meaning thus does not lie in the world – indeed, meaning consists in limiting the world, or in giving limits to the world. Weber goes on to indicate first that humans are 'cultural beings,' that is, beings who can give significance to the world. He establishes this not empirically but, in a conscious echo of Kantian metaphysics, by the assertion that this is the 'transcendental presupposition' of every cultural science.

A 'transcendental presupposition' calls us to the idea of a 'transcendental deduction,' the term by which Kant designated the elaboration of that which has to be the case for a given entity to have existence at all. A transcendental deduction cannot be directly demonstrated, but one can show that its supposition is required for sense to be made at all. In the *Critique of Pure Reason*, Kant shows (definitively, one may say) that we know reality through the forms of sense and the categories of understanding. We know the world that our mind constructs and makes available to us – there is nothing else, and nothing else is needed. These categories are the transcendental presupposition of our understanding.

This means that an investigation of the world through social science will also be for Weber an acknowledgement of who we are – of the fact that we are cultural beings, since only as cultural beings do we know the world. (If you realize that you are looking at the world through a lens, what you see in the world will eventually tell you something about the lens, even if you cannot independently examine the lens.) In taking over this language, however, Weber has also historicized it. He continues the passage cited above with the assertion that the possibility of social science is premised on the existence of a particular type of individual, namely the '*historische Individuen*,' whose nature it is to lend meaning. They make meaning and cannot help doing so, because they are historical beings. This is what it means to be human.

On the surface, Weber appears here to be making a distinction somewhat analogous to that made in Hegel and common among the neo-Kantians, some of whom had been his friends and intellectual allies.[9] There the social or human sciences (*Geisteswissenschaften*) are differentiated from the natural sciences (*Naturwissenschaften*) in terms of differing relations of the truth pursued to the activity of pursuing it. This distinction itself had its origin in Hegel's distinction of the mathematical sciences, whose truth lay outside themselves, from philosophy, whose truth was part of its activity.[10] For Weber, as for Hegel and the neo-Kantians, the objects of investigation of the natural sciences are built by theory: these objects do not affect us and have no scientific existence independently of our cognition of them as scientific entities. For example, how we predict the tides does not affect what the tides are. Tides have neither intention nor purpose; since they cannot confer meaning on their activity or on that of others, they are distinct from whatever we make of them scientifically. Hence in the natural sciences, most centrally perhaps in mathematics and physics, 'objectivity' is a necessary part of the theoretical construct. One cannot imagine a natural science that would not be what one would call objective: objectivity poses no problem.

In fact, however, Weber's point is somewhat different from that made by Hegel and the neo-Kantians. For Weber, those who practice or pursue 'objectivity' in the realm of social science and social policy have to be understood and have to understand themselves as 'historical beings,' that is, as never transcendent to the object of investigation. Furthermore, since social science is about human beings, that is, beings who confer meaning, and is itself a conferring of meaning, it must in its activity reflect the premise of human culture, namely that meaning has been and is being conferred. It must do so not only prior to the social scientist's activity, but also in that activity itself. This is the premise of Weber's understanding of 'objectivity' in the social sciences.[11]

In slightly humbler language, this means that Weber seeks a social science whose standpoint does not claim to escape from the strictures it lays on the subject matter of its own analysis. Weber does not want to develop a social science that somehow claims to escape the world of which it is a part and which gave birth to it.[12] Thus, in 'Science as a Vocation,' Weber does not remain with the distinction of *Geistes-* and *Natur-Wissenschaften*, but suggests rather that there is a parallel between Kantian epistemology and Lukácsian esthetics: at best the neo-Kantian distinction has pragmatic value. 'Kant ... took for his point of departure the presupposition: "Scientific truth exists and it is valid," and then asked: "Under which presuppositions of thought is truth meaningful and possible?" '[13] Note that for Kant, according to Weber, truth itself is a *presupposition*. Thus the 'transcendental premise' of the social sciences cannot be truth, but rather the fact that human beings give meaning from a 'particular point of view,' that is, a set of historical presuppositions. It is not, however, from just any point of view, as if points of view were a matter of free choice, of which animal cage to get into in a zoo. The points of view in question are those that are available to us, and while one could in principle always develop a 'new' one, there are only the points of view that there are.

Points of view – what Nietzsche would have called perspectives – correspond to the particularities of the human condition, to the forms of life that are available to us as humans. Among these, Weber says, some are 'more meaning-ful' than others. It is the meaningfulness to human beings – that is, that we encounter them as important in our lives – that gives us subject-matter to have a science about. Thus Weber can refer to the question of 'the scarcity of means' as the 'fundamental social economic problem.'[14]

None of this should be taken to imply that any source of meaning is in any way privileged in the sense of being universal. It makes an epistemological difference if one sees scarcity as a universal given of the human condition, or as something that humans encounter and have to deal with when they encounter it. Meaning cannot, therefore, even in this case, be derived from the 'facts themselves' (Weber places the expression in quotation marks) because all social science starts from the concerns that a social scientist has as a particular being in history. It follows from this that for Weber whatever we mean by 'objectivity' cannot rest simply on the 'facts' or on 'being true to the facts,' since the 'facts' are always what has been selected from a world that in its chaotic multiplicity far exceeds any attempts we can make to exhaust it.[15]

To this Weber adds a number of claims. Even though social science must by its nature pursue 'causal explanations,' it cannot pursue 'general laws.' A general law would in fact require transcending the historicity of the investigator for the explanation of the 'world as a whole' rather than explaining something that is individual.[16] While Weber does not want to escape the historicity of the investigator, it is also important to note that when Weber talks of an 'investiga-tor' and 'meanings' that the investigator has, he does not mean meanings in what one might see as a narrow, 'subjective,' individual sense. At the beginning of *The Protestant Ethic and the Spirit of Capitalism*, for instance, Weber places the author, and by extension all those who would write on matters of general concern, under the compulsion of their own past: 'Any product of Western civilization is *bound* to ask himself ...'[17]

The meanings that are the subject matter of the social scientist are those he must investigate in response to and out of his own historicity; one might be tempted to say that they derive from the particular 'thrownness' of the investigator into the world. It is thus impossible to do social science without acknowledging who and what one is in history. Or, more accurately, doing social science must at the same time also be an acknowledgment of one's place in history. As we shall see in more detail below, the central faults that social scientists can make all come from the unwillingness or refusal to so acknowledge themselves.

Much as Nietzsche would have had it, the social scientist in fact understands the past only by what is most powerful in the present. In this anti-Hegelian mode – we know that Weber thought perverse the influence of Hegel on Germany[18] – Weber writes, still in the 'Objectivity' essay: 'The number and type of causes which have influenced any given event are always infinite and there is nothing in the things themselves to set some of them apart as alone meriting attention ... Order is brought to this chaos only on the condition that in every case only a part of concrete reality is interesting and significant to us, because only it is related to the cultural values with which we approach reality.'[19] There are two intertwined problems here. The first has to do with the cultural values of which we are the issue, and the second with the reason that those cultural values lead us to want to make sense of the world.

I shall first approach the question, 'What, now, are the conditions that govern the significance(s) that we can attribute to cultural phenomena?' It is clear that for Weber an infinity of meanings can logically be attributed.[20] But it is equally clear and much more important to understand that this in no way implies to him that we are beings who can/will give that infinite sense. It is always the case, perhaps, that something else can be made of the world, but this statement has no meaning until something else is actually made of the world. There is, as I noted above, no reservoir of interpretations waiting to be fished from. The world for Weber, as for the early Wittgenstein, is, and is only, everything that is the case.[21]

We are not logical beings for Weber, but historical ones. Thus, understanding our attribution of meaning to cultural phenomena – doing social science – results in Weber not so much in the discovery of ourselves or in the revelation of our self to our selves, as in the practical acknowledgment of who we in fact are, that is, of our position in history. Weber emphasizes here that there are reasons for us to insist on self-ignorance.[22] It is clear that as historical beings we are certain kinds of beings and do not have a choice not to be those beings. Though we might want to insist that we are not what we have been, that stance will, for Weber no more than for Freud, make us other than who we are.

So the question one must first ask is 'What kind of historical beings are we?' To this, the simplest answer that Weber gives is that we are creatures who live under the conditions of general rationalization of social relationships, namely the 'bureaucratization of all forms of domination.' By 'bureaucratization of all forms of domination' Weber does not mean simply the system of organization by which large institutions govern their day-to-day affairs. In *Economy and Society* he argues that the general nature of *Herrschaft* ('authoritarian power of command,' translated most often as 'authority' or 'domination') designates: 'The situation in which the manifested will (command) of the ruler or rulers is meant to influence the conduct of one or more others (the ruled) and actually does influence it in such a way that their conduct to a socially relevant degree occurs as if the ruled had made the content of the command the maxim of their conduct for its very own sake.'[23]

Weber apologizes for what he terms the 'awkward' quality of the definition, pointing especially at the 'as if' formula.' The 'as if' in fact allows him to suggest that obedience occurs in the manner of a Kantian categorical imperative ('for its very own sake') even though the command exists because someone has influenced the behaviour of another. Leaving aside the sociological complexities in this statement, what is important here for our purposes is that authoritatively engendered behaviour is experienced as if it were autonomy. That is, it is the nature of the modern state that the ruled think that the rules under which they live are in fact rules for everyone, that is, their rules. What then is the autonomy experienced under the 'bureaucratization of all forms of domination'?

Bureaucracy, argues Weber, is a situation in which 'obedience is thus given to norms rather than to the person.'[24] 'Bureaucracy is the form of authoritative legitimacy in which obedience is due to and rests on norms rather than persons. It is thus a form of domination in which commands are linked not to human beings but rather to abstract and non-personal entities. There is "objective" discharge of business ... according to calculable rules and "without regard for persons." '[25]

In this, bureaucracy is set by Weber in opposition to the political, for politics, Weber says, 'means conflict,' that is, a relation between persons. 'Bureaucracy,' Weber suggests, 'failed completely whenever it was expected to deal with political problems.' The two forms are 'inherently alien' to each other.[26] In part this seems to be because bureaucracy effaces or disguises the fact that there is ruling going on at all. Officials, even at the highest level, tend, says Weber, to think of themselves merely as the first official of their enterprise. Rules replace ruling, and 'it is decisive for the modern loyalty to an office that in the pure type, it does not establish a relationship to a person ... but rather is devoted to impersonal and functional purposes.'[27] Here Weber attaches himself again to Nietzsche and to the latter's anxieties about 'all herd and no shepherd.'[28]

This situation has abrogated to itself, Weber seems to indicate, much of the aura that used to surround the old churches. Indeed, the process of depersonalization is not limited to politics. He writes:

> The political official – at least in the fully developed modern state – is not considered the personal servant of the ruler. Likewise, the bishop, the priest and the preacher are in fact no longer, as in early Christian times, carriers of a purely personal charisma, which offers other-worldly sacred values under the personal mandate of a master, and in principle only responsible to him, to everybody who appears worthy of them and asks for them. In spite of the partial survival of the old theory, they have become officials in the service of a functional purpose, a purpose which in the present-day 'church' appears at once impersonal and ideologically sanctified.[29]

There are, however, political consequences for both individual and society when the procedures of bureaucratized domination supplant the choices of politics. Weber argues that to the degree that election (through some kind of voting, such as a plebiscite) plays no major role in the structuring of an organization, then that organization will more easily tend to rationalize its procedures, that is, to make them rule-governed. In fact, over the long term, bureaucratic organization must devalue any power obtained through election, since that tends to lessen the claim to rational competence. Weber writes:

> [T]he 'separation' of the worker from the material means of production, destruction, administration, academic research [soldiers, civil servants, assistant professors] and finance in general is the common basis of the modern state, in its political, cultural and military sphere, and of private capitalist economy. In both cases, the disposition of these means is in the hands of that power whom the bureaucratic apparatus ... directly obeys or to whom it is available in case of need. This apparatus is equally typical of all those organizations; its existence and function are inseparably cause and effect of this concentration of the means of operation ... Increasing public ownership in the economic sphere today unavoidably means increasing bureaucratization.[30]

A deadly process is initiated. Alienation encourages bureaucratization encourages the sense of autonomy. To the degree that rational competence becomes a basis for social organization, the introduction of anything new to a framework (that is, not legitimated in terms of that framework) will necessarily have to come from beyond that organization. In a bureaucracy, the political problem is to find the sources of the new, sources that must come from outside the rationalized structure.[31] 'The decisive question,' Weber proclaims in *Parliament and Governance in a Reconstructed Germany*, 'about the future of Germany's political order must be: How can parliament be made fit to govern?'[32] The reason this is now the central problem, he argues, is that 'Bismarck had dishabituated [Germany] from worrying about public affairs ... [and] the nation [had] permitted itself to be talked into accepting something ... which in truth amounted to the unchecked rule of the bureaucracy.'[33] It is a matter of recruitment: since the 'essence of politics is ... struggle, the recruitment of allies and of a voluntary following,' it is impossible to get training in this difficult art 'under the career system of the *Obrigkeitsstaat* [the administrative state].'[34]

For Weber, over the long run, rationalization of social relationships runs counter to all forms of political democracy. At first, he allows, political democratization tends to increase and enhance social rationalization, for it encourages the notion that all individuals are to be treated on the same basis. But political decision-making procedures, he insists, are ultimately non-rational. The tendency to rationalization, therefore, will be to reduce the importance of procedures such as voting in the face of more thoroughly rationalized and rule-governed processes. To the degree that this happens, specifically 'human' solutions (ones that involve persons and thus rest on ultimately non-rational choices) will be increasingly devalued.

They will be attacked on the grounds that they are irrational, or non-rational, means to an end. The attack, however, will also be an attack on the idea that the means for social policies should be human means. Rules which make, or appear to make a claim to universality, in effect deny the historical and human quality of decisions and policies. Weber writes: 'It is decisive for the specific nature of modern loyalty to an office, that, in the pure type, it does not establish a relation to a person, like a vassal's or disciple's faith in feudal or patrimonial relations of authority. Modern loyalty is devoted to an impersonal functional (*sachlichen*) purpose (*Zweck*).'[35] For Weber there is a danger that persons, and thus the non-rational, will be eliminated from the modern world.

One should note at this point, however, that Weber is caught in a paradox. The historical nature of human beings in the present is to be increasingly without a historical nature. Before exploring his approach to this paradox, a number of additional factors which complicate the world even more must be examined.

In relation to the conduct of political and social life, the entire quality of human relations is affected by the rationalization of society. Weber notes that rationalization tends to promote situations where business is discharged according to calculable rules and without regard for 'persons.' Furthermore, the notion of legitimacy that corresponds to this pattern of authority tends to reinforce it in the minds of those subject to it. We think, for instance, that there is something wrong, unjust, if an individual waiting to pay his or her bill at the cashier's is given either special treatment or denied equal treatment because of race, sex, religion, or social origin. In this case, the person would have been treated in terms of his or her particular characteristics, that is, not in terms of universal categories. Even a hundred years ago in the West, this would not have been so widely the case. What we want is for everyone to be treated the same – there are attractive things about bureaucracy and the rationalized pattern of authority.

These processes extend themselves into other realms. The discharge of business without regard for persons – *sine ira et studio* – is 'also the watchword of the market place and, in general, of all pursuits of naked economic interests.' Hence the bureaucratization of society means in fact the domination of those classes (defined in purely economic terms here) that will profit from the market, that is, of the rich. Weber continues explicitly: 'If the principle of the free market is not at the same time restricted, [this] means the universal domination of the "class situation." '[36] Bureaucratization, in other words, tends to encourage the domination of the market over politics, or, more precisely, over what is left of politics.

A Marxist analysis might have said that the domination of the market over politics encourages bureaucratization. Weber and Marx see the same things, but as they arrive at their diagnoses from very different paths, their conclusions are correspondingly different. In particular, Weber does not understand class consciousness as resulting from the obvious domination of politics by economics. Rather, he argues, no common consciousness is formed. By eliminating persons, and replacing them with roles, there is no need for a common consciousness. 'Bureaucracy develops the more perfectly, the more it is "dehumanized," the more completely it succeeds in eliminating from official business love, hatred, and all purely personal, irrational, and emotional elements which escape calculation. This is appraised as its special virtue by capitalism.'[37]

Bureaucracy is thus the front of a great historical process of rationalization that has as its consequence the increasing destruction of affective or status relations between individuals and the progressive domination of the economic over the political.[38] The bureaucrat is in fact the vanguard of history, implicitly a participant in a vast revolutionary process that has totally transformed all relationships. Weber sketches this out in the last pages of the 'Bureaucracy' section of *Economy and Society*. The democratic ethos is tied in with specific substantive questions (on rights, for example) that are not a necessary part of a rational legal system;[39] the non-rational legal system is instrumentally oriented. Such instrumentality can make use of 'rights' and so forth, but rights are clearly only instruments to its instrumentality. In fact, Weber claims, instrumentality has become the world historical *Zweck* for the West.[40] Where there arises a conflict between the substantive parts of the democratic ethos – treating an individual not only fairly, but with dignity, for example – there also arises an incompatibility between bureaucratic procedures and democracy. This incompatibility will most especially be of importance to those in the lower classes, since by what we noted above, they will be increasingly subject to those who have money, to those classes, that is, who will naturally come to dominate the bureaucracy.

This is a little known part of Weber, where although in no ways 'Marxist,' he deals with the same constellation of circumstances as does Marx. He writes: 'The propertyless masses especially are not served by the formal "equality before the law" and the "calculable" adjudication and administration demanded by bourgeois interests.'[41] Thus, for Weber, those who suffer under the bureaucracy the most from the historical process are the working classes.

This is in fact far more complex than most standard arguments about the 'rise of mass society.' It is a mistake to see Weber's position as a sad, grey regret of the decline of the aristocracy in face of the rise of the plebs and faceless anonymity. He is, rather, reasserting an argument that he had made elsewhere against Gustav Schmoller, Wilhelm Roscher, and others,[42] to the effect that although it is in the nature of the bureaucracy to be 'neutral' and instrumental, it is not and cannot be the practice of the bureaucracy to so remain. In fact, Weber argues that the practice of bureaucratic domination goes 'hand in hand with the concentration of the material means of management in the hand of the master,'[43] and that this process occurs in both business and public organizations.

This is the central development of modern society. As Robert Eden has pointed out,[44] to live by the division of labour as a member of the bureaucracy is to partake of the most widespread revolutionary process in the world. Marx had argued in the *Communist Manifesto* that it was in the nature and to the glory of the bourgeoisie that it wipe out all structures that threatened to become permanent. 'All that is solid melts into thin air,' he wrote, signifying that the Faustian urge of the bourgeoisie would tolerate nothing to remain in the form it was in, neither human relations nor commodities.[45] Weber's vision is a cousin to Marx's but with real family differences. It is also true for him that bourgeois society, as expressed socially in rationalized structures, tends to eliminate anything that is solid. But the 'solids' that melt – love, friendship, passion, hatred, marriage, honour, and so forth – are specifically human relations, not just those of the stages prior to the full realization of the bourgeoisie. For Weber, the bureaucracy leaves nothing as it was and transforms previous orders into its own rational vision. To be a bureaucrat is not only not to be a person, but to participate in a historical transformation of the world, far more extensive than any that particular political groups or parties could advocate. Bureaucrats are the locomotive of the train of historical rationalism, destroying all other structures of domination.[46]

Rationalization and bureaucratization are ensured both an objective and a subjective basis of perpetuation. As Weber remarks at the end of *The Protestant Ethic*: 'The Puritan wanted to work in a calling; we are forced to do so. For when asceticism was carried out of monastic cells into everyday life, and began to dominate world morality, it did its part in building the tremendous cosmos of the modern economic order.'[47] In such conditions, ruling is impossible without a bureaucracy.[48] Furthermore, Weber tells us, since bureaucracy bears no necessary relation to any given political economic system, the drive towards perpetuation will take place under both socialist and capitalist states.[49]

Weber implies, indeed asserts, that under no foreseeable conditions will life in other than a rationalized society henceforth be possible. Here his attitude towards the division of labour is importantly different from that of his other two great social scientist contemporaries, Marx and Durkheim. The dream of doing away with the division of labour that had attracted Marx as well as the utopian socialist seems to Weber a pointless one. There was no hope for what Lenin was at about the same period to foresee, the slow re-emergence of 'the elementary rules of social life that have been known for centuries.'[50] We live, rather, in the image made famous at the end of *The Protestant Ethic*, in an 'iron cage,' or better, a 'steel box' (*stahlhartes Gehäuse*), outside of which there is nothing we can see.

Nor does Weber think, as did Emile Durkheim, that the social division of labour is necessary because society and justice are found upon it.[51] Rather, Weber thinks, as does Marx, that the historical process and not the functional basis of society is the most important thing to look at in understanding the human world. Weber thinks that rationalization – a form of theodicy – is the force which is the animation of history, and that none of us has a choice, if we are honest with ourselves, but to acknowledge ourselves as a subject of that force. Thus, what Marx had seen as the source of our alienation – the socially forced and necessary division of labour – is for Weber the fundamental precondition and characteristic of our life.[52] It is still 'alienation' for Weber, but with the difference that there is nothing else to be alienated from. Thus we can no more live without the division of labour implied by bureaucracy than we can get off the track of history.[53]

There is no way around this problem. The inevitability of bureaucracy has nothing to do with its power or potential power. Indeed, as Weber wrote to his friend and student Michels in November 1906, 'indispensability in the economic process means nothing, absolutely nothing in the power position and power chances of the class.'[54] The importance of the bureaucracy derives solely from the fact that it comes to structure alterations in its own image; and the ruler, Weber says, is helpless unless 'he finds support in Parliament,' that is, from an outside and non-rational source.

We have been examining the historical characteristics of the world that govern the significance we can attribute to cultural phenomena. How, then, do beings such as those described above – ourselves – understand the world while fully acknowledging their position in it? If the world is for Weber, as noted above, inexhaustible chaos, then the source and validity of the understanding of this world must be derived not from 'facts' about the world, but from the quality or character of a person of knowledge. What kind a person must one be – what must one have acknowledged about one's historicity – in order to be able to make, to be entitled to make, 'objective' claims about our condition?

The answer is best approached by an examination of the ability to elaborate what Weber calls 'ideal types.' Much has been written both for and against this notion, but the role of the ideal type in establishing the right to make claims about the world has generally been overlooked. The ideal type is for Weber an artificial construction – it is not found, but built. Therefore, he says, it is a 'utopia,' not intended to describe or reflect reality but rather to provide for an 'unambiguous means of expression to such a description.'[55] Weber seems to mean by this that there has never been in history any set of circumstances that looked 'just like' capitalism or even the 'spirit of capitalism.' Rather, Weber's elaboration of capitalism derives from his own ability to understand and accept himself as a historical being, under the compulsions of his age. The 'spirit of capitalism' is thus the assemblage of all those traits that 'in their singularity draw upon and respond to (entnommen) their truth from the meaningful traits of our culture.'[56] It is a thought experiment,[57] which has as its aim to make sense of all the experiences of our own that we are able to acknowledge. At the beginning of The Protestant Ethic, Weber had found himself placed under compulsion to investigate the rationalization process. The whole rhetorical structure of the book has as its aim to allow him at the end hermeneutically to close the circle of his thought and reaffirm the compulsion with which he had started his book. The Puritan had a choice, but we moderns are 'compelled to live' in the rationalized world.

From this conclusion, three things seem to follow. First, to the degree that we are aware of the inchoate complexities that make up who we are, our construction of ideal types will be better. Self-knowledge is the prerequisite for doing good social science in that it allows us to know the parts of our self that are constructing the world we encounter. It is not the case that we factor out our 'subjectivity,' but that we know that we have factored it in. One remembers here a story Marianne Weber reports, that when her husband was asked why he learned so much and what his vast knowledge meant, he responded: 'I want to see how much I can bear.'

Second, the ideal type has a 'moral' intent integral to his 'scientific' one. It compels the acknowledgment of one's own stance and status and thus keeps one from pretending to a transcendence to which one is not entitled. In 'Science as a Vocation,' speaking of the origins of the ideal type, Weber writes that there appeared '[i]n Greece, for the first time, a handy means by which one could put the logical screws on somebody so that he could not come out without admitting either that he knew nothing or that this and nothing else was the truth ... Thus [Weber continues] if we are competent in our pursuit ... we can force the individual, or at least we can help him, to give himself *an account of the ultimate meaning of his own conduct.*'[58]

Lastly, the criterion for a 'better' ideal type will be power. 'There is,' Weber notes, 'only one standard: that of success in the recognition (*Erkenntnis*) of concrete cultural phenomena in their interdependence, their causal determination (*ursachliches Bedingtheit*) and their significance.'[59] The ideal type is a 'clearly thought out' construct: it is this clarity that allows it to construct for us a historical and human realm that functions in the same manner as a transcendent noumenal realm. In Kant, the noumenal realm was a realm whose existence had to be accepted, despite the fact that direct apprehension of it was not possible, in order to account for the fact that we made sense to each other (as we clearly do). In Weber, the ideal type plays the role of the noumenal realm; its status, however, is completely 'this-sided.'

The knowledge we obtain from using the ideal type will be 'objective' as an ordering of the world in categories whose power it is to show ourselves to ourselves as meaningful beings. It functions in a transcendent manner in that it shows us why it is our necessary human burden to make sense. We do not, as with Kant, make sense because of qualities that we have 'naturally.' Rather, in Weber, the equivalent of the noumenal realm is itself a historical product and can be grasped only through his kind of historical sociology. Towards the end of the 'Objectivity' essay, Weber writes: 'The objective validity of all knowledge of experience (*Erfahrungswissen*) rests on and only on the ordering of given reality according to categories which are subjective in a specific sense, namely as presenting the presuppositions of our knowledge, and are tied to the presupposition of the value of that truth which the knowledge of experience alone is able to give us.'[60]

Objective knowledge thus rests on a 'presupposition.' In other words, to be capable of gaining 'objective knowledge,' we must share this presupposition, which can only be a presupposition given or made available to us by our history. Weber goes on immediately to make an extraordinary assertion. To anyone by whom 'this truth is not valued – and the belief in the value of a scientific (*wissenschaftlicher*) truth is the product of a given culture and not given in nature (*Naturgegebenes*) – to him we have nothing to offer of the means (*Mitteln*) of our science.'[61]

To be able to have accepted 'objective truth' as a criterion for one's own life means to be a man of science; however, as Weber informs us in 'Science as a Vocation,' that also means to have accepted what historical sociology enforces on us: the permanence of the division of labour, the necessity of specialization, the demagification of the world, the end of amateurishness. To have accepted and acknowledged as oneself these qualities of the modern world means to have accepted as oneself the position of member of the professional middle classes, of the bourgeoisie. Therefore to acknowledge oneself as a bourgeois is a precondition for being able responsibly to make a claim to scientific truth. Only such a person can face what Weber calls the 'fate of the times,' which he enjoins us to 'bear like men.'[62]

But what is it, one should ask, that the (bourgeois) truth seeker 'bears?' It is precisely not the dispassionate image of the social scientist, such as that presented by Edward Shils in his introduction to his translation of the *Methodology*. It is a demand that one take upon oneself the various and now irreconcilable fragments into which the modern world has been shattered. It is, for Weber, as if our world had returned to a state before there was coherence, not that it had moved to a new and different one.

> We live as did the olden world, not yet disenchanted of demons and gods, but in another sense: just as the Hellene at times sacrificed to Aphrodite and then to Apollo and before all to the gods of his city, so do we still, but in a manner disenchanted and disrobed of the mythic but inwardly true plasticity of that stance (*der mythischen, aber innerlich wahren Plastik jenes Verhaltens*). The destiny of our culture is, however, that we will become more and more clearly conscious of these struggles, after our eyes have been shut for a millennium by the allegedly or presumably exclusive orientation towards the great fervor (*pathos*) of the Christian ethic.[63]

For Weber, as for Nietzsche in *Beyond Good and Evil*,[64] and, for both, contrary to a millennium of Christianity, we must refuse to make sense of the whole world, and must take that meaninglessness on us as far as we can. Since the world for Weber does not and cannot cohere, the danger that confronts us is that we are going to be tempted to make it cohere, and that we will do so with insufficient self-knowledge, in, as it were, an uncontrolled fashion.

If we move to the realm of politics, important consequences follow from this position. There is first of all a political dilemma: the demands of the time require that all people take upon themselves what is properly theirs to do, and to seek no meaning beyond that. This, of course, will not link them together – they will not be a true people. At the end of 'Science as a Vocation,' Weber says that: 'It is not accidental that our highest art is intimate and not monumental, nor that today, only in the smallest communities (*Gemeinschaftskreise*) something pulsates from person to person, in pianissimo, which corresponds to that which erstwhile, as prophetic pneuma, swept through the great communities in a storming fire and welded them together.'

Against this, Weber's analysis of the social and economic conditions of advanced industrial societies and of Germany in particular had indicated, first, that an increasingly large group of people will suffer under the structural developments in such societies – the working class being especially oppressed; and, second, that as the world becomes demagified, there will develop an increasingly large group of those who suffer from that process and for whom any available apparent integration of their world will suffice. Hence the fundamental modern political problem becomes that of theodicy, to find an answer to the question, 'Why do I suffer?'

Weber must pay special attention to the dynamics of how new communities are formed, for formed they will certainly be. His understanding is that the only dynamic available to modern society is the political 'prophet,' the charismatic leader who can resolve the epistemological nihilism in which humans find themselves. Much has been written in criticism of Weber on this count, the most extreme version being that by Mommsen, who accused Weber of laying the groundwork for fascism.[65] This is a complex question, raising matters that cannot be dealt with here. Weber certainly holds out a hope for the charismatic plebiscitarian leader, but he also, I think, establishes such stringent criteria for such a leader as to make the emergence of a real one close to impossible. What is often ignored here is that on this score his mode immediately becomes Augustinian. In the year 410, Augustine had with great circumspection come to the conclusion, over the course of his conflict with Bishop Donatus and his (to be) heretic followers, that under certain conditions coercion should and could be used in the name of Christian love. The salvation of souls was of an importance so paramount that humans could be coerced against their immediate (and misunderstanding) wills to accept baptism. This raised immediately the question of who should do the coercing, that is, of the qualities that a prince must have. Augustine argued that only those who were acting from true love could be entitled to use such coercion.[66]

In a similar manner, in 'Politics as a Vocation,' Weber discusses the personal characteristics that the political leader must have in order to be entitled to act so as to weld people together into a community. Under what conditions does the political leader exist: the answer is that he exists under the same conditions as everyone else, except that he has the ability to 'bear' it. In 'Politics as a Vocation' Weber spends much time describing both the bureaucratization of the world and the necessity of accepting it, while concomitantly insisting on the reality that we are 'placed into different life-orders, each under differently understood laws.'[67] The premises of the political sphere are thus approximately those of the scientific one. Any action, including a political action, will constitute an attribution of meaning; we know that all general claims to meaning are invalid; yet the world is filled with those who have not the self-discipline to hold unto themselves the world in all its chaos. We must make something of the world and not take our action as other than it is. 'Seeing how much I can bear' is the premise of facing both the scientific and political worlds as they are.

What then do we make of the rage of those who claim to love (in Weber's list) 'the future of socialism' or 'international peace' or 'the fatherland' more than their souls?[68] This formulation gives us, according to Weber, the problem as it now stands: What are we to make of those who claim to be able to use violence in the name of a transformation of the chaos of the world? At a slightly more conceptual level, this is for Weber the problem of those who claim to be ethically justified in their political actions.

It is for Weber in the nature of ethics that any particular claim must be subsumable under a general claim. For instance, the claim 'I promise to meet Sheila at four o'clock' must be derivable from a general and abstract claim that 'one ought to keep one's promises.' Among other things ethical situations have the characteristic of requiring of their players that reasons be offered when ethical principles have been infringed. If I do not meet Sheila, I must offer an excuse as to why not. That excuse will very likely be an explanation of what kept me from meeting Sheila such that it was not my fault that I missed our appointment. Politics, for Weber, cannot be the realm in which the failure to complete a particular action (or the unintended consequences of a particular action) can be excused. No true leader can ever plead intentions. The dialogue with Ludendorff after the First World War, in which Weber calls upon Ludendorff to sacrifice himself for events that were not his 'fault,' makes this plain.[69]

It does no good in politics to plead that one 'didn't mean it'; and, since politics is the legitimate use of violence, the only question can be what might make it legitimate.

When Rousseau had famously confronted this question in the beginning of the *Social Contract*,[70] his answer had been to elaborate the boundaries of legitimacy in volitional time and space, that is, to lay the ground for the legitimacy of the modern state. Weber seems to suggest that this solution has come to an end. Legitimacy once stopped at the border and was recognized as doing so. (That is why international politics was such a threat for Rousseau.)[71] In the modern age, however, where borders are of less importance and ideologies transcend national boundaries,[72] the very possibility of legitimacy is in question. Weber does not, I think, argue, as some commentators claim, that the legitimate is whatever the people accept.[73] Weber's fear, rather, is precisely the fact that there is nothing that the people will find to be legitimate, that they will not have the criteria by which to recognize legitimacy, and thus that they will turn to almost anything. (In somewhat the same spirit Oswald Spengler suggested, after Hitler's rise to the Chancellorship, that '*Wir brauchen einen Helden, nicht einen Heldentenor.*')[74] The course of legitimacy must come, in politics as it had in religion, from 'true' prophecy.[75]

Weber's account here is both frustrating and enticing. The true political leader, who is entitled to lead a state (that is, to make reality for others), must 'become conscious of these ethical paradoxes and of his responsibility for what can become of himself under their pressure.'[76] The danger that threatens is that of succumbing to the 'diabolic.' Indeed, anyone will be 'helplessly taken over (*hilflos preisgegeben*)' 'by the devil unless 'he sees him.' (It is an old Teutonic belief that the devil will get you unless you see him first.) This is a matter of grasping the consequences that will befall one from one's actions. Here the focus in Weber moves to the notion of maturity. The ability to see what may become of oneself derives not from age, or even experience, but from a kind of Aristotelean notion of maturity. 'A man, whether old or young in years' is how Weber refers to him, drawing directly on Aristotle's *Nicomachean Ethics*.[77]

Weber, however, sees maturity in terms different from Aristotle's. It is a kind of 'trained relentlessness' (*geschulte Rücksichtslosigkeit*) in looking at the realities of the world, a refusal to avoid anything. It is an insistence that all possible targets, whether obscure social scientists or the top political leaders of Germany, be ruthlessly attacked. (The only exception that Weber will make to this is for friends, such as Robert Michels.) But just as 'historical materialism is not a cab to be taken at will,'[78] so also is it the lot of the historical sociologist to deal with all aspects of the world that his science makes available to him.

Tellingly this trained relentlessness gives one the ability to face the realities of life and 'bear and be adequate to them inwardly as an adult' (*sie zu ertragen und ihnen innerlich gewachsen zu sein*). Weber's choice of words is important and striking here. Anyone who cannot so do is still a 'political infant.' Indeed, 'nine out of ten' of those whom Weber meets are such even when, perhaps especially when, they claim to be 'mature.'

At this point Weber introduces his term for those who cannot face the realities of the world as a grown-up. In the political realm, they are *Gesinnungspolitiker*, a word often translated as 'politicians of conviction,'[79] but better rendered as 'politicians of disposition' or 'ideologists.' They are those who interpret the world in such a manner as to avoid facing the realities of their position and thus the consequences their actions will entail for the world. Those who claim that they are going to eradicate the 'false and the base,' says Weber, are 'spiritual lightweights' who have 'become enraptured with romantic sensations.'

For Weber, maturity – being an adult – is the recognition that any action is taken under circumstances where the consequences of that action are not only not apparent, but do not over the long term add up to make sense (as Hegel had thought they would). The acceptance of this, and the avoidance of the plea of good intentions, no matter what the outcome, is what distinguishes an adult from a child. Mistakes are to be attributed to insufficient skill and commitment. Politics, as Hannah Arendt has remarked in a similar vein, 'is not the nursery.' It does no good to say 'I didn't mean it.'[80]

What then does it mean to be mature? Weber presents the following as his summary of the qualities of character of those who have faced up to their historical position:

> [I]t is immeasurably moving when a mature *(reif)* man – whether old or young in years – who truly feels this responsibility for consequences and acts with a whole soul in terms of the ethic of responsibility, arrives at some point where he says, 'I can do no other; here I stand.' This is something truly impressive *(ergreift)*. For this situation truly must be possible at some point for each of us who is not inwardly dead. Insofar as the ethics of disposition and the ethics of responsibility are not absolute contraries, but complements, which only in combination constitute a genuine person (*echten Menschen*), one who can have the 'calling for politics.'[81]

A – perhaps the – central point of this extraordinary passage is that one must act with 'a whole soul' in terms of the ethics of responsibility. That means that all those components of one's action which are not taken in the terms of this ethic must simply be cast aside and not be part of one's self. In other words, everything that I am must be expressed in terms of what I do.

This is a choice, somewhat analogous to the exhortation of the English Puritans to 'choose ye this day which God ye shall serve.' That their English brethren insisted on differing with this choice was only a cause for disdain, and a reinforcement of their belief that they were doing it right. In the *Methodology*, for instance, Weber insists on the choice:

> The fruit of the tree of knowledge, which is distasteful to the complacent but which is, nonetheless, inescapable, consists in the insight that every single important activity and ultimately life as a whole, if it is not to be permitted to run on as an event in nature but is instead to be consciously guided, is a series of ultimate decisions through which the soul – as in Plato – chooses its own fate, i.e. the meaning of its activity and existence.[82]

The reference to Plato is breathtakingly bold. It is presumably to the end of the *Republic*, in which the dead souls return to life after choosing their next self. It is a choice that they will forget: *Lethe* (forgetfulness) will be the precondition of the unforgetting truth (*aletheia*) of their next life. In Weber, as with Nietzsche's doctrine of eternal return, there is no forgetfulness: all the choices that one has made are to be there, once and for all. In this, the person will be given, like a work of art.[83] Here we see the aesthetic basis of the Weberian notion of maturity. The person is a work, a conscious delimiting of the world so as to make possible its perfection. For Weber, the final justification of the leader with a calling for politics who is entitled to lay hands on the 'spokes of the wheel of history' are Luther's words before the Diet of Worms: 'Here I stand; I can do no other.'

It is clear that the man in this position has the entitlement to go beyond, or perhaps to do without, the demands and calls of morality. His actions are justified simply in terms of his ontic self – the fact that he is, and as a being who is, has a claim to be understood. Actions cannot be subsumed under a higher law, for they provide the terms of their own justification. Most actions, Weber is quite clear, do not spring from this level. Though we are all beings that are, our activity responds to a 'higher' or more 'superficial' level, in the sense that the actions correspond not to how we are, but to something like how we would like to think of ourselves or who we would like to be. These are the ethics of disposition.

It is also clear that Weber does not think that the possibility of having a calling for politics is available to anyone, for any reason, at any time. The Augustinian emphasis on character, here appearing as the idea of maturity, requires not only that certain tests be met if one is to claim such entitlement, but also that one be suspicious of any claim that one may make of oneself.[84] Weber is here the modernist Protestant, a position not less powerful for being identified in older terms. He immediately warns his audience in 'Politics as a Vocation' that a test of the justification of making such claims will take at least ten years of passage through the 'polar night of icy darkness and hardness,' through which few have passed without succumbing to temptations. Succumbing to temptations means for Weber not to have 'measured up to the world as it really is in its everyday routine,'[85] that is, in its tedious, unheroic, slow, *alltäglich* qualities – precisely those qualities of the person I have called bourgeois.

The important and often missed point here is that for Weber, for most humans, life is, or should be, routine; the most dangerous thing for people is to think that they can do more than what is before them – to have a modern version of hubris or original sin. He notes that since most of us are not 'sober (*schlicht*) heroes,' we must go about 'our daily work' – which is to be the rationalized beings that we are and are becoming.

Weber is concerned to distance his audience from their desires, much in the manner that the man who truly has a vocation for politics must have a perspective on himself. This concern manifests itself especially in the way that Weber's texts refuse to engage the expectations of their audience. He gave the lecture 'Politics as a Vocation' to an audience in Munich in late 1918. It was a group caught up in the Bavarian revolution; the Soviet was in power. The lecture was a major event of the time, for in the aftermath of the defeat Weber had perhaps more prestige than any other German figure. In the audience were not only heady young students and distressed bourgeois, but notables such as Rilke and Jaspers.

Weber begins his lecture by asserting that he is going to disappoint his audience – that what they expected will not be forthcoming: '*Der Vortrag, den ich auf Ihren Wunsch zu halten habe, wird Sie nach verschiedenen Richtungen notwendig enttäuschen.* [This lecture, which I give at your request, will necessarily dis-illusion and disappoint you in a number of ways.]'[86] Weber finds his audience possessed with the need and the desire for an answer to the question of what is to be done. (Likewise, in a companion lecture, 'Science as a Vocation,' he will address the audience's desire to overcome their anxieties about what can be known.) To make people come to terms with the actuality of their position in history – with what it means to be who they are – he cannot simply tell them that they are wrong, he must dis-illusion (*enttäuschen*) them.[87]

The self-knowledge to which Weber's text enjoins his audience as a prerequisite does not take them out of the world. Instead it throws them back into it and places their feet on their own ground. Contrary to Marx, who hoped to escape from the everyday minutiae of the division of labour, and contrary also to Emile Durkheim, who suggested that happiness was to be found in the divisions of labour, Weber seeks neither escape nor happiness.[88] But he does find in this world, as it is given to us as our history, the only possibility for humanness. It is worth noting that similar considerations were the basis for Nietzsche's insistence that we are doomed by our genealogy to pursue truth. Where Nietzsche had decided that such a pursuit must end in nihilism, Weber tried, quite consciously,[89] to counter these nihilistic conclusions.[90]

One may object to my portrait of Weber as presenting a man without salvation and a world without redemption. What, one might retort, has become of the portrait of the hero who appears so often in Weber's writings? It would seem that if Weber tries to show us how to 'set to work to meet the demands of the day,' as he puts it at the end of the 'Politics as a Vocation' lecture, he also and importantly gives us a portrait of a responsible Caesar who may make all things new.[91] It is clear that there appears to be something correct in this portrait. Consider the end of the lecture: 'Certainly all historical experience confirms the truth – that man would not have attained the possible unless time and again he reached out for the impossible. But to do that a man must be a leader, and not only a leader but a hero as well, in a very sober sense of the word.'[92]

Some actions do escape the everyday, the *alltäglich*. They are the actions of those who truly have the calling for politics, and they are, for Weber, something like works of art. They provide the terms of their own justification. Weber, however, is concerned to make sure that no one be able to claim this aesthetic entitlement easily, without, as it were, having earned it. The choice he gives us is one of fire and ice – with no possibility of honestly being able to claim the fire. For most of us, the honourable course consists in finding/doing what is ours to do – our 'damned duty' – with the recognition that this and only this can constitute an acceptance of our human condition. Knowing oneself is for Weber as much an imperative as it was for those pre-Platonic Greeks whom he seem to have admired. External conditions gave one multiple selves: the only answer was to restrict the self to that which could be controlled, and refuse the rest. In practice this is the source of Weber's insistence on specialization and professionalism. This insistence is to solve a problem for a self whose multiplicity and essential contestability has now become historically unavoidable.

Weber is centrally concerned to avoid the easy claim to be able to act in the name of an other. In doing so he gives us a very stark world which does not allow for action based on probable surmise or assured continuities. Sartre once wrote that probability is the necessary predicate of that which comes to be, meaning by this statement that all volitional activity is based on the proposition that what will be, can be. Weber suggests that this claim no longer holds – that the world has become demagified – disenchanted – and petrified. Only magic will change the structures, and while we may hope for a magician, Weber is careful to make sure that we can never claim to be one, and probably not claim to recognize one.

## NOTES

1 Here the decisive text was Wolfgang Mommsen, *Max Weber und die deutsche Politik* (Tübingen 1959; 2d ed. 1974); see also Mommsen, *The Social and Political Theory of Max Weber* (Cambridge: Polity 1989).

2 This is, for instance, what was made of Weber even in the presentation by Raymond Aron; see my analysis in 'History and Choices: The Foundations of the Political Thought of Raymond Aron,' *History and Theory* 11, no. 2 (1972).

3 Cited in Ed. Baumgarten, *Max Weber: Werk und Person* (Tübingen: Mohr 1964), 554.

4 See Tracy B. Strong, *The Idea of Political Theory* (Notre Dame 1990), chaps. 1 and 3. The best of the new work on Weber (some of it dates back many years) is collected in Peter Hamilton, ed., *Max Weber: Critical Assessments*, 4 vols (London: Routledge 1991).

5 See Harvey Goldman, *Max Weber and Thomas Mann* (University of California Press 1990).

6 Max Weber, *Wirkschaft und Gesellschaft: Grundriss der verstehenden Soziologie* (Tübingen: Mohr 1956), 584 (hereafter wc). Translated in Max Weber, *Economy and Society*, 2 vols, ed. Guenther Roth and Claus Wittich (Berkeley and Los Angeles: University of California Press 1978) (hereafter es).

7 Max Weber, 'Politics as a Vocation,' *Gesammelte Politische Schriften* (Tübingen: Mohr 1958), 552ff (hereafter gps). Trans. in H. Gerth and C.W. Mills, eds. *From Max Weber* (New York: Oxford University Press 1958), 121ff (hereafter gm).

8 Max Weber, 'Die 'Objektivität' socialwissenschaftlicher and sozialpolitischer Erkentnis,' in *Gesammelte Aufsätze zur Wissenschaftslehre*, Herausgegeben von Johannes Winckelman (Tübingen: Mohr 1973), 180 (hereafter wl). Translated in Edward Shils and Henry A. Finch, eds, *The Methodology of the Social Sciences* (New York: Free Press 1949), 81 (hereafter mss). See the discussion in David Goddard, 'Max Weber and the Objectivity of Social Science,' *History and Theory* 12, no. 1 (1973), 1–22, especially 10–17.

9 Among them Hermann Rickert and Wilhelm Dilthey. See Guy Oakes, 'Max Weber and the Southwest German School: The Genesis of the Concept of the Historical Individual,' in W. Mommsen and J. Osterhammel, eds, *Max Weber and His Contemporaries* (London: Allen Unwin 1987), 434–46, especially 434–5.

10 G.W.F. Hegel, *The Phenomenology of Spirit* (Oxford and New York: Oxford University Press 1979), 23ff.

11 See H.H. Bruun, *Science, Values and Politics in Max Weber's Methodology* (Copenhagen: Munksgaard 1972), especially 131ff.

12 Compare to Paul Feyerabend, ' "Consolations for the Specialist": Why should a science be allowed to put an end to that which gives it birth?' and 'Problems of

Empiricism,' in R. Colodny, ed., *Beyond the Edge of Certainty* (Englewood Cliffs, NJ: Prentice Hall 1965), 145–260.

13 WL 610, GM 154. See John Seery, 'Marxism as Artwork: Weber and Lukács in Heidelberg, 1912–1914,' *Berkeley Journal of Sociology* 27 (1982), 129–65; Goddard, note 8 above, 3 n5.

14 WL 161, MSS 64. I use Shils's translation, which, although very free, conveys here Weber's point. Lawrence Scaff, in 'Weber before Weberian Sociology,' has a related point in his analysis of 'labour relations' in Weber.

15 See 'Science as a Vocation,' WL 601f, GM 146f. For parallels in Nietzsche see Alexander Nehamas, 'Immanent and Transcendent Perspectivism in Nietzsche,' *Nietzsche Studien*, vol. 12 (Berlin: Gruyter 1983), 473–90, and my 'Response,' following. See also my 'Texts and Pretexts,' *Friedrich Nietzsche and the Politics of Transfiguration*, 2d ed. (Berkeley and Los Angeles: University of California Press), chap. 10, and my 'History and Choices: The Political Theory of Raymond Aron,' *History and Theory*.

16 Note that 'individual' here could mean 'capitalism.'

17 Max Weber, *The Protestant Ethic and the Spirit of Capitalism* (New York: Scribners 1958), 12 (hereafter PESC). Emphasis added.

18 Paul Honigsheim, *On Max Weber* (New York: Free Press 1968), 12; see W. Schluchter, *The Rise of Western Nationalism: Max Weber's Developmental History*, trans. G. Roth (Berkeley and Los Angeles: University of California Press 1981), 21.

19 WL 177–8, MSS 78.

20 See WL 213–14, MSS 111.

21 This is, of course, almost the first line of Wittgenstein's *Tractatus Logico-Philosophicus*.

22 WL 194–5, MSS 94.

23 ES 946.

24 ES 954.

25 ES 975.

26 'Parliament und Regierung im neugeordnetend Deutschland,' GPS 329 n1, 351; ES 1399, 1417 (henceforth PG).

27 ES 958–9.

28 See my discussion in *Friedrich Nietzsche and the Politics of Transfiguration*, chap. 7, and Alexander Nehamas, *Nietzsche: Life as Literature* (Cambridge: Harvard University Press 1988).

29 ES 959.

30 PG, ES 1394.

31 ES 961. See the discussion by Erik Olin Wright, 'To Control or to Smash the Bureaucracy: Weber and Lenin on Politics, the State and Bureaucracy,' *Berkeley Journal of Sociology* 19 (1974–5), 69–108, especially 70f. Wright, however, focuses too much on a liberal-revolutionary dichotomy.

32 ES 1426.

33 ES 1413.

34  ES 1414.

35  ES 961.

36  ES 975.

37  ES 975.

38  See Karl Löwith, 'Marx and Weber,' *Gesammelte Abhandlungen: Zur Kritik der geschichtlichen Existenz* (Stuttgart: Kohlhammer Verlag 1960), 1–3.

39  See Max Weber, *The Religion of China* (New York: Free Press 1968), 226–49.

40  See the beginning of PESC.

41  ES 980; see ES 990ff.

42  See Manfred Schön, 'Gustav Schmoller and Max Weber,' in Mommsen and Oster-hammel, note 9 above; and Guy Oakes, 'Introduction,' *Roscher and Knies* (New York: Free Press 1975).

43  ES 980.

44  Robert Eden, *Political Leadership and Nihilism* (Tampa: University Presses of Florida 1983).

45  See the discussion of this passage from the *Manifesto* in Marshall Berman, *All That Is Solid Melts into Thin Air: The Experience of Modernity* (New York: Simon & Schuster 1982), chap. 1.

46  ES 1002.

47  PESC 181.

48  ES 990; cf. Mommsen, *Max Weber und die deutsche Politik*, 97, 121 (first edition).

49  ES 988.

50  V.I. Lenin, 'State and Revolution,' in *Selected Works*, vol. 1, part 1 (Moscow Foreign Languages 1950), 74.

51  See the letters from Marcel Mauss cited in Raymond Aron, *Memoires: 50 ans de réflexions* (Paris: Juillard 1983), 71.

52  Compare the argument about Marx and Durkheim in Steven Lukes, 'Alienation and Anomie,' in Peter Laslett and W. Runciman, eds, *Politics, Philosophy and Society*, series I and II (Oxford: Blackwell 1967), 134–55.

53  GPS 321–2, ES 1394. I thus agree with Scaff, note 54 below, and with Frederic Jameson, 'The Vanishing Mediator: Narrative Structure in Max Weber,' *New German Critique* (Winter 1974), as well as with Bryan Turner, *For Weber* (London: Routledge & Kegan Paul 1981), that there is a 'structuralism' in Weber, although I see it as much more diachronic than do they.

54  Cited from Mommsen, *Max Weber und die deutsche Politik*, note 1 above, 97; see Lawrence Scaff, 'Max Weber and Robert Michels,' *American Journal of Sociology* 86, no. 6, 1269–1286, especially 1281–3.

55  WL 191, MSS 90.

56  WL 192, MSS 91.

57  See Thomas Kuhn, 'A Function for Thought Experiments,' *The Essential Tension*

(Chicago: University of Chicago Press 1978), 240–65.

58  WL 596, 608; GM 141, 152. I believe that I first understood this point from work done by Rolf Kolden around 1965.

59  WL 913, MSS 92.

60  WL 213, MSS 110. M. Merleau-Ponty recognizes his affinity to Weber on this point in *Les aventures de la dialectique* (Paris: Gallimard 1961), chap. 1.

61  WL 213, MSS 110–11; see 'Science as a Vocation,' WL 610–11, GM 154. This is a parallel point to Nietzsche's question about the 'value of truth' in *Jenseits von Gut und Böse*, Introduction.

62  'Science as a Vocation,' WL 612, GM 155.

63  'Science as a Vocation,' WL 604–5, GM 148–9. Gerth and Mills mistranslate the passage in their edition. Jameson, note 53 above, 61ff, uses their translation in his very interesting discussion of this passage.

64  F. Nietzsche, *Beyond Good and Evil*, para. 39: 'It might be a basic characteristic of existence that those who would know it completely would perish, in which case the strength of a spirit should be measured according to how much of the "truth" one could still barely endure.'

65  Mommsen, *Max Weber und die deutsche Politik*, see note 1 above.

66  Augustine, letter 185, in *Letters*, vol. 3 (New York: Catholic Publishers 1953). See the discussion in Peter Brown, *Augustine of Hippo* (Berkeley and Los Angeles: University of California Press 1975), especially 233–43.

67  'Politics as a Vocation,' GPS 554, GM 123.

68  'Politics as a Vocation,' GPS 558, GM 126.

69  GM, 'Introduction,' 41–2.

70  'Man is born free and is everywhere in chains. How did this situation come about? I do not know. *How can it be made legitimate?* I think I can provide an answer.' *Social Contract* vol. 1.

71  Stanley Hoffmann, 'Rousseau on War and Peace,' *American Political Science Review* (June 1963), 317–33.

72  See 'Politics as a Vocation,' GPS 557, GM 125; see the analogous recognition in Arno Mayer, *From Wilson to Lenin: Political Origins of the New Diplomacy, 1917–1918* (New Haven: Yale 1959), chap. 1.

73  See John Schaar, 'Legitimacy in the Modern State,' in Phillip Green and Sanford Levinson, eds, *Power and Community: Dissenting Essays in Political Science* (New York: Pantheon 1969).

74  See Tracy B. Strong, 'Oswald Spengler – Ontologie, Kritik, and Enttäuschung,' in P. Ludz, ed., *Spengler heute* (Munich: Beck 1980), 74–100.

75  Cf. Jameson, note 53 above, 68.

76  This and following citations from 'Politics as a Vocation,' GPS 557ff, GM 125ff.

77  Aristotle, *Ethica Nicomachia* (Oxford: Clarendon 1963), 1095a, 6–10.

78  'Entitlement and Legitimacy: Weber and Lenin on the Problems of Leadership,' in

Fred Eidlin, ed., *Constitutional Government and Democracy*. Festschrift for Henry Ehrmann (New York: Westview Press 1983).

79 Gerth and Mills, for instance, give it as 'politics of conviction.'

80 Hannah Arendt, *Eichmann in Jerusalem: A Report on the Banality of Evil* (New York: Viking 1974), 279.

81 PV, GPS 559, GM 127.

82 MSS 18.

83 See my *Friedrich Nietzsche and the Politics of Transfiguration*, 2d ed. (Berkeley and Los Angeles: University of California Press 1988), chap. 10.

84 Arthur Mitzman, *The Iron Cage: An Historical Interpretation of Max Weber* (New York: Knopf 1970), is still the best, if an unsatisfactory, account of Weber's life. Until the account of Weber's treatment with the psychiatrist Binswanger are published we will remain in the twilight on these matters.

85 PV GPS 560, GM 128.

86 GPS 505, GM 77. '*Enttäuschen*' permits the double meaning of 'take away illusions' and 'disappoint.'

87 See the discussion of this point in the excellent essay by Wolfgang Schluchter, *Wertfreiheit und Verantwortungsethik: Zum Verhaltnis von Wissenschaft und Politik bei Max Weber* (Tübingen: Mohr 1971).

88 On Marx and Durkheim, see Steven Lukes, 'Alienation and Anomie,' in P. Laslett and W.D. Runciman, eds, *Politics, Philosophy, and Society*, vols 1 and 2.

89 See Eden, note 44 above.

90 I am not clear on his success. See my ' "What Have We to Do With Morals": Nietzsche and Weber on History and Ethics,' *History of Human Sciences* (August 1992).

91 This image plays an important role in the work of Wolfgang Mommsen, as well as that of Ernst Nolte, 'Max Weber vor dem Faschismus,' *Der Staat* 2 (1) (1964), 295–321 among others.

92 PV GPS 560, GM 128.

# 7

# The Politics of Time: Subjectivity and Modernity in Max Weber

TERRY MALEY

> His eyes are staring, his wings are spread. This is how one pictures the angel of history. His face is turned toward the past. Where we perceive a chain of events, he sees a single catastrophe which keeps piling wreckage upon wreckage and hurls it up in front of his feet. The angel would like to stay, awaken the dead, and to make whole what has been smashed. But a storm is blowing in paradise ... [It] irresistably propels him into the future to which his back is turned, while the pile of debris before him grows skyward.[1]
> — Walter Benjamin

In his incessant political battles and writings, in his methodological reflections, in his searing analysis of the seemingly irresistable march of an increasingly instrumental rationality through Occidental culture, Max Weber struggles to come to grips with the cultural significance of a modernity which has outlived and superseded the Enlightenment. Those practices and institutional arrangements which, in the eighteenth century, were to make people free, had, by the end of the nineteenth, given way to the rationalization of the world. The advent of huge structures of bureaucratic, disciplinary domination and rationalized, large-scale capitalism fundamentally reorganized the time and space within which we in the West live. Weber's *fin de siècle* Europe is a time beyond Enlightenment. Increasingly, it is a time beyond History. A time without a past, what was once History threatens to mutate into a never-ending present, an utterly indeterminate future with no hope of redemption.

In his work and in his life, Weber is obsessed with the loss of the history and agency of a certain kind of individual. In the thoroughly disenchanted world of modernity, it is historical and personal depth, a connection to or embeddedness in historical time and experience, which are destroyed and irretrievably lost. In all of his work after his breakdown of 1898, Weber is obsessed with the recovery/reconstruction of an historical time in which agency and meaning are still possible. In an age in which philosophies of history and metaphysics were collapsing all around him, Weber wants a *deep historical understanding* of how the modern world, with its vast powers, tensions, and contradictions, came to be our world. He desperately wants to know if, and to what extent, it is still possible to find/create values in this world, and to act meaningfully within it. The rationalized, post-Enlightenment universe no longer provides any grounds for doing so. Throughout his tormented life, Weber agonizes over what it means to live and act in this new, immense, impersonal time.

This time, the configuration of developments we can call modernity has, since at least the sixteenth century, witnessed the rising star of the natural sciences; their increasing, pervasive deployment in the domination of nature; the bureaucratic, disciplinary regulation of everyday life; industrial capitalism; and the emergence of vast structures of domination and discourses of power. The Enlightenment thought that these forces, guided by a benevolent reason which was still the inherent property of an autonomous individual, would set humankind free.

But when we delve into Weber's tortured, fragmented oeuvre, we are repeatedly confronted with the realization that the promises of the Enlightenment had been decisively disappointed. From Weber's vantage point as a member of the German 'bourgeois classes' in *fin de siècle* Europe, the Enlightenment's 'charisma of reason,' its metaphysics of progress, and its benign, utopian dreams all lay in ruins, undermined by the development of the very historical conditions which had, in part, given rise to it. In Weber's work, the dream had long since imploded and been renounced. From the 'endless struggle for dominance' among nations, which Weber pronounced in his 1895 Freiburg address, to the slaughter of the first truly modern World War, the Enlightenment's 'rosy blush' had turned to crimson beneath glittering towers of steel which housed the new, depersonalized regimes of discipline and order.

In modernity, reason undergoes a prolonged series of elaborate, complex, and far-reaching mutations. Initially, it is freed from the enchantments of myth and, later, from the last vestiges of the domination of religious eschatologies. In the nineteenth century, it is increasingly severed and cut adrift from the humanism of the Enlightenment, or from any trans-historical or transcendent ontological postulates or substantive roots. It is emptied of its normative substance. By the twentieth century, it was becoming embedded in abstract discourses of power, in the bureaucratized, regimented, institutional structures and practices of the factory and the office, in the interstices of mass culture, in the psyche of no longer autonomous but separate individuals. It is displaced by a logic of calculability, by rationalities whose instrumentality renders it incapable of generating and sustaining an autonomous sphere of substantive ends.[3] Freed from utopian, metaphysical 'illusions' and ends, we witness the mutation of what was progressive in reason into a rationality which is left thoroughly functional and instrumental. It can be pressed into service by a wide array of knowledges which have no allegiance to anything resembling the humanism of the Enlightenment. Circumscribed, reduced, and fundamentally altered, reason becomes rationality, an instrument of power.

Rationalization, in its totalizing, modern form,[4] renders the collapse of metaphysics decisive. With the collapse of metaphysics goes the collapse of meta-narratives and their overarching meanings, their 'reality principles.' The communities, places, histories, and forms of domination from which the master narratives of modernity grew and which sustained them are radically altered by this process. From stories of creation and salvation to philosophies of history, all of the teleological narratives of the past that once offered an account of the origins of Being and a corresponding resolution or closure to the human drama, a place and a time beyond which it is not necessary to venture, are threatened by the relentless historical advances which Weber traced with such morbid lucidity and with which he struggled so intensely throughout his life. Particularly after his breakdown, Weber was 'deeply engaged' with these 'powers that dominate the soul of modern man: bureaucracy, science, violence, and the "intellectualism" that has destroyed the spiritual resources on which humankind has fed for three thousand years or more.'[5]

This historical configuration, marked by the obliteration of the dreams of Enlightenment and the dawning of a thoroughly disenchanted world, a world without meaning, heralds, for Weber, the emergence of what I will call the *politics of disenchantment*. The politics of disenchantment is characterized by a vision of heroic individual action in a devastated, rationalized cultural and historical universe. Its central, foreground figure is the charismatic yet responsible hero (either political or scientific) who acts passionately but with an eye to consequences. He acts in the full knowledge that his actions occur in a world which no longer provides any metaphysical ground or foundation for them. With this awareness in hand, the new politics of heroic action seeks to revitalize a kind of agency which can survive in the machine world of the 'iron cage.' In his post-first World War essay 'Parliament and Government in a Reconstructed Germany,' Weber poses the decisive question: 'Given the basic fact of the irresistible advance of bureaucratization, the question about the future forms of political organization can only be asked in the following way: How can one possibly save any remnants of individual freedom?'[6]

Weber's distress at the thought of 'the irresistible advance of bureaucratization' and the consequent eradication of any remnants of freedom is emblematic of an agitated, extremely active resistance to the erosion of the ideal of the autonomy of the person, an ideal which Weber nonetheless ambivalently recognizes as an outmoded one in Western culture.[7] Through this resistance and the notion of responsibility which is central to his conception of heroic action and the mature personality, Weber attempts to articulate a new context in which subjectivity can survive in a meaningless universe. This effort becomes a defining feature of post-Enlightenment modernity.

As rationalization, capitalism, and bureaucracy extend themselves ungraciously into every crevice of culture and the psyche, more holistic experiences of history and place, of rootedness and embeddedness in time and in living communities, are irretrievably destroyed. The sense of historical time in which more 'organic' communities are embedded is replaced by modern *regimes of temporality*. Historical time is increasingly replaced by the discourses and practices which render temporality abstract, quantifiable, rigid. The *temporal regimes of modernity* – particularly what has been referred to as 'chronometric time' – are characterized by what the French theorist Joseph Gabel referred to as the reification of time. In modernity – and now in increasingly severe and dislocating ways in post-modernity – people's relations to time and place have been fundamentally altered in ways which have far-reaching effects. Historical time is increasingly rearranged, fractured, and made abstract by rationalized institutional structures and discourses.

Although he does not name it in this way, Weber is deeply engaged with this problematic. As I will suggest later on in the chapter, recent discussions of post-modernity which highlight the loss of historical depth and the spatialization of time in Western culture have allowed us to see this problematic more fully and explicitly. While not normally associated with Weber scholarship, the location of the problematic of the spatialization of time *within* the process of rationalization provides an important context within which to understand Weber's attempt to reconstitute individual agency and subjectivity. To foreshadow, in Weber's attempts to redefine the agency of the political actor we find the *politicization of temporality* and the opening up of both the past and the future as contested, contradictory terrains and sites of meaning. This politicization provides the context or frame for interpreting the cultural significance of the political hero in Weber's work. The significance of the hero in Weber's imaginary of resistance to domination is not intelligible without the discursive moves which allow for the redefinition and politicization of temporality. This occurs first and most self-consciously in some of the early methodology essays which Weber published in the *Archiv für Sozialwissenschaft* during and shortly after he began to more or less recover from his 'devastating nervous collapse' of 1898. It is given substance and its distinctively political meaning in *The Protestant Ethic and the Spirit of Capitalism*, Weber's first major substantive work after his breakdown. In ways I will suggest towards the end of the chapter, his attempts, although completely at odds with recent, post-modern discussions/critiques of Enlightenment accounts of knowledge, power, and subjectivity, can, in fleeting moments, be seen as an imprisoned precursor to a post-modern sensibility.

The politics of the charismatic hero acting in a disenchanted world is bound up with a new sense of time and historicity in which Weber wants to situate us. I want to suggest that in Weber's work, the *historical* context in which subjectivity had been constructed by the Enlightenment is problematized and partially deconstructed. He wants to recast the sense of time in the iron cage in such a way that people can act meaningfully within it. This intervention cannot take place without an attempt to reconstitute an image of the acting subject not as an agent of historical change, but as someone who makes the world meaningful by acting in accordance with consciously chosen values. Weber tries to situate this idea of the person in a new sense of historical time – one that is fluid, open-ended. This intervention involves locating the new, self-consciously meaningful subjectivity of the heroic actor in a historical temporality which is, in principle, outside of and somehow beyond the criteria of efficiency which define the instrumental rationality of both the capitalist market and the formal, rule-bound technical expertise of the hierarchical bureaucratic organization. In this effort, Weber tries to create a new space and time in which people can act as a way of counteracting the reification of historical time which the rationalization of the world generates. From 1902–3 on, the images of both a new subjectivity and a radically new temporality run like a pulse through all of Weber's work. Let me first briefly characterize the role of *The Protestant Ethic* in this process, and locate those aspects of Weber's portrayal of the Puritan in which temporality is redefined and politicized. I will then show how Weber grounds this new notion of time in the essay 'Objectivity in Social Science and Social Policy,' relate this change in Weber's political sensibility to his breakdown, and then move on to discuss regimes of temporality in modernity. This leads to a discussion of how the new, open temporality in Weber's methodology builds up to the politicization of choosing in the stark, compelling imagery of the 'warring gods.'

The substantive argument of *The Protestant Ethic* regarding the influence of the Calvinist ethic of ascetic renunciation on the development of early capitalism in Western Europe is widely known. As Wolin points out, however, so much ink has been spilled trying to determine the validity of the thesis of *The Protestant Ethic* that its political import has been largely overlooked. Rather than try, once again, to assess the merits of the thesis itself, I will focus on the political meaning of the images of temporality and heroic personality in Weber's portrayal of the Puritan.

In *The Protestant Ethic*, Weber enters into the Puritan's state of permanent uncertainty with a vengeance. Accepting the doctrine of predestination, the Puritan worked arduously in the hope of winning salvation. Even though the Puritan believed that his individual fate had already been determined, he could never know whether he had been chosen or elected.[8] The Puritan laboured so intensively because he believed that he was acting in the service of God.

But the world in which the Puritan finds himself is already meaningless. This does not lead to despair, however. Instead, the Puritan is obsessed, driven. He 'accumulates ferociously, with a controlled frenzy.' He does this by strictly regimenting his actions in the world. He submits without moderation to discipline, relying on rational planning, methodical conduct, self-supervision ...[9] He is a 'fanatical figure who brings an intensity to the task which converts the deed into a heroic, spiritual triumph.'[10]

The Puritan's feverish accumulation and extreme asceticism, both strictly subordinated to the higher end of a calling, gave his relentless activity on earth a meaning which welded the personality together. The coherence of the Puritan's personality depended on a complete consistency between belief and life, between thought and action. Working continuously towards salvation and in the service of a calling gave the strenuous effort needed to sustain continuous accumulation its 'highly developed ethical' quality.[11]

There is a complex politics of time in *The Protestant Ethic*. It is embedded in Weber's celebration of the bourgeois hero, which itself is a highly politicized image of the coherent acting person. This image of the person is embedded in a complex nexus of temporal coordinates which are not politically or ideologically innocent. There are a number of related dimensions to this which I will now begin to unfold.

There are two overlapping temporal contexts in *The Protestant Ethic*. One has to do with the market, and its reification of time. The other is an undetermined, fluid time which Weber deploys as a deep background in *The Protestant Ethic*, and which he will make explicit in the subsequent methodology essays. Both come together as the lived experience of perpetual uncertainty in Weber's portrayal of Protestant asceticism, where the chronic insecurity which Hobbes had first imagined in the infamous state of nature, the uncertainty endemic to a ferociously competitive, burgeoning market society, finds its way into the image of the Puritan working furiously to win salvation. In the *endless* pursuit of a salvation which can never be known, the chronic uncertainty of the competitive market is reified, and projected into an unknowable future beyond this world. I will return to the reified time of the competitive market towards the end of the chapter. First, I would like to explicate the open-ended notion of time more fully.

In his defence of *The Protestant Ethic* thesis and in the methodology essays, Weber repeatedly insisted that he wanted to understand the unique cultural significance of certain religious ideas on early capitalist development in Europe from a particular point of view which both limits and creates the object of investigation. In order to do this – to understand the Protestant ethic as an Ideal Type – he must presume that history is not inherently progressive or determined in any teleological sense. In *The Protestant Ethic*, we find a definitive repudiation of the Enlightenment's metaphysics of progress, in both its Marxist and naive liberal forms. As Jameson and others have noted, Weber argued incessantly against evolutionary and teleological conceptions of historical progress.[12] This is because Weber saw notions of historical time which claimed to be either scientifically or naturally progressive as forms of flight or escape from reality, as an abdication of one's responsibility to face up to the 'demands of the day.'

For Weber, then, historical temporality is not determined or closed. In his essay, 'Objectivity in Social Science and Social Policy,' written for the *Archiv für Sozialwissenschaft und Sozialpolitik* in 1904, Weber explicates in an extremely self-conscious way the notion of historical time which formed the backdrop to *The Protestant Ethic*. It begins with the portrayal of history as open, fluid time. 'The concrete form' in which values are chosen and acted upon 'remains perpetually in flux, ever subject to change in the dimly seen future of human culture, the vast, chaotic stream of events which flows away through time.' Weber continues, '[A]s soon as we attempt to reflect on the way in which life confronts us in immediate, concrete situations, it presents us with an infinite multiplicity of successively and co-existently emerging and disappearing events ... Life, with its irrationality and its store of possible meanings, is inexhaustible.'[13] This is obviously much more than a theory of 'choice,' rational or otherwise, for it entails both a notion of culture and historical temporality.

There are two dimensions to the idea that reality is a 'vast, chaotic stream of events which flows away through time.' The first, framed by the interminable battles Weber waged against philosophies of history, is the ground-clearing notion that history is inherently unstructured, that it has no telos, and that it doesn't 'mean' anything at all. What one values and how one acts are destined to remain perpetually in flux, ever subject to change in the dimly seen future '... the vast, chaotic stream of events which flows away through time.' For Weber, it is this time in which we can come to life, and, with an almost Nietzschean excess, live fully in the infinite multiplicity of the vast, chaotic stream of events. In this time, life is inexhaustible, and the future is alive with possibility. With this Weber counters both positivist and Marxist positions and their views of history, as well as what he saw as purely 'subjectivist,' 'irrational' flights from reality. The second is that the future is open as a horizon of possibility, that 'its store of possible meanings is inexhaustible.' Because reality 'remains perpetually in flux,' it is 'ever subject to change.'

These formulations are extremely significant. They retain the fluid, qualitative sense of a *temporality not yet reified*, one open to movement and change. The portrayal of reality as open, fluid time allows Weber to reconstruct history ideal-typically, as narratives of unique significance against the dull, grey background of a rationalized world. The presupposition of a fluid, undetermined history creates an open-ended time which is, in principle, open to possibility and intervention. It is a historicizing and politicizing moment, in which actors who, he hopes, will still retain some faint, dim resemblance to the heroic Puritans, can intervene and rupture the apparently seamless web, the 'masterless slavery' of bureaucratic rationalization and domination. It is a new time in which the responsible political hero can act in the world in a meaningful way. The idea of an open-ended notion of historical time is indirectly implicated in the ideal-typical nature of Weber's representation of Protestant asceticism.

Wolin notes that the 'ideal type' is crucial for Weber because it is that place in the methodology where the social scientist can inject significance – values which define the object of investigation from a particular point of view – into the practice of research. Values thus assume a political role in the methodology. The ideal type, as the repository of significance, is the theoretical vehicle and rhetorical mechanism which allows Weber to open up the past and thereby to politicize it. The past is opened up as a contested interpretive terrain because the ideal type allows the social scientist to reconstruct/create unique historical events, liberating history from the tyranny of all objectivist or determinist conceptions of historical progress or development. The ideal type is thus the methodological route to the politicization of historical time; it is that conceptual space in which Weber constructs his highly charged image of the Puritan. Once historical time is, in principle, open to the intervention of significance and particular points of view, the interpretive acts of social scientists, acts of defining and naming the past, present or future, become political ones.

Such is the case with *The Protestant Ethic*. Through the ideal type of the Puritan, Weber is able to respond to a host of competing visions and allegiances, to Marxist, religious, and philosophical images of the determined (and therefore depoliticized, for Weber) nature of historical time. It allows Weber to 'celebrate the moral and political superiority of the capitalist hero of the past over the Proletarian hero of the present and future.' Its directly political significance lies in the fact that *The Protestant Ethic* is a complex work 'concerned with the historical legitimation of capitalism.' *The Protestant Ethic*, as Wolin also notes, 'contains the most extensive formulation of Weber's ideal conception of the political actor, and the most polemical.'

Weber's portrayal of time as open, fluid, subject to human intervention and significance, is contextualized and placed in perspective by his well-known remarks at the close of *The Protestant Ethic*: 'The Puritan wanted to work in a calling; we are forced to do so. This order (the tremendous cosmos of the modern economic order) is now bound to the technical and economic conditions of machine production which today determine the lives of all individuals who are born into this mechanism ... with irresistible force.'[4] Or, as Wolin suggests, 'Weber knew that he was composing a portrait of the last hero before the age of rationalization set in and rendered both heroes, Marx's and his own, anachronisms.'[5]

Both Marx's Promethean hero and Weber's own were being rendered anachronistic because the conceptions of historical time – both linear and developmental – that the nineteenth century had inherited from the Enlightenment, were being obliterated by the temporality specific to instrumental rationalization, by chronometric time.

Chronometric time is the time of modern scientific calculation; 'this is time which is measured,' abstract. It signifies the reduction of time to that which can measure things as exact, precisely defined quantities. It is the temporality of capitalism: '[A]s that which highlights the division of labour and social life, this abstract time belongs to the imperative of productivity, and is substituted for the rhythms of work and celebration.'[6] It is implicated in bureaucratic structures, in discourses of power and disciplinary regimentation, and in the rationalization of the modern world in general.

It is deeply implicated in the spread of instrumental rationality in Western culture. With the predominance of both science and capitalism, it has been enshrined as the ruling principle and experience of temporality in the twentieth century. Modernity had also produced historically developmental time (Hegel, Marx) and linear, progressive time (Condorcet, Comte, J.S. Mill). But the chronometric temporality of the rationalized factory and the bureaucratic apparatus had become culturally predominant by the end of the nineteenth century, the development of capitalism having effectively destroyed the metaphysical presuppositions of the other two temporalities and the conceptions of history which went with them. It is implicated in the generalization of rationalization, beyond what Marx had shown to be true in the factory,[7] out into every crevice of culture and the psyche.

The effect of chronometric time is a certain endlessness. Both the capitalist principle of accumulation and the repetitive performance of routinized tasks in a highly specialized division of labour are defined by this endlessness and are its principal material embodiment in modernity. To take Weber's famous example, the Puritan can never accumulate enough, nor can he work too hard. Ross

Perot was worth 3 billion dollars in 1992. By 1996, he could be 'worth' 5 billion; there is no inherent limitation to competitive accumulation. Accumulation counts ... how much you have.

There is a phenomenological dimension to this as well, an experience of time. It is not an abstract conception of history as progressive or developmental,[18] but an experience of time as never-ending, the endless repetition/production of more. Whether more of the same or more multiplicity makes little difference. Marx had identified it in the experience of alienated labour; it is the performance of the same task over and over hundreds of times under the sign of ever more choice, variety, an endless stream of newer, bigger, better, more variegated product. It is also implicit in Weber's notion that, in the modern world, all things are, in principle, calculable.[19]

Endlessness in this sense is necessarily divorced from any resting place beyond this world, or from any moment of rest or culmination in it. Chronometric temporality produces endlessness as its pervasive cultural, socio-psychological effect under capitalism, where accumulation and indeed 'reality' are seen as unlimited, or unbounded by any metaphysical constraints or religious dogmas, by any historical or natural determinations. This kind of endlessness under the regime of chronometric time in modernity is reifying in its social effects. It profoundly influences an experience of what it means to be a person who acts in the world. I would now like to elaborate on some of the implications of the relation between what it means to be a person in Weber's sense and this notion of reified time.

According to the French theorist Joseph Gabel,[20] a reified experience of existence is a depersonalizing and dissociative one involving both a loss of contact with duration and the devaluation of persons. 'It is a whole way of Being-in-the-world involving two schizophrenic elements: the state of being crushed by the world and a spatialization of duration.'[21] In his clinical work with people suffering from schizophrenia, Gabel noted that they often perceived the world and themselves in reified ways. Their way of 'being-in-the-world' was one of severe dislocation from social relationships. Schizophrenia, for Gabel, is an extreme, individualized form of what Marx had identified as alienation. People become unhinged from their pasts, from others, from their bodies, from the social time in which they create the world with others. Schizophrenics often expressed feelings of absolute futility, uselessness, abject meaninglessness, and suffered from paranoid delusions in which *things* haunted them. They felt crushed by the world, or trapped in it, and felt it too much to bear.

People living through schizophrenic experiences are often engulfed by delusional worlds in which both their sense of time and sense of self seem to have been completely fractured or splintered. The delusional world is populated by objects and things, and not by real, living people. Divorced from both past and future, the present becomes reified or frozen as an eternal, never-ending, repetitive condition from which there is no escape. Gabel theorized that these states had to do with the fact that those people had become *dissociated or dislocated from time*. They come to exist in a universe without any historical sense of time. All of these symptoms point to what Gabel referred to as the 'spatialization of time.' For Gabel 'both alienation and schizophrenia share the tendency to turn time into space.'[22]

Space for Gabel is temporally one-dimensional. It may have depth and width; you can put things in it, or move through it. It can be contested, and because it is socially and historically constructed, it is political. But it is temporally static; it does not move or change in time.[23] To create space, or rearrange it, or move things through it, involves action and agency, both of which occur only in time. Time, in any of its previously mentioned incarnations (particularly linear and historical or developmental time) does change and move. Space does not change apart from, or outside of, the time in which people act. People have histories; in a reified temporal universe, things, objects, do not. Things do not appear to exist in time, they exist only in space. Only chronometric time does not change or move. It shares this feature with space; it is abstract, quantifiable. This is because it is already spatialized.

In a world characterized by structures of spatialized temporality, people are easily separated from their own agency, from their capacity to reach back into and draw sustenance from their pasts, and to envision new futures. In a spatialized temporal universe, it becomes extraordinarily difficult for people to experience their own histories and actions as self-determined *and* socially generated. For Gabel, '[a]s a prisoner in a universe where space takes the place of duration, people in a reified world cannot understand history as the expression of creativity and spontaneity ...' In a reified universe of experience, 'temporality loses its qualitative, changing, fluid character; it is transformed into a rigid, exactly delimited continuum, filled with quantitatively measurable things; it is transformed into space.'[24]

The highly bureaucratized institutional spheres which were the objects of Weber's attention – the factory, the capitalist firm, the office, the army – are the quintessential social structures and spaces, the cites of reified temporality in the modern world. In Weber's time, these spheres were just beginning to be dominated by the regime of spatialized temporality on a truly massive scale. Today, in the post-modern vortex of mass-market products, simultaneous global information technology, simulacra, and neon images, it is the entire culture which, in its fragments, is subject to the dislocating, depersonalizing effects of spatialized time.

Living in a world of spatialized temporality also has consequences for the formation of personality. People living in spatialized temporal structures – and Weber's world of autonomous value spheres is a paradigmatic case – themselves become fragmented, unhinged from time and from their own histories. Increasingly, subjectivity is socially constructed in such a way that affectivity, meaning, and understanding, those dimensions which used to constitute a 'whole personality,' now 'slide past' one another, in Lawrence Grossberg's apt formulation. They are not necessarily connected *within the person* any longer; to the extent that they are, the inner connections are increasingly tenuous.[25] The tenuous coherence of the personality consists of a 'unity' of contradictions and tensions; personality becomes an unstable unity in fragmentation, a never-ending struggle to achieve a coherence which is no longer simply given. In Weber's world, people will find themselves dislocated from time, from a sense of history, from themselves. In modernity after Enlightenment, and increasingly in the hyper-reality of the post-modern cityscape, there is no continuous, social time in which people live, and which holds personalities together by providing a temporal or historical continuity between the past, present, and future. Nor can there really be any sense of community because communities are temporal, historical associations.[26] As Portis has noted, the attempt to be an active participant in one's history or one's future 'assumes that one is part of either an actual or a potential community, for only community provides the individual with a link to the future.'[27]

In the case of the Puritan, living ascetically and working continuously in the service of a calling provided the link to a reified future, one not of this world, one not subject to human agency or intervention. Still, working in the service of a calling gave the Puritan's relentless activity on earth a meaning which fused his personality together. It was the 'moral imperative' which gave continuous work directed at accumulation, and the strenuous effort needed to sustain it, its 'highly developed ethical' quality.[28] The Puritan's personality depended on complete consistency between belief and life, between thought and action.

The intensity, iron discipline and compulsive coherence of the Puritan hero are those characteristics which were psychically necessary both for Weber, in his private life, and for his image of what it means to be a person capable of 'facing up to the times.' One of liberalism's most fundamental 'truths,' the autonomy and rationality of the individual, would not make sense to us without this coherence. Like the rational (male) individual of Enlightenment fame, the consistency of the Puritan's personality is essential for the identity of the person.

Those characteristics to which I just referred also weld the personality together in the rapidly shifting, chronically uncertain cultural terrain of a modernity no longer anchored in the progressive temporal metaphysics of the Enlightenment. In this context, the very idea of the person, as conceived by the Enlightenment, is fundamentally threatened. The demand for 'complete consistency' in the life of the Puritan, as well as in Weber's own experience, is the reaction of the bourgeois individual to a world which has undermined his capacity for autonomous action. Paradoxically, it is the very experience of an endless, unbounded time which produces the need for coherence. Coherence and an endless time are symbiotically related for the person destined to live in a disenchanted world ruled by the regime of chronometric time. The need for a consciously chosen coherence does not exist in the same way in a cultural world in which temporality is more structured, given, 'natural,' or magical, in which the experience of life is structured by a metaphysical, culturally meaningful experience of history.

Without the Puritan's religious roots and temporal context, however, the compulsive, coherent behaviour of the bourgeois loses its 'highly developed ethical quality.' As the experience of time in modernity is liberated from myth, superstition, and religious foundations, and as it is increasingly defined and limited by the abstract determinations of rationalized bureaucratic structures and an ever more pervasive capitalism, the coherence of the bourgeois personality becomes simultaneously both more difficult to achieve and more meaningless.

Weber seems painfully aware of precisely this as he traces the historical formation of the heroic bourgeois personality in *The Protestant Ethic*. In his simultaneous celebration and politicization of the historical formation of that personality (and in the contemporaneous methodology essays), Weber also strains to put himself back together. As I noted earlier, *The Protestant Ethic* is Weber's first major work after the breakdown.[29] I see it, in part, as an ambivalent, excessive attempt to reconnect himself to his history, to his past, to his social class and his nation.[30] In *The Protestant Ethic*, Weber reconstitutes his contradictory identity as 'a member of the bourgeois class' by constructing an exalted heroic image of meaningful agency rooted in the past. The Calvinist hero is one who, after all, 'shatters the powers of church and state, ushering in a new era of universal history.'[31] In a time of enormous historical change, in which the liberal individual of the Enlightenment and Marx's proletarian hero were being superseded by the rationalization of the world, Weber, in *The Protestant Ethic*, vicariously projects an image of coherence, rational self-discipline and ethical certainty into the past.[32] The need for coherence, certainty, and ethical purity or rigour is symptomatic of a consciousness of its tenuousness in the present, both historically and in Weber's own life. Weber's struggle with the precarious coherence of identity in the rapidly shifting 'flux' of modern culture becomes intelligible in a different way when seen against the deep background of his collapse.[33]

Weber suffered what has been described as a 'devastating nervous disorder' in 1898.[34] Before his breakdown, Weber had achieved considerable success early on in his career. Prior to his collapse he had risen mercurially in his reluctantly chosen profession. Through his work for the *Verein für Sozialpolitik* in the mid-1890s, Weber quickly developed a reputation as a enormously well-read, brilliant, politically active young scholar, one we would now think of as a compulsive overachiever, a workaholic who was wilful, charismatic, and driven.

For Weber, like the Puritan, only more self-consciously, constant activity had been important to psychic stability. He reports having felt the need to be crushed by an enormous workload. A punishing self-discipline and self-control had both held him together and made him immensely productive.

Portis, drawing largely on Marianne Weber's biography, tells us that Weber revealed signs of what would now be recognized as both traumatic and anxiety neuroses. He could not sleep, was subject to 'uncontrollable emotions' and periodic bouts of rage. He manifested hysterical symptoms physically, suffering from partial paralysis, exhaustion, and phobias. He was unable to read or work continuously or to address an audience. His 'chronic habituation to work' collapsed. In a letter, he spoke of an 'icy hand' having let go of him. For more than four years he could not participate at all in the political debates which had so engaged him. The severity of Weber's condition was absolutely debilitating for long periods of time from 1898 to 1902, and intermittently after that for the rest of his life. Later, after Weber began to recover, anything which interfered with his self-control was disorienting and unsettling. He was subsequently 'forced by his shattering experience to demand complete consistency between belief and life.'[35]

In most of the Weber commentary, the breakdown is either mentioned in passing, as an unfortunate interruption of his work, or not mentioned at all.[36] It is not usually seen as relevant to the 'work' or in any way related to the specific substantive concerns which were to occupy Weber after he had more or less recovered. But I think that its significance lies in how the experience of the collapse contextualizes Weber's subsequent, strenuous efforts to resuscitate aspects of the Puritan's personality in the disenchanted world of the iron cage, efforts which were not self-consciously present in the same way in Weber's work before the breakdown.

The *conscious* demand for 'complete consistency between life and work' also becomes an explicit and important issue in Weber's work only after the breakdown.[37] To put this differently, Weber's collapse is emblematic of the agonizing difficulty of maintaining the coherence and consistency of the personality, of which the Puritan had been a model, in a meaningless, disenchanted world beyond Enlightenment. Weber's struggle to reconstitute himself and a form of subjectivity[38] appropriate to the present involved not only the writing of *The Protestant Ethic*, but, as we have seen, the elaboration of a specific historical temporality in which people are fated either to choose to act within, or to flee from, the iron cage.[39]

Later, as Weber haltingly recovers from his breakdown, he becomes increasingly concerned with the effects and structures of a world *in which time has become reified* and with how a modern echo of the Puritan hero can sustain both moral integrity and personal coherence in a rationalized world. He becomes more concerned with how the coherent personality must act in a world in which notions of history can no longer keep it together by connecting it to the past and the future.[40] It is only after the breakdown, with the writing of *The Protestant Ethic* and the methodology essays, that Weber begins to explicitly formulate the kind of person who is to act in a historical time which is not teleologically determined or metaphysically bounded, but which is open to possibility and, perhaps occasionally, to heroic intervention.

In addition to what I have been calling the 'open' notion of time which Weber presupposed in *The Protestant Ethic* and which he elaborates more fully in the methodology essays, there is another image of temporality in Weber's work. It is one which exemplifies his implicit acceptance of the reified temporality of the capitalist market as a necessary boundary within which modernity is fated to unfold in the foreseeable future. Let me cite an example of this temporal sensibility, and then show how it stands in tension with the 'open time' of the 'Objectivity' essay.

In 1895, Weber delivers his inaugural address at the University of Freiburg.[41] In the Freiburg speech, Weber declares himself a member of the bourgeois classes. He also aggressively accepts the *endless struggle* among nations for dominance. There is no suggestion that politics, life, or the world might be meaningless.[42] Nor is politics all that it was to become in his later work, namely responsible leadership in action.[43] Before the breakdown, there is a strong, almost overbearing emphasis on politics as Machtkämpfe, where nations are 'locked in an endless struggle for existence and domination in a world of hostile forces.'

Underneath its more agonistic, Nietzschean dimension, Weber's conception of the *eternal struggle* for dominance among nations discloses an acceptance of the market of competing political forces in and between the emerging liberal democracies of *fin de siècle* Europe.[44] When Weber refers to either the struggle between individuals in the market, or the struggle between irreconcilable values and life-orders, the 'warring gods' of modernity to which he alludes so often in his work,[45] it is always endless: it is always destined to be eternal.

My intention in citing this instance of Weber's early political sensibility is not to dwell on his well-known penchant for a kind of macho Machtpolitik fashionable in German bourgeois political circles at the time. Rather, it is to explicate the notion of temporality embedded in it and how it is integral to a certain dimension of liberalism and the politics of modernity. It is the temporality of the capitalist market, and it entails the assumption that time is a never-ending 'struggle for dominance' among individuals. In its post-Enlightenment form, this notion of endless do-or-die competition has none of the progressive metaphysical justifications in which capitalism had been able to clothe itself in the nineteenth century. It reverts to its beginnings. In liberal thought, the notion of life as 'an endless struggle for existence and domination in a world of hostile forces' can be seen in its pristine, most lucid form in Hobbes's state of nature in *Leviathan*.

In Hobbes's fiction of the pre-social state, we are confronted with an image of unremitting competition between isolated individuals. In the absence of the binding authority of the state, civil law, or ethical norms, Hobbes's protohumans relentlessly seek 'power after power' over others.[46] In the 'natural' state, they are compelled to do so by the fear of violent death. As such, Hobbes's 'natural' man is not yet productive; he is a liberal, pre-Enlightenment fiction who is not yet concerned with the universalizing humanism of the Enlightenment.[47] Instead, he tends towards the destruction and/or domination of others, and suffers paranoid delusions of obliteration by everyone and no one in particular.[48]

It is in the state of nature that we see the temporality of the market in its primordial form.[49] Historical time, in any of its modern forms, is not in evidence here; it has been obliterated and utterly reified in Hobbes's stark depiction. The protohumans moving ceaselessly within the state of nature do not come from anywhere; they have no past, and they do not have a future. And without a historical context, they are, of course, completely depersonalized, and can be conceived of abstractly, as *things* to be dominated, used instrumentally, or obliterated. Thus, in the state of nature the future becomes merely the interminable, brutal repetition of the every-present struggle for survival and dominance.

Hobbes's state of nature is the quintessential image of reified temporality, a temporality which is integral to the structures of the rationalized market which Weber accepts as the boundary of modernity. I now want to relate this discussion to Weber's conception of how the heroic personality is formed in the confrontation with the 'warring gods' of modern culture.

In *Science as a Vocation*, Weber tells us that in modernity, 'Many old gods ascend from their graves; they are disenchanted and hence take the form of impersonal forces. They strive to gain power over our lives and again resume their eternal struggle with one another.'[50] The compelling imagery of the gods is scattered throughout Weber's work. For him, the struggle between the 'warring gods,' which are fated to be locked in an endless, eternal, and agonistic conflict, is intimately associated with his vision of meaningful subjectivity and agency. The fully formed, mature personality of the heroic actor, the most meaningful, 'real' form of agency, for Weber, can only emerge from the life-and-death struggles and confrontations with one's inner gods and demons. Only the fully formed personality, in the form of the leader who understands and has successfully negotiated the depth and intensity of the struggle, can imagine not what might lie beyond the iron cage, but how to live and act within it. For Weber, the emergence of the truly heroic personality, one who 'is aware of a responsibility for the consequences of his conduct and really feels such responsibility with heart and soul,'[51] is a truly rare and moving experience. What is important here is that for Weber, it is an experience that is still possible, even palpably real, in the iron cage.

The 'tremendous cosmos of the modern economic order' is the historical and cultural context within which the warring gods, now as abstract, impersonal forces, are fated to do battle. The iron cage or modernity is a capitalist one. Historically, capitalism has smashed communities. It has dislocated people from their pasts, from their places, from each other. It has dislocated people's lived experience of a real connection to their collective past and future. Capitalism spatializes time. Spatialized time is impersonal, abstract. The spatialization of time allows the temporal and social context in which people live to be constantly in flux, unstable. As Weber noted, the 'masterless slavery' of capitalism has been rendered more abstract and rigid by the rampant spread of bureaucratic structures, whose depersonalizing effects were even more severe, dehumanizing, and soul-destroying for Weber than those of capitalism itself.[52]

To recall, in *The Protestant Ethic* and in the methodology essays, Weber presents us with a new image of historical time – one that is open and fluid – in which he posits the possibility of heroic agency – acts of choosing ultimate values and acting in accordance with them. Weber wants to 'preserve that which is valuable in people' in the depersonalized world of modernity. But if historical time is opened up, in the context described above, only to have agents and values do eternal battle in the shifting, chronically uncertain 'marketplace of meaning,' then the result will be something less than heroic action. I have this question: Is heroic action really possible in the context of a highly bureaucratized, ferociously competitive, time-destroying capitalism? Or, more precisely: Exactly what is the *meaning* of heroic action in such a context? And has this kind of action lost the context that could make it meaningful?

Capitalism reifies values; it turns them into things, objects; and reduces them to instrumentalities in the competitive struggle for dominance. In this context, the incessant competition among values will nullify the acts of valuing themselves. In the liberal market societies of late modernity, the struggle has reproduced immense hierarchies of power and colossal inequalities of wealth. Now, at the close of the twentieth century, the prospects for attenuating this state of affairs in the post-modern vortex of a high-tech, immensely competitive, global, capitalist economy seem even slimmer than they did in Weber's time. Weber's explicit acceptance of this context means that his attempt to situate the valuing individual in a new, open historical reality is condemned to perpetually negate itself; it is a context that necessarily precludes heroic action. If it does not preclude heroic action, at the very least, it makes heroic action exceedingly difficult.

Given all this, there is another problem. The hero, for Weber, is the 'inquiring, passionate self'; Weber accepts that as a given. The values which the person is supposed to struggle to choose in the process of self-formation are given to us by culture, even if they are, as I have just argued, reified in the iron cage of modern capitalism. But the struggle itself is assumed to occur within the 'soul' of the individual; its intensity must be generated from 'within.' Weber thus works with what Jameson has, in another context, called a 'fundamental depth model of inside and outside.'[53] In his discussions of post-modernism as the new 'cultural dominant' in the West, Jameson has called our attention to 'a new depthlessness' which has emerged alongside other constitutive features such as the spatialization of temporality,[54] 'a weakening of historicity,' or what I have called the loss of history, and the 'waning of affect.'

If we accept, for the moment, the notion of a new cultural depthlessness which follows from the spatialization of historical temporality and the consequent loss of history or the loss of a connection to both past and future, then the cultural/historical time and space, or the entire context, presumed by the depth model with which Weber was working cannot be assumed to exist in the same way any longer. Or, one cannot still have a depth model of the individual if the culture as a whole, which had been the ground or source of the formation of that kind of person, has lost its connection to a certain kind of historical time and cannot provide that kind of historical or personal depth any longer. In this cultural constellation, the distinction between inside and outside, or individual and society, cannot sustain itself. Without the personalizing and socializing effects of embeddedness in a historical community *which is* the depth within the individual, people cannot effectively resist the homogenizing effects of rationalization for long, if at all. In this context, the very capacity of Weber's individual to choose, to act coherently, or to value others in their uniqueness, difference,[55] and particularity is something Weber cannot begin to address.

What we are left with, then, are three major problems with what I earlier called Weber's politics of disenchantment. The first two have to do with the idea of choice, and the third concerns the temporal context in which choices are supposed to occur. First, there are serious problems with the idea of choice as Weber conceives it. As much as one can understand his desire to compel people to make meaningful choices in a meaningless world, the question remains, 'can they be genuine choices' in the context I have just outlined? For Weber, they can only be genuine if they are not predetermined or delimited by the will of another,[56] that is, if they come from 'within' the individual.

As I have indicated, there are serious problems with both autonomy and choosing in the context of extremely hierarchical, very competitive, rigidly capitalist social structures such as those which currently prevail in the West. Given the market-bound conditions in which all acts of choosing take place, to the extent that choice is possible, those who have access to resources, information, cultural and real capital, will be vastly more capable of making choices than their social inferiors/others. They will be more coherent, more rational, and will likely come to occupy socially dominant positions, if they do not do so already. Those who are not, who are different, resistant, destitute, somehow grotesque, or debilitated are likely to be obliterated or excluded, marginalized, left to wander, in anonymity, silence, and obscurity in the interstices of the cage or the streets of the city. The question I am raising is: What is the status of the choices and values of those who are substantially dominated, persecuted, or marginalized? In many cases the larger context to which I have been referring has seriously damaged people's capacity to make meaningful choices in Weber's sense.

Second, Weber's struggle to preserve a world of responsible choice and an appreciation of difference has, in post-modernity, given way not only to the instrumentalization of all values, but to their trivialization as well. As Jameson and other post-modern critics have noted, global capitalism is having a field-day wreaking havoc on the terrain of culture, popular or otherwise; values are as commodifiable or marketable as anything else. To choose values responsibly is not to treat them instrumentally or interchangeably, but to temporalize them and one's relations to others. The extent to which this is possible, in Weber's sense, in a world in which the 'struggle' between 'values' has been appropriated, subsumed, and marketed to death by global capital (think of the so-called cola wars) is doubtful.

Third, as mentioned above, Weber wants an open, fluid temporality in which acts of choosing can be meaningful. But if our social and historical context has actually resulted in the spatialization of time and the loss of historical depth, then the idea of choice, the guiding light of modern individualist ethics, having lost its context, loses much of its meaning as well.

In the image of the warring gods, Weber problematizes and deconstructs the historicity of the Enlightenment, the rule of reason-as-progress-in-history. But he does not problematize the idea of the irreconcilable conflict among values which emerges from the ruins of the Enlightenment's collapse. Given the notion of the heroic actor, which he takes as given, he cannot problematize either the notion of choosing or the context in which he wants to set these choices.

For Weber, it is our fate in the twentieth century to come to terms with modernity without enlightenment. It was his self-appointed task to draw the contours and fathom the depths of this vast, world-historical mutation. Most of all, Weber compulsively needed to understand the deep cultural significance and necessity of this development for the present. He needed to know what significance capitalism and rationalization had for what it meant to be a person living and acting in this disenchanted, post-Enlightenment world. In Weber's myriad attempts to trace the cultural significance of the disenchantment of the world in modern times, we find a profound self-understanding of modernity. It is an understanding of a rationalized world beyond reason; it is an understanding filled with ambivalence, passion, rage at its seeming inexorability, a paralysing anxiety, morbid lucidity ... and a strange kind of longing. In these and other respects, Weber reveals himself to be the quintessential post-Enlightenment modern, trying to reconcile contradictory impulses, desires, and ways of knowing, struggling to forge a unity, a compulsive coherence, out of the fragments of his own life, yet perpetually on the precipice of chaos, collapse, and meaninglessness. I have traced a few moments of that struggle. Yet, as an image of its contradictions, as a unity of its tensions, Max Weber is still the exemplary self-consciousness of modernity.

NOTES

1 Walter Benjamin, 'Theses on the Philosophy of History,' in *Illuminations* (New York: Shocken Books 1969), thesis no. 9.

2 I am reminded of an extreme example of the phenomenon described here; George Orwell's *1984*. In the opening pages we read of Winston Smith looking out over the 'glittering towers' of the ministries which dominate what used to be London's Whitehall and Westminster. Orwell's chilling novel is a stark, arresting portrayal of the absolute reversal of the dreams of the Enlightenment. The imagery in *1984* of the urban centre where Winston lives is reminiscent of that in Fritz Lang's film

*Metropolis* or Terry Gillam's *Brazil*. Weber's image of the 'iron cage' bears a strong family resemblance to these visions of modernity.

3  Gil Germain puts this well when he states that Weber's 'attempt to revive a sphere of autonomous ends has not materialized.' See chapter 11 for his contribution to this volume.

4  Alkis Kontos, in chapter 10 of this volume, correctly makes the point that for Weber, the problem in modernity is not rationality per se, but rather the *totalizing* effect of rationalization.

5  Sheldon S. Wolin, this volume, chapter 13.

6  The essay is reprinted in G. Roth and C. Wittich, eds, *Economy and Society* (Berkeley: University of California Press 1978), 1403 (appendix).

7  L. Scaff, in *Fleeing the Iron Cage* (see note 33 below), is one of the few Weber commentators who has drawn attention to this important nuance in Weber's conception of the individual.

8  See chap. 4 of *The Protestant Ethic*, 'The Religious Foundations of Worldly Asceticism.'

9  Ibid., 413.

10  S. Wolin, note 5 above.

11  M. Weber, *The Protestant Ethic and the Spirit of Capitalism* (New York: Charles Scribner 1958), 69.

12  See F. Jameson, 'The Vanishing Mediator: Narrative Structure in Max Weber,' *New German Critique* 1 (1973), 52–89.

13  See Max Weber, 'Objectivity in Social Science and Social Policy,' in *The Methodology of the Social Sciences*, trans. and ed. Edward Shils and Henry Finch (New York: The Free Press 1949), 72.

14  M. Weber, (see note 11 above), 181.

15  S. Wolin, note 5 above.

16  See Jean Baudrillard, 'Modernity,' *Canadian Journal of Political and Social Theory* 11, no. 3 (1987), 63–74.

17  Weber was fully aware of Marx's critique of capitalism, and even though he disagreed with Marxism and its prophetic metaphysic of universal emancipation, he was sympathetic to Marx's analysis and critique of capitalism. Gerth and Mills, and Löwith were among the first to bring the affinities between Marx and Weber to light for the English-speaking audience. Others followed. In the 1960s, against the conventional Parsonian/positivist American interpretation of Weber as a value-free sociologist, I.M. Zeitlin argued that Weber had been strongly influenced by Marx and that there are affinities between them. Recently, the relationship has been further explored, and its implications debated. The Antonio and Glassman collection delves much more deeply into the relationship between the two thinkers and its implications. The useful introduction to the Whimster and Lash volume (below) is good on situating Weber's relationship to Marx in the context of the positivist appropriation of Weber in the United States in the 1960s.

See H. Gerth and C.W. Mills, eds, *From Max Weber: Essays in Sociology* (New York: Oxford University Press 1958); K. Löwith, *Max Weber and Karl Marx* (London: Allen & Unwin 1982); I.M. Zeitlin, *Ideology and the Development of Sociological Theory* (Englewood Cliffs, NJ: Prentice-Hall 1968); R. Antonio and A. Glassman, eds, *A Marx-Weber Dialogue* (Lawrence: University of Kansas 1985); S. Whimster and S. Lash, eds, *Max Weber, Rationality and Modernity* (London: Allen & Unwin 1987).

Although Weber did not deploy the discourse of alienation in his many prophetic pronouncements on the fate of those destined to live and work in the iron cage, he was, in his more philosophical and political moments (which were many), describing the existential milieu of a reified temporal world. Marx's solutions were vastly different; the two thinkers would not have agreed on what constituted subjectivity, historical emancipation, and a host of other issues. But when Scaff, for example, notes that one has to come to grips with the influence of Nietzsche and Marx on Weber, he is clearly correct.

18 Jean Baudrillard has characterized the three dimensions of the modern temporality as chronometric, developmental, and linear. The last is characteristic of the liberal Enlightenment's view of evolutionary progress; the second of Marx's view of history. The first is the time of abstract calculation and quantification. As such, it is an integral part of how capitalism destroys a sense of history, how it reduces history and the experience of lived and living time to abstract, measurable units which seem to exist outside of time. See Baudrillard, note 16 above, 67.

19 M. Weber, 'Science as a Vocation,' in Gerth and Mills, 129–58.

20 Gabel's concentration on the schizophrenic structure of reified thought and experience lets me employ his notion of the reification of time in the interpretation of the temporality of modernity in Weber. By way of clarification, I am not suggesting or implying either (1) that Weber was schizophrenic, or (2) that the rationalized world is schizophrenic. Reification, however, does exist on a continuum; something of the experience of spatialized temporality is shared, in differing degrees, by the schizophrenic, the alienated factory worker, and the compulsive consumer.

Although Gabel's work has now been 'superseded' in important respects by post-modern theorizations of the spatialization of culture and temporality (Jameson, Deleuze and Guattari, and Baudrillard come to mind), it is important for locating notions of post-Enlightenment but still modern temporalities in Weber's thought. Gabel's theorization of a reificational phenomenon such as the spatialization of time serves as an important precursor to post-modern discussions such as Jameson's. See F. Jameson, 'Post-Modernism, or the Cultural Logic of Late Capitalism,' *New Left Review* 146 (July-August 1984). I rely here on Gabel's major text, *False Consciousness: A Study in Reification*, trans. M. Thompson and K. Thompson (London: Open University Press 1975).

21 J. Gabel, note 20 above, 25.

22 Ibid., 32.

23 Gabel's notion of space is rather literal, and has been supplemented, or even supplanted, by the new political geographers and recent, post-modern discussions of the politics of space, whether in architecture or on the streets of the inner city, and the spatial media of communication. See, for example, *Collapsing Space and Time: Geographic Aspects of Communication and Information*, ed. S. Brunn and T. Leinbach (London: Harper-Collins 1991). See also the work of Ed Soja, for example, 'The Post-Modernization of Geography: A Review,' *Annals of the Association of American Geographers* 77 (2), 289–323.

24 J. Gabel, note 23 above, 148.

25 See Lawrence Grossberg's essay, 'Putting the Pop Back into Post-Modernism,' in *Universal Abandon?*, ed. Andrew Ross (Minneapolis: University of Minnesota Press 1988), particularly 180. The phenomenon that Grossberg notices in post-modern popular culture falls under the heading of 'the waning of affect,' a notion that Fredric Jameson introduced in his well-known discussion of the nature of post-modern culture under late capitalism. See F. Jameson, 'Postmodernism, or The Cultural Logic of Late Capitalism,' *New Left Review*, no. 146 (1984), 53–92. Jameson talks about the spatialization of time as well as the 'schizophrenic' nature of experience in post-modernity.

26 E. Portis makes this point in his recent work *Max Weber and Political Commitment: Science, Politics and Personality* (Philadelphia: Temple University Press 1986), 123.

27 Ibid.

28 Weber, note 11 above, 69.

29 Commentators as different as Hennis and Scaff agree that we should not see the essay on Rocher and Knies, written just prior to *The Protestant Ethic and the Spirit of Capitalism*, as carrying the same weight as the latter. Scaff is right when he notes that the essay, supposedly in honour of his former teachers of the German Historical School of political economy, was rambling, incoherent, chronically bitter, and at times petty. See L. Scaff, *Fleeing the Iron Cage*, note 33 below.

30 This effort at 'reconstitution' may be indirectly related to Weber's strident and problematic nationalism. Weber's strongly nationalist proclivities were already present in his Freiburg inaugural address of 1895 and were part of how he conceived of political economy prior to his breakdown. The strongly ethical and duty-bound love of the nation was widely shared among German liberals in Weber's time. The Puritan in the PE is not incompatible with this, and we are aware of the echoes of the Puritan in Weber's life. Among those who have commented on Weber's nationalism are E. Portis, note 26 above; W. Mommsen, in his well-known works; W. Hennis; L. Scaff; and I.M. Zeitlin.

31 See S. Wolin, note 5 above.

32 In his *Law, Custom and Social Order: The Colonial Experience in Malawi and Zambia*

(Cambridge: Cambridge University Press 1985), Martin Chanock has formulated, in the context of an entirely different discussion, precisely what Weber's recreation of the Puritan hero represents.

In colonial central Africa, an idealized account of customary law was projected back into the past during a time of rapid social change and great uncertainty. As Chanock puts it: 'The desire for certainty, purity, power and control was vicariously projected back into the past by those who felt the lack of control in the changing and uncertain present under alien rule and unpredictable economic conditions.'

Although the details are different, this is exactly what is going on in Weber's portrayal of the Puritan. I would like to thank Sandra Badin for bringing Chanock's excellent work to my attention. See S. Badin's review of Chanock's book, 'Law Custom and Social Order: A Review,' unpublished (1992).

33  Scaff makes the point that Weber never really recovered from the collapse of 1898, that its effects stayed with him for the rest of his life. See Lawrence Scaff, *Fleeing the Iron Cage: Culture, Politics and Modernity in the Thought of Max Weber* (Berkeley: University of California Press 1989). If this was so – and from Marianne's biography and the other sources we have, it seems that it was – then it also seems reasonable to venture that Weber's life and work cannot be completely dissociated. To suggest that they were entirely separate is to assume that they could be neatly compartmentalized. The fact that certain of Weber's key themes either found expression in his written work only after the breakdown, or appeared in dramatically different form, suggests that the separation was, at best, difficult to maintain. This provides the rationale for the following section on how Weber's breakdown contextualizes some of his most important substantive concerns.

34  In this section on Weber's collapse I rely on the recent study by Edward Portis, note 26 above, and also on the new English edition of Marianne Weber's biography, *Max Weber: A Biography*, trans. Harry Zohn, intro. Guenther Roth (New Brunswick, NJ: Transaction Books 1988).

35  E. Portis, note 26 above, 109.

36  E. Portis's recent work is a notable exception. He deals extensively with the breakdown, amassing a considerable amount of useful biographical material. Portis does a good job of giving us a vivid, much fuller picture than most do of Weber's condition from 1898 to 1902–3.

Portis suggests that Weber could not reconcile incompatible intellectual commitments to both science and politics. In addition to being intellectually incompatible commitments, science and politics also require, Portis suggests, different personal characteristics. Weber's inability to reconcile in himself the two incompatible intellectual commitments led to the breakdown. This view rejects the Freudian assumptions regarding Oedipal conflict put forward by Mitzman and, in a different vein, by Jameson, almost twenty years ago.

In the light of recent post-modern criticism, the assumption that science and politics can be strictly separated, and that they *require* conflicting, or opposite, personal characteristics, is highly debatable. Regarding the latter point, that science and politics require opposing personal characteristics, Wolin, correctly, I think, makes precisely the opposite point. He suggests that Weber bases both his later Political and Scientific heroes on the model of the earlier Puritan. Both the Politician and the Scientist are compelled to make choices: they must both renounce any claims to definitive knowledge of the Good or Truth; they must both possess the virtues of passion, distance, commitment to a vocation, and a certain objectivity. If Wolin is correct in supposing that 'post-modern' social science is somehow fundamentally political in nature, and that the practice of science is not an objective, disinterested one, then Portis's strict separation of politics and social science becomes strained. Portis does not really engage the issues raised by Wolin, Hekman, and others in recent critiques of a rigid separation between science and politics.

Scaff notes the breakdown, but, given the lack of conclusive evidence, does not speculate on the causes. See E. Portis, note 26 above; A. Mitzman, *The Iron Cage: An Historical Interpretation of Max Weber* (New York: Knopf 1970); F. Jameson, 'The Vanishing Mediator: Narrative Structure in Max Weber,' *New German Critique* 1 (1973), 52–89.

37 Four years before the breakdown, in an 1894 article, Weber shows us some of what was to fuel his scathing, post-breakdown critiques of the disenchanted machine-world of modern bureaucratic capitalism. 'We want to protect and sustain that which appears valuable in people: self-responsibility, the deep impulse toward achievement, toward the spiritual and moral excellence of humanity' (cited in Scaff, note 33 above, 71).

But this notion of the personality is decidedly different from that of the Puritan. It does not have the edge, the need for 'compulsive coherence,' and the 'demand for complete consistency' which we find in Weber's work and in his life after his partial recovery.

38 Portis is one of the few commentators aware of the fact that Weber articulates a new idea of the person in the early methodology essays, written around the time of *The Protestant Ethic* and just after. I think Portis is correct about this; it is the specific nature of the new idea of the person which we would see differently. See Portis, note 26 above. Harvey Goldman's recent work on Weber's conception of the person in *The Protestant Ethic* is also relevant here. See H. Goldman, *Max Weber and Thomas Mann: Calling and the Shaping of the Self* (Berkeley: University of California Press 1988).

39 Weber did begin work, in 1902–3, on a number of other projects before *The Protestant Ethic* and the 'Objectivity' essay. These essays – on Roscher and Knies, and others such as Eduard Meyer – were attempts to demolish the pretences of the scientific school of historical economics. But they were also, as Scaff notes, at times tortured,

'obscure pursuits' (p. 76) marked by 'disingenuous and ill-tempered argumentation' (p. 75 n7). *The Protestant Ethic* and the 'Objectivity' essay were written as Weber seemed to move out of this initial phase of recovery. Scaff relies on Lowith's explanation of this shift from 'negative criticism' to more 'systematic topics.' In the initial 'fragments' (Scaff, p. 75), Weber is concerned with the 'radical demolition of illusions' regarding modern science, culture, and 'our present orientation of life in general' (p. 76). Perhaps these invectives were necessary before Weber could articulate a more 'positive' view of personality and historical time.

40  I am thinking of Marx as a contrast in this respect. His critique of capitalism provided the proletariat with an explanation of their past oppression, with an image of how to remake their experience of the present, and with an image of how the future would look once they had remade it through their own activity.

41  See M. Weber, 'The National State and Economic Policy (Freiburg Address),' trans. K. Tribe, *Economy and Society* 9 (1980), 428–49.

42  See Wolin, note 5 above.

43  'Politics as a Vocation' is probably the fullest and clearest articulation of Weber's view of politics, and of what is personally necessary if one is to become engaged with the 'diabolical forces' that are the politicians interlocutors.

44  This aspect of Weber's politics and his Hobbesian assumptions regarding political conflict have been well captured in David Beetham's *Max Weber and the Theory of Modern Politics* (London: Allen & Unwin 1974).

45  Most notably in the 'Religious Rejections of the World and Their Directions' (the Intermediate Reflection), 'Politics as a Vocation,' and 'Science as a Vocation,' all in H. Gerth and C.W. Mills, note 17 above.

46  See T. Hobbes, *Leviathan*, ed. C.B. Macpherson (New York: Penguin 1968), 161, 169, 186–7.

47  This situation – an apparently timeless ahistoricism in which the struggle of each against all is thought to be interminable – has been fundamental to liberalism since Hobbes. The variations in liberalism can be accounted for by the varying resolutions which theorists have provided to this very problematic ontological assumption. The most noteworthy of these variations in the English-speaking West are eloquently sketched in C.B. Macpherson's *The Life and Times of Liberal Democracy* (London: Oxford University Press 1978).

48  James Glass, in *Delusion: Internal Dimensions of Political Life* (Chicago: University of Chicago Press 1985), has noted precisely this dimension of Hobbes's state of nature. He compares it, quite strikingly, to the delusional utterances of schizophrenics, who live in a reified world in which time has become, in our terminology, spatialized. The delusional imagery and language in both Hobbes's state of nature and in schizophrenic utterance is completely removed from any social or historical sense of time. It is literally out of (historical) time, and no longer embedded in it. The link Glass makes

between Hobbes's state of nature and the fractured, vivid discourse of schizophrenia bears directly on my discussion of spatialized temporality. It lets us think of Hobbes's state of nature as a universe in which schizophrenic, reificational phenomena predominate because time has become spatialized. Divorced from any of the conceptions of historical or even linear time which have characterized modernity, the state of nature is a lucid, paranoid delusion. In it others are depersonalized, rendered into objects which must be conquered, controlled or destroyed before they do the same to you.

49  My sketch of Hobbes is loosely based on Macpherson's classic text, *The Political Theory of Possessive Individualism: Hobbes to Locke* (Oxford: Oxford University Press 1963). I want to mention Macpherson explicitly because his position is the point of departure for the sketch of Hobbes.

If, as Macpherson has suggested, Hobbes's state of nature is one in which the gross insecurities and enormous psychic stress of competition in a nascent market society were read back into an eternal, 'natural' condition, then, by extension, the reification of time, and the obliteration of history we find there, are also implicated in market societies and their social relations. Behind the discussions of reified temporality and post-modernity, the spirit of Macpherson's thought informs my encounter with Weber.

50  sv, 149.

51  pv, 127. The issue of responsibility and who is capable of facing up to it is complex in Weber's conception of the political actor. Weber often implies that only some individuals will be up to the hard realities of politics. So, 'Only he has a calling for politics who is sure that he shall not crumble when the world from his point of view is too stupid or too base for what he wants to offer' (128). Only moments earlier, however, in *Politics as a Vocation*, after telling his audience that to see a mature personality reach the point when he must say, 'Here I stand: I can do no other,' is 'something genuinely human and moving' (127), Weber says, 'And every one of us who is not spiritually dead must realize the possibility of finding himself at some time in that position.' The implication is that we may all find ourselves in the position of having to accept responsibility for the consequences of our actions, but that only few will really be able to do so genuinely.

52  Roth and Wittich, note 6 above, 1186.

53  See F. Jameson, note 20 above, 62.

54  Earlier in the paper, I traced the notion of the spatialization of temporality back to Gabel's existential psychiatry. While Jameson is, I think, entirely correct in pointing to spatialized time as a 'constitutive feature' of our post-modern situation, Gabel's work was not concerned with the issues and problematics of post-modernism or post-structuralism. His major work was completed (in the original French) in the early 1960s, but he had been working on the problematic of spatialization for more than

twenty years prior to that. He had identified the problem of spatialized temporality and the reification of time almost forty years before it was explicitly treated in post-modern discourse in North America. Gabel began writing before the Second World War, that is, not long after Weber's death.

This bit of intellectual-biographical detail is important for my argument because it means that the phenomenon of spatialized time was identified *as a problematic of modernity* shortly after Weber's time. In other words, my use of spatialization does not simply lift the idea from recent post-modern studies and apply it, inappropriately, to a time to which it does not belong. There is a historical and cultural link between the spatialization Jameson has identified in post-modernity and what I have referred to as the reification of temporality in both the institutional structures with which Weber was concerned and in his own notion of the endless struggle between the warring gods. In post-modernity, the spatialization of time has spread to virtually epidemic proportions; it has become a pervasive cultural effect. Regarding Weber, my argument is that the reification – that is, spatialization – of time was already a constitutive feature of the iron cage, and that it even found its way, in its market form, into Weber's image of the highest realm of human experience, the struggle within the individual between the warring gods of culture.

55  Scaff has noted that for Weber, the ideal types, in which particular significance is inscribed, constitute an 'awareness of difference.' Weber had a very complex and difficult relationship to the idea of difference in the sense that Scaff seems to mean it. In his own polemics and exchanges with colleagues, he was often brutal and dismissive in his criticisms. If you disagreed with Weber, it was difficult to avoid his open wrath. He was even abrupt to the point of being abusive with colleagues and friends whom he greatly respected, such as Michels. Towards those who had gone too far in espousing, for instance, 'subjective flights' from the world, such as Otto Gross, Weber's fury was unrestrained. Yet, as Scaff correctly notes, Weber remained fascinated with attempts to flee the iron cage, and was often personally sympathetic and helpful to those on the margins. See Scaff, *Fleeing the Iron Cage*, note 33 above, 110–11.

56  I am thinking here of Weber's well-known definition of power at the beginning of *Economy and Society*: power consists of being able to realize one's will over and against the resistance of others. Genuine choice, then, would involve something like the capacity to 'realize one's will' without the interference of others, that is, autonomously. It is the capacity for individual autonomy in Weber's formulation of choice which is problematic.

**PART III** THE DILEMMAS OF RATIONALIZATION

# 8

# Mannheim and the Early Frankfurt School: The Weber Reception of Rival Traditions of Critical Sociology

RAYMOND MORROW

## I. POST-WEBERIAN SOCIAL THEORY

To speak of post-Weberian social theory is simply to acknowledge the epochal significance of Max Weber's work (which is often most enlightening when most wrong-headed to his opponents), and to recognize that certain fundamental issues of social theory – especially in the Marxist tradition – can no longer be thought about in the same way. In the present instance, the focus of attention will be a specific response to the political left of Weber which began in the Weimar Republic and was continued in exile.

If the metaphors of domination for Marx were concretely the alienation of the sweatshop, and more abstractly the process of commodification, for Weber the accent shifted to the theme of formal rationalization, a notion captured in the image of dwelling in an 'iron cage' (Weber, 1958: 181) or a 'casing hard as steel' (Weber, 1978: 170) – variant translations of the notion of a 'stahlhartes Gehäuse' (Weber, 1964: 379). Weber's response was a stoic resignation coupled with flashes of utopian hopefulness: 'No one knows who will live in this cage in the future ... whether entirely new prophets will arise, or there will be a great rebirth of old ideas and ideals, or, if neither, mechanized petrification, embellished with a sort of convulsive self-importance' (Weber, 1958: 182). Weber's stance here bears an uncanny resemblance to Rilke's poetic image of a panther trapped in a cage, gazing tiredly through the endless bars of his imprisonment (Rilke, 1982: 24–5). Like Weber's relation to his own theory of politics and science, the panther's powerful will remains paralysed within his supple, circling movements, except for the occasional moment when the image of liberation tempts the eye of his imagination. Unlike Weber, however, left post-Weberian theorists actively struggled for a way out of the cage. Early Frankfurt Critical Theory sought to revive the notion of a revolutionary smashing of the bars of domination, only to retreat later to the realization that taking away the bars did not resolve the problem of the internalization of domination. Mannheim's sociology of knowledge and democratic planning, in contrast, optimistically proposed that domination as imprisonment could be overcome by rationally controlling exits and entries in such a way as to create a compromise between necessary domination and democratic freedom.

The present chapter can thus be situated within the framework of recent concerns with a 'Marx-Weber debate' (Wiley, 1987) or 'Weber-Marx dialogue' (Antonio and Glassman, 1985). Yet it does so in a very selective and contextually bound way. Rather than confront Marx and Weber directly – a problematic exercise in any case, given the differences between writing in the mid-nineteenth century and the early twentieth century – the objective will be to consider the first fully developed version of this debate which flourished in the Weimar Republic and on into exile (Löwith, 1982 [1932]).

The first phase of this process has been recently documented with respect to the contemporaries of Weber, where only the figures of Ernst Bloch and George Lukács assume an important place in relation to a Marx-Weber confrontation (Karádi, 1987; Beirsdörfer, 1986). More specifically, it will be argued that such a Marx-Weber dialogue had its most illuminating origins in a second phase defined by two rival programs for a 'critical sociology' which emerged in Frankfurt in the 1920s and early 1930s: the Critical Theory of the early Frankfurt School as defined in the work of Horkheimer, Adorno, and Marcuse, and the theoretical program initiated by the sociology of knowledge as developed by Karl Mannheim.[1] Indeed, without an understanding of this transitional generation of debate (cf. Frisby, 1983), it is difficult to make sense of the confrontations that have marked the postwar reception of Weber (e.g., Stammer, 1972, to Lash and Whimster, 1987).

This essay traces rival receptions of Weber which both appropriate different aspects of his work, and yet reject many of his fundamental assumptions. More systematically, the discussion attempts to outline the logical structure of the leftist variants of post-Weberian social theory in Weimar Germany and the period of exile through the Second World War. In most general terms, the problematic of leftist post-Weberian social theory was linked to the confrontation of two provocative and closely related theoretical strategies: the Lukácsian reading of Marx (which anticipated the discovery of Marx's Early Manuscripts) and the Lukácsian Marxist reading of Weber. The first became the strategy of what is often referred to – somewhat misleading – as Hegelian Marxism, most closely associated with the earliest, neo-Marxist phase of the Frankfurt School tradition, and the parallel but independent work of Gramsci in Italy (Kilminster, 1979).

The second strategy – the Lukácsian (or Hegelian) Marxist rereading of

Weber – followed from the imperative of rethinking this new understanding of Marx in relation to Weber's astute criticisms of what he understood to be Marxism and historical materialism. As well, it took place in the context of coming to terms with the rise of fascism and the failure of the Soviet experiment. Such rethinking took many different forms, but the two most fruitful versions proceeded from antithetical starting points: the second phase of development (in the late 1930s) of the Frankfurt School's critique of technology as a 'dialectic of enlightenment,' as opposed to Mannheim's sociology of knowledge and later conception of a structural sociology of mass society and theory of democratic planning.

On the one hand, the Hegelian Marxists in the first phase of the early Frankfurt School (Horkheimer, Adorno, Marcuse) initially viewed the new understanding of Marx (initiated by Lukács and Karl Korsch) as convincingly undermining the criticisms of their neo-Weberian contemporaries; accordingly, during the Weimar period they were not concerned with taking Weber very seriously, a factor exacerbated by their own precarious and marginal position and the dominance of Weber's students. Only in the period of exile, following the rise of Hitler and their own disillusionment with their previous revolutionary expectations, did the Frankfurt theorists begin – very selectively to be sure – to reread Weber, incorporating above all aspects of his theory of rationalization and historical pessimism into a fundamentally transformed version of historical materialism and Critical Theory – the basis of what has been referred to as Weberian Marxism. But the result was in no sense an effort at comprehensive synthesis; rather, it entailed a very selective borrowing of certain themes – the theory of bureaucracy and rationalization – for recasting the whole problematic of Marxist theory as a critique of the dialectic of Enlightenment.

On the other hand, there was a second starting point represented primarily in the work of Mannheim: a Weberian rereading of Lukács's Marx, coupled with a Marxian rereading of Weber from the perspective of a generalized Marxian (hence anti-Weberian) epistemology. In this respect, Mannheim's strategy represents, along with Löwith's revelation of surprising elements of convergence between the two (1982 [1932]), one of the most important pioneering efforts to reconcile Marx and Weber. In preference to the term bourgeois Marxist, Mannheim's approach will be referred as a Marxisant Weberianism, given Mannheim's ultimate subordination of the project of radical emancipation – so central to the Marxian tradition – to the reformist tasks of social reconstruction and social order. And yet even this characterization is misleading, given that he was fundamentally at odds in many respects with Weber at the levels of epistemology, method, politics, theory of society, and social psychology – all in ways which derived their primary inspiration from his critique of Marx and Lukács, as well as his rarely noted but continuous opposition to Critical Theory. In that respect he comes much closer to a Marx-Weber synthesis, but one which ends up, in the last analysis, in opposition to neo-Marxist and Critical Theory, despite important elements of convergence.

The idea of the sociology of knowledge was closely linked to Mannheim's systematic formulation of *Wissenssoziologie* – a term laden with political and ideological overtones which aroused considerable controversy in the 1920s and '30s (Meja and Stehr, 1982). In the present context, however, the term will be used to refer to Mannheim's more general theoretical program as well, which in his later writings was clearly constructed as an alternative to both early Frankfurt School Critical Theory (i.e., Hegelian Marxism in the tradition of their mentor Lukács) *and* orthodox Weberian sociology in its various forms. Thus, Mannheim's theoretical program is grounded in the sociology of knowledge and its related epistemological claims, but also includes a conception of a structural sociology and a historical and interactionist social psychology.

Despite their differences, however, both early Critical Theory in its second phase and Mannheim's Marxisant Weberianism based on the sociology of knowledge shared an aspiration for a 'critical sociology' mediated by a critique of Weber *and* Marx.[2] The decisive aspect here is that Mannheim's sociology of knowledge did break decisively with Weber's epistemological and methodological approach, as well as political position, though his later work on democratic planning lost the critical edge of his earlier work.[3] Nevertheless, in this general sense both Critical Theory and Mannheim attempted to develop the foundations for rival programs for a critical sociology which originated in the Weimar Republic and continued into exile into the 1950s. In the Anglo-American sociological vocabulary of the period, they represented two of the most important and influential variants of left-wing forms of 'mass society' theory (though they were not usually clearly distinguished until the full retrieval of the Critical Theory tradition in the 1970s).

As we shall see, both of these rival post-Weberian theoretical programs ultimately failed with respect to the goals they set for themselves: the Frankfurt appropriation of Weber's theory of rationalization culminated in the impotence of a theory of 'total administration,' and Mannheim's cheerful effort to plan away the problems of instrumental rationality never adequately confronted the problem of the political economy of the planning process. Yet it will be suggested that only by deciphering the enduring significance of these efforts, hence standing on the shoulders of this desperate and transitional generation of theoretical giants, that we can fully appreciate the contradictory heritage inherited, above all, by Jürgen Habermas – and originally bequeathed by Weber's critique of Marxism.

## II. THE CHALLENGE OF MANNHEIM: CONTINUITIES AND DISCONTINUITIES

Mannheim's relationship to Weber is complex, subtle, and changed over time. Nor has (to the author's knowledge) this issue ever been subjected to the detailed, systematic scrutiny which it deserves;[4] and it would be much easier to carry out if the book on Weber which Mannheim had told a publisher in 1929 was already a manuscript of 300–350 pages had been preserved (Woldring, 1987: 410). The present discussion makes no pretense to fill this gap, but will attempt to sketch out in broad strokes some points of similarity and difference which link up with the overall question of contrasting the two strategies of critically appropriating Weber in question.

Mannheim was certainly deeply indebted to Weber, so much so that his Frankfurt School critics generally derisively referred to Mannheim's sociology of knowledge and general sociology as simply warmed-over Weberianism and hence a form of 'traditional theory' (e.g., Adorno, 1967: 37; Frankfurt Institute, 1973: 197). But this polemical response – motivated by the political divisions in the Weimar context – tends to obscure Mannheim's fundamental opposition to Weber on issues of epistemology, method, normative theory, theory of society, and politics. One only has to recall the vigorous and often acerbic responses of Weber's German disciples to Mannheim's sociology of knowledge to be reminded of the important differences (e.g., von Schelting, 1982 [1934]).[5]

Though the present discussion will focus on these differences, it should be mentioned at the outset – for the matter will come up again in a later context – that there were some fundamental continuities between Weber and Mannheim which were the focus of attack by their Marxist opponents. First, Mannheim, like Weber, remained sceptical of the Marxian theory of revolution; instead, he sought a radical reformist political strategy which he saw best represented in aspects of German social democracy, though not all of its theoretical assumptions (see, e.g., Kettler and Meja, 1988). In contrast, though formally identified as a nationalist liberal in the German context, Weber was no unsympathetic to the importance of a reformist working-class party as a necessary component of a stable democratic society.

Second, Mannheim shared with Weber a rejection of the Marxist theory of ideology as the dogmatic application of a particular philosophy of history as the 'science' of history. As well, he followed Weber in viewing the relative predominance of ideal and material factors as historically contingent. But even on both of these issues, as exemplified in his sociology of knowledge, Mannheim's overall epistemological position (e.g., his defence of an evaluative conception of ideology analysis) led him far beyond those faithful to a neo-Weberian position (e.g., von Schelting or, today, Bendix).

Third, Mannheim tended to broadly accept Weber's substantive sociological analyses of religion, economic history, bureaucracy, politics, and so forth, but this sympathy was generally complemented by qualifications of Marxist inspiration, or readings which drew out the continuities between Marx and Weber. On the whole, therefore, his position attempted to transcend the dominant polarization of Marx and Weber in the Weimar period of German sociology, a situation which made Mannheim's stance anathema to Marxists and Weberians alike, even though it was rather popular among many students towards the end of the Weimar Republic and contributed to his remarkably rapid rise to a university professorship (cf. Kettler, Meja, and Stehr, 1990).

Mannheim's critique of Weber revolved around two fundamental issues which went to the very heart of Weberian sociology and which were, successively, the primary preoccupations of the two main phases of Mannheim's career: the theory, ideology, knowledge, and sociological methods, and later a theory of mass society and democratic planning. The following discussion will thus develop the notion of Mannheim as a Marxisant Weberian and argue that this entailed a critique and appropriation of Weber which cannot be adequately described as either Marxian *or* Weberian. Rather, his thinking reached out for – though did not fully realize – a synthesis within which both Marxian and Weberian categories could be re-integrated. Accordingly, the following discussion will focus on his critical dialogue with Weber and stress the way in which he fundamentally transforms Weber's sociology via a critical sociology of knowledge and a structural theory of society which anticipates the possibility of the reconciliation of functional and substantial reason.

In the present context, the central issue regarding Mannheim's sociology of knowledge, culminating in *Ideology and Utopia*, is the relative significance of Lukács and Weber in his effort to generalize Marx's theory of ideology. Past commentators have tended to place stress on the decisive influence of Lukács's *History and Class Consciousness* (1968), a point echoed by the general hostility of most Weberians to Mannheim's approach. More recently, however, it has been argued that *Ideology and Utopia* 'was an attempt to come to terms with the position Weber articulated at the end of his life and that the role of Lukács's book was secondary' (Loader, 1985: 96). As Loader suggests, the answer to this question revolves around whether Mannheim adhered to the following Lukácsian themes:

(1) Was Mannheim's view of history teleological, that is, did he believe that history could be grasped in its totality? (2) Did he believe that one sector of society, be it a spiritual aristocracy or a the proletariat, had the ability to achieve this teleological comprehension? (3) Did he believe that theory could

verify praxis, either from an aristocratic or a proletarian standpoint? (4) Did he view the relationship of science (theory) and politics as one of (a) subordination (*Überwindung*), (b) dialectical transcendence (*Aufhebung*), or (c) clarification for responsibility (*Verantwortung*)? As I have already indicated, I contend that the answer to all three of these questions, with the exception of 4c, is no and that, therefore, Mannheim was closest to the position of Max Weber. (Loader, 1985: 100–101)

There are two basic problems, however, with this type of interpretation. First, it is built around the assumption that three basic positions were influential for Mannheim (the monadic historicism of people like Troeltsch, Lukács's Marxism, and Weber's politics of responsibility) and that in the end he was closest to Max Weber. As a consequence, insufficient attention is given to the originality and distinctive character of Mannheim's overall theoretical position, which does not neatly fit into any of the three options set out by Loader.[6] Though strictly speaking Mannheim does not adhere to the four Lukácsian positions set out by Loader, this cannot be taken to imply that he reverts back to Weber instead, with the partial exception of taking seriously the latter's conception of the ethics of responsibility in politics as a point a departure, though not an adequate solution. In fact, it could easily be shown that while Mannheim rejected each of these Lukácsian positions in their extreme form, he equally rejected the Weberian alternatives: (1) instead of a teleological theory of history, Weber's methodological individualism which rejected on methodological grounds any analysis of society as a totality or history as a developmental process; (2) in place of a proletarian mission, a theory of charismatic leadership as the solution to the problem of utopian renewal in the crisis of capitalism; (3) as opposed to a theory of knowledge based on praxis from a privileged social position, a positivist variant of social scientific theory; (4) in place of revolutionary dialectics, a theory of political decisionism which largely denied intellectuals any visionary or prophetic role. On all four of these points Mannheim developed positions which cannot be reduced to those of either Lukács *or* Weber, even as he drew upon and criticized both.

Second, Loader's argument turns essentially on viewing Mannheim's conception of the relationship between intellectuals and politics as basically an extension of Weber's approach. Though there is some merit to seeing this continuity – as a kind of social democratic revision of Weber's nationalist liberalism, its significance is vastly overrated by Loader because he does not take into account the rather different theories of knowledge and society underlying Mannheim's approach.[7] To see the significance of this, it is useful to review briefly Mannheim's response to the four questions identified by Loader and how they undermine the thesis of the continuity between Weber and Mannheim, aside from the trivial sense in which they both advocate a politics of responsibility in place of revolutionary dialectics. But the conception of knowledge underlying the assessment of 'responsible' action, and the theory of society which might guide the determination of 'responsible' actions, are quite distinct.

First, though Mannheim rejects Lukács's philosophy of history as arbitrary, he always remained enough of a historicist to view the task of sociology in terms of its ability to grasp historical epochs as a totality, and in opposition to Weber's methodological individualism, to analyse society as a structural whole (a theme whose implications will be developed in the next section).

Second, Mannheim does not altogether abandon the notion that the dynamic of social change can best be understood in relation to the rise and fall of social groups and classes which may have a variable (declining or emergent) position within the new form of society in the making. Clearly, his theory of intellectuals does entail in a muted form a generalization of the Lukácsian Marxist theme of a privileged social position in particular historical transitions. What he rejects, of course, is basing this conclusion on a teleological theory of history.

Third, Mannheim's hostility to Durkheimian positivism, his sympathy with the Marxian principle of the interrelationship between knowledge and practice, his later embracing of American pragmatism, and his complementary theory of democratic planning are all suggestive of a position very distant from Weber in the context of the theory/practice relationship. Though Marxists tended to argue that Mannheim's relationism was ultimately no different from Weber's value relativism and epistemological positivism, it did open the door to a type of non-dogmatic critique of ideology which was excluded by Weber's value-neutral approach and its strict separation of facts and values.[8] With respect to political ideologies, this suggested a historical conception of truth based on the notion of the objective possibilities in a given socio-historical context – the primary responsibility of progressive utopian movements. Though this contextual understanding of the theory/practice relationship is distant from any notion of a proletarian theory/praxis approach of the Lukácsian variety, it is also sharply at odds with Weber's decisionism and sharp division between science and politics.

Fourth, though Mannheim rejected a revolutionary model of politics (whether in its Marxist-Leninist or Critical Theory versions), and was sympathetic to the principle of the politics of responsibility in the Weberian sense, his whole account of the tensions between ideology and utopia leave room for elements of a politics of conscience or ultimate values rooted in substantial reason – themes which were central to his overall critique of Weber's theory of bureaucracy and rationalization, as we will see in a moment.

Forced into exile in England in 1933 following the rise of Hitler, Mannheim turned away from his earlier concerns with epistemology and knowledge towards an analysis of the 'crisis' of his time. Again the works of this period can be read as a prolonged dialogue with and critique of Weber's theory of bureaucracy and rationalization. Ironically, at the very moment when the Frankfurt School theorists began to turn to Weber's theory of rationalization to cope with interpreting the new stage of 'crisis,' Mannheim was developing a critique of it, and an alternative to Weber's pessimistic diagnosis of modern society as an 'iron cage.'

Even at the outset of his career, Mannheim's historicist leanings precluded any identification with Weber's methodological individualism and extreme nominalism: 'Max Weber's exaggerated theoretical nominalism led him to construe these formations so that they coincided with the intended "meanings" of individual experiencing subjects' (1982: 224). Mannheim thus distinguished throughout his career between three types of sociology: general (e.g., Simmel's 'formal sociology'), comparative (e.g., Weber), and structural (e.g., Marx) (Mannheim, 1956: 56–8 and 1953: 204–8). Weber is charged with not advancing to the structural level, 'mainly because within his individualistic and nominalistic frame of reference he had no access to singular historical phenomena' (1956: 57). In contrast, 'What the student of social change may learn from Marx is not his political and propagandistic casuistry, but the structural approach to change and to the dynamics of history' (1956: 58).[9] Clearly, Mannheim sides with those who contend that sociology should operate not only at the concrete, empirical level of 'social integration' in the manner of Weber, but also at the level of 'system integration,' that is, the deployment of a generalized functional method:[10]

> Max Weber's oversimplified conception of the 'meaning' of action – as an intended or unconscious aim – prevented him from realizing the objective or functional meaning of behaviour. One may well assume such a meaning without construing it à la Hegel as a goalward drift of events. Second, the structural interpretation of behaviour does not obviate the causal. (1956: 77)[11]

The application of this approach to such a structural sociology assumes the form of a sketchily developed theory of mass society in his *Man and Society in an Age of Reconstruction* (1940), which is based on the methodological assumption that 'it is the total structure of society alone which reveals the real function and meaning of the parts' (1940: 26). The basic argument is that in a mass society the potentials for mass democratization are undermined by capital concentration and centralization, rationalization and the monopolization of expert knowledge, bureaucratization, and the concentration of military power (1940: 47ff). Societal crisis and breakdown are thus linked to the transition of an unregulated liberal society to a regulated one providing a new basis for social order. The primary choice was whether this would assume some kind of totalitarian form or a democratic one.

The basis for Mannheim's optimistic reappraisal of Weber's theory of bureaucracy and rationalization is a three-stage developmental model which assumes different forms in various phases of his own work.[12] At the level of societal development, his approach could be read as a kind of reworking of Toennies's *Gemeinschaft/Gesellschaft* distinction and Durkheim's theory of organic solidarity.[13] The primary difference is that he works with trichotomous rather than dichotomous distinctions, thus identifying two stages within the *Gesellschaft* or organic solidarity phase.

Mannheim's theory of planning represents the concrete outcome of his critique of Weber's conception of the relationship between intellectuals and politics (Weber, 1946: 77–156). In the context of the sociology of knowledge (Mannheim, 1936: 109–91), this critique required the presupposition that the progressive elements of an intelligentsia adequately informed by a theory of society could in fact develop a cultural-intellectual synthesis capable of transcending the war of competing ideologies. Weber, of course, rejected the assumption that there could be any rational resolution of the struggle between competing worldviews.

In the context of Mannheim's theory of planning, a similar critique of Weber is developed. As opposed to the notion of any inexorable expansion of functional rationalization, Mannheim argues for the possibility of a higher level of synthesis in various spheres which could facilitate the transition to a new level of systemic integration – a democratically planned society – in which the negative effects of functional rationalization could be brought under control. As he notes against Weber's analysis of the negative effects of functional rationalization, 'it would be false ... to believe that this process must *unconditionally* and *under all circumstances* lead to the catastrophes which it so often produces to-day' (1940: 61).

In support of this point, Mannheim perceived a series of interlinked triadic developmental processes which created the conditions of possibility for transcending Weber's fatalistic perspective. Most generally, this entailed the movement from substantive irrationality, through functional rationality, and then substantial rationality. Similar progressive possibilities are envisioned in moral development (horde, individualistic, group solidarity), analytic thought (chance discovery, invention, planning), forms of political society (traditional, liberal, democratic), and types of sociology (systematic, comparative, structural).

Though the latter does not strictly correspond to the other developmental forms as historical sequences, the advent of a structural sociology is the decisive element required for the theory of planning which could overcome the negative aspects of functional rationalization.

Such a structural sociology has two crucial aspects which distances it from any conventional Weberian conception of sociology. On the one hand, it presupposes analysing society as a structural totality, a possibility ruled out by Weber's methodological individualism. On the other hand, it presupposes the development of a sociological social psychology which could provide knowledge of the mediating processes required for a system of democratic planning and social control.

A complementary aspect of Mannheim's critique of Weber's theory of rationalization is recognition of the continuing importance of the irrational or non-rational aspects of social life. Weber's theory of disenchantment (*Entzauberung*) is premised on the inevitable decline the religious foundations of culture, whereas Mannheim (implicitly drawing again upon Durkheim) postulates the functional necessity of a theological dimension for any form of society (what he refers to as 'paradigmatic experiences' in his later work (cf. Woldring, 1987: 344–52). Indeed, he attributes much of the irrationality at the stage of mass democratization as a consequence of the disorientation following from disenchantment. His theory of planning presupposes that it would be possible to construct alternative forms of cultural synthesis, including functional alternatives to religion or transformations of traditional religion, consistent with social stability, freedom, and relative equality.[14]

It is also important to note the counterfactual dimension of Mannheim's argument as developed in the 1930s. He is discussing the conditions of possibility of such a democratically planned society, not predicting its emergence; to this extent, he was admitting that the third stage of these triadic developmental processes was only an emergent, contingent possibility rather than a fully realized actuality. At various points he also noted the processes mitigating against their realization – themes stressed above all by his Frankfurt opponents. The decisive point in relation to Weber is his challenge to the thesis of the inexorability of functional rationalization in its negative forms.

III. THE EARLY FRANKFURT SCHOOL: FROM UTOPIA TO DESPAIR

From the founding of the Frankfurt Institute of Social Research until its movement into exile after 1932, Critical Theory was conceived in direct opposition to Weberian sociology. Löwith writing in 1932 captures this polarization aptly: 'Like our actual society, which it studies, social science is not unified but divided in two: *bourgeois sociology* and *Marxism*. The most important representatives of these two lines of inquiry are Max Weber and Karl Marx' (1982: 18). But the heritage of both Marx and Weber was up for grabs in the years following the First World War in the Weimar Republic, and the Frankfurt Institute – and the atmosphere of the University of Frankfurt generally – represented a unique opportunity for research of Marxist inspiration to be conducted independently of any party influences.[15] Under these circumstances, a certain familiarity between opposing viewpoints became possible, and out of this dialogue emerged the respective theoretical programs of Critical Theory and Mannheim.[16]

Despite respect for Weber's brilliance and his concrete studies, and the fact that someone like Lukács had cordial associations with Weber's Heidelberg circle (and had borrowed from Weber's theory of rationalization to reconstruct a theory of alienation qua reification), the notion of any basis for a synthesis or mutual accommodation of the two traditions was anathema in the early days of the Frankfurt School.

In the context of Horkheimer's classic distinction between 'traditional' and 'critical' theory, Weber (along with Mannheim) was relegated to the former. Weber's (and Mannheim's) criticisms of Marxism could be ignored as based on an inadequate understanding of Marx's general theory, a point reinforced by the recovery of Marx's Early Manuscripts. As for Weber's critique of socialism and the Soviet revolution, the Critical Theorists remained confident that a transformation of the relations of production, along with the new understanding of Marx, could in principle overcome any supposed 'iron law of oligarchy' or any ostensible inevitable bureaucratization of the revolutionary process.[17] Only with the increasingly evident failure of the Soviet experiment toward the end of the 1930s, along with the success of both authoritarian and democratic state capitalism, do Adorno, Horkheimer, and Marcuse turn back to Weber for a fundamental rethinking of historical materialism.

The antipathy of Critical Theory for Weberian sociology (with which Mannheim was somewhat unfairly closely associated) is outlined initially in Horkheimer's famous distinction between 'traditional' and 'critical' theory and is coupled with a bold vision of an interdisciplinary materialist research program. In this connection, both Weber and Mannheim are noted as examples of 'traditional' theory, a term which rather uneasily came to embrace everything other than Critical Theory: 'There can be no doubt, in fact, that the various schools of sociology have an identical conception of theory and that it is the same as theory in the natural sciences' (1972 [1937]). Against Mannheim's sociology of knowledge, Horkheimer and Marcuse argue: 'The abstract sociological concept of an intelligentsia which is to have missionary functions is, by its structure, an hypostatization of specialized science. Critical theory is neither "deeply rooted" like totalitarian propaganda nor "detached" like the liberalist intelligentsia' (1972 [1937]: 223–4).

As well, the theory of culture and ideology developed in the work of early Critical Theory fundamentally transformed the significance of the theory of domination (*Herrschaft*) by introducing a social psychological basis for a theory of authority fundamentally at odds with Weber's theory of legitimation. Whereas the classic Weberian distinction between traditional, rational-legal, and charismatic forms of legitimation simply provided a value-neutral description of authority relations, Critical Theory opposed this strategy with a critique of ideology and a social psychology of self-victimization which had its roots in Freudian theory (cf. Held, 1980: 111–47).

Despite a persistent and somewhat unfair classification of Mannheim's approach as a version of neo-Weberian sociology, early Critical Theory's initial critical response to Weber actually converges on most points with that of Mannheim: a rejection of his methodological individualism and resulting inability to analyse society as a totality, his non-critical conception of ideology and normative relativism, his nationalist liberal political orientation, and his pessimistic interpretation of the process rationalization.

But the points of divergence between early Critical Theory and Mannheim were also significant and were linked to areas where Mannheim remained more or less Weberian: a rejection of the Marxian theory of history and proletarian revolution, and the search for a scientifically credible method for empirically studying the social genesis of knowledge which transcended the materialist-idealist polarization.

On two other important issues Mannheim's position diverged from both Weber *and* early Critical Theory. On the one hand, he held out the possibility that the sociology of knowledge could provide the foundation for a non-dogmatic version of ideology critique and point the way to a new cultural synthesis which might overcome the Babel of conflicting ideologies. On the other hand, this possibility also opened way for a politics guided by an 'ethic of responsibility' which would allow intellectuals to play a strategic role in realizing the objectively possible (relatively utopian) in the given historical situation.

The real confrontation between Critical Theory and Weber came only with the crisis of Critical Theory in the mid-1930s with the failure of the German working class to revolt and increasing disillusionment with the Soviet experiment in its Stalinist phase. Though the resulting appropriation of the Weberian theory of rationalization under the heading of the thesis of the 'dialectic of Enlightenment' is well known, it needs to be complemented by two other closely related aspects of the Weberian influence upon later Critical Theory: the revised theory of the state embodied in the concept of state capitalism, especially as it developed under the influence of Friedrich Pollock; and the epistemological contortions and evasions revealed by efforts to convincingly postulate an 'objective reason' which might overcome instrumental rationalization.

The seeds for a return to Weber can be found in Critical Theory's use of Lukács's theory of reification, which was of particular interest to Adorno's early efforts at cultural analysis. Though Lukács's use of the concept of reification also anticipated Marx's theory of alienation, its original formulation had been strongly influenced by Weber's theory of rationalization. Initially, however, reification is held, following Lukács, to be a specific consequence of rationalization within capitalism, a theme developed most intensively by Adorno in his study of popular music.

By the end of the 1930s, however, disillusionment with the Soviet experiment (which is expressed along Weberian lines as a critique of bureaucracy), along with the failure of working-class revolutionary movements, culminates in returning to Weber's more pessimistic formulations regarding rationalization. Within the Frankfurt inner circle this reappropriation of Weber took two forms: a moderate version in Marcuse and a radicalized version in the writings of Adorno and Horkheimer, which will be the focus of the present discussion.[18]

Adorno and Horkheimer radicalize Weber's thesis, tracing the process of rationalization not to capitalism as such, but to the Enlightenment conception of reason underlying modern science – the 'dialectic of enlightenment' (Horkheimer and Adorno, 1972 [1944]). Wellmer provides a succinct formulation of the Weberian components of this strategy:

> Simplifying, one could describe the basic strategy of the philosophers of the 'Frankfurt School' (Horkheimer, Adorno, and Marcuse in particular) as follows: they adopted the negative dialectics of progress from Weber and, at the same time, criticized his notion of formal and instrumental rationality as a 'truncated' conception of rationality which did not allow him even to conceive of the *possibility* of a rational organization of society which would be in accord with an emphatic conception of reason ... This is a way of thinking which for Weber would indeed have been impossible. For Weber, in a disenchanted world, no rational justification of norms, values or forms of social organization was possible ... The Frankfurt philosophers, on the other hand, did acknowledge that Weber's 'truncated' conception of rationality corresponded to the reality of advanced industrial societies ... For this reason they also could agree with Weber – against Marx – that the *immanent* logic of the capitalist modernization process pointed *not* to the emergence of a classless society but rather to the emergence of a closed system of

instrumental and administrative rationality, rooted in the reified consciousness of individuals ... The dialectics of progress became a negative one,
aiming at the destruction rather than the realization of reason (Wellmer,
1985: 44).

Historical events and the critique of instrumental reason also contributed to
another decisive break with the orthodox Marxist tradition in the context of the
theory of the state with respect to both capitalism and Soviet Communism; this
shift was decisively influenced by arguments deriving from Weber (cf. Arato and
Gebhardt, 1978: 3–25; Held, 1980: 40–76). Indeed, these issues brought about a
split within the Frankfurt School related to the relative primacy of the economic
and the political. Those who held to more orthodox Marxist positions argued
that fascism was the inevitable outcome of the changing political economy of
capitalism. And, as for the Soviet case, the response was silence because of the
absence of a coherent theoretical basis for explaining Stalinism, aside from a
'betrayal' of the revolution thesis along Trotskyist lines.

In contrast, the positions developed by Pollock (1975) and Horkheimer were
in fact derived to a great extent from Weberian assumptions and 'based on the
powerful insight that validates the effort from the start: the change in the
function of political economy, the end of the primacy of the economic under
industrially advanced contemporary social formations and the necessity of the
replacement of political economy as the framework and object of Marxism as
critique' (Arato and Gebhardt, 1978: 22).

The lines of reasoning developed depended on assumptions largely consistent
with Weber and, in certain respects, with Mannheim. The Weberian element
here was twofold. First, the contention that there was no inherent reason why
the new form of (more or less authoritarian) state capitalism could not provide
a new form of capitalism followed from Weber's earlier insistence on the
primacy of the political and his tendency (shared by Mannheim) to dismiss a
mechanistic theory of revolution based on economic contradictions. Mannheim, of course, drew upon this assumption of the autonomy of the political
as part of his optimistic theory of democratic planning. For the new stage of
Critical Theory, in contrast, the critique of Mannheim's theory of the state had
become the new object of critique. The second Weberian element appropriated
by the Frankfurt School (and already shared by Mannheim) provided a theoretical basis for a critique of the Soviet experiment: the theory of rationalization
and bureaucratization.

But the Critical Theorists appropriation of Weber's theory of rationalization
rejected the epistemological basis of his position, that is, the sharp contrast
between an instrumental reason capable of scientific calculation and substantial

reason as essentially irrational. In Horkheimer's formulation, Weber's position is characterized as a 'subjectivistic' conception of reason because of the resulting denial of 'objective' truth:

> The difference between this connotation of reason and the objectivistic conception resembles to a certain degree the difference between functional and substantial rationality as these words are used in the Max Weber school. Max Weber, however, adhered so definitively to the subjectivistic trend that he did not conceive of any rationality – even a 'substantial' one by which man can discriminate one end from another. If our drives, intentions, and finally our ultimate decisions must a priori be irrational, substantial reason becomes an agency merely of correlation and is therefore itself essentially 'functional'. Although Max Weber's own and his followers' descriptions of the bureaucratization and monopolization of knowledge have illuminated much of the social aspect of the transition from objective to subjective reason (cf. particularly the analyses of Karl Mannheim in *Man and Society*, London, 1940), Max Weber's pessimism with regard to the possibility of rational insight and action, as expressed in his philosophy ... is itself a stepping-stone in the renunciation of philosophy and science as regards their aspiration of defining man's goal (1974 [1947]: 6).[19]

But the thesis of the negative dialectic of enlightenment proposed by Horkheimer and Adorno calls into question the grounds on which 'objective reason' could still be sustained as either a rational construct or a practical possibility. At least in Marx's original formulation there was an essential continuity between the unfolding of technical rationalization, the transformation of society, and the realization of substantial (objective) reason. But as Wellmer points out: 'However, by stressing the radical *discontinuity* rather than the historical *continuity* between the history of class society and the liberated society, it obviously risks ending up with a new form of utopianism, which would be the back side of its radical negativism – a form of utopianism, i.e., in which the future would be related to the present only by a radical but abstract negation' (1985: 45).

The fundamental difficulty of this argument is that it 'ultimately took the tone of an impotent protest against Weber's claim; that in a world without religion or metaphysics, the idea of "objective reason" can have no place' (Wellmer, 1985: 47).[20] Again, the mode of reasoning here is virtually the converse of that of Mannheim, who claims to have recovered a new basis of continuity by proposing the objective possibility of democratic planning as an alternative to Weber's inexorable process of formal rationalization. But Mannheim's vision of continuity foundered not only on an inadequate consideration of the political economic processes and groups that might cripple or distort this process; he also presupposed a form of theoretical value consensus which also required a form of 'objective reason' – of substantial rationality – which conflicted with his own critique of the Hegelian-Marxist tradition. Horkheimer and Adorno's vision of discontinuity, in contrast, could not point to the conditions of possibility for either the articulation or realization of the objective reason their approach had postulated. At best, it could provide a negative critique of the limitations of Mannheim's vision in practice: the welfare state.

## IV. THE FIRST MARX-WEBER CONFRONTATION: A CONTRADICTORY LEGACY

The theoretical programs of Horkheimer's Institute for Social Research – at least in its Weberian Marxist form in the late 1930s and 1940s – and Mannheim's vision of a synthetic structural sociology based on the sociology of knowledge are both remarkably convergent and divergent. The similarities include: the effort to draw upon both Marx and Weber to provide an interdisciplinary, normatively grounded critical sociology capable of dealing with the crisis of mass capitalist society and the rise of fascism; stress upon the cultural bases of order and change and the unique if changing role of intellectuals in guiding processes of transformation; recognition of the autonomous effects of processes of functional rationalization as a problematic (originally defined by Weber) which goes beyond the original Marxian formulation; a turn to social psychological theory to complement the traditional macrosociological focus of classical European theory; a failure to convincingly ground the value assumptions (based on objective or substantial reason) underlying their 'utopian' visions of an alternative to the crisis of capitalism; and, ironically, the failure of both theoretical programs to fully institutionalize a tradition of research.

The points of divergence are also equally striking, though they have often been overemphasized given the animosities dating back to their rivalry in the Weimar Republic: Critical Theory's virtual abandonment of its interdisciplinary empirical research program in the name of an anti-positivist critique of the dialectic of Enlightenment which renders all empirical social science suspect, as opposed to Mannheim's insistence upon a structural sociology and pragmatic social psychology as the theoretical basis for a new planned social order; Mannheim's idealistic plea for a form of democratic planning which was at complete odds with the Weberian themes appropriated by the later phase of Critical Theory; Mannheim's concern with a social psychology which could provide the forms of social control necessary for a planned society, as opposed to Critical Theory's conception of a social psychology of domination analysing the very processes which would undermine Mannheim's reformist project; Mannheim's preoccupation with overcoming the irrationality of disorder in the mass society of advanced capitalism through planning, as opposed to Critical Theory's concern with the total administration as the primary source of irrationality in a one-dimensional state capitalist society; Mannheim's conviction of the necessity of a new ethical basis for cultural integration, in contrast to Critical Theory's agreement with Weber that religion could no longer ground the cultural order, and that there was no alternative basis for such a grounding.

In most respects, Mannheim's diagnosis was more historically accurate in that his theory of planning in fact anticipated the type of welfare state that has become the typical form of advanced capitalist liberal democracies in the postwar period. Yet at the same time, the surprising ease with which social order was re-established in the emergent postwar welfare states deprived his theory of the critical edge which it possessed in the 1930s. Even though C. Wright Mill's version of a radical sociology attempted to preserve such a critical thrust with a theory of power elites, even his position was eclipsed with the revival of neo-Marxist theory and critical theory in the 1970s.

In contrast, Critical Theory had preserved a critical moment which had been largely lost in Mannheim's effort to reconcile conflicting viewpoints and his tendency to gloss over the deeper political economic contradictions of advanced capitalism, the persistence of class conflict, the full implications of the industrialization of culture, the distortions of emergent forms of social character – all obstacles to effective democratic planning oriented towards substantial rationality. In the first two decades of postwar reconstruction, however, Critical Theory was almost completely marginalized. Most of those who had previously adhered to Marxist positions recanted under the rubric of 'the god that failed,' assuming liberal and social democratic stances which closely resembled Mannheim's optimistic diagnosis.

Nevertheless, though neither approach fully comprehended or anticipated the realities of the post-Second World War era, taken together they represent the most prescient early diagnoses of the issues which would in fact dominate social theory in advanced capitalism in the last half of the twentieth century. Only with the rise of the New Left, along with the discovery (and translation) of the major works of the Frankfurt tradition in the 1970s, did the full implications of the project of Critical Theory become apparent. But even the retrieval of the older Frankfurt tradition had run its course by the mid 1970s, when its inadequacies, whether in its original neo-Marxist version or its later critique of the dialectic of Enlightenment, became increasingly evident. In West Germany, the result was a resurgence of more orthodox Marxist tendencies and in Latin countries the rise of structuralist Marxism. At this point, it might seem that the neo-Weberians were on the verge of having the 'last laugh' as the two most important challenges to Weber – the rival programs of Critical Theory and the sociology of knowledge – appeared inadequate to the task of diagnosing and confronting the crisis of advanced capitalism, and as an ironic consequence were increasingly displaced by the revival of a neo-Marxist orthodoxy even less able to do so.

Yet the emergence of the work of Jürgen Habermas in the late 1960s, its continuous development in the subsequent two decades, and its fairly rapid international diffusion had the effect of breathing new life within the tradition of Weberian Marxism and reopening the Marx-Weber dialogue. Despite fundamental differences with his Frankfurt mentors, Habermas's work can be viewed in the trajectory of the Frankfurt School and in apparent explicit opposition to the variant of Marxisant Weberianism which Mannheim valiantly attempted to develop.

Yet one of the most paradoxical features of contemporary developments in critical theory – specifically the more recent work of Habermas – is that on certain fundamental issues he sides more often with Mannheim's general *strategy* (though not for the most part his specific solutions) than with that of his own Frankfurt mentors. As Habermas has pointed out in an interview, he differed from his mentors in three basic ways: their inadequately grounded conception of science and the relation of theory to the empirical disciplines, a failure to fully come to terms with the normative groundings of Critical Theory, and an insufficient sense of the importance of protecting, despite their limitations, liberal democratic institutions (Habermas, 1986: 97). On all three points Habermas was thus siding with Mannheim's strategy (though not generally his specific solutions) in attempting to develop a critique of – and alternative to – early Frankfurt Critical Theory.

First, like Mannheim, the overall architectonic of this theoretical program has been to provide a response to Weber's critique of historical materialism in order to reaffirm the scientific credibility of a reconstructed formulation and its relation to the other empirical disciplines. Though Mannheim is typically criticized by positivists and non-positivists alike for his relativistic relationism, Hekman makes the case for the convergence of his work with Gadamer and for viewing him 'as a forerunner of anti-foundational social science ... Far from being unthinkable ... the groundless philosophy of social science that Mannheim proposes offers a number of distinct advantages ...' (1986: 79). As in the case of Mannheim, the point of departure for Habermas has been an epistemological reconstruction, an attempt to generalize Marxian theory and open the way for a reflexive, and self-critical, anti-foundationalist theory of knowledge (Habermas, 1987b; 1988). Like Mannheim, this has also entailed efforts to clarify the relationship between critical social thought and specialized, empirical fields.

Second, he recognized – in the context of justifying the normative grounds of historical materialism – with Mannheim that without an answer to Weber's conception of the opposition of formal and substantial reason, there was no choice between dogmatism (objective reason) and relativism (subjective reason). Whatever the failings of his answers, Mannheim was again groping for the right questions for coming to terms with the normative crisis of historical materialism.

Third, like Mannheim, he has attempted to respond to the Weberian assumption of the ultimate incompatibility of instrumental and substantial reason with a plea for participatory democracy and democratic planning. For this reason, in his latest work in social theory he has even subjected Critical Theory's use of Weber's theory of rationalization to a searching critique which in fact revises his own earlier position (Habermas, 1984). Habermas's concern with rehabilitating the concept of the 'public sphere' as a critical concept has many parallels with the intentions behind Mannheim's conception of democratic planning, even if the latter did not fully appreciate the possibilities of 'technology as ideology,' a theme which could have been in principle developed within the sociology of knowledge.

Why this uncanny resemblance between the theoretical strategies of Habermas and Mannheim, despite crucial divergences in the outcome? The answer follows from the formal logic of the discursive context in which both authors worked. Mannheim's position was developed as an explicit effort to anticipate a synthetic position which could effectively play off the strengths and weaknesses of Weber and Marx, given the failure of both to adequately deal with the crisis of the Weimar Republic, as well as the general crisis of capitalism.

Similarly, Habermas was confronted some three decades later with inheriting a version of Critical Theory which had become increasingly unable to deal with the changing nature of advanced capitalism, a problem exacerbated by the appropriation of the Weberian theory of rationalization. As in the case of Mannheim, this entailed playing off in a new context the strengths and weaknesses of Weber and Marx as the point of departure for a 'reconstructed' historical materialism. And at this point there is even a partial convergence in content as well as strategy between Habermas and Mannheim: postulating the ideal of a democratic public sphere, coupled with a rational justification of normative (substantial) reason, as the conditions of possibility for an alternative to the Weberian theory of rationalization and its tragic Marxist complement in the theory of the dialectic of Enlightenment.[21]

Implicitly and unconsciously, then, in Habermas's work the old wounds inflicted in the rivalry between the two camps of a post-Weberian critical sociology have been perhaps partially healed as the debate has moved on – beyond Mannheim, as well as beyond the critique of the dialectic of Enlightenment (Habermas, 1984; 1987a). But then the Frankfurt School and Mannheim thought they too had banished Max Weber's ghost by incorporating themes from his unsystematic edifice into theoretical programs that would transcend the antinomies of his thought. Ironically, from this perspective both the notion of Weberian Marxism and a Marxisant Weberianism are misleading – and even oxymoronic – given the way in which both theoretical programs rejected fundamental epistemological, methodological, and theoretical assumptions of Weber's sociology and political philosophy. Equally misleading are characterizations of Habermas's theoretical program as 'Weberian' in any general sense.

Why then has the critique of Weber played such a powerful role in post-Weberian social theory? Why this chronic – and seemingly necessary – tendency to misleadingly label theories as Weberian which were in fact both opposed to each other, as well as to his most fundamental normative, epistemological, and methodological assumptions? Above all, it reflects the power of Weber's questions, if not his personal solutions, and the spell they have cast on his opponents who, despite themselves, stand on his tragic shoulders in search of the light guiding the way out of his anticipations of the icy darkness – of the barbarism of instrumental reason.

## NOTES

1  The present essay develops some of the themes regarding the relation between Mannheim and the early Frankfurt School originally presented in my unpublished doctoral dissertation (Morrow, 1981), but adds the specific focus on their contrasting receptions of Weber. Given the synthetic character of my essay, no systematic attempt has been made to support non-controversial assertions with references to original sources, though general references are often made to the many competent secondary sources. In particular, no effort has been made to document the basic positions of Weber, which are largely taken for granted and not detailed in the present discussion.

2  To be sure, this characterization assumes a definition of 'critical' which is somewhat broader than that employed within the Frankfurt tradition, but confirmed indirectly by C. Wright Mills's reliance upon Mannheim for his own radical sociology.

3  This does not justify the assertion, however, that 'Mannheim's later work, concerned almost exclusively with social planning, is, from the point of view of social theory, uninteresting' (Hekman, 1986: 78). For a contrasting view, see Kettler and Meja, 1988.

4 Insightful if fragmentary comments on the Weber-Mannheim relation can be found in the many essays and introductions by David Kettler, Volker Meja, and Nico Stehr, as well as their book on Mannheim (1984); from the perspective of a focus on Weber, Sica (1988) is also helpful.

5 Again, this contrasts, ironically, with the radical American reception of Weber and Mannheim in the work of C. Wright Mills where we find the essentials of a left-Weberian approach inspired by Mannheim.

6 As Woldring puts it, 'Mannheim attributed many sociological insights to Weber and also accepted Weber's ideal types in his own methodology; in the sociology of culture and especially in his ideas on the mission of the intelligentsia, however, Mannheim opposes Weber' (1987: 223). For an account of Mannheim's social theory which gives full justice to its distinctiveness – and difficulties – as an alternative to both Marx and Weber, see Kettler, Meja, and Stehr (1984).

7 As Kettler, Meja, and Stehr (1984: 54) point out: 'Although Mannheim invokes Weber's conception of politics as dependent ultimately on choices which no knowledge can dictate, his own conception of the insight to be derived from comprehensive understanding of the political situation and his extension of the clarifying impact which authentic political knowledge can have upon the political field of action fundamentally alter the meaning of the Weberian formulas he invokes.'

8 This is most evident in his defence of an evaluative approach to ideology and recognition of the importance of a critique of false consciousness (Mannheim, 1936: 88–97). Unlike the Frankfurt Critical Theorists, however, he sought more secure, empirically based, methodological foundations for ideology critique, as well as a less dogmatic epistemological 'relationism.'

9 One of the limitations of those who otherwise correctly stress the 'hermeneutic' aspect of Mannheim's methodology in the sociology of knowledge (e.g., Simonds, 1978; Hekman, 1986) is that they do not take into account his aspirations for a structural analysis of society – a theme which even appears in his earliest work. Though the realization of these intentions in his theory of mass society may have been seriously flawed, their ultimate relation to the project of the sociology of knowledge needs to be taken into account, rather than dismissed as an uninteresting aberration resulting from his exile experience.

10 The distinction between 'social integration' and 'system integration' was originally developed by Lockwood (1964) and has more recently been employed by Habermas.

11 In this context, the editors of this posthumously published text add references to Parsons and Merton to confirm that methodological point. But it should be stressed that Mannheim derives his understanding of a structural method – employing a generalized form of functional analysis – from Marx and should not be construed a 'functionalist' in the Parsonian sense, though one could say he employed a conflict functionalist method which was not specifically Marxian, and rather more Weberian

in content, as, for example, in the early work of Alvin Gouldner.

12 For a useful summary of these typologies and their appearance even in Mannheim's early work, cf. Loader (1987: 128–45).

13 As Woldring notes, Mannheim rarely cites Durkheim in his later work despite obvious affinities and attributes this to Mannheim's 'critical attitude toward positivism, increasing by the year; apparently he did not want to run the risk of being interpreted positivistically' (1987: 289).

14 For a searching account of Mannheim's lifelong struggle with dealing with the rational and the irrational, see Kettler, Meja, and Stehr (1990). They stress how exile in England undermined the more fruitful dialogue with religious thought and the irrational, which had taken place through involvement with Paul Tillich's religious circle in the Weimar Republic and confrontations with Lukács, Horkheimer, Adorno, and others.

15 For detailed accounts of this early work, see BonB, 1982; Dubiel, 1978; Sollner, 1978.

16 For contrasting analyses of this dialogue and its implications, see Schmidt, 1974; Jay, 1974; and Dubiel, 1975.

17 The essence of this orthodox position was later fleshed out in rather vulgar terms in Lukács's *Destruction of Reason* (1974 [1954]). Though by the 1950s the Frankfurt Critical Theorists no longer hold such a reductionist view of Weberian sociology, Lukács's caricature was probably not as far from the position of Horkheimer, Adorno, and Marcuse as in the early 1930s.

18 Marcuse's account remains more moderate primarily because he continued to hold to the Marxian thesis that the transformation of the relations of production would transform the effects of functional rationalization. His later book on the Soviet Union (Marcuse, 1961) served in part to defend Marx's original vision from its historically distorted form. Even in his more pessimistic moments, where the autonomous power of science and technology is seen to produce a one-dimensional society, he can still envision an alternative conception of science which might allow the reconciliation of man and nature. On this aspect of Marcuse's work, especially in relation to Habermas, cf. Alford, 1985.

19 This theme was later developed in greater detail in Marcuse's essay (1968 [1964]: 201–26). But at this point Marcuse is forced to admit that Weber's critique of the project of overcoming instrumental reason was valid: 'For Max Weber this possibility was utopian. Today it looks as if he was right' (1968: 225).

20 Wellmer, here, is of course echoing Habermas, and goes on to discuss how Habermas's overall theoretical strategy is built around an effort to overcome the aporias of such a radical Weberianized Marxism – a question which is beyond the confines of this essay.

21 Mannheim, of course, though critical of positivism, was not able to anticipate the scientization of politics which would severely distort planning processes in the postwar

welfare state, even though Adorno's savage critique along these lines had been circulated privately to Mannheim, though not published until much later (Adomo, 1967: 35–49) to avoid sectarian rivalries among the Weimar immigrants in exile (Buck-Morss, 1977: 226).

## REFERENCES

Alford, C. Fred. 1985. *Science and the Revenge of Nature: Marcuse and Habermas.* Tampa/ Gainesville: University of South Florida Press/University of Florida Press.

Antonio, Robert J., and Ronal M. Glassman, eds. 1985. *A Weber-Marx Dialogue.* Lawrence: University of Kansas Press.

Arato, Andrew, and Eike Gebhardt, eds. 1978. *The Essential Frankfurt School Reader.* New York/Oxford: Urizen/Basil Blackwell.

Beiersdörfer, Kurt. 1986. *Max Weber und Lukács: Über die Bieziehung von Verstehender Soziologie und Westlichen Marxismus.* Frankfurt/New York. Campus.

BonB, Wolfgang. 1982. *Die Einübung des Tatsachenblicks: Zur Struktur und Veränderung empirischer Sozialforschung.* Frankfurt am Main: Suhrkamp.

Buck-Morss, Susan. 1977. *The Origins of Negative Dialectics: Theodor W. Adomo, Walter Benjamin and the Frankfurt Institut.* New York: Free Press.

Dubiel, Helmut. 1975. 'Ideologiekritik versus Wissenssoziologie in der kritischen Theorie.' *Archiv für Rechts und Sozialphilosophie* 61: 223–38.

— 1978. *Wissenschaftsorganisation und politische Erfahrung. Studien zur frühen Kritische Theorie.* Frankfurt am Main: Suhrkamp.

Frankfurt Institute for Social Research. 1973 (1956). *Aspects of Sociology*, trans. John Viertel. Boston: Beacon Press.

Frisby, David. 1983. *The Alienated Mind: The Sociology of Knowledge in Germany 1918–1933.* London and New Jersey: Heinemann/Humanities Press.

Habermas, Jürgen. 1984. *The Theory of Communicative Action*, vol. 1, *Reason and the Rationalization of Society*, trans. Thomas McCarthy. Boston: Beacon.

— 1986. *Autonomy and Solidarity: Interviews*, ed. and intro. Peter Dews. London: Verso.

— 1987a [1981]. *The Theory of Communicative Action*, vol. 2, *Lifeworld and System: A Critique of Functionalist Reason*, trans. Thomas McCarthy. Boston: Beacon Press.

— 1987b [1985]. *The Philosophical Discourse of Modernity: Twelve Lectures*, trans. Frederick Lawrence. Cambridge, MA: MIT Press.

— 1988. *Nachtmetaphysiches Denken: Philosophische Aufsätze.* Frankfurt am Main: Suhrkamp.

Hekman, Susan J. 1986. *Hermeneutics and the Sociology of Knowledge.* Notre Dame and London: University of Notre Dame Press.

Held, David. 1980. *Introduction to Critical Theory: Horkheimer to Habermas.* Berkeley and Los Angeles: University of California Press.

Horkheimer, Max. 1972. *Critical Theory: Selected Essays*, trans. Matthew J. O'Connell et al. New York: Herder and Herder.

— 1974 [1947]. *Eclipse of Reason*. New York: Seabury.

— and Theodor W. Adorno. 1972 [1944]. *Dialectic of Enlightenment*, trans. John Cumming. New York: Herder and Herder.

Jay, Martin. 1973. *The Dialectical Imagination: A History of the Frankfurt School and the Institute of Social Research, 1923–1950*. Boston: Little, Brown and Co.

— 1974. 'The Frankfurt Critique of Mannheim.' *Telos*, no. 20: 72–89.

Karádi, Éva. 1987. 'Ernst Bloch and Georg Lukács in Max Weber's Heidelberg.' Pp. 499–514 in *Max Weber and His Contemporaries*, ed. Wolfgang J. Mommsen and Jürgen Osterhammel. London: Allen & Unwin.

Kettler, David, Volker Meja, and Nico Stehr. 1984. *Karl Mannheim*. Chichester, London and New York: Ellis Horwood/Tavistock.

— 1990. 'Rationalizing the Irrational: Learning From Karl Mannheim.' *American Journal of Sociology*.

Kettler, David, and Volker Meja. 1988. 'The Reconstitution of Political Life: The Contemporary Relevance of Karl Mannheim's Political Project.' *Polity* 20: 623–47.

Kilminster, Richard. 1979. *Praxis and Method: A Sociological Dialogue with Lukács, Gamsci and the Early Frankfurt School*. London, Boston, Henley: Routledge & Kegan Paul.

Loader, Colin. 1985. *The Intellectual Development of Karl Mannheim*. Cambridge: Cambridge University Press.

Lockwood, David. 1964. 'Social Integration and System Integration.' Pp. 244–57 in *Explorations in Social Change*, ed. G.K. Zollschan and W. Hirsch. London: Routledge & Kegan Paul.

Löwith, Karl. 1982 [1932]. *Max Weber and Karl Marx*, ed. and trans. Tom Bottomore and William Outhwaite. London: George Allen & Unwin.

Lukács, George. 1968 [1923]. *History and Class Consciousness*, trans. Rodney Livingstone. London: Merlin Press.

— 1974 [1954]. *Die Zerstörung der Vernunft. Band III: Irrationalismus und Soziologie*. Darmstadt and Neuwied: Luchterhand.

Mannheim, Karl. 1936. *Ideology and Utopia*, trans. Edward Shils. New York: Harcourt Brace & World.

— 1940. *Man and Society in the Age of Reconstruction: Studies in Modern Social Structure*, trans. Edward Shils. New York: Harcourt, Brace & World.

— 1952. *Essays on the Sociology of Knowledge*, ed. Paul Kecskemeti. London: Routledge & Kegan Paul.

— 1953. *Essays on Sociology and Social Psychology*, ed. Paul Kecskemeti. London: Routledge & Kegan Paul.

— 1956. *Essays on the Sociology of Culture*, ed. Ernest Mannheim and Paul Kecskemeti. London: Routledge & Kegan Paul.

— 1982 [1922–4]. *Structures of Thinking*, ed. and intro. David Kettler, Volker Meja, and Nico Stehr. London, Boston, Henley: Routledge & Kegan Paul.

Marcuse, Herbert. 1969. *Negations: Essays in Critical Theory*, trans. Jeremy J. Shapiro. Boston: Beacon.

— 1961. *Soviet Marxism: A Critical Analysis*. New York: Vintage.

Meja, Volker, and Nico Stehr, eds. 1982. *Der Streit um die Wissenssoziologie*. 2 vols. Frankfurt am Main: Suhrkamp.

Mommsen, Wolfgang J., and Jürgen Osterhammel, eds. 1987. *Max Weber and His Contemporaries*. London: Allen & Unwin.

Morrow, Raymond A. 1981. *The Sociology of Knowledge and the Frankfurt School: Karl Mannheim and the Origins of Critical Sociology*. Dissertation: York University.

Pollock, Friedrich. 1975. *Stadien des Kapitalismus*, ed. Helmut Dubiel. Munich: C.H. Beck.

Rilke, Rainer Maria. 1982. *The Selected Poetry of Rainer Maria Rilke*, trans. and ed. Stephen Mitchell. New York: Random House.

Schelting, Alexander von. 1982 [1934]. 'Die Grenzen der Soziologie des Wissens.' Pp. 756–890 in *Der Streit um die Wissenssoziologie*, vol. 2, ed. Volker Meja and Nico Stehr. Frankfurt am Main: Suhrkamp.

Schmidt, James. 1974. 'Reply to Martin Jay.' *Telos*, no. 21: 168–80.

Sica, Alan. 1988. *Weber, Irrationality, and Social Order*. Berkeley, Los Angeles, London: University of California Press.

Simonds, A.P. 1978. *Karl Mannheim's Sociology of Knowledge*. Oxford: Oxford University Press.

Söllner, Alfons. 1979. *Geschichte und Herrschaft: Studien zur materialistischen Sozialwissenschaft 1929–1942*. Frankfurt am Main: Suhrkamp.

Stammer, Otto, ed. 1972 [1965]. *Max Weber and Sociology Today*. New York: Harper Torchbooks.

Weber, Max. 1946. *From Max Weber*, trans. and ed. Hans Gerth and C. Wright Mills. New York: Oxford University Press.

— 1958 [1904–5]. *The Protestant Ethic and the Spirit of Capitalism*, trans. Talcott Parsons. New York: Charles Scribner's.

— 1964. *Max Weber, Soziologie, Weltgeschichtlichen Analysen, Politik*, ed. Johannes Winckelmann. 3d ed. Stuttgart: Kröner Verlag.

— 1978. *Weber: Selections in Translation*, ed. W.G. Runciman, trans. E. Matthews. Cambridge: Cambridge University Press.

Wellmer, Albrecht. 1985. 'Reason, Utopia and the Dialectic of Enlightenment.' Pp. 35–66 in *Habermas and Modernity*, ed. Richard J. Bernstein. Cambridge, MA: MIT Press.

Whimster, Sam, and Scott Lash, eds. 1987. *Max Weber, Rationality and Modernity*. London: Allen & Unwin.

Wiley, Norbert, ed. 1987. *The Marx-Weber Debate*. Newbury Park and Beverly Hills: Sage.

Woldring, Henk E.S. 1987. *Karl Mannheim: The Development of His Thought*. New York: St. Martin's Press.

# 9

# The Comedy of Enlightenment: Weber, Habermas, and the Critique of Reification

ASHER HOROWITZ

Universal history must be construed and denied.[1]

– T.W. Adorno

I

Nowhere is the spell that Max Weber has cast over subsequent political thinking stronger than in the tradition of Western Marxism. It is this very spell, specifically the appropriation of Weber's universal-historical analysis of rationalization leading to the spectre of an 'iron cage,' that in large part accounts for Jürgen Habermas's attempt in *The Theory of Communicative Action* to dispel the pessimism associated with the critiques of rationalization advanced by Lukács, Horkheimer, Adorno, and Marcuse. In Habermas's work an alternative theory of reification is taking shape that owes as much to Weber as do the theoretical efforts of Habermas's predecessors. As with the work of those predecessors, Habermas remains critical in his appropriation of Weber's diagnosis of the losses in freedom and meaning attendant on capitalist modernization. Yet his critical appropriation of Weber's theory of rationalization amounts to a reversal of the significance rationalization held not only for earlier Western Marxism, but for Weber himself. The *Theory of Communicative Action* needs Weber both to help account for the disenchantment of the world and, ironically, to account for the 'aporias' of the Frankfurt School which Habermas would like to transcend. A revised theory of disenchanted rationality takes the place of Critical Theory's disenchantment with rationality.[2]

---

Many thanks to David Shugarman, Bryce Weber and Christian Lenhardt for our long talks about TCA. Any errors in this essay are, of course, my own.

What distinguishes Lukács, Horkheimer, Adorno, and Marcuse from Marx in Habermas's eyes, is that they all, like Weber, have blurred the distinction between rationalization and reification. In Marx, by contrast, as in the Enlightenment tradition in general, that distinction and the commitment to rationalization remain strong: 'For Marx, socialism lies on the vanishing line of a rationalization of the lifeworld that was misguided by the capitalist dissolution of the traditional forms of life.'[3] For Habermas everyday life has simultaneously been rationalized in the direction of a communicative ethic, *and* reified. The balanced or measured approach he sees himself as taking to the universal-historical phenomenon of rationalization would reopen the possibilities of a rational praxis.[4] Disenchantment and reification must be seen, according to Habermas, as parallel processes of the universal history of rationalization rather than as a single dialectical process. This can be done through the reconstruction of dialectical theory in terms of a reformed Weberian theory of action in functional relation with a reformed Parsonian systems theory. These two '*disjecta membra* of a dialectical concept of totality' (TCA I, 343) can, in a bilevel conception of the social whole, restore hope in the practical rationality for which a critical theory must aim. 'Only if we differentiate Gesellschaftshandeln into action oriented to reaching understanding and action oriented to success can we conceive the communicative rationalization of everyday action and the formation of subsystems of purposive-rational economic and administrative action as *complementary* developments. Both reflect, it is true, the institutional embodiment of rationality complexes, but in other respects they are *counteracting* tendencies' (TCA I, 341; emphasis added). Neither Western Marxism nor Weber, nor Marx for that matter, was able to make that differentiation or carry it through. Habermas's critical reconstruction and absorption of Weber thus comprises two major 'moments' not clearly differentiated in the text. The first is a moment of critique in which disenchantment (or communicative rationalization) and societal rationalization, with the latter's inevitable losses in freedom and meaning, are carefully distinguished analytically. The second is a moment of appropriation in which, with the aid of Parsons and Luhmann, Habermas will offer a revised theory of reification, of the loss of freedom and meaning – one that ends up neither in what Habermas conceives of as the ultimately empty gesture of the Frankfurt School or in the latent terrorism of Lukács's Hegelianism.[5] It is therefore to Weber's theory of rationalization that Habermas recommends we look if, unlike Weber himself, a critical theory of society is not to fix upon universal history as the fateful and catastrophic destruction of the very subjectivity it creates and of the form of linguistically mediated intersubjectivity it eventually generates. In restoring what he believes to be Marx's and Condorcet's hope for the fulfilment of the modern project, a reformed Weber will supply an essential aspect of the theory of the rationalization of the life-world and an ethic to go along with it.

II

Much of Habermas's critical reconstruction of Weber's rationalization thesis depends on and departs from recent strains in Weber scholarship that insist on understanding his work in terms of universal history.[6] But universal history is itself recast in the terms of a neo-evolutionary systems theory. According to Habermas, Weber did not exhaust the systematic scope of his theoretical approach; he failed to trace the development of general structures of conscious-ness, remaining mired in the investigation of the substantive problematic guiding rationalization – that is, the problem of theodicy (TCA I, 196–8).[7] The evolutionary potential of Weber's history of disenchantment may thus be turned against the implications of his rationalization thesis.

According to Habermas, Weber's rationalization thesis follows a social-scientific logic in which one phenomenon, in this case 'Occidental rationalism,' the explanandum, is causally referred to an antecedent phenomenon, in this case 'the disenchantment of religious-metaphysical worldviews' – the explanans (TCA I, 158–9, 165). Briefly put, Habermas's principal objection to this is that between the explanans and the explanandum falls a shadow for which Weber cannot account, the shadow of *selective* rationalization. Habermas will *not* allow that the *moral structures* underlying Occidental rationalism – most importantly, formal law and the vocational ethic – lead with any inevitability or fatality to the losses in freedom and meaning associated with the spread of purely purpos-ive-rational action in the contexts of bureaucratic organizations and legal domination. A reconstructed theory of rationalization must, then, distinguish between a sort of basic rationalization that is universal in the history of culture and particular-cultural process in which universal rationalization is selectively realized in concrete historical time and which may be surplus from the point of view of the structural logic of universal rationalization itself (TCA I, 165–8).[8]

The rational reconstruction of the developmental logic of world-view struc-tures must be kept strictly separate from the empirical analysis of those world views. This would allow for the possibility of selective rationalization within *every* stage along the universal path of development of structures of conscious-ness, including that of modernity. '[T]here emerges a sharper contrast between the possibilities for orientation contained in the modern structures of conscious-ness that issued from the process of disenchantment and the profile of those parts of this spectrum of possibilities that were actualized, that is, translated in fact into institutions and motivations – a profile characteristic of capitalist

society' (TCA I, 198). According to Habermas disenchantment gives us modernity, capitalist rationalization gives us its discontents.

The fact of the matter is that the process of disenchantment, although it leads
to a universalist and post-traditional ethic, is in and of itself not a sufficient,
but only a necessary condition of the Protestant ethic that historically became
intertwined with capitalist rationalization (TCA I, 198–9). More than disenchantment, in the sense of the differentiation of irreducible cognitive-value spheres
open to independent development, is needed to explain the selective route of
rationalization undertaken in the modern West. The question Weber missed is
whether capitalist rationalization is merely a partial realization of the modern
structures of consciousness, and, if so, how to explain this selective path. 'Weber
did not hesitate to equate *this* particular form of rationalization with rationalization as such' (TCA I, 221).

The vocational ethic of Protestantism, which was the historical grounds for
the institutionalization in the personality system of the purposive rationality of
capitalism, is not the pure end product of the course of disenchantment carried
out in the religious development of the West. Weber himself sees that the
momentum of rationalized salvation religion carries within itself 'the strictly
universalistic conception of moral principles, the form of an autonomous
self-control on the basis of internalized and highly abstract action orientations,
and the model of a complete reciprocity of relations among members of an
unlimited communications community' (TCA I, 227). The Protestant ethic turns
out to be a distortion of this more fundamental structure of the decentred
modern consciousness. And the distortion is introduced via the 'particularism
of grace' at the core of Protestant theology. But the particularism of grace is
not an inherent part of the logic of disenchantment; rather, it is the logic of
disenchantment switched onto that track which has greatest elective affinity
with the needs of the capitalist entrepreneur for the objectification of interpersonal relations. 'In principle the spell of traditionalism could also have been
broken without separating off an ethically neutralized system of action' (TCA I,
226). Thus disenchantment and rationalization do not lead to capitalism, as
with Weber, who saw in the Protestant ethic the only religious ethic sufficient to
produce the inner-worldly asceticism needed to establish a methodical conduct
of life along the lines of purposive-instrumental rationality. Instead, the interests of the carrier-strata of modern capitalism account for the one essential
aspect of that world image under which disenchantment is selectively distorted.
Capitalist rationalization, at the level of systems differentiation, accounts for
the one-sided and unbalanced process of rationalization that has been the
concrete history of the West over the last half millennium. With the estab-
lishment of the quasi-categorical distinction between disenchantment and

rationalization, and with the reversal of the causal relationship between the Protestant ethic in its full-blown form and capitalism, Habermas has chiseled out a niche in the previously continuous Weberian universal history of rationalization within which an alternative theory of reification can be built on the basis of a reappropriation of Weber's understanding of modernity.

Critical Theory had, according to Habermas, given up on the critical potential of bourgeois culture (TCA 2, 382) at the same time that it had read the negative aspects of bourgeois rationality into the very hominization of man. It had conceived this process as though it unfolded along a single continuum. The following passage will be worth quoting in full: 'The basic concepts of Critical Theory placed the concepts of individuals directly vis-à-vis societal mechanisms of integration, which were only extended inward, intrapsychically. In contrast to this the theory of communicative action can ascertain for itself the rational content of anthropologically deep-seated structures by means of an analysis which, to begin with, proceeds reconstructively, that is, unhistorically. It describes structures of action and structures of mutual understanding that are found in the intuitive knowledge of competent members of modern societies. There is no way back from them to a theory of history that does not distinguish between problems of developmental logic and problems of developmental dynamics' (TCA 2, 382–3).[9]

Armed with the distinction between developmental logic and developmental dynamics, Habermas can proceed to the absorption of Weber's understanding and diagnosis of modernity into a theory of reification as the colonization of the life-world. Basic to Weber's understanding of modernity, according to Habermas, is the differentiation of three irreducible value spheres, each of which follows its own inherent logic. These value spheres coincide with Habermas's own delineation of cognitive-value spheres into the cognitive-instrumental, the normative and the aesthetic-expressive (TCA 1, 153–4). For Weber, the tension between these value spheres grows, giving rise to a dialectic of rationalization that issues in the tendency for one of these spheres, the purposive-instrumental, to overwhelm the normative and to split the aesthetic-expressive off from the other two.

Now, Habermas is concerned, perhaps above all, to deny two theses he attributes to Weber which, taken together, would vitiate the usefulness of the theory of rationalization for a reconstructed theory of reification: (1) that the value spheres differentiated in modern culture are mutually antagonistic to the extent that their mere differentiation amounts to the appearance of the 'seeds of destruction' (TCA 1, 241); and (2) that these seeds sprout with the process of secularization. A secular culture of antagonistic value spheres, lacking the unifying competence of religious-metaphysical world-views, becomes a society in which 'differences' between competing 'validity claims' turn into conflicts of action (TCA I, 241): 'reason splits itself up into a plurality of value spheres and destroys its own universality' (TCA I, 247). In a formula, Weber attributes the loss of freedom to the loss of meaning, and the loss of meaning to a further disenchantment (secularization) which he sees, ambivalently, as both fatal and salutary. Habermas's theory of reification will seek to reverse this formula: it is the loss of freedom under capitalist conditions of rationalization that create the loss of meaning via the colonization of the life-world.

Weber was correct, in Habermas's view, to identify as the core of modernity the differentiation and institutionalization of mutually irreducible value spheres. His error lay in construing these value spheres as incompatible, as fomenting a new polytheism in which there would be an endless struggle between different gods and demons; but for Habermas 'the pluralism of value *contents* has nothing to do with the differences among the aspects of *validity* under which questions of truth, justice and taste can be differentiated out and rationally dealt with as such' (TCA I, 250; emphasis added). Once modernity is seen as the objectification of a *formal* structure of cognitive validity claims open in principle to discursive argumentation, that is, when the logic of development is kept distinct from the dynamics of development, Habermas, in abstraction from all contents, can claim that there is no inherent antagonism among these spheres; he can claim even more, that 'the unity of rationality in the multiplicity of value spheres ... is secured precisely at the formal level of the argumentative redemption of validity claims' (TCA I, 249).

For Habermas, modernity involves a twofold rationalization: a differentiation of cognitive spheres together with a simultaneous development within each sphere towards cumulative learning, based upon the freedom each sphere has now gained to be guided not by traditional norms, but by communicatively achieved understanding (e.g., TCA I, 340). Whether Habermas succeeds in restoring harmony among the new gods Weber spoke of is a question to which I shall return below.

If secularization, the rise of a new polytheism, does not amount to a loss of meaning, but rather to a gain in clarity and distinctness in which both the mythic and religious-metaphysical collapse of ontic and normative dimensions is overcome, then the loss of freedom involved in the bureaucratization of society must be ascribed to a different source. Weber, working under what Habermas takes to be the confusion of value contents and validity claims, was led thereby to de-emphasizing the role of legal institutions guided by universalistic norms. Instead he chose to dramatize his vision of the 'iron cage' or of a 'new Egyptian despotism.' But Weber should have realized, according to Habermas, that modern law, a principal component of Occidental rationalism, with its positivity, legalism, and formality, can arise only on the basis of a universalistic, post-traditional value rationality. Modern law cannot be merely an expression of purposive rationality: 'It is only within normatively established limits that legal subjects are permitted to act purposive-rationally without concern for conventions. Thus for the institutionalization of purposive-rational action [without which neither the modern economy nor the modern state, that is, the abstract steering media of money and power, could function], a kind of normative consensus is required' (TCA 1, 255–6).[10]

Habermas's alternative theory of reification begins from the assumption that Weber's descriptions of the loss of freedom and the loss of meaning amounts to a valid 'diagnosis of the times.' It is Weber's aetiology which is oversimplified. To render this diagnosis fruitful it is necessary to reconstruct his theory with improved conceptual tools and, above all, to trace the pathological effects of class structure (TCA 2, 303–4).

Weber's theory of bureaucratization captures 'the development of media-steered subsystems from the viewpoint of the lifeworld' (TCA 2, 316). But Weber had only a dim notion of the difference between purposive rationality and the systemic rationality which, under conditions of capitalist economic development, leads to the colonization of the life-world. Colonization takes place when (1) 'formally organized domains of action emerge which are no longer integrated through the mechanism of mutual understanding, which sheer off from lifeworld contexts and congeal into a kind of norm free sociality' (TCA 2, 307), and further, when (2) systemic crises can be avoided 'only at the cost of disturbances in the symbolic reproduction of the lifeworld – i.e. of "subjectively" experienced, identity-threatening crises or pathologies' (TCA 2, 305). The paradigmatic locus for this increasing process of colonization is the modern bureaucratic organization, whether public or private. In the bureaucratic organization, all three components of the life-world that depend on symbolic reproduction – personality, culture, and norms – are 'neutralized' by the establishments of 'zones of indifference' between the organization and what is progressively reduced to the status of its 'environment,' that is, the private meanings and motivations of its individual members, the cultural traditions of the groups it deals with as clients or customers, and the morally regulated context of intersubjectivity inherent in the life-world (TCA 2, 308–9). Within bureaucratic organization 'communicative action forfeits its validity basis' (TCA 2, 310). A similar process takes place at the macro-sociological level, where the characteristic form of bourgeois society as a complementarity of private and public spheres, which, in the *logic* of development, is simply the result of the mediatization of the life-world necessary to the level of systems differentiation in modernity, is transformed by the penetration of their rationalities into those areas necessary for social reproduction that necessarily require mutual understanding (TCA 2, 330).

In Habermas's reconstructed theory of reification, the colonization of the life-world is a function of the displacement of class conflict and its attendant crises into the administrative system (TCA 2, 343). With the expansion of the welfare state, instead of class conflict following a Marxian logic in which initially defensive economic struggles lead to the appearance of increasingly revolutionary demands for democratic will-formation (TCA 2, 344),[11] the public sphere that first appeared under the auspices of the bourgeois Enlightenment and the political participation tied to it are subject to a process of 'real abstraction' analogous to that developed in Marx's theory of value in reference to concrete labour power (TCA 2, 350). Reification is derived not from the loss of meaning, à la Weber. It is not secularization that unhinges the possibility of a culturally unifying value rationality which could afford the necessary basis for containing the expansion of pure purposive rationality in the direction of an iron cage *or* a totally administered society. The loss of freedom is brought on, not by the logic of the modern system itself, not by the logic of development, but merely in the dynamics of development by the increasing extension of formally organized domains of action and their increased 'internal density' into domains that are inherently arenas of coordination through reaching understanding mediated by language (TCA 2, 351). This colonization accounts for the loss of meaning, for the 'fragmented consciousness' (TCA 2, 355) of the contemporary life-world: 'In place of the positive task of meeting a certain need for interpretation by ideological means, we have the negative requirement of preventing holistic interpretations from coming into existence' (TCA 2, 355).

According to Habermas, Marx's situation of alienation recedes further and further into the background as a narrow capitalist rationalization colonizes the decentred life-world that was emerging prior to capitalism itself. The potential of the decentred life-world to institutionalize a communicative ethic is disrupted by the purely formal rationality of abstract steering media (TCA 2, 349). But this turns out to be all for the best, since the theory of alienation lacks criteria by which to distinguish the destruction of traditional forms of life (which belongs to the process of disenchantment, constituting the logic of development) from the reification of post-traditional forms (rationalization according to a selective profile, constituting the dynamics of development). Nor does the concept of alienation fare better in indicating a criterion of modern praxis, since it refers not to any deviation from a norm that can be recognized through the reconstruction of the logic of development, being suited only to contrast an instrumentalization of life from a life that is represented as an end in itself (TCA 2, 340–1). The Weberian understanding of reification, once reconstructed and rid of the 'secularization hypothesis,' is better and more suitable since Weber, at least implicitly, understood that the paradox of rationalization, the reification effects attendant upon the development of modern society, are not a function of a clash between action orientations of two different types, but between *two different principles of sociation* (TCA 2, 318). It is better because it avoids Marx's romanticist appeal to the concrete expressiveness of a life lived for its own sake, while at least partially recognizing the universalistic morality that is the inherent outcome of the process of disenchantment. It is more suitable since it can be used to analyse the overextension of abstract media of coordination in all domains of social life without falling into the trap of economic reductionism.[12]

III

Objections have been raised that the *Theory of Communicative Action* is removed from political practice, that it tends, as Habermas accused Critical Theory of tending, to distance theoretical knowledge from any politics of self-transformation.[13] And while it is true that Habermas presupposes the desirability of a high degree of the mediation of practice by a theoretical knowledge of the distance between the logic and possibilities of development on the one hand, and the empirical dynamics of development on the other, this line of criticism tends to avoid engaging the actual political implications of Habermas's alternative theory of reification.[14] Habermas's redemptive criticism of the modern project is clearly aimed at the moralization of politics via the mediating function of post-conventional law. Post-conventional, modern law is, according to Habermas, experienced as legitimate only when it is judged to be the outcome of a 'rational consensus.' It is now a structural necessity underlying the degree of differentiation of the modern societal system to recognize basic rights and popular sovereignty as essential elements of bourgeois constitutionalism. Within bourgeois constitutionalism, 'the model for justifying basic norms is an uncoerced agreement, arrived at by those affected in the role of contractual partners who are in principle free and equal' (TCA 1, 260-1). The content of moral universalism is the formal freedom and equality of independent individuals. This itself is basic to the content of the modern life-world that Habermas wishes not only to read back into the logic of development of cognitive structures, but to project as its final term, its telos. Weber, it turns out, would be not so much wrong in his positivization of law (TCA 1, 262-9) as inconsistent in not carrying through his ambivalence about rationalization into the sphere of law itself. For modern law presents itself to Habermas with a Janus face, as the medium at one and the same time for bringing systems rationality (and with it the inevitable mediatization of the life-world) back under the rule of moral reason *and* for the mediatization of the life-world itself, with all its fateful possibilities for being colonized and technicized. Public law, which is one of 'the institutions that anchor steering mechanisms like power and money in the lifeworld could serve as a channel *either* for the influence of the lifeworld on formally organized domains of action, *or* conversely, for the influence of the system on communicatively structured contexts of action' (TCA 2, 185).

Weber's universal history of rationalization traced the reification of the life of the modern individual to the institutionalization of a thoroughly disenchanted world image. In the objectification of everything outside the conscious subject of action, everything but that subject loses objective value, and subjectivity threatens to become meaningless. But in his late essays in particular Weber turns to the possibilities open to the modern subject for the recovery of freedom and meaning. The subject of action in a disenchanted world regains the meaning of dignity in the methodical assertion of particular values by acting in such a way that the values asserted could in principle be brought into existence in spite of and against a world that is fundamentally indifferent.[15] Unlike the religious ethics of the past that strove with various degrees of magical residue to undo the irrationality of the world through an intellectual sacrifice that discovers meaning where none is to be found, Weber's ethic of heroic individualism aims at bestowing meaning where there in fact was none to begin with. Like Kant before him, Weber understood it to be man's duty to justify God (or the world) to man. This is why Weber ultimately conceived of the two ethics of absolute ends and of responsibility to be mutually supplementary rather than opposed. The two ethics can 'only in unison constitute a genuine man.'[16] But Weber's genuine man, who 'somewhere reaches the point where he says: "Here I stand; I can do no other," ' may only appear, strictly speaking, once the discovery of meaning is held to be impossible. That in turn presupposes the existence of irreconcilable value spheres. Insofar as this is a virtuoso ethic it constitutes a very slender thread upon which any sort of value rationality can be reintroduced into the political life of modern states. It leads inexorably and with manifest irony to plebiscitary leader-democracy resting upon charisma. Or as Wolfgang Mommsen summarized this dilemma: 'The greatest possible freedom through the greatest possible domination.'[17]

From a Weberian point of view, the political meaning of Habermas's *Theory of Communicative Action* could be taken as an effort to supply scientific grounds for the continuing vitality of the charisma of reason accessible to the mass of men. The answer to the problem of reification, the reintroduction of value rationality into the political life of modern states, as with Weber, is anchored in the structure of the modern world-view. In Habermas's version of this world-view, however, it is the common possession (or at least common capability) of individuals who are simply competent speakers of a natural language. A decentred consciousness is the product of the logic of the development of cognitive structures once the momentum of systems differentiation has swept away (1) myth and ritual; (2) metaphysics, theology, and traditionalism; and (3) done the work of institutionalizing the value generalization upon which the modern social system rests. The potential for disenchanted value-rational political order is inhibited only by the selective rationalization institutionalized in capitalist modernity, not by any causality of fate *or* by a dialectic of enlightenment. Once rationalization and disenchantment are seen as essentially separate processes – the former belonging to the dynamics, the latter to the logic of development – it becomes possible again to revive the theoretical project of the Enlightenment's utopia of reason. More than that, it is now possible to demand that the pursuit of the utopia of reason is the only rational response to the dilemma of reification.

The rational ethic of responsibility that is the implicit outcome of the universal history Habermas reconstructs out of the *disjecta membra* of modern social theory is certainly an egalitarian ethic. It is so not only in the sense that it has as its content the assertion of universal formal equality and liberty, but also in the sense that it is intended as an ethic that can be realized not by a very few who possess the psychological and material prerequisites of Weber's vocation for politics, but by all adult members of society. A rationalized life-world, free from the distorting effects of colonization by systemic rationality, would constitute itself as the public space of free discussion elevated by the Enlightenment into *the* principle of free sociation: 'The rationalization of the lifeworld both makes it possible to differentiate off autonomized subsystems and at the same time opens up the utopian horizon of a bourgeois society in which the formally organized spheres of action of the bourgeois (the economy and the state apparatus) *form the foundation* of the post-traditional lifeworld of the homme (the private sphere) and the citoyen (the public sphere)' (TCA 2, 328; emphasis added). It is no accident that Habermas here adopts Rousseauian forms of speech. The general affinity between the utopia of reason Habermas projects as the political fulfilment of modernity and that outlined in *The Social Contract* as the rule of a general will founded in the mutual recognition of individuals of their formal liberty and equality is a function of the attempt to moralize politics on a non-metaphysical basis. As in the *Social Contract*, so too in the utopia of reason, 'communication was represented as standing on its own feet, setting limits to the internal dynamics of autonomous subsystems, bursting encapsulated expert cultures, and thus escaping the combined threat of reification and desolation' (TCA 2, 329). In analogous fashion the sovereignty of the general will both restores the freedom and dignity of individuals who would otherwise be enslaved to the *amour propre* inflamed by the system of private property in the market.[18] Thus modern society, considered from the side of systems theory as a set of autonomous subsystems in which social action is coordinated formally by abstract media of exchange, both depends on and its potentially subject to the decentred modern consciousness that is simultaneously its outcome. The *mediatization* of society and the rationalization of the life-world are internally related and dialectically dependent upon one another. But the colonization of the life-world is by no means an unavoidable side-effect of either 'the secularization of worldviews [or] the structural differentiation of society' (TCA 2, 330).

IV

In order to provide an alternative to the theories of reification advanced both by Weber and by Critical Theory, both on Habermas's right and his left, as it were, he must establish that the *conflict* between the two principles of sociation, which the selective rationalization of capitalism deflects along the route towards technicizing the life-world, is in no way inherent or essentially related to what he identifies as disenchanted rationality itself. The prospects for turning back reification, then, depend ultimately and over the long run on the inner structure, or perhaps better, the non-conflictual quality, of the rationalized life-world of the decentred modern subject. But this is precisely where the formalism of Habermas's approach runs up against what may be the insuperable obstacle of a 'Weberian thorn' similar to that Habermas had seen Critical Theory encountering.[19]

According to Habermas the inner structure of the modern decentred life-world is free of the conflicts among separate substantive value spheres that Weber traced in 'Religious Rejections of the World and Their Directions' and which he made central to the ethic of responsibility outlined in 'Politics as a Vocation' and 'Science as a Vocation,' Habermas's three 'cognitive value spheres,' although irreducible, do not seem to admit of possibly being inherently conflictual because they all appear with the same structure of validity claims that are redeemable in argumentative discourse. The substantive values presupposed in each of these spheres, roughly the values of instrumental success, moral rightness, and conscious self-expression, are united procedurally insofar as they share this formal similarity. The iron cage that Weber saw as the logical outcome of a conflict of action orientations leading to (1) the progressive evaporation of the claims of moral consciousness under the impact of secularization and (2) the sundering of sensuality from the imperatives of instrumental realism, is therefore only true at the descriptive level. It is an effect to be attributed neither to the substance of any action orientation in and of itself nor to the potential for conflict that different substantive values in fact *do possess*. The potential of an iron cage is purely a function of the selective rationalization introduced along with modern capitalism. A critical theory need not in any way, therefore, go back behind capitalism in order to comprehend or criticize reification.[20]

Yet it is significant that Habermas himself admits that he has no explanation for the appearance of this direction of selective rationalization except for capitalism itself (TCA 2, 327–8). And we have already seen that capitalist selective rationalization is the outcome of the particularization of grace which is in turn to be attributed to the elective affinity it has with the material interests of the capitalist entrepreneur (see above). This must seem like a circular and highly arbitrary theoretical manoeuvre dictated simply by the need to guarantee the innocence of reason when it is decentred rationality. Could there not be something within the necessary preconditions of capitalist selective rationalization that predispose the disenchantment process, at least in the West, to just that principle of selection? As Habermas would have it, it seems to be simply an unfortunate accident, and any attempt at its genetic explanation must draw the line at pointing the finger of guilt at reason. It is ironic that Habermas, who dons the mantle of Weber's 'austere insight' into the impossibility of objective reason and virtually rests his entire case for modernity on the presumption that modern thought recognizes nothing secure from doubt, 'no exemptions from the critical power of hypothetical thought' (TCA 1, 212) should draw back at such a point.

Yet Habermas does draw back at a number of points from examining more closely the potential for inner conflict of the structure of the modern world-view. This is no trivial matter, but one of essential importance to the value and visibility of Habermas's alternative theory of reification. If reification, as the colonization of the life-world, is to be resisted and possibly even reversed, this could occur, as Habermas would have it, only through the reassertion on the part of the life-world of its primacy.[21] The motivation and capacity for the redirection and limitation of uncoupled steering media must come from within the decentred life-world. The contest between the two different principles of sociation must end up in a balance of power in favour of that principle that is essentially mediated by speech. If the decentred life-world does not carry within it a means, in Habermas's terms, of reconciling and balancing the claims of the three distinct and irreducible cognitive-value spheres, then it is difficult to imagine how decentration, the universal-historical process of disenchantment, could be anything but simply an aspect of cognitive reification.

The problem appears clearly enough in the following passage, in which

Habermas is attempting to put to rest the Weberian notion that it is not the relativity of basic value positions that are a problem for the re-establishment of value-rationality, since the basic contrast is between the pre-modern modes of thought still tied to magic and the modern view of the world: 'He [Weber] is convinced that the "distillation of the specific peculiarity of every sphere that crops up in the world" brings out ever harsher incompatibilities and conflicts that are grounded in the inner logics of the value spheres. But this critique refers not to the differentiation of the inner logics of individual value spheres but to some value spheres becoming predominant at the expense of others. We must at least regard it as an empirical question, whether the tensions among the ever more rationalized spheres of life go back in fact to an incompatibility of abstract standards of value and aspects of validity, or rather to a partial and therefore imbalanced rationalization ... [W]e may not in any case place the aspect of validity ... on a level with any value contents whatever, with any historically changing particular patterns of value. Rather these validity claims form a system – however fraught with internal tensions – that did indeed first appear in the form of Occidental rationalism but that, beyond the peculiarity of this specific culture, lays claim to a universal validity binding on all "civilized men" ' (TCA I, 183–4). This passage approaches the heart of the issue, but that issue is too quickly laid aside.

What does it mean to say that the question of whether the tensions among value spheres go back to irreducible abstract standards or to imbalanced rationalization is *an empirical problem*? How could empirical considerations possibly be used to adjudicate this problem without recourse to some non-empirical concept of 'tension'? How could such a concept be constructed free of prior, higher-order value propositions? It seems to me much more likely that a necessary level of tension would be differentiated from tensions that were a product of 'imbalance' simply by implicit reference to an ethnocentric preference for the standards and values of 'civilized men.'[22]

In the second place, is not Habermas himself responsible for an inverted version of just that collapse of value contents with aspects of validity that he attributes to Weber? Certainly value contents and aspects of validity are analytically distinct. But the *formal analogy* between aspects of validity – that they are all subject to argumentative redemption in discourse – that *crosses* the three spheres does not in itself establish the possibility of argumentation between values that belong to different spheres themselves. And as one quite sympathetic critic of Habermas puts it, 'everything turns, of course, on how one conceptualizes ... the "permeability" between the various realms.'[23] It is no wonder that some of Habermas's gentler critics see the next step in his theoretical enterprise as necessarily involving a move in the direction of an aesthetic conception of 'balance' among the three.[24] And it is once again ironic that even if this were possible, it would mean, at least formally, a regression in Habermas's own terms towards a blurring of the outlines of the concept of reason that he bemoans in Critical Theory. Or else it would mean the discovery or construction of an aesthetic meta-standard according to which the three spheres could be reconciled and balanced; but this itself, at least *formally*, could be read as an effort to reduce the ostensibly irreducible to a new objective concept of reason, not merely the use of objective reason as an 'ironically distanced' critical foil. In *The Theory of Communicative Action* at least, not only is this route not taken, but Habermas as much as admits the fact that, given the criteria of rationality he is employing, it is at the very least unlikely. For in a moment of almost uncharacteristic candour he allows for the existence of different *degrees of discursive binding force* in the three spheres (TCA 1, 249; emphasis added).[25] How likely is our decentred modern subject to weigh moral and expressive-aesthetic considerations equally into the 'balance' with purposive-instrumental propositions that are capable to a significantly higher degree of standing up to the tests of truth? Rather than continue this line of inquiry, however, Habermas will persist with the inversion of the collapse he attributes to Weber by putting his trust in the 'communicative infrastructure' of the decentred life-world to resolve such problems in advance: 'In the communicative practice of everyday life, cognitive interpretations, moral expectations, expressions and valuations have to interpenetrate and form a rational interconnectedness via the transfer of validity that is possible in the performative attitude' (TCA 2, 327). What standard of rationality is available to test the particular relations of mutual permeation and balance among the three irreducible spheres? How is linking them through the performative attitude more rational than decisionism?

Third, and finally, Habermas offers no argument whatsoever to discount the possibility that Weber's critique of the conflicts and incompatibilities between the rationalized value spheres of modern life could be attributed to *both* the selective (or imbalanced) rationalization of capitalism *and* to the course of disenchantment (or decentration) undergone in Western civilization or even civilization itself. There is no reason offered, except perhaps the appeal to trust in the communicative infrastructure of everyday modern life, why we might not reasonably view the capitalist selective rationalization of the inner structure of modernity merely to be an *intensification* of the potential for reification that sets in with disenchantment itself. But his *is* the structure of the response of the Frankfurt School to the problem of reification. And although Habermas's critique of Weber may be sufficient to force upon Weber's theory the recognition that reification, the loss of meaning and freedom attendant upon the rationalization of action, receives a qualitative boost with specifically capitalist modernization and cannot be reversed without at lest the 'political' supersession of capitalism, it is *not* sufficient to undo the dialectical relation between disenchantment and reification that both Weber and the Frankfurt School detect in the history of domination as such.

Habermas's alternative theory of reification sets up the critical potential of bourgeois culture against its own distortions. Modernity in its deep inner structures is supposed to possess the resources to correct its empirical deficiencies. The only thing wrong with the modern, really, is that it has never been tried.[26] The formidable and manifold intellectual resources of the *Theory of Communicative Action*, and especially the elaborately linked strategies of drawing sharp distinctions (1) between the logic of development and the empirical dynamics of development on the one hand, and (2) between the life-world and systems differentiation on the other, have as their aim a critique of reification that would, paradoxically, bar its transcendence. The conflict between the two principles of sociation that Habermas identifies as the source of reification appears, strictly speaking, unavoidable and unresolvable.[27] At best the conflict can be redressed in favour of a blurry 'performative' concept of balance rooted in the priority of the life-world. Yet the decentred modern life-world owes its fragmentation, with Weber and contra Habermas, not simply to colonization by delinguistified steering media, but to the inadequacy of its merely formal or performative unity.

What Habermas actually proposes is a utopia of reason in which state and civil society, *homme* and *citoyen*, are permanently at war. This the very same political solution to the conflicts of capitalist modernization that Marx already subjected to devastating criticism in *On the Jewish Question*. It elevates and idealizes the morality of the subject of the relations of abstract exchange into the model of social individuality. Habermas, like Rousseau and Marx earlier on, is correct in recognizing that, contra Weber, abstract exchange relations guaranteed by positive law presuppose a form of universalistic moral consensus. Yet moral universalism as the obverse of exchange relations is not the opposite of or solution to reification. Formal-universal morality is one of its conditions. Weber was more aware of this than the Marxian Habermas; yet only paradoxically, insofar as he identified the non-reified with the spheres of illusion or of intimacy: 'Precisely the ultimate and most sublime values have retreated from public life either into the transcendental realm of mystic life or into the brotherliness of direct and personal human relations. It is not accidental that our greatest art is intimate and not monumental, nor is it accidental that today only within the smallest and intimate circles, in personal human situations, in *pianissimo*, that something is pulsating that corresponds to the prophetic *pneuma*, which in former times swept through the great communities like a firebrand, welding them together.'[28] Weber assumed that escape from reification, rather than a rising above it, could be accomplished only outside of the political sphere altogether. And all who would cleave to the prospect of bringing direct and personal human relations into the political sphere, to breaking down the hard boundaries between the private and the public, must be guilty of the self-deception involved in holding to an absolute ethic of conviction.[29]

Weber's reasons for disallowing the possibility of political community based upon direct and personal human relations are fundamentally similar to those of Habermas. Both are committed, after all, to the exponential gain in instrumental rationality, to the systems-rationality of expanded possibilities for self-preservation, that are manifestly connected with rationalization, in the one case, or with increased systems differentiation, in the other. And, like Weber, Habermas sees the gain in the possibility of heroic individual freedom as resting upon this basis.

As we have seen, it is the uncoupling of abstract steering media which 'form the foundation' of the politico-moral potential of the post-traditional life-world. Habermas, too, is committed to an 'ethic of responsibility,' of *Mundigkeit*, in which the autonomy of the abstract subject of purposeful action is presupposed as the most highly prized value. Thus, whereas Adorno could explicitly reject a communicative ideal as not reaching the extra-linguistic object[30] Habermas must stop short, despite occasional worries that emancipation as 'the participatory transformation of administrative decision structures' might mean a culture 'that would have no content.'[31]

Having absolutely separated modern disenchantment from capitalist rationalization Habermas is able, in contrast to both Weber and the Frankfurt School, to conceive once again of the undoing of reification – only now as the triumph of bourgeois morality. Yet in order to do that Habermas must not only ontologize the 'I' of grammatical speech who appears, if only *in potentia*, at the end of universal history; he must also radically discount the psychic costs involved in the universal history of disenchantment in which this 'I' is constructed. There is a surreptitious 'transfer of validity' of prescriptive force to the reconstructed logic of development that entails a radical devaluation of all that belongs outside the ego of communicative action and its progress. Again Weber's paradoxical estimate of modernity is better suited to taking this into account than the blithe evolutionism that identifies the reconstructed logic of development with progress. Perhaps Weber's supersensitivity as a neo-Kantian to the apologetic functions of the 'naturalistic fallacy' was not, as Habermas suggests, exaggerated. '[W]hether one designates progressive differentiation,' Weber insists in 'The Meaning of Ethical Neutrality,' 'as "progress" is a matter of intellectual convenience. But as to whether one should evaluate it as "progress" in the sense of an increase in "inner richness" cannot be decided by any empirical discipline ... But whoever wishes to state a value judgement regarding the fact of differentiation as such ... and seeks a point of view from which this can be done, will come upon the question as to the price which is "paid" for this process (insofar as it is more than an intellectualistic illusion). We should not overlook the fact ... of a diminishing power to stand the stress of everyday life and that the publicity which the individual feels the increasing need of giving to his "experience," can perhaps be evaluated as a loss in the sense of privacy and therewith in the sense of propriety and dignity. At any rate, in the sphere of the evaluation of subjective experience, "progressive differentiation" is to be identified with an increasing "value" only in the intellectualistic sense of an increase in self-awareness or of an increasing capacity for expression and communication.'[32]

It is not only the psychic cost of ostensible progress that is avoided in Habermas's universal history of rationalization, it is the grounds for a possible transcendence of reification that are systematically repressed. The fragmented consciousness and the sense of desolation that he attributes, contra a right-Weberian culture criticism, not to the process of secularization, but to the pressures for excessive delinguistification that appear with the displacement of class conflict – that fragmented consciousness and that desolation are already present in the course of disenchantment prior to the selective rationalization of capitalist modernization. Neither the unity nor the balance of the *disjecta membra* of objective reason can be retrieved at a purely formal and procedural level. The conflict between the two principles of sociation is a function of the decentred consciousness which, in turn, is *itself also a function* of cumulative systems differentiation. This is why Dallmayr is right to detect an endemic ambivalence in the status and role Habermas grants to communication. At times communication remains the permanent horizon that participants cannot globally thematize and that binds them in an intersubjectivity that is prior to purposive-teleological action. At other times communication appears as a mechanism of action coordination to be implicitly judged by its role in facilitating expanded systems reproduction. Thus Habermas's 'stress on coordinating functions – intimately associated with rationalization processes – is bound to cast doubt on Habermas's linguistic turn, by revealing language either as a usable means or else a property or "competence" of individual speakers (a construal not radically at odds with the traditional philosophy of consciousness).'[33] The meta-critical strategy by which the subject-object opposition inherent in the philosophy of consciousness is to be transcended and left behind in the philosophy of language turns out to simply be a displacement of the subject-object opposition onto the plane of principles of sociation. The philosophy of language circles back to the same old subject as that presupposed by the formally rejected, and much despised, philosophy of consciousness. Thus Habermas, although he recognizes reason as embodied, has, as David Levin has pointed out, no content to offer for it. Even the turn towards need interpretation ignores, in his hands, the roots of need interpretation in the body of felt experience.[34]

By abjuring the Frankfurt School's appeal to an inner nature whose logic defies the clear and distinct outlines of the grammar of propositions (TCA 2, 388–9 and 382–3) Habermas then, ironically, repeats the misplaced optimism of the reliance on a formal limit to formalism that he attributed, along with critical theory, to Lukács: 'Along the front between system and life-world, the life-world evidently offers stubborn and possibly successful resistance *only* when functions of symbolic reproduction are in question' (TCA 2, 351; emphasis added).[35] Although Habermas claims that *reification itself* cannot be ultimately attributed to an inherent *conflict* between the two principles of sociation, it seems that somehow the *resistance* to reification can. Inner nature returns but, as Weber already noted, 'only in the intellectualistic sense of an increase in self-awareness or of an increasing capacity for expression and communication' (see above). Inner nature returns not against 'progress' but *as* 'progress' – as moral perfectibility. The answer to reification is no longer to be found in the consciousness of the proletariat but in the conscience of the bourgeoisie.

v

If there are strong reasons for believing that Habermas's alternative Weberian theory of reification inverts the failings he attributed to the appropriation of Weber on the part of Lukács and Critical Theory, this does not mean that the critique of reification must 'retreat' either to the heroic individualism of Weber's virtuosi of disenchanted authenticity, or to an avant-garde of proletarian class consciousness, or even to the proletarian *conscientia abscondita* from which a negative dialectics begins. If it is not too unfair to read *The Theory of Communicative Action*, as I have been doing, as an extended response to *The Dialectic of Enlightenment* that attempts to restore the critical and emancipatory potential of the project of enlightenment, then it would appear that the strategy of that work is built around a very curious instance of amnesia.

Throughout Habermas's treatment of Weber's reception by the Frankfurt School, Marcuse's work is lumped together with that of Horkheimer and Adorno. Whatever the merits or shortcomings of Habermas's account of the trajectory of Horkheimer and Adorno's work, this all too conveniently overlooks the fact that Marcuse, in his well-known essay 'Industrialization and Capitalism in the work of Max Weber,' subjected Weber to a critique that, very much like

Habermas, takes the former to task for conflating rationalization with capitalist industrialization.[36] By itself this episode of forgetting would be only of scholastic interest. However, the strategy behind which Habermas accuses Critical Theory of having retrogressed, a theoretical critique based upon the distinction between the logic and dynamics of development, is one at least as old as Marx's critique of Hegel's conflation of alienation with objectification in the *Economic and Philosophic Manuscripts of 1844*, and is the strategy that Marcuse retained in *Eros and Civilization*. The latter is a work that could also be suitably read as a response to *The Dialectic of Enlightenment*, but it is one in which, like Horkheimer and Adorno, reification is traced back to the very hominization of the species. The two strategies are not incompatible. It is possible, although Horkheimer and Adorno do not advance it, to totalize the critique of reason, yet at the same time, via a distinction between basic and surplus rationalization, identify the unrealized potential in reason's distorted development. It would appear in fact that only by construing universal history in terms of a single process, from which rationality cannot be abstracted from any, even its most 'advanced,' moments, is it possible to envision the dialectical transcendence of reification. This is accomplished in *Eros and Civilization* to the extent that the history of rationalization is systematically related to the vicissitudes of the instincts, to the development of the social body that, in Levin's evocative parlance, needs and dreams its own society. The outcome in this case is substantially different, however, insofar as it leads to the notion of a libidinal rationality that would *also* be conceivable as an 'institutionalization' of an alternative selective profile of the general features of a logic of development that has been blocked, cut off, and repressed. A libidinal rationality, however, would appear to any strictly formalist theory, like the *Theory of Communicative Action*, with the taint of an appeal to a substantive conception of reason, a 'regression' to objective reason. The paradox lies, however, in the fact that decentred rationality is an implicit idealization of the bourgeois subject, whose potential, granted, is not realized in the process of capitalist modernization that historically created that potential.[37]

Habermas's bi-level theory of society only becomes a dialectical theory insofar as the historical interaction of life-world and system is overlaid by the strict distinction between reconstructive logic and empirical dynamics of development. But it is the strictness of this latter distinction, amounting to the hypostatization of an analytic device, that abruptly brings his dialectic to a premature conclusion in a bourgeois utopia. Anything less, I suspect, would for Habermas amount to historicism with its twin evils of the moral relativism he associates with Gadamerian hermeneutics on the one hand, or the 'fatalism' and aporetic impasse attributed to the Frankfurt School, on the other. The free modernity Habermas envisions is still, like Weber's, but despite itself, committed to the performance principle insofar as it is systematically based upon a denial of the surplus-repressive conditions that have shaped the whole process of disenchantment-cum-rationalization.[38]

Like Weber, Habermas is drawn into accepting the overdrawn dichotomy between an ethic of responsibility and an ethic of commitment. Responsibility – realistic and rational praxis – is identified with that which can be realized without historical rupture, with that which has already been realized in principle. As with Hegel, freedom has already been realized, in principle, in the idea of the modern state. History no longer holds forth the possibility of any surprises.[39]

Habermas's response to the *Dialectic of Enlightenment* echoes Marcuse at the same time that it forgets him. *The Theory of Communicative Action* sets out, in a way (see above), to construct a theory of basic and surplus rationalization. Against the charge, from both conservatism on the right and the Frankfurt School on the left,[40] that enlightenment turns into myth, the 'fulfilment' of the modern project rests upon that kind of distinction. Yet it is a distinction that Habermas cannot follow through on without challenging the asceticism that is as much constitutive of reification as is the capitalism which is its finest flower. To do that, however, Habermas would have to replace the procedural ideal of a communicative utopia with a substantive concept of rationality. This, in turn, would require the affirmation of the *value* of happiness, or at least of the striving for happiness as the material basis of all valuation, including normative valuation. It would require the recognition of the erotic basis of all subjectivity. Yet Habermas's Kantian orientation, like that of Weber, and unlike the more Rousseauan orientation of the Frankfurt School, finds fulfilment simply in the dignity of the autonomous subject acting simultaneously against the world and effectively in it. There is no room here for a separation between the realms of necessity and freedom or for a life lived for its own sake. At best the utopia of reason is not one of reconciliation and does not truly reply to the problems that Weber and Adorno posed, or it is perhaps libidinal rationality in its alienated form.

Habermas's comedy of enlightenment, like Weber's tragedy, attempts to establish once more that enlightenment is the opposite of myth, but unlike Weber, that it has its own possibilities of reconciliation. In this sense, Habermas's comedy does not try to overcome the dialectic of enlightenment, but to argue that it never existed. This comedy is by no means cheap or complacent: it shares with Kant the austere concern for the realization of a difficult, if not impossible task, one in which freedom is *aufgegeben* rather than *gegeben*. Yet Weber's very identification of thoroughgoing enlightenment with a heroic-tragic vision remains paradoxically truer to the tasks of critique. In 'Science as a Vocation' Weber, who himself had made a fundamental commitment to the god or demon of science, notes that 'civilized man, placed in the midst of the continuous enrichment of culture by ideas, knowledge, and problems, may become "tired of life" but not "satiated with life." He catches only the most minute part of what the life of the spirit brings forth ever anew, and what he seizes is always something provisional and not definitive, and therefore death for him is a meaningless occurence. And because death is meaningless, civilized life as such is meaningless; by its very "progressiveness" it gives death the imprint of meaninglessness.'[41] Weber at least recognized that freedom under modern conditions had for its reward only the futile achievement of dignity in the bleak recognition of the self in transitory performance. Fulfilment, or satiation with life, was something belonging to the archaic. At the end of the *Theory of Communicative Action* Habermas admits that 'the test case for a theory of rationality with which the modern understanding of the world is to ascertain its own universality would certainly include throwing light on the opaque figures of mythical thought ... and indeed in such a way that we not only comprehend the learning processes that separate "us" from "them," but also become aware of what we have unlearned in the course of this learning.' (TCA 2, 400). It is not so much that Habermas lacks a conception of happiness[42] as that he has not confronted the historical dialectic of civilized virtue with happiness. This will not be possible until, like Critical Theory, Habermas's concept of learning learns to include rather than attempt to abolish the archaic, and like both Weber and Critical Theory, his critique learns to 'hate intellectualism as the worst devil.'[43]

## NOTES

1  T.W. Adorno, *Negative Dialectics*, trans. E.B. Ashton (New York: Seabury Press 1979), 320.

2  J. Whitebook, 'Reconciling the Irreconcilable: Utopianism after Habermas,' *Praxis International* 8:1 (April 1988), 73, 78–9, recognizes that Habermas's turn to a pragmatic, linguistically construed model of intersubjectivity based upon a reconstruction of the developmental structures of the modern decentred consciousness constitutes a rupture with the Frankfurt School that no amount of effort to imbue with utopian content can disguise (p. 82).

3  J. Habermas, *The Theory of Communicative Action*, trans. T. McCarthy (Beacon Press: Boston 1983), vol. 1, *Reason and the Rationalization of Society*, 343, hereafter referred to as TCA 1; vol. 2, *Lifeworld and System: A Critique of Functionalist Reason*, trans. T. McCarthy (Boston: Beacon Press 1987), hereafter referred to as TCA 2.

4 In this connection Habermas's communicative ethics has recently become an important part of the liberal-communitarian debate in the English-speaking countries. See David Rasmussen, ed. *Universalism vs. Communitarianism: Contemporary Debates in Ethics* (Cambridge, MA: MIT Press 1990), particularly the articles by Ferrara, Doppelt, Baynes, and Cohen.

5 Thomas McCarthy, 'Complexity and Democracy: The Seducements of Systems Theory,' in his *Ideas and Illusions: On Reconstruction and Deconstruction in Contemporary Critical Theory* (Cambridge, MA: MIT Press 1991), 152–80, argues quite persuasively that by ceding too much ground to systems theory Habermas tends to undermine his own professed political ideals and unnecessarily weakens the utopian thrust of critical theory.

6 See, e.g., Friedrich H. Tenbruck, 'The Problem of Thematic Unity in the Works of Max Weber,' *British Journal of Sociology* 31, no. 3 (1980), 316–51; Guenter Roth and Wolfgang Schluchter, *Max Weber's Vision of History: Ethics and Methods* (Berkeley: University of California Press 1979); Wolfgang Schluchter, *The Rise of Western Rationalism* (Berkeley: University of California Press 1981). Wolfgang Mommsen, *The Age of Bureaucracy: Perspectives on the Political Sociology of Max Weber* (Oxford: Basil Blackwell 1974), also falls into this general category despite his critical stance with respect to Weber. Habermas cites the work of Robert Bellah in English, and in the German literature, the work of R. Doebert in particular (TCA 2, 432, n21). Perhaps the best example of the older literature outside of the work of Parsons is that of Reinhard Bendix, *Max Weber: An Intellectual Portrait* (New York 1960).

7 According to Habermas it was primarily Weber's historicist heritage, rejecting the possibility of discovering laws of development, that prevented him from doing justice to the 'less dubious' aspects of systems functionalism. Added to this was the influence of neo-Kantian epistemology, which was supremely sensitive to the naturalistic fallacy (TCA 1, 153–4).

8 The characterizations of 'basic' and 'surplus' are not those of Habermas but my own allusions, which I believe are not only justified by the general structure of Habermas's argument against Weber but exemplified in the overall strategy of *The Theory of Communicative Action*.

9 J. Whitebook, 'Reason and Happiness: Some Psychoanalytic Themes in Critical Theory,' in R.J. Bernstein, ed., *Habermas and Modernity* (Cambridge, MA: MIT Press 1985), 140–60, takes up the same idea about Critical Theory having opposed *individuals* directly to the mechanisms of societal integration in at least qualified defence of Habermas's departures from that tradition. For a quite different view of the concept of repression, and its use in the work of Herbert Marcuse, see Gad Horowitz, *Repression: Basic and Surplus Repression in Psychoanalytic Theory: Freud, Reich, Marcuse* (Toronto: University of Toronto Press 1977).

10 This normative consensus 'stands under the idea of free (discursive) agreement and

autonomous (willed) enactment, and ... is characterized by formal properties of value rationality.' (Ibid.)

11  'In this respect, the organized labour movement aimed in the same general direction as the bourgeois emancipation movements.' (Ibid.)

12  According to Habermas, a part of the decisive weakness of the theory of value is that the genesis of reification is seen to be a result of processes taking place below the level of interaction, thus rendering interaction relations themselves amenable to treatment as mere derivatives (TCA 2, 342).

13  See, e.g., Fred Dallmayr, *Polis and Praxis: Exercises in Contemporary Political Theory* (Cambridge, MA: MIT Press 1984), 251–3; David Ingram, *Habermas and the Dialectic of Reason* (New Haven: Yale University Press 1987), 17–18; Dieter Misgeld, 'Critical Theory and Sociological Theory,' *Philosophy of the Social Sciences* 14 (1984), 97–105.

14  One notable exception is Nancy Fraser, 'What's Critical about Critical Theory: The Case of Habermas and Gender,' in S. Benhabib and D. Cornell, eds, *Feminism as Critique* (Minneapolis: University of Minnesota Press 1987), 31–56, who sees that there is a 'more basic battle line' than that between system and life-world (p. 55). Another is McCarthy, 'Complexity and Democracy,' note 5 above, and 'Reason and Rationalization: Habermas' "Overcoming" of Hermeneutics,' in *Ideals and Illusions*, note 5 above, 127–51.

15  See Karl Loewith's classic essay, 'Weber's Interpretation of the Bourgeois-Capitalistic World in Terms of the Guiding Principle of "Rationalization," ' in Dennis Wrong, ed., *Max Weber* (Englewood Cliffs: Prentice-Hall 1970), 101–22.

16  Weber, 'Politics as a Vocation,' in H.H. Gerth and C.W. Mills, eds, *From Max Weber* (New York: Oxford University Press 1969), 127.

17  W. Mommsen, 'Max Weber's Political Sociology and His Philosophy of World History,' *International Social Science Journal* 7 (1965), 41; cf. David Beetham, *Max Weber and the Theory of Modern Politics* (London: George Allen & Unwin 1974).

18  A. Horowitz, *Rousseau, Nature, and History* (Toronto: University of Toronto Press 1987), especially chap. 6.

19  Habermas refers to a 'Weberian thorn' in the side of Critical Theory (TCA 1, 377) because, realizing with Weber the collapse of the philosophic tradition that had conflated philosophic norms and ontic claims, it was unable to ground its own norms, or at least give a rational account of them insofar as it had also limited rationalization, like Weber, to instrumental action (TCA 1, 270, 339–42).

20  For Habermas the aporias of the Frankfurt School are traceable to its adoption of the Weberian perspective on rationalization which takes to their logical extreme the consequences of the philosophy of consciousness (TCA 1, 366–85). Most sympathetic followers and critics of Habermas, such as Wellmer, Ben-Habib, Whitebook, Honneth, and even Ingram, do not question the advisability of Habermas's basic innovations insofar as they allow a retreat from a totalizing critique of reason. One

of the few exceptions to this rule among commentators upon Habermas's linguistic turn is Jay Bernstein, 'Art Against Enlightenment: Adorno's Critique of Habermas,' in A. Benjamin, ed., *The Problems of Modernity: Adorno and Benjamin* (London: Routledge 1989), 49–66, who points out that for Adorno the significance of autonomous art lay both in its protest against differentiation (pp. 50, 59) and in its offering of an image of what things could be for a 'historical reason'; art, even in its semblance, is a model for an alternative form of praxis that has not succumbed to the regimentation and enforced identification of universalizing systems. For Bernstein the totalizing critique of reason along with the performative contradiction that critique necessitates do not invalidate the analysis of reason undertaken in *The Dialectic of Enlightenment*. The problem is not that critical theory, in totalizing its critique of reason, deprives itself of the possibility of a rational foundation for normative judgement; the problem is the opacity of reason to itself, presumably something that cannot be revealed outside of a totalizing critique (p. 54).

21 Thus, as Kenneth Baynes points out, 'Rational Reconstruction and Social Criticism: Habermas' Model of Interpretive Social Science,' in Michael Kelly, ed., *Hermeneutics and Critical Theory in Ethics and Politics* (Cambridge, MA: MIT Press 1990), 122–45, Habermas's model of interpretive social science must strive to avoid the reification of the life-world to which hermeneutic and phenomenological analyses are prone (p. 135).

22 Thus S. Benhabib, *Critique, Norm and Utopia* (New York: Columbia University Press 1986), who makes a number of important criticisms of the way in which Habermas construes a communicative ethic as the proper legacy of modernity, also limits the binding quality of communicative rationality: '[T]he constituents of communicative rationality like decentration, reflexivity and the differentiation of value spheres can be said to have "universal significance and validity" only in a weak sense' (p. 279). Yet it is not clear how the 'weak universality' Benhabib grants Habermas's construal of his (albeit flawed) communicative rationality – that, for example, a cognitive capacity such as reflexivity is binding 'for us' (p. 274) but not binding for cultures in which it has not developed – is unlike being a little pregnant or somewhat dead. Surely, if anything is a yes/no proposition it is universality, especially when that universality refers to quasi-transcendental conditions. If 'weak universality' refers simply to processes that cannot be easily reversed/unlearned/transcended, why grant those processes universality even in a weak sense? Surely if one of Benhabib's aims is to recover a utopian dimension that is increasingly deflated in Habermas, and especially by his reliance on evolutionary theories (p. 277), then she should be willing to entertain the possibility that utopia might require a great deal of unlearning. In a later article, 'In the Shadow of Aristotle and Hegel: Communicative Ethics and Current Controversies in Practical Philosophy,' in Kelly, ed., *Hermeneutics*, note 21 above, 1–31, Benhabib still claims that universalism is not a dogmatism in favour of modernity

because it can be challenged within the conversation itself. Yet she admits that her 'historically self-conscious universalism,' as an outcome of a sort of Rawlsian 'reflective equilibrium,' has the status of a 'thick description' of 'the moral presuppositions of the cultural horizon of modernity' (p. 8). A number of other commentators, such as McCarthy, 'Reason and Rationalization,' note 3 above, 134–8; Ferrara, 'Universalisms: Procedural, Contextualist, and Prudential,' in Rasmussen, ed., *Universalism*, note 4 above, 16–18; and Carol Gould, 'On the Conception of the Common Interest: Between Procedure and Substance,' in Kelly, ed., *Hermeneutics*, note 21 above, 267, all seem to agree that, in Ferrara's words, Habermas generalizes 'the parochialism of modernity' and begs the question of the intrinsic desirability of the modern form of life. Albrecht Wellmer, 'Practical Philosophy and the Theory of Society: On the Problem of the Normative Foundations of a Critical Social Science,' in S. Benhabib and F. Dallmayr, eds, *The Communicative Ethics Controversy* (Cambridge, MA: MIT Press 1990), 293–329, concludes that the ultimate justification of a universalist communicative ethic is not possible or that its justification is its 'historical elaboration' (p. 328). If this is the case it is difficult to see in what way Habermas's development of both universal pragmatics and his development of an evolutionary systems theory as a reconstructive science have (as McCarthy suggests) helped at all in overcoming what he perceives to be the shortcomings of hermeneutics. It would amount to saying that modernity has the structural-cognitive resources to identify its own shortcomings by its own criteria. Yet one does not need to be a 'modernist' to see this; nor is it sufficient as a justification of modernity.

23 J. Whitebook, 'Reconciling the Irreconcilable,' note 2 above, 83.

24 For example, Ingram, note 13 above, 177–88; Martin Jay, 'Habermas and Modernism,' in R. Bernstein, ed., *Habermas and Modernity*, 125–39.

25 He goes on to add that 'even today we lack a pragmatic logic of argumentation that satisfactorily captures the inner connections between the forms of speech acts. Only such a theory of discourse could explicitly state wherein the unity of argumentation consists and what we mean by procedural rationality after all substantial concepts of reason have been critically dissolved.' (Ibid.)

26 J. Whitebook, 'Reconciling the Irreconcilable,' note 2 above, suggests that Habermas's reconciliation with modernity leads to 'Hegelianism in the bad sense, namely a complacency toward the status quo rationalized as a theory of modernity,' (p. 73) and attributes efforts by 'Habermasians' such as Wellmer and Benhabib to reintroduce utopian elements into a theory which is no longer utopian to a certain bad conscience (p. 82).

27 But see McCarthy's 'Seducements of Systems Theory,' note 5 above, who suggests that critical theory does not need systems theory in order to explain tendencies towards reification, and that without its pull the possibility of at least *political* de-differentiation becomes once more open as a matter of degree (pp. 176–7). Cf. Jean

Cohen, 'Discourse Ethics and Civil Society,' in Rasmussen, *Universalism*, note 4 above, 83–105, who, like Habermas, conceives rationalized societal systems to put strict limits on differentiation and as a result ends up sounding like John Stuart Mill, that is, torn between imperatives of democratic development and economic accumulation.

28  Weber, 'Science as a Vocation,' in Gerth and Mills, note 16 above, 155.

29  Weber, 'Politics as a Vocation,' in Gerth and Mills, note 16 above, 128.

30  In 'Subject and Object,' one of Adorno's last essays, the formal mutuality of communication between moral agents is identified as 'infamous because the best there is, the potential of an agreement between people and things, is betrayed to an interchange between subjects according to the requirements of subjective reason. In its proper place, even epistemologically, the relationship of subject and object would lie in the realization of peace among men as well as between men and their Other.' A. Arato and E. Gebhardt, *The Essential Frankfurt School Reader* (New York: Urizen 1978), 500. Cf. McCarthy, 'Reason and Rationalization,' note 3 above, who argues that we need not go back to metaphysics in order to conceive a reconciliation with nature (p. 148–9).

31  Habermas, 'Walter Benjamin: Consciousness Raising or Rescuing Critique,' in *Philosophical-Political Profiles* (Cambridge, MA: MIT 1985), 160.

32  Weber, 'The Meaning of Ethical Neutrality,' in E.A. Shils and H.A. Finch, eds, *The Methodology of the Social Sciences: Max Weber* (New York: The Free Press 1949), 28; see also Weber's discussion of the Mormons and the 'Indians,' 26. It is interesting to note that one of the most trenchant criticisms of the program and self-understanding of communicative ethics, that of Karl-Heinz Ilting, 'The Basis of the Validity of Moral Norms,' in Benhabib and Dallmayr, *Communicative Ethics*, note 22 above, 220–55, accuses it of having committed an 'intellectualistic fallacy,' that is, of overlooking the fact that the rules that need to be followed for the sake of knowledge are not binding in the same way as moral norms. According to Ilting, the rules that must be presupposed in order to generate knowledge are hypothetical imperatives; morally binding rules, as necessary limitations of an unbounded freedom that cannot be renounced, draw their force from an act of free recognition. In this quite Rousseauan way, Ilting derives a universalist political ethic from a theory of moral meta-norms that recognizes the essentiality of the will (see especially pp. 231–9), and is thus not divorced from the problem of happiness.

33  Dallmayr, note 13 above, 237.

34  David M. Levin, 'The Body Politic: The Embodiment of Praxis in Foucault and Habermas,' *Praxis International* 9:12 (April and July 1989), 112–32. Levin, drawing upon Merleau-Ponty's late reflections on the reversibility of 'the flesh,' makes the important suggestion that critical theory needs not only a theory of what body society produces, but of what society our bodies dream and need. He recognizes that Marcuse was the only one among the Frankfurt School thinkers to embark on this task, but thinks he

was still too embroiled in a Freudian (and behind him, Nietzschean) theory of drives to advance such a theory beyond an expressive/aesthetic dimension. Habermas's ethical/political theory supplies that dimension, but only at the cost of excessive linguistification. Yet as G. Horowitz, note 9 above, has demonstrated, Marcuse's theory of basic and surplus repression can be restated, drawing upon both ego psychology and object relations theory, to include an account of moral development. It could be further argued that the aesthetic in Marcuse, as in Adorno, serves at least as an image of a rational ethic of happiness. Cf. Bernstein, note 20 above.

35 See also TCA 2, 350–1.

36 In H. Marcuse, *Negations: Essays in Critical Theory* (Boston: Beacon Press 1969), 201–26; see especially 204, 222, and 223: 'Weber's analysis ... has fallen prey to the identification of technical reason with bourgeois capitalist reason ... Put differently: Max Weber's analysis of capitalism was not sufficiently value-free, inasmuch as it took into its "pure" definitions of formal rationality valuations peculiar to capitalism. On this basis, the contradiction developed between formal and material (or substantive) rationality, whose obverse is the "neutrality" of technical reason vis-à-vis all outside material valuations.' This omission is all the more puzzling given the strategic attention Habermas paid to it earlier in his 'Technology and Science as Ideology,' *Towards a Rational Society*, trans. J.J. Shapiro (London: Heinemann), 81–122.

37 See Iris Young, 'Impartiality and the Civic Public,' in Benhabib and Cornell, *Feminism as Critique*, note 14 above, 57–76, who finds, despite the promise of Habermas's theory of communicative action for a conception of normativity that does not oppose reason and affectivity, that because of his commitment to impartiality he 'exhibits the logic of identity' (p. 70).

38 McCarthy, 'Reason and Rationalization,' note 3 above, 150, rightly points out that the 'separation of domains of reality and types of validity claims, of an ego that stands over against nature, society and its own feelings and desires, must eventually allow for a nonregressive reconciliation with self, others and nature if the "dialectic of enlightenment" is to lose its sway over our lives' (p. 150).

39 As Agnes Heller points out in 'Habermas and Marxism,' in John B. Thompson and David Held, eds, *Habermas: Critical Debates* (Cambridge, MA: MIT Press 1982).

40 Habermas locates himself in such terms in the course of a characterization of enlightenment and counter-enlightenment in TCA 2, chap. 6, 'Intermediate Reflections: System and Lifeworld.'

41 In Gerth and Mills, note 16 above, 140.

42 Whitebook, 'Reason and Happiness,' note 9 above, 152.

43 Weber, 'Science as a Vocation,' in Gerth and Mills, note 16 above, 152.

# 10

# The World Disenchanted, and the Return of Gods and Demons

ALKIS KONTOS

> History never confesses, not even her lost illusions, but neither does she
> dream of them again.
>
> – Maurice Merleau-Ponty

'Tell the emperor that my hall has fallen to the ground. Phoibos [Apollo] no longer has his house nor his mantic bay nor his prophetic spring; the water has dried up.' This is the Delphic Oracle's response, one of its final utterances, to Emperor Julian's envoy.[1] After a long, supreme reign, the god of light disappears; ruins, desiccation, and silence follow. The temple is now an empty shell.

In a totally different time and place, Albert Camus affirms life against death, mortals against gods. Sisyphus and Prometheus are his mythic protagonists. With evocative lyricism Camus issues 'a lucid invitation to live and to create, in the midst of the desert.'[2] With Pindar, he urges the human soul: '[D]o not aspire to immortal life but exhaust the limits of the possible.'[3] Facing the brutal fact of mortality under empty, silent skies should give birth to rebellion, not despair. Awareness of the absurd and its ensuing consciousness render the rebellious mortal life challenging and *preferable* to the amorphous infinity of immortality.

Between the lamenting god of the Delphic Oracle and Camus stands the mad genius with his dancing Zarathustra; Nietzsche proclaims the violent death of

For Maria del Pilar who knows of paradoxes and understands Lorca's verse: 'Aunque sepa los caminos/ Yo nunca llegaré a Córdoba' (Though I know all the roads/ I may not reach Cordoba).

Thanks are due to Pia Christina and Simone Tamar for their help in the preparation of this manuscript, and, of course, for being constant sources of enchantment.

God and our utter desolation; then Turin, 1889: a horse, a tearful embrace, the darkness of the mind.[4]

The oracular, sorrowful pronouncement of the passing of an era and its nostalgia for the past on the one hand; Camus's resilient, measured celebration and courageous determination on the other; against the fragmented, shattered horizons of modern existence, the deafening echo of Nietzsche's prophetic word, full of horror, pronouncing on our totally transfigured historical existence and on the struggle of our unborn future hour. Paradoxes and antinomies, the agony and splendour of the human spirit in the vast landscape of our modern wasteland.[5]

These paradoxes and antinomies constitute the substance of Weber's idea of disenchantment. The Oracle and Camus are tentative boundaries, the contours within which Weber's articulation of the struggle of modernity can become audible: threnodies and heroics; the desperate and valiant labour to tame Nietzsche's word; they provide the architectonic structure for my treatment of the Weberian theme of disenchantment.

I shall argue the significance of disenchantment; I declare the dialectics of enchantment/disenchantment/re-enchantment to be the normative conceptual ground upon which our understanding of Weber's philosophy of history and ontological postulate rest; Weber's elaboration of the dialectics of the disenchantment of the world and his claim that re-enchantment is surfacing again are not signs of a confused mind;[6] there are complex polarities inherent in the historicity of the human condition, in the encounter and confrontation of ontology and culture, ontology and politics. I shall argue that neither contradiction nor confusion exists here. The modern human predicament is complex and paradoxical. But let me commence my argument from its logical starting point: conceptual categories and the dialectics of the Weberian cosmos.

## I. THE WORLD ENCHANTED

In the beginning, in the pristine hour of the youth of the world, the world was enchanted. In Weber's sense, the world was conceived as inhabited and guided by divine spirits whose powers were mediated and negotiated through rituals and sacrifices. The world was a place of mystery and wonderment; human activity and calculation, creativity and energy, knowledge and practice could not, nor were they presumed able to, either prevail over the world or exhaust its mystery. The world, Nature, stood before the mortals as inexhaustible, mysterious, imbued with spirits, unconquerable. Human survival and comfort did not imply the possibility or desirability of omnipotence. Effective, efficient human action did not warrant it.

The world stood before its ancient inhabitants neither as a hostile territory nor as a gentle, idyllic, hospitable garden. Calculation, effort and energy were called forth. The primitive, ancient ancestors of ours had to make choices, practical decisions; taxing, demanding options were exercised by them. But they did not think of themselves as masters or sole inhabitants of the earth. The world was cohabited with other creatures, spirits, forces. A multiple, complex, labyrinthine web unfolded before the eye of the primitive human mind.

Effective, practical mastery of the vital contours of the world meant continuous ritualistic interaction with the spirits of the world, that mysterious other dimension beyond mere matter, beyond the visible. The order and logic of the world, of the cosmos as a whole, could not be treated as the subject of a complete, exhaustive comprehension. No human calculation, method, practice, or imagining aimed at, or was believed capable of, performing such a task. The world in its vastness and complexity remained immune to full penetration by the human mind. Yet the human mind was neither demoralized nor frustrated by this. Weber most forcefully argues that primitives knew all they needed to know about the world. He tells us that modernity does not yield greater knowledge of the world than that of past epochs. He states:

> Does it mean that we, today ... have a greater knowledge of the conditions of life under which we exist than has an American Indian or a Hottentot? Hardly. Unless he is a physicist, one who rides on the street-car has no idea how the car happened to get into motion ... [H]e knows nothing about what it takes to produce such a car so that it can move. The savage knows incomparably more about his tools.

Weber concludes:

> The savage knows what he does in order to get his daily food and which institutions serve him in this pursuit. The increasing intellectualization and rationalization do *not*, therefore, indicate an increased and general knowledge of the conditions under which one lives.[7]

It was not human inadequacy that militated against the penetration of the secrets of the world, nor was it the natural massiveness and solidity of the world that rendered it inexhaustible and impenetrable. It was the *spiritual* dimension of the world, its enchanted, magical quality that rendered it infinite, not amenable to complete calculability; spirit could not be quantified; it permitted and invited mythologization.

With the idea of enchantment, Weber introduces, in a rudimentary and fundamentally primordial sense, the spiritual, inexhaustible nature of human existence. With the spirits of the primitive world, the mysterious and incalculable enter the cosmos as vital features of it. The idea of enchantment is *simultaneously* anthropologically-historically specific *and* metaphorical. The term is rooted in the archaic, magical origins of religion. The characteristics of the anthropologically-historically specific idea of an enchanted world are: mystery and a plurality of spirits.[8] It is from these features that Weber will later on enunciate his critique of the modern disenchanted world; he will decry the loss of these features; a routinized, conformist, calculable universal emerges; no mystery, no spirits, no wonderment; a demythified world is fabricated.

Weber's treatment of enchantment in its concrete anthropological-historical mode, magical primitiveness, insists on the presence of features such as plurality of spirits, magic, mystery. Yet the *qualitative* appropriation of their meaning, the awareness of their implication and significance, could only take place, if at all, at an embryonic level at that most pristine moment of human existence. The awareness of the deeper meaning of enchantment emerges at a later historical time. The primitive is not conscious of the metaphysical and existential importance of the meaning of enchantment. When Weber speaks of the primitive world as an enchanted place, he treats it in contradistinction to the modern world, a disenchanted world: a despiritualized and despirited world devoid of meaning; a mechanical, dispassionate world, the world of modern existence.

The enchanted world of the primitive is *not* Weber's prototype of enchantment, however. The full meaning of enchantment is not developed under primitive conditions. The image of the world as an enchanted place, the belief in divine spirits, spirituality, and mystery come to acquire a deeper and more significant meaning when they correspond to a consciousness imbued with moral complexity. This developmental moral trajectory of consciousness is clearly present during the intellectual growth of classical Greece. At this historic juncture an intellectual and cultural sophistication emerged which accentuated consciousness. The choice between gods and demons became simultaneously a more theoretically lucid and ethically conscious choice than in earlier primitive times.[9]

Simply stated, Weber must claim that the progressive emergence and growth of rationality is the very process of disenchantment *and* that at the same time this process yields a sharpened awareness of the meaning of enchantment. The process of disenchantment will ultimately, of course, sweep away enchantment and its heightened awareness, but not for ever. Enchantment and disenchantment are not static over the immense span of historical time, yet they are always differentiated – enchantment: mystery, wonderment, polytheism (actual or metaphoric); disenchantment: their absence and the emergence of meaninglessness.

Weber's position, stated simply and comprehensively, is as follows: the primordial condition of the world, including its most primitive origins, was one of enchantment. This implied, in a rudimentary sense, a specific image of the world and a corresponding attitude towards life. The image and attitude of the enchanted world stand in stark contrast to those of the disenchanted world. The enchanted world from its primitive beginnings to later epochs of enchantment undergoes protracted transformations and mutations. These transformations mirror the proclivity of social life towards disenchantment. It is on the way to disenchantment that enchantment reaches a stage where belief in divine spirits and mystery is coupled with intellectual lucidity characteristic of conceptual and philosophical *theoria*.[10]

Ancient Greek polytheism and philosophical thought capture Weber's idea of the apogee of enchantment prior to the rise of modernity. Weber's normative ontological idea of enchantment takes its bearings from the axiological imperative he assigns to existential and ethical choice-making, which he associates with character formation and maturation. This creative choice-making he roots in the tension of responsible, conscious evaluations of vital and equally legitimate claims and counter claims. Plurality versus one-dimensionality constitutes the crux of the matter. In Weber's terminology polytheism, gods and demons, characterizes the situation best. Conformity, monotheism, dogmatism of any kind are anathema to Weber. Moral and intellectual atrophy ensues whenever they prevail. Spiritual deadening, the near death of the soul, results from routinized habitual blind ethical obedience and passivity.

Not the right choice, not the right path matter in and of themselves, but *the making* of the right choice, *the choosing* of the right path; and to do so time and again. This agonizing and exhilarating process is the fertile ground of human development; it is the humanizing context, the sanctified space and mode of the mysterious, magical moment of the appropriation of the meaning of existence and of the creativity of the self-determined, thinking, passionate self. This is Weber's ontological vision. Heart and mind, passion and intelligence unite; the soul vibrates.

When Weber speaks of enchantment he always means a polytheistic firmament. And when he idealizes and praises enchantment, the pantheon of gods and spirits, of gods and demons, he speaks of tension: vying ultimate claims which cannot be, once and for all, fully harmonized and resolved. They are perennial; the constant stuff of a fully dynamic existence and meaningful life. The primitive lives in an enchanted world because the many spirits of a magical, mysterious cosmos exist there. The world of the ancient Greeks is an enchanted world; polytheistic, inexhaustible, full of wonderment. But there also exists a crystallized culture of philosophical theorizing and speculation. A conceptual self-awareness is cultivated and celebrated there. Hence a difference which leads Weber to grant to that epoch a superior status.

This accentuated, sharpened awareness of the dialectics between an enchanted cosmos and the individual, the self and others, which Weber attributes to ancient Greek culture, allows him to silently bypass the world of the primitive or savage. Though enchanted, the latter appears to be shrouded more in ritual than illuminated by consciousness, more in instinctual sensibility than conscience; the world of the primitive lacks the philosophical crystallization of a fully blossomed awareness and ethos, a veritable philosophy of life and existence. For Weber, consciousness and conscience together constitute the full meaning of the dance of an enchanted soul. And though the primitives dance in a world of spirits they do so without the lucidity of the intellect, without the choreography of a theoretical perspective regarding the dance of life.

## II. NATURE AND CULTURE

For Weber, the enchanted world not only reaches a certain plateau in self-perception; it can also be spoken of retrospectively, from the perspective of a disenchanted world, as the world of Nature. The enchanted world then is treated by Weber as one in which a symbiosis, an organic unity, is struck between humans and Nature. In an enchanted world, Nature provides a meaningful, stabilizing foundation to existence; it moderates and gives orientation to life activity; it secures existential satisfaction. Mental and psychological anxiety does not prevail. Satiation and, above all, meaning reign supreme.

Human existence so embedded in the bosom of Nature is possible only when and where Nature is imbued with the life of divine spirits. Weber's remarks on Nature in this context reveal a further elaboration of the *substantive meaningfulness of enchantment*. It is this aspect of enchantment, naturalness, that is crucial to Weber's critique of the disenchanting force of science.

It is this naturalness, in contradistinction to the cultural wasteland of a disenchanted world, that Weber wishes to stress in his reference to 'Abraham, or some peasant of the past,' who 'died "old and satiated with life" because he stood in the organic cycle of life; because his life, in terms of its meaning and on the eve of his days, had given to him what life had to offer; because for him there remained no puzzles he might wish to solve; and therefore he could have had "enough" of life.'[11] Weber compares this to the disenchanted world, its perpetual, meaningless cultural life. This idea is expressed again when we read: 'the peasant, like Abraham, could die "satiated with life." The feudal landlord and the warrior hero could do likewise. For both fulfilled a cycle of their existence beyond which they did not reach. Each in his way could attain an inner-worldly perfection as a result of the naive unambiguity of the substance of his life.'[12] Weber's references to Abraham and peasant life, feudalism, and warrior heroes should be interpreted as emphasizing the organic cycle of life and its meaningfulness; this cycle constitutes an intrinsic part of the enchanted world. This is an era after the primitive's enchanted world. It is not so much the biblical figure of Abraham – founder of Judaism and, of course, a believer in monotheism – who is at issue. The naturalism in the references is an integral part of the enchanted epoch of the world. It is a moment within its progressive development. If the Abraham references were to be granted autonomy, Weber's insistence on the theme of polytheism, actual and metaphoric, would become flagrantly contradictory, if not utterly incoherent.

Weber speaks of the enchanted world as an actual anthropological condition and as a metaphor, an imaginative image of human existence. He refers to three moments of enchantment or to three enchanted worlds. The world of the primitive, the world of peasant life (Abraham), and the world of ancient Greece. Weber does not treat these moments systematically, nor does he always differentiate them as distinct developmental stages. Though we could cast them in a broad historical developmental pattern, Weber distinguishes them *and* connects them in a grand generalized image of the enchanted world of the past contra the disenchanted world of modernity. The primacy given to ancient Greece integrates the images and imagery of enchantment under the rubric of Nature, polytheism, and myth, and stresses the significance of the intellect and consciousness.

It is precisely this moment or epoch that Weber will use as a model in order to speak of the re-enchantment of the world. Weber clearly and unequivocally treats this moment of enchantment as *the* supreme mode of enchantment, as enchantment *par excellence*. In the context of modernity, however, the Greek culture of polytheism and philosophy cannot be revived *in toto*. Hence, Weber alludes to transformations.

Nature is no longer the horizon upon which the humanly meaningful can be projected. Meaning cannot be grafted upon the magical texture of Nature, for we have lost Nature forever. Abraham and peasant life are only suggestive of what we have lost; they are meant to expose the poverty and barren mess of our existence, our meaningless lives. This is very much like Rousseau's savage whose image permits a social critique of modernity. As an actual way of life it remains utterly inaccessible, lost in the ruins of time and the structures of a disenchanted world. It was an ordered, finite, and meaningful cosmos. That is all that Weber wants to convey through the references to Abraham.

In turn, the fecundity of the reference gains its richness only when placed in the context of the other two moments or images of enchanted worlds: that of the primitive and that of ancient Greece. Even then the full power and significance of the Weberian theme can be unveiled only when we bear in mind that references to enchantment and disenchantment are references respectively to meaningful and meaningless worlds. The comparative scrutiny to which Weber subjects the two conceptual images moves constantly and rapidly from the particular to the general, comprehensive, composite portraits of the two worlds. Thus, Weber's remarks about Abraham and peasant life should be read only as references to a meaningful Natural cycle which sustains and nourishes social existence. By comparison, the denatured social life of the modern world knows no goal or boundaries; its infinite, destabilized energy drowns meaning.

### III. THE DIALECTICS OF DISENCHANTMENT

The process of disenchantment has been going on since time immemorial.[13] It is intrinsic to the civilizing process, the genesis of culture and the increased complexity of social structures and life itself. Central to this process is the force of rationalization; religion, science, bureaucracy and capitalism play a pivotal role in this whole process. Weber's treatment of the rise of capitalism and the role played by religious doctrines in this respect is well known.[14]

The force behind disenchantment is rationality or, more precisely, rationalization. Rationality, unlike reason, is concerned with means, not ends; it is the human ability to calculate, to effectively reach desired goals. It emanates from purposive practical human activity. It is this-worldly in origin. It has infinite applicability and an extraordinary expansiveness under certain circumstances. Indeed, it can be quite imperial. It transforms what it touches and, finally, it destroys the means-ends nexus. As a process, rationalization creates its own infinity; it transvaluates and undermines ends. It empties life of passion and the world of enchantment; it assaults and seeks to asphyxiate the human spirit. It twists, constrains, and contorts the human soul to the point of numbness.

According to Weber, rationalization can apply to a variety of human interests or activities:

> There is, for example, rationalization of mystical contemplation, that is of an attitude which, viewed from other departments of life, is specifically irrational, just as much as there are rationalizations of economic life, of technique, of scientific research, of military training, of law and administration. Furthermore, each one of these fields may be rationalized in terms of very different ultimate values and ends, and what is rational from one point of view may well be irrational from another.[15]

The two major factors that contribute to the rationalization of the world and, inevitably, to its disenchantment are religion and science. Religion disenchants in its progressive movement towards monotheism. Since Weber takes plurality of claims, polytheism, to be central to an enchanted world, the presence of vying spirits is necessary in order for the individual to be exercised in the making of crucial choices. The presence of a single god establishes, as far as ethical choices are concerned, a monopoly, one-dimensionality: the individual is deprived of the soul-searching process of self-discovery and self-growth. Monotheism is a single dogma, a commandment, hence anti-enchantment, in Weber's perspective.[16]

Religion, when confronted with the irrationality of the world, is forced to rationalize its dogma. The irrationality of the world, the fact of human suffering, must be explained rationally; it must be made reasonable by providing a justification for it. The brilliant essays 'Politics as a Vocation,' 'Science as a Vocation,' 'The Social Psychology of the World Religions,' and 'Religious Rejections of the World and Their Directions' capture the dialectics of religious beliefs and historical, existential realities. Weber states: 'This problem – the experience of the irrationality of the world – has been the driving force of all religious evolution. The Indian doctrine of karma, Persian dualism, the doctrine of original sin, predestination and the *deus absconditus*, all these have grown out of this experience.'[17] The problem of theodicy and soteriology is central here. It is beautifully summed up by Weber as follows:

> The age-old problem of theodicy consists of the very question of how it is that a power which is said to be at once omnipotent and kind could have created such an irrational world of undeserved suffering, unpunished injustice, and hopeless stupidity. Either this power is not omnipotent or is not kind, or, entirely different principles of compensation and reward govern our life – principles we may interpret metaphysically, or even principles that forever escape our comprehension.[18]

Theodicy is religion's failed attempt to deal with the irrational nature of human suffering. Irrationality is the nemesis of religion: it forces religion to articulate its dogma more explicitly, to become progressively more deeply entrapped in the quagmire of rationalization. Indeed, religion has only two options: rationalization of its dogma or flight into mysticism.[19] Human suffering cannot be justified in rational, human terms.

It is important to realize that the spiritual dimension of life, which Weber identifies as a fundamental feature of enchantment, is not identical to the spiritual concerns and dogmas of formal religion and theology. Weber is referring to a specific spiritual, moral attitude towards the world which springs from and discloses a certain personality, a character. Religion, instead of being a source and a sustenance of the spiritual, in Weber's sense, unwittingly becomes its enemy and destroyer.

Science, religion's secular counterpart, plays, according to Weber, an even greater role in the drama of disenchantment.[20] Science renders the world a landscape amenable to exhaustive knowledge and, inevitably, to control. The world is matter to be moulded and mastered. Science masters the mechanisms of the world, the empirical realities of life. Science, by the very nature of its activity and scope, enters into a process of progressive discovery and invention which must and will be superseded, surpassed. This situation gives rise to a sense of obsolescence, of futility. Weber compares scientific work to artistic creation. Art's achievements are permanent; they cannot be relegated to museums as pieces of historical importance only for the expert. Art's story is a continuous, coherent, interconnected and interdependent development of episodes in the drama of human existence. Obsolescence is alien to it. Each artistic achievement stands as *a constant* source of fascination, immune to the passage of time; it is timeless in its meaning though born in a specific historical epoch.

Science's achievements are by definition impermanent. An endless, infinite chain of discoveries is the task of science; hence each discovery must be overshadowed by yet another scientific discovery. This impermanence of the concrete, the specific, this very flux of discoveries harbours meaninglessness; it governs the whole spectrum of scientific discovery. Progress negates individual discovery. Weber's point is meant to stress the inexorable march of scientific progress which supersedes *all* past discoveries and achievements. It is not so much that scientific discoveries are devoid of prestige and fame. Yet there is an inherent transience to scientific discovery.

It is this ephemeral aura that Weber wishes to stress by comparing science to art, whose achievements are permanent. Weber does not differentiate the individual scientist-discoverer from the flow of scientific discovery and progress as a whole. However, his argument regarding the stream of endless, infinite progressive discoveries without transhistorical permanence remains crucial. Without mysteries or riddles, the world stands before us empty, a wasteland, a nullified entity imprisoned in the perpetual flux of a process the very recurrence of which cannot evince meaning.

Science more than any other single human endeavour rationalizes the human mind and the world. Science, as the technique of means, stands incapable of responding to fundamental human questions, questions of meaning, life and death, of why should we live or how should we live our lives. Questions concerning ultimate values force science into silence; they disclose its limits.

Weber argues that science cannot and does not address the most vital of questions: that of meaningfulness. Science answers to our practical concerns; it can tell us whether a specific course of action is viable or not; it can decipher the possible from the impossible; it cannot determine what should be our desirable course. The normative realm does not belong to the scientific domain. Clarity regarding means, feasibility of action and its consequences, falls within the jurisdiction of science. Science can be our indispensable servant regarding only such matters. Though silent regarding ultimate ends, science has established its method as the conclusive form of validation; the royal road to verification. Without scientific access to ultimate values, yet seduced and mesmerized by the spectacular success of science, we are at a loss as to ultimate values. The irreconcilability of ultimate values appears abysmal, permanent. Subjectivity and relativism reign. The process of disenchantment reaches its climax in our age.

## IV. THE WORLD DISENCHANTED

Hence Weber's melancholy metaphors. Petrification, darkness, mechanization – emptiness, inner death; no spirit, no vision. Routine, non-creative energy; a world of shadows without true substance. An iron cage. Prisoners of a denatured culture, subjects of massive, bureaucratized institutions, victims of the ferocity and impersonality of capitalist market society; prisoners oblivious to the meaning of freedom. Exiles unable to recall visions of the promised land. Modern urban life: totally detached from Nature, insular, dispirited, lonely. With uncompromising disdain Weber remarks: 'For of the last stage of this cultural development, it might well be truly said: "Specialists without spirit, sensualists without heart; this nullity imagines that it has attained a level of civilization never before achieved." '[21]

The great void. Hence Weber's threnody. In concrete socio-political terms Weber speaks of new institutional structures and practices; he speaks of modern culture, our fate. Historical circumstances brought about new irreversible configurations. Gone are the days of the polytheistic images of the cosmos. Gods and demons took flight from our modern world; exiled from the human soul, they have vanished.

Bereft, we stand alone, utterly alone, as Nietzsche prophesied. The great hour of enchantment is gone. We have entered the long arid season. The grand transformative power of politics, charismatic leadership, which Weber calls 'the specifically creative revolutionary force of history,'[22] the secular descendant of the prophetic tradition of the Hebrews, is also gone; it has evaporated into thin air, its vitality killed by bureaucratic structures and self-interests.[23] Pettiness replaces courage.[24] A comprehensive, qualitative deterioration is diagnosed by

Weber; he views it as the 'spirit' of the modern age. New structures and images have seized the mind and confounded the soul. A veritable cultural and societal transfiguration has occurred.

This transfiguration of the world is Weber's grand theme. Its dialectics constitutes the vicissitudes of the human spirit and the loss of enchantment; intellectual, material, structural impediments towards a full recovery constitute the narrative of the Weberian epos, the penetrating study of cultures, civilizations, and religious beliefs.

The elaboration of the notion of a disenchanted world is not confined to the two eloquent essays 'Politics as a Vocation' and 'Science as a Vocation.' There the concept receives its most extensive and explicit treatment. But the *idea* of disenchantment permeates a great deal of Weber's writings.[25] Even though he does not use the term very frequently, his explorations and analyses of societies and civilizations, his relentless scrutiny of the ruinous passage of time, abound with a sense of loss, dissolution, and extinction. Yet, he also heralds new modes of being, new existential trajectories and visions.

Weber's imagery speaks of loss and death; it is merciless, haunting. A melancholy eloquence prevails. The theme of disenchantment as a whole is a threnody. It laments the loss of meaning, passion, and spiritual vibrancy in Western civilization. Yet, paradoxically, although there are moments of almost paralysing pessimism, this lament does not conclude in despair.

Weber hurls his utterances like a biblical prophet, a creature of the blazing desert. He declares: 'Not summer's bloom lies ahead of us, but rather a polar night of icy darkness and hardness ...'[26] We shall live, he tells us, in an 'iron cage';[27] a 'mechanized petrification' will overcome us;[28] we shall inhabit a disenchanted world.[29] But Weber does not simply and brutally foretell our imminent, horrendous fate, a fate to which, in all probability, the world as a whole will succumb. Prophecy is mixed with analysis and prescription; new vistas are unveiled.

Modernity, the climax of disenchantment and of progress (scientific and intellectual), is not for Weber a satanic curse. He delineates the drama of modernity without a concluding lament. His most pessimistic utterances are coupled with alternative possibilities. The famous remark about specialists without spirit, sensualists without heart, is preceded by another possibility; 'No one knows who will live in this cage in the future, or whether at the end of this tremendous development entirely new prophets will arise, or there will be a great rebirth of old ideas and ideals ...'[30] The fabrication of 'the shell of bondage which men will *perhaps* be forced to inhabit some day, as powerless as the fellahs of ancient Egypt'[31] calls for a seriality of preconditions not always expressed as inevitabilities.[32]

The final verdict points towards a rather muted or, perhaps, sober spiritedness and determination. Not stoicism but a tamed excitation pervades the atmosphere; options are adumbrated on the distant horizon; new Herculean labours await us; new heroics, echoes of a past long silenced are audible again. Neither a polar night nor a fool's paradise awaits us as our future. Disenchantment speaks of the loss of what Weber takes to be a normative image of the individual and society, his ontology, which constitutes his evaluative criterion; critique of disenchantment is affirmation of a specific human essence and world-view. Affirmation of enchantment is *confirmation* of the dehumanization suffered under the reign of a disenchanted world. Disenchantment stands for Weber just as alienation stands for Marx and anomie for Durkheim.

Rationality, the very achievement of the West, with relentless vehemence turns against its creators and proceeds to transform their world into a spiritual wasteland. Weber does not see a return to a less anguished past either as possible or as desirable. He seems to be simultaneously extolling rationality and condemning its monstrous effects. He decries the loss of enchantment in the world, yet he speaks of the past without unbearable, painful nostalgia.

No golden age past or future is mentioned; no *ante lapsum* condition lures Weber. His preference seems to be for the future, a future which lies beyond the immediate, impending dark times. This future is not devoid of rationality nor does it promise a magical transition to a blissful social condition. Weber speaks of re-enchantment, yet he does not suggest a return to a past enchanted world, nor does he allude to a time to come in the near future when the *structures* of a disenchanted world would disappear.[33]

Rationality, rationalization, systematization, intellectualism or intellectualization, which for Weber are essentially one and the same, and disenchantment, are inseparable. The one implies the other. More precisely, disenchantment is the direct consequence of the spread of rationalization.[34] A disenchanted world is, of necessity, a rationalized world. Nowhere can we find the one without the other.[35] The issue is not rationality per se, but a deranged, totalized rationalization which yields disenchantment. The mere presence of rationality does not result in disenchantment. After all, science as a rational tool is not discarded by Weber. His studies of religion, economy, urbanization, bureaucratization seek to show how rationality became totalized and hence disenchanting.

Metaphorically, rationalization devours the very substance, the spiritual quality, of an enchanted world and thus it empties it of meaning. The progressive growth, spread, and dominance of rationalization force enchantment to recede, to dissipate and vanish. A rationalized world is, therefore, a disenchanted world and vice versa; but a world in which rationality exists, even if to a significant degree, need not be a disenchanted world. It is the *totalization* of rationalization which causes the world to be disenchanted.

The enchantment-disenchantment thesis is neither Weber's romanticized naivete nor his ideological blindness.[36] On the contrary; it is a normative category which is meant to offer us a critical perspective; a ground upon which to stand and pronounce meaningful and authoritative value judgments regarding the world of facts which, sociologically speaking, must and does include belief systems and ultimate values. The human quest for meaning, the panorama of the cultural manifestations of human behaviour in the context of institutional structures and practices, can be qualitatively evaluated, judged.

Enchantment-disenchantment permits Weber an ethical perspective which anthropologically and philosophically ushers in a *qualitative* critique of the *quantitative* factual universe. And more: it allows, indeed demands, a *prescriptive* attitude towards the sociological description of phenomena.

Without reference to it ultimate values, ends, would be part of a narrative which falls outside the jurisdiction of any authoritative, reasoned articulation of value judgments. Without this normative grounding, the mediocre and base could not be judged inferior to the lofty and sublime. The prison of subjectivity and the culture-bound character of social life are instantly ruptured in the light of the critique of disenchantment. The observer-narrator becomes judge-evaluator. Thus humanity can be affirmed contra inhumanity, the heroic contra cowardice.[37]

The negative aspects of modernity are critically narrated by Weber under the general theme of rationalization and particularly under the metaphor of disenchantment. 'Neutrality' evaporates before the spectrum of the torment of the spirit. Yet, ironically, modernity carries new possibilities, new challenges. The melancholy awareness of the ruins and loss that the passage of time brings about does not eradicate the promise of new and renewed challenges and visions. The past must be mournfully acknowledged as gone forever. The new must be seen simultaneously in the light of the old and in its actual novelty. History can instruct us, but we do not live in the past. No eternal recurrence occurs here; yet nothing is born *ex nihilo*. Unchartered territories offer themselves; new adventures in the primordial odyssey of the mysterious dialectics between spirit and matter, soul and society, mind and culture emerge once again.

Like Machiavelli who registers the glorious past and urges his contemporary new princes to seek glory in a significantly altered socio-political environment, Weber with sorrow must bid farewell to his charismatic leaders, prophets, and the enchanted world of old. But the modern landscape is not totally desolate; nor does it remain transfixed in its disenchanted state. To Weber, exemplary heroism, courage, and integrity are still possible. Politics can still be a genuine vocation; so can science. Politics and ethics need not be in utter disunity. Heroics and authenticity are revived once again, but in a transformed world, in a new cultural context.

## V. RE-ENCHANTMENT OR THE RETURN OF GODS AND DEMONS

The iron cage is not hermetically sealed. Signs of life still exist. Weber tells us: 'We live as did the ancients when their world was not yet disenchanted of its gods and demons, only we live in a different sense. As Hellenic man at times sacrificed to Aphrodite and at other times to Apollo ... so do we still nowadays, only the bearing of man has been disenchanted and denuded of its mystical but inwardly genuine plasticity.'[38] And again, further on, he reminds us that today, 'Many old gods ascend from their graves; they are disenchanted and hence take the form of impersonal forces. They strive to gain power over our lives and again they resume their eternal struggle with one another.' And referring to 'the stern seriousness of our fateful times' which we must be able 'to countenance' he states: 'Our civilization destines us to realize more clearly these struggles again after our eyes have been blinded for a thousand years – blinded by the allegedly or presumably exclusive orientation towards the grandiose moral fervour of Christian ethics.'[39] And more unequivocally he declares: 'When this night shall have slowly receded ...'[40]

The cosmos as a whole and our life experiences are mediated constantly by our mind and heart, by mental images and beliefs, aspirations and fears. Modernity is the massive growth of certain cultural patterns and practices. The rise and collapse of the prison house of culture is immensely slow. Weber sees in the modern context of externality the passing of ancient ways of life and the crystallization of new ones. But he declares the re-emergence of a single, primordial, and indestructible force; a force which could be rechanelled, a force which like the mythological Phoenix rises from its ashes; this force is none other than the human essence.

Yet, when it awakens anew it must act in a transformed world, in a world of new ideas, new cultural patterns, which render the life of the mind and heart more complex, difficult, and challenging. The re-enchanted world is a new, austere, arid world, a desert where humans must act out and express their once again enchanted being. It is the difference between the past-enchanted world on the one hand and the modern once-again enchanted individual soul under siege by the rationalized structures of a denatured world on the other that renders modernity simultaneously lamentable and challenging. Weber says:

If anything, we realize again today that something can be sacred not only in spite of its not being beautiful, but rather because and in so far as it is not beautiful. You will find this documented in the fifty-third chapter of the book of Isaiah and in the twenty-first Psalm. And, since Nietzsche, we realize that something can be beautiful, not only in spite of the aspect in which it is not good, but rather in that very aspect. You will find this expressed earlier in the *Fleurs du Mal*, as Baudelaire named his volume of poems.[41]

But the human essence will thrive and vibrate again on the same primordial principle, the tension of polytheism, the making and remaking of existential decisions, decisions involving ultimate values, decisions which galvanize the human character, decisions which affirm, confirm, and nurture the human personality. In the absence of charismatic leadership and its volcanic ruptures, heroic leadership is still possible.

Weber's new hero is not a hopeless or helpless creature. Dynamic and self-confident, the modern soul stands before a disenchanted world, aware of its inadequacies, ready to seek its amelioration, never intoxicated with the illusion of omnipotence, never paralysed by despair and resignation. Weber's once-again enchanted individual with courage and heroic resilience and aspiration seizes upon the fateful, dark times of modernity; between gods and demons a primordial, human-all-too-human struggle commences. Weber's once-again enchanted individual-hero with maturity and responsibility utters: 'Here I stand; I can do no other.' Neither defeatism nor resignation exists here. Whoever can speak so is one 'who *can* have the "calling for politics." '

In such an individual the ethic of ultimate ends and the ethic of responsibility are in unison. In Weber's view, the two ethics 'are not absolute contrasts but rather supplements.' Only in such unison can the two ethics 'constitute a genuine man ...'[42] It is the individual's ethos which harmonizes ultimate values, not a dogma or doctrine. The irreconcilable values are reconciled in the actions of such an individual. Such an individual is their incarnate unity. And Weber declares such unity as 'something genuinely human and moving.'[43]

Weber's message to the children of modernity is this: 'Only he has the calling for politics who is sure that he shall not crumble when the world from his point of view is too stupid or too base for what he wants to offer. Only he who in the face of all this can say "In spite of all!" has the calling for politics.'[44] And politics 'takes both passion and perspective.'[45] Mind, heart, and soul are called forth. One must reach for the impossible in order to attain the possible. But to do so, Weber warns us, a leader and a hero is needed. 'And even those who are neither leaders nor heroes must arm themselves with that steadfastness of heart which can brave even the crumbling of all hopes.'[46] For Weber reminds us that:

'Successful political action is always the "art of the possible." Nonetheless, the possible is often reached only by striving to attain the impossible that lies beyond it.'[47] Such is our destiny.

> The fate of our times is characterized by rationalization and intellectualization and, above all, by the 'disenchantment of the world.' Precisely the ultimate and most sublime values have retreated from public life either into the transcendental realm of mystic life or into the brotherliness of direct and personal human relations. It is not accidental that our greatest art is intimate and not monumental, nor is it accidental that today only within the smallest and intimate circles, in personal human situations, in *pianissimo* that something is pulsating that corresponds to the prophetic *pneuma*, which in former times swept through the great communities like a firebrand, welding them together.[48]

The fire of charisma, the *pneuma* of genuine prophecy is gone; Apollo's temple is bereft. No genuine prophecy, no new religion can be construed at will, artificially, intellectually. The result would be a spiritual monstrosity.[49] The prophet for whom we 'yearn simply does not exist.' Who should answer our most crucial question? 'Which of the warring gods should be serve? Or should we serve perhaps an entirely different god, and who is he?'[50] Such is the crisis of disenchantment, of our dark, icy, hard times. Weber tells us, 'this process of disenchantment ... has continued to exist in Occidental culture for millennia ...'[51] Now it has reached its apogee. To those 'who cannot bear the fate of the times' in a humanly befitting manner, Weber's advice is to return to the wide-open 'arms of the old churches.'[52] Weber's other options, which he names with contempt, are: to become 'bitter or banausic;' to 'simply and dully accept world and occupation;' 'mystic flight from reality.'[53]

What is to be done? Shall we yearn and tarry for new prophets and saviours? Weber urges a different course of action. 'We shall set to work and meet the "demands of the day," in human relations as well as in our vocation. This, however, is plain and simple, if each finds and obeys the demon who holds the fibres of his very life.'[54]

We should not dream of the past, just as history does not dream of its lost illusions; we should heed Camus's invitation. Weber tells us: 'The fate of an epoch which has eaten of the tree of knowledge is that it must know that we cannot learn the *meaning* of the world from the results of its analysis, be it ever so perfect; it must rather be in a position to create this meaning itself. It must recognize that general views of life and the universe can never be the products of increasing empirical knowledge, and that the highest ideals, which move us most forcefully, are always formed only in the struggle with other ideals which are just as sacred to others as ours are to us.'[55] Gods and demons; Nietzschean struggles.

Re-enchantment is the human awakening, the recovery of our true, genuine being; but this recovery of our essential plasticity does not occur in the bosom of Nature; it takes place in the iron cage of modern culture.[56] We cannot flee the iron cage; it is our context, our fate. The spirits and gods of the enchanted world of the past, the world of Nature, now surface as impersonal forces, abstractions, ideas and ideals; ultimate values.[57]

Weber suggestively indicates that the process of disenchantment yields to a re-enchanting recovery of the self, a radical recovery of our essential spirituality, but in the context of a disenchanted, rationalized world.[58] Re-enchantment is then not a mere romantic yearning on Weber's part. It is rooted in the very dialectics of his notion of enchantment and disenchantment; of his understanding of human essence and historical time. The dynamics of re-enchantment as a profound recovery of our inner resources pitted against the massive presence of a disenchanted external world is clearly present in Weber's thought; it is an intrinsic feature of his world-view even though he does not accord an extensive treatment to it.

This qualitative split between the re-enchanted human and the external socio-cultural disenchanted world constitutes the homelessness and exile of the modern self. The now re-enchanted human soul confronts the disenchanted externality. It cannot demolish the iron cage. But neither can the iron cage of rationality and Culture extinguish the now re-enchanted inner being.

For Weber the denatured world of Culture as the context of re-enchantment suggests difficulties and tensions, constrictions and restrictions. They adumbrate his vision of the modern heroic personality. Neither moral relativism nor arbitrariness is suggested here. Just as the ancient polytheistic pantheon was not a personal, individualistic construct, so it is with abstract ultimate values. Severe constriction of the public space and uncertainty regarding the impact of leadership, since the loss of the magisterial sweep of charisma, do not suggest for Weber a subjectivist, arbitrary moral horizon.[59] The otherwise irreconcilable ultimate values find relief and coherence in the moral fibre of the authentic character and ethos of the distinctly modern re-enchanted being, one who has the strength of character 'to be able to countenance the stern seriousness of our fateful times.'[60]

Charting a course between paralysing pessimism and naive optimism, Weber proclaims: 'Certainly all historical experience confirms the truth – that man would not have attained the possible unless time and again he had reached out for the impossible.'[61] In the midst of a deadly, barren wasteland, within the iron cage, we must dare to dream the impossible. Such is the genuinely majestic splendour, mysterious magic, demonic grandeur of the human soul.

NOTES

1 This response was given on the occasion of the contemplated revival of the Delphic Oracle. Joseph Fontenrose, *The Delphic Oracle: Its Responses and Operations* (Berkeley: University of California Press 1981), 353.

2 *The Myth of Sisyphus and Other Essays*, trans. Justin O'Brien (New York: Vintage 1955), v.

3 The motto for these essays is from Pindar, Pythian III; it reads: 'O my soul, do not aspire to immortal life, but exhaust the limits of the possible.' Camus initially emphasizes the desire, almost lust, for life, immortal life, only to choose a more sober and moderate but exhilarating route: finite life informed by the Absurd and rebellion. It is in his *The Rebel* and his novel *The Plague* that exhausting the limits of the possible receives its most mature articulation.

4 Nietzsche rushes, embraces a horse beaten with a whip by its coachman, and bursts into tears. Milan Kundera, *The Unbearable Lightness of Being*, trans. Michael Heim (New York: Harper and Row 1984), tells us: 'Nietzsche was trying to apologize to the horse for Descartes' and for the cruelty of the human race (p. 290).

5 The notion of exile is central to Camus. Imprisonment, enslavement, emptiness, desolation, and exile constitute Weber's lexicon regarding disenchantment. On exile in Camus and disenchantment in Weber, see Alkis Kontos, 'Memories of Ithaca,' in *Ethnicity in a Technological Age*, ed. Ian A. Angus (Edmonton: University of Alberta 1988), 95–8.

6 Leo Strauss, *Natural Right and History* (Chicago: University of Chicago Press 1953), chap. 2, devoted to Weber. Strauss gives a severe critique of Weber in which Weber is not always recognizable. He stresses the tension between reason and revelation. Also Allan Bloom, *The Closing of the American Mind* (New York: Simon and Schuster 1987), 210–11, 213, 369; Eric Voegelin, *The New Science of Politics* (Chicago: University of Chicago Press 1952), 13–23. But see: Maurice Merleau-Ponty, *Adventures of the Dialectic*, trans. Joseph Bien (Evanston: Northwestern University Press 1973), chap. 1; Sheldon S. Wolin, 'Max Weber: Legitimation, Method and the Politics of Theory,' *Political Theory*, chapter 13 of this volume, especially 297–306. A perceptive but highly eulogizing piece is *Karl Jaspers on Max Weber*, ed. John Dreijmanis (New York: Paragon House 1989).

7 'Science as a Vocation' [sv], in *From Max Weber: Essays in Sociology*, trans. and ed. H.H. Gerth and C. Wright Mills (New York: Oxford University Press 1958), 139 (emphasis in original). Weber's thesis on the primitive mind finds support in the work of Claude

Levi-Strauss, especially *The Savage Mind* (Chicago: University of Chicago Press 1966).

8  Weber speaks of 'mysterious incalculable forces,' sv, 139. On polytheism see sv, 147–8 and 'Politics as a Vocation' [PV], in *From Max Weber*, note 7 above, 123; on polytheism metaphorically, *The Methodology of the Social Sciences* [MSS], trans. Edward Shils and Henry Finch (New York: The Free Press 1949), 5, 17. PV and SV abound with references to gods and demons. The sociological studies of religion give the anthropological-historical trajectory of mysteries and spirits. On the plurality of gods, Weber's pantheistic universe and the agonistic spirit of choice-making see Fredric Jameson, 'The Vanishing Mediator; Narrative Structure in Max Weber,' *New German Critique* 1 (winter 1974), 61. On choice-making, treated negatively, see Alastair MacIntyre, *After Virtue: A Study in Moral Theory* (Notre Dame: University of Notre Dame Press 1984), 26–7. But see Weber, MSS, 18 on soul, fate, and choice-making. Though Weber introduces plurality of spirits in conjunction with primitive enchantment and choice-making, he stresses the Hellenic age as his prototype of choosing between rivalling gods: Aphrodite and Apollo, Aphrodite and Hera, Dionysus and Apollo. sv, 148; PV, 123. And reference is made to Plato's discovery of the dialectic of logical argument. SV, 140–1.

Weber, in *Ancient Judaism*, trans. Hans H. Gerth and Don Martindale (New York: The Free Press 1967), suggestively points out that 'prerequisite to new religious conceptions is that man must not yet have unlearned how to face the course of the world with *questions of his own*. Precisely the man distant from the great culture centers has cause to do so ... Man living in the midst of the culturally satiated areas and enmeshed in their techniques' does not address such questions for much is taken for granted. And Weber adds: 'The possibility of questioning the meaning of the world *presupposes the capacity to be astonished* about the course of events' (206–7) (emphasis added). Disenchantment militates against both questioning and the capacity to experience astonishment, for 'one can, in principle, master all things by calculation.' And Weber concludes: 'This means that the world is disenchanted.' sv, 139.

9  Re-enchantment will be precisely this, but instead of choosing between rival gods the choice would be made between rival abstract principles, ideals, or values. Weber's references to gods and demons is, in this context, metaphoric. Metaphors illuminate reality, they are not reality itself, thus they are misleading if taken literally; see Alkis Kontos, 'Domination: Metaphor and Reality,' in *Domination*, ed. Alkis Kontos (Toronto: University of Toronto Press 1975), 225.

10  See Weber's remarks on Plato's *Republic*, Indian logic, and Aristotle. sv, 140–1.

11  sv, 140.

12  'Religious Rejections of the World and Their Directions' [RRWD], in *From Max Weber*, note 7 above, 356.

13  sv, 138–9.

14  See: Norman Birnbaum, 'Conflicting Interpretations of the Rise of Capitalism:

Marx and Weber,' *British Journal of Sociology* 4 (1952), 125–41; Anthony Giddens, 'Marx, Weber and the Development of Capitalism,' *Sociology* 4 (1970), 289–310; Anthony Giddens, *Capitalism and Modern Social Theory: An Analysis of the Writings of Marx, Durkheim and Max Weber* (Cambridge: Cambridge University Press 1971).

15 Author's introduction, in *The Protestant Ethic and the Spirit of Capitalism* [PE], trans. Talcott Parsons (New York: Charles Scribner's Sons 1958), 26.

16 And more polemically, Weber states: 'The grandiose rationalism of an ethical and methodical conduct of life which flows from every religious prophecy has *dethroned* ... *polytheism* ...' (emphasis added), sv, 148; and: 'Our civilization destines us to realize more clearly these struggles again, after *our eyes have been blinded* for a thousand years – *blinded by* the allegedly or presumably exclusive orientation towards *the grandiose moral fervour of Christian ethics*' (emphasis added), sv, 149. The irrationality of the world and of human suffering cannot be accounted for rationally. Theodicy is a doomed endeavour. But Weber's paramount hostility is reserved for monotheism – the constriction and extinction of plurality so indispensable to choice-making.

17 PV, 123.

18 PV, 122.

19 RRWD and 'The Social Psychology of the World Religious' [SPWR], in *From Max Weber*, note 7 above, capture best Weber's ideas on the movement and evolution of religious beliefs and dogmas in a world of utter irrationality.

20 'Scientific progress is a fraction, the most important fraction, of the process of intellectualization which we have been undergoing for thousands of years ...' sv, 138, 139. He is critical of science, but he does not wish to eliminate. He wishes to reduce science to its vital and indispensable role.

But beyond the instrumental utility of science, Weber, ultimately, views science as meaningless. He quotes Tolstoy's words: 'Science is meaningless because it gives no answer to our question, the only question important for us: "What shall we do and how shall we live?" ' sv, 143. On science and meaninglessness see Peter Lassman and Irving Velody, eds, *Max Weber's Science as Vocation* (London: Unwin Hyman 1988), chap. 13, especially 193ff. On scientific activity Wolin brilliantly points out: 'Like the Calvinist, scientific man accumulates, only his activity takes the form of knowledge; yet what he amasses has no more lasting value than other things of the world. Scientific knowledge is always being superseded' (413).

21 PE, 182. On the aesthetic and erotic spheres and religion see RRWD; on passion, heart, soul, and mind-head see PV, 115–17, 127–8. Weber's disenchanted individuals are very much T.S. Eliot's 'The Hollow Men': 'We are the hollow men ... Shape without form, shade without colour,/ Paralysed force, gesture without motion ...' See T.S. Eliot, *The Complete Poems and Plays 1909–1950* (New York: Harcourt Brace & World 1971), 56.

22 *Economy and Society* [ES], ed. Guenther Roth and Clause Wittich (Berkeley: University of California Press 1978), chap. 14, 'Charisma and Its Transformation.' Charisma

'manifests its revolutionary power from within, from a central *metanoia* of the followers' attitudes' (1117; also 1116, 1111–12).

23 ES, 1132. Weber tells us: 'The future belongs to bureaucratization ... Bureaucracy is distinguished from other historical agencies of the modern rational order of life in that it is far more persistent and "escape-proof." History shows that wherever bureaucracy gained the upper hand, as in China, Egypt and, to a lesser extent, in the later Roman empire and Byzantium, it did not disappear again unless in the course of the total collapse of the supporting culture ... In contrast to these older forms, modern bureaucracy has one characteristic which makes its "escape-proof" nature much more definite: rational specialization and training.' ES, 1400–1. Weber speaks of bureaucratic 'castration of charisma.' ES, 1132. Weber writes: 'Not ideas, but material, and ideal interests, directly govern men's conduct. Yet very frequently the "world images" that have been created by "ideas" have, like switchmen, determined the tracks along which action has been pushed by the dynamic of interest.' SPWR, 280.

24 PV argues for an ethos, specific qualities necessary, indeed indispensable, for 'heroic' political leadership.

25 PE abounds with references to disenchantment. The author's introduction in the work, written in 1920 to introduce the whole series on the Sociology of Religion, clearly delineates the devastating march of rationalization. ES makes repeated reference to disenchantment.

26 PV, 128.

27 PE, 181, 182.

28 PE, 182.

29 SV, 138–9, 155.

30 PE, 182.

31 ES, 1402 (emphasis added).

32 ES, 1402. Weber speaks conditionally: 'if,' 'might,' 'perhaps.' And in SV Weber insists the process of re-enchantment is already under way.

33 Gregory Baum, 'Does the World Remain Disenchanted?' *Social Research* 37 (1970), 153–202, assumes Weber to be claiming the permanence of disenchantment. Weber argues the opposite. Weber's position is accurately grasped and masterfully argued by Karl Löwith, *Max Weber and Karl Marx*, trans. Hans Fantel, ed. Tom Bottomore and William Outhwaite (London: Allen and Unwin 1982). Löwith stresses the fact that the structures of the disenchanted world remain, yet humanity is not totally extinguished within the iron cage (p. 52). On Weber's philosophy of history see Gabriel Kolko, 'A Critique of Max Weber's Philosophy of History,' *Ethics* 70 (October 1959), 21–36.

34 Unlike Jacques Ellul, in the *Technological Society*, trans. John Wilkinson (New York: Vintage 1964), Weber does not assign to rationality an inherently evil quality. For Weber, the problem is not rationality per se but a rationalized world. The monstrosity is a totally rationalized, disenchanted world. The Satanic is absent; religion is not the

answer, according to Weber. See Herbert Marcuse, *Negations: Essays in Critical Theory*, trans. Jeremy J. Shapiro (Boston: Beacon Press 1968), chap. 6. See Löwith, note 33 above, chap. 2, on Weber's ambiguity and ambivalence regarding rationality.

35  In SV Weber speaks of 'intellectualist rationalization' of 'the process of intellectualization which we have been undergoing for thousands of years'; 'this process of disenchantment, which has continued to exist in Occidental culture for millennia'; the 'fate of our times is characterized by rationalization and intellectualization' and, above all, by the 'disenchantment of the world' (139, 138, 139, 155 respectively).

36  See Ernest Gellner, 'The Rubber Cage: Disenchantment with Disenchantment,' in his *Culture, Identity, and Politics* (Cambridge: Cambridge University Press 1987).

37  For Weber the metaphysical premises upon which values rest 'are never demonstrable by science' MSS, 24–5, 17, 19. SV argues the inability of science to deal with questions of ultimate values and meaning. For Weber this does not negate science – its utility regarding means – nor does it imply that ultimate values are automatically rendered totally and absolutely subjective, relativistic. Where science does not have an authoritative voice, philosophy and personality (ethos) do. SV, 151–2; PV, 117ff, 127–8. Weber is fighting *against* the belief that science is our grand arbiter. To Weber all matters of evaluation, value-judgments, are 'scientifically undemonstrable.' MSS, 6, 8; also 10 regarding science's 'inestimable service.' In SV Weber states: 'No science is absolutely free for presuppositions, and no science can prove its fundamental value to the man who rejects these presuppositions' (153); but see p. 152 where one can be made 'to give himself an *account of the ultimate meaning of his own conduct*' (emphasis in original). See also MSS, 58–9 regarding scientific analysis of empirical reality and its validity for others, even if from other cultures – the Chinese is Weber's example. But see W.G. Runciman, *A Critique of Max Weber's Philosophy of Social Science* (Cambridge: Cambridge University Press 1972), 55.

38  SV, 148 (emphasis added).

39  SV, 149 (emphasis added).

40  PV, 128.

41  SV, 147–8.

42  PV, 127 (emphasis in original). All quotation are from p. 127. The ethic of responsibility and the ethic of ultimate ends find their unity and reconciliation not on a theoretical plane but in the maturity of the personality of the political actor, one who has the 'calling for politics' and who has 'the knowledge of tragedy.' PV, 117. Weber refers approvingly to Machiavelli: '[I]n a beautiful passage, if I am not mistaken, of the *History of Florence*, [he] has one of his heroes praise those citizens who deemed the greatness of their native city higher than the salvation of their souls.' PV, 126; and MSS, 18 on soul, choice, and fate.

43  PV, 127.

44  PV, 128.

45  Ibid.

46  Ibid.

47  MSS, 23–4.

48  SV, 155.

49  Ibid.

50  SV, 153.

51  SV, 139.

52  SV, 155.

53  PV, 128.

54  SV, 156.

55  MSS, 57.

56  PV, 128. For Weber, '[A]ll "culture" appears as man's emancipation from the originally prescribed cycle of natural life. For this very reason culture's every step forward seems condemned to lead to an even more devastating senselessness.' RWD, 356–7. On the importance of the organic versus the cultural dimension see Lawrence Scaff, 'Fleeing the Iron Cage: Politics and Culture in the Thought of Max Weber,' *American Political Science Review* 81, no. 3 (September 1987), especially 742–4. The issue is placed in a much broader context in Scaff's recent, excellent book-length study, *Fleeing the Iron Cage: Culture, Politics and Modernity in the Thought of Max Weber* (Berkeley: University of California Press 1989).

57  The emergence of re-enchantment, its genesis and timing, suggests a Weberian dialectics of ontology, irrationality, and the human drive for meaning. This is not developed by Weber; my essay only adumbrates the schema of the enchantment-disenchantment and re-enchantment theme. Regarding the conflict of gods and demons, the tension of choosing a fate which yields meaning and befits the human essence see MSS, 16–18, PV, SV.

58  Löwith's and Scaff's work is crucial on this issue. Also H. Stuart Hughes, *Consciousness and Society: The Reorientation of European Social Thought 1890–1930* (New York: Vintage Books 1961), 322.

59  Arendt's concept of public space is instructive here, especially her treatment in *Men in Dark Times* (New York: Harcourt, Brace and World 1968). For an engaging treatment of authenticity contra moral relativism see Charles Taylor, *Sources of the Self* (Cambridge: Harvard University Press 1989) and *The Malaise of Modernity* (Concord, Ont.: House of Anansi Press 1991). Weber states in MSS: 'It is really a question not only of alternatives between values but of an irreconcilable death-struggle, like that between "God" and the "Devil." Between these, neither relativization nor compromise is possible' (pp. 17–18). And he adds: '[E]very single important activity and ultimately life as a whole, if it is ... to be consciously guided, is a series of ultimate decisions through which the soul – as in Plato – chooses its own fate, i.e., the meaning of its activity and existence.' Weber explicitly states that only the 'crudest misunder-

standing' could 'claim that this standpoint is ' "relativistic" ' (p. 18). Regarding charges of a nihilistic proclivity voiced against Weber see Lassman and Velody, 197; and an ontology and essentialism in Weber see ibid., 203.

60 SV, 149.
61 PV, 128. In MSS, 23–4 Weber refers to successful political action as the art of the possible and he adds: 'Nonetheless, the possible is often reached only by striving to attain the impossible that lies beyond it.'

# 11

# The Revenge of the Sacred:
# Technology and Re-enchantment

## GILBERT G. GERMAIN

> No one knows who will live in this cage in the future, or whether at the end
> of this tremendous development entirely new prophets will arise, or there
> will be a great rebirth of old ideas and ideals, or, if neither, mechanized
> petrification, embellished with a sort of convulsive self-importance.
>
> – Max Weber[1]

I

It is intriguing that the person who presented us with an image of modernity
as stark and uncompromising as the 'iron cage' should have entertained the
prospect of alternative futures. After all, a cage, like a prison, restricts and
homogenizes experience so that the 'same day' is relived by its inhabitants in
perpetuity. There is no future – no tomorrow – for these persons, because every
'tomorrow' is merely a replay of a self-same today. Likewise there is no past, at
least not in a meaningful sense, for every 'yesterday' is simply the trace of a
today grown old. Time as history, therefore, eludes those who inhabit a cage.

Given that Weber sees the future as indeterminate, recognition of which
affirms the very notion of a future, and hence, of history, we must conclude that
he assumed the iron cage of modernity could be breached. For if Weber's iron
cage were utterly incorruptible, it would constitute history's endpoint and
denote history's end.

Still, it is difficult at times to perceive modernity, as Weber portrays it, as
anything but self-perpetuating. That Weber chose the image of an iron cage to

The author gratefully acknowledges the permission of the State University of New York
Press to reprint material from chapter 2 of his book *A Discourse on Disenchantment: Reflections
on Politics and Technology.* © 1993 State University of New York Press.

symbolize the modern condition, with its connotations of confinement and permanence, reinforces the argument that he perceived humanity to be trapped by forces beyond its control. Specifically, the forces of which Weber speaks are those that contributed to the rise of the 'modern economic order,' forces that now have assumed a commanding power. Weber says as much when he asserts that 'the care for external goods' is no longer worn on the shoulders of mankind 'like a light cloak.' Rather, 'fate,' he concludes, has decreed that 'the cloak should become an iron cage.'[2] The inhabitants of the new world are forced, therefore, according to Weber, to seek out a life within the existing economic order, having lost their capacity to make this order respond to needs that transcend the order's own exigencies.

What, then, are we to make of Weber's claim that in the future 'new prophets may arise,' or that 'old ideas and ideals' may be reborn? How could fundamental change originate from within a societal order that appears so intractable that Weber saw fit to analogize it to an iron cage? The answer lies, I will argue, in the fact that despite appearances, Weber refuses ultimately to conceive the modern capitalist economy, and the overarching societal order of which it is a part, as a system. What is meant by 'system' will be addressed shortly. For now, it suffices to say that other observers of the modern condition, who, like Weber, are partial to the view that humanity has lost control of the productive forces it created, but who, unlike Weber, adopt a systems approach to their analysis of this development, come to a very different conclusion as to what the future may hold.

The task ahead, then, is to locate the tension in Weber's thought that permits him to see the future as open-ended, despite evidence which points towards the perpetuation of current societal forces. In order to draw out and highlight this tension, I will contrast the Weberian discourse on modernity with that of Jacques Ellul, whose systems theory bias presents us with an iron cage devoid of such a tension, and consequently much less amenable to dissolution or substantive change than Weber's. The purpose of drawing this comparison is twofold. On the one hand, as alluded to above, it serves the heuristic function of allowing us to see more clearly the source of Weber's perplexing ambivalence towards the future of the iron cage. On the other hand, such a comparison will enable us to identify some of the shortcomings of Weber's account of the modern condition. While by no means suggesting, in the process, that Ellul's reading of modernity is without its serious flaws, the systems theory approach upon which it is based offers us insights into the origin of what may now appear to be Weber's misguided optimism.

II

It is necessary, when evaluating Weber's response to the phenomenon of the iron cage, to incorporate into the analysis the Weberian notion of 'rationalization,' or its more value-laden equivalent, 'disenchantment.' For the iron cage constitutes the endpoint of a specific historical process, the culmination of a process that Weber refers to as either rationalization or disenchantment.

*Die Entzauberung der Welt* – the disenchantment of the world – is the expression Weber uses most frequently to convey his vision or philosophy of history. As such, it bears a certain surface resemblance to Hegel's 'phenomenology of spirit' or Marx's 'dialectical materialism.' However, for Weber the movement of Occidental history is best accounted for not in terms of a protracted struggle for political freedom and equality or for proletarian ownership of the means of production, but as a progressive emptying of magic from the world. Hence the iron cage is the child of a disenchanted world, a world without magic or mystery, where it is assumed, as Weber says, that 'one can, in principle, master all things by calculation.'[3]

The concepts 'mastery' and 'calculation' are central to an understanding of disenchantment. To start with, a disenchanted age is informed by the belief that no process or event – be it natural or social – is beyond rational comprehension and hence beyond mastery as well. A disenchanted age therefore cannot countenance indecipherability, the fact that certain things may be intellectually impenetrable. To admit to such a possibility would be to undercut the claim, implicit in a disenchanted world, that all things in principle are capable of being mastered by a controlling mind.

For Weber, the intellect that disenchants the world, that demystifies the world and makes it an object of rational comprehension, does so by employing a specific form of reasoning – a calculative mode of reasoning. The technical term Weber uses to describe this intellectual operation is *Zweckrationalität*, commonly translated as purposive, formal, or means-ends rationality.[4] Purposive rationality denotes a kind of reasoning devoted to calculating the best or most efficient means to attain a given end. It refers, in other words, to an instrumental or strategic mode of reasoning, a form of reasoning that is not intrinsically directed towards a particular purpose or goal. It follows then that, for Weber, the world becomes disenchanted as this value-neutral mode of reasoning extends into and reorders every domain of human experience.

This is not the place to review Weber's frustratingly complex and often incomplete account of the disenchantment of the world, a process that has its roots in the birth of Western philosophy and natural science.[5] For our purposes it is sufficient to note that for Weber modernity is characterized by the restructuring of action in accordance with the principles of goal-directedness and technical efficiency. Hence, the rationalization of the economic sphere in a disenchanted world – the realm of the iron cage, proper – has produced, in capitalism, a system premised on the deliberate and calculating pursuit of economic self-interest, free from the constraining values of tradition and sentiment, such as the religious ethic of brotherliness.[6] The contemporary legal order, in contrast, has evolved into a complex body of abstract legal maxims, which, precisely because of its involution, tends to lose sight of those substantive ends that ground it and lend it meaning. Likewise, the rationalizing of human interaction within the public sphere has produced the modern bureaucracy with its impersonal formalism, efficient structuring of channels of communication and command, and growing demand for 'technical expertise' from those 'specialists without spirit' of whom Weber speaks.[7] Even the arts, as witnessed in a number of aesthetic revolutions during the early part of this century, turned in on themselves to display a similar fascination with form and process at the expense of content.

All of these developments indicated to Weber the loss of spirit within the social realm. They point to the loss of any value or vision within society capable of leading it beyond its own parameters, to self-transcendence. As a consequence, the disenchanted world retreats within itself – encloses or encages itself – and fixes its attention on matters related to its own self-management.

As with Weber, Ellul's critique of modernity focuses on the impact the proliferation of calculative reasoning has had on the ends that traditionally furnished our social order with its normative coordinates. Ellul explores this development in his account of the genealogy of 'technique,' a genealogy that bears a striking resemblance to Weber's theorizing on disenchantment.

Ellul is well aware, along with Heidegger, that technique – understood as *techne* or technical know-how – preceded modern science chronologically. What distinguishes it from modern technical reasoning is that, in its initial, pre-modern configuration, technique was contextualized within, and hence constrained by, a comprehensive background of meaning. However, upon the dissolution of its ontological ground, technique began to assume an autonomous status.[8] Like Weber, Ellul links the rise of technical reasoning in part to the decline in belief in a transcendent world that serves as a repository for eternal truths.

Divorced from all valuative considerations, technique for Ellul is concerned solely with the determination of the most efficient means to attain given end. As he puts it, technique is no longer conditioned by anything other than 'its own calculus of efficiency.'[9] Ellul sums up his description of technique by saying that it comprises 'the totality of methods rationally arrived at and having absolute efficiency ... in every field of human activity.'[10] Importantly, his description of technique lets it be known that technique is not to be confused with technology *qua* hardware. Rather, technique refers to rationalized 'know-how,' or to calculative rationality.

## III

It is here, with Ellul's understanding of technical rationality, that we see the beginnings of a rift developing between Ellul and Weber, one which helps explain the divergence in their respective prognoses for the future. Weber, to repeat, took purposive rationality to be solely concerned with determining the most efficient means of attaining a given end. However, unlike Ellul, Weber refused to equate purposive rationality with what might be called 'objective rationality,' because for Weber purposive rationality is subject-driven. In other words, when one reasons in a purposive manner, one does so according to one's subjective evaluation of the appropriateness of the means chosen. This evaluation need not, according to Weber, coincide with the best or most efficient decision based on purely technical considerations. In short, calculating actors are always susceptible to making strategic errors.

Weber expresses this tension between the two kinds of calculative reasoning in his juxtaposing of purposive rationality and 'objectively correct rationality,' or *objecktive Richtigkeitsrationalität*.[11] The latter, as stated, refers to the calculation of means with the aid of objective or scientific knowledge.

Weber is not altogether clear, when he associates the disenchanting of the world with the rise of means-oriented reasoning, whether he had in mind its purposive or its objectively correct variant. There are, however, good reasons to assume he was referring to both. Science and its interrelated technologies, for one, are obviously premised on the assumption that there is one best way to achieve a desired end. The goal of a technical operation optimally is not merely 'to get the job done,' but to do it in the most efficient manner possible. If the substantive end of a car manufacturer, for example, is to make cars and sell them for a profit, then the production process must make use of 'the totality of methods rationally arrived at,' as Ellul would say, in order to maximize profits and thus successfully fulfil its mandate. In contrast, one would assume that individual actors are generally less likely than institutions – that is, businesses, bureaucracies, governments, etc. – to take advantage of technically correct knowledge in their deliberations, given the variance between individual actors' access to, and interest in, such knowledge. These two forms of calculative reasoning need not be antagonistic. In fact, they are often mutually supportive. We see, for instance, in reference to the example above, an automotive industry on this continent that functions internally in accordance with the principle of technical efficiency, yet whose external objective (that is, delivering people to cars) is entirely dependent on the nature of the purposive rational strategies of the public – that is, on variances in personal taste, in perceived value, and so on.

Assessing Weber's stand on the status of means-oriented rationality in modernity is not an easy task. Perhaps the only thing we can say with certainty is that for Weber a rationalized world is not a strictly technicized world. It cannot be because Weber interprets the guiding ethos of the rationalized world – the ethos of calculative rationality – in a sufficiently subtle way as to account for the input of non-technical (read: non-objective) forces, namely, those associated with the subjective determination of correctness.

Beyond this we must remember that, for Weber, non-technical forces also gain entry into and shape the technological order through the substantive value commitments of individual actors. Weber's contribution to the methodology of the social sciences illustrates well his understanding of the distinction between scientific understanding and value. Very briefly, Weber argued that all scientific analysis, and by that he meant all attempts to give an objective, rational account of some aspect of the world, are framed by the interests or values of the scientist doing the analysing. This means that the scientist brings to phenomena a particular value-orientation that determines what in 'infinite reality' is deemed worthy of being known.[12] The scientist thus confronts a world framed by his own interests. However, once so situated, the scientist, according to Weber, engages himself with the world in such a way as to produce results that are explanatory and not merely interpretive of that world.

For Weber the epistemological distinction between determining the end or value of an action, on the one hand, and determining the means to reach that end, on the other, applies not just to scientific analysis, but to any kind of purposive action. Thus, for instance, the writing of this essay, and my attempt in it to adhere to objective standards of rational discourse in an effort to make my overall argument intelligible – in short, writing as a purposive enterprise – is underpinned by a more fundamental belief in the value or worth of such an activity. The perceived value of such an exercise cannot, Weber argues, be determined rationally in the technical or scientific sense of the term. In other words, my understanding of modernity as garnered through the insights of Weber and Ellul does not suggest, in itself, why, or even if, it makes sense to spend time commenting on their insights rather than performing some other activity, like reading a novel or golfing, for example. And so, while persons have the power to articulate their commitments, and hence to reason substantively with respect to them, Weber claims that the source or motivation for one's actual adherence to a particular end is beyond rational explanation. We see, then, that for Weber reasoning and valuing are distinct and incommensurable operations. The business of calculating the means to action – the 'end' of technical reasoning – is superimposed upon a fundamentally unrelated operation that selects the end these means are to realize.

When Weber speaks of modernity in terms of an iron cage, he is expressing his concern over what he takes to be an imbalance of forces within the contemporary social order, an imbalance that sees ends all but subsumed under means. This means that in a disenchanted world the vast bulk of available resources is expended in an effort to amplify the powers of administrative control within the social order, as witnessed in the extension of technical control over nature, in the continued pursuit of economic prosperity, in refining the powers of social and political management, and so on. The cultural commitment to the project of mastery in turn presupposes an ever greater need for masters, for managers, technicians, and other types of functionaries. This development led Weber to conclude that modernity is characterized in part by a 'loss of freedom,' by the inability of growing numbers of persons to live and work in accordance with goals that transcend those embedded, implicitly, as is often the case, within the existing social structure. Weber seems to say that it is only to be expected that, in a world where means are fetishized, the capacity to set for oneself such goals is being lost.

Ellul takes Weber's account of the technological order a step further. As noted, Weber maintains that calculative reasoning and valuing are fundamentally incommensurable operations. It follows then that no matter how well entrenched the technological order becomes, there lies beneath its well-oiled surface the multiform and protean realm of ends, enfeebled, to be sure, but not beyond revitalization, in Weber's estimation. Importantly, Weber assumes that any prospect for the revitalization of the kingdom of ends must originate from within individual actors, since institutions are by definition functional machines given over to the means-ends mentality and thus not likely sources of newly emerging value. Implied in this line of reasoning is a belief in the ineradicability of human freedom, a belief that the thoughts and actions of individuals are not simply determined by the ethos that prevails within their social order. If Weber thought otherwise, the technological ethos informing the iron cage would ensure the perpetuation of the status quo, a prospect which, we have seen, Weber does not take to be a given. Weber, therefore, must pin his hopes for the future – indeed, for *a* future – on the acts of extraordinary individuals, on those persons whose vision transcends the limited horizon of the technological order.[13] As we will discuss later, Weber looks to politics to find such persons.

Ellul is able to radicalize Weber's portrayal of modernity precisely because he takes issue with Weber's general sociological orientation. Following Durkheim's lead, Ellul asserts that 'the sociological does not consist of the addition and subtraction of individual actions. I believe that there is a collective socio-logical reality, which is independent of the individual. As I see it, individual decisions are always made within the framework of this sociological reality, itself pre-existent and more or less determinative.'[14] By adopting this position, Ellul is able to argue that the proliferation of technique in modernity has not merely enervated the realm of ends, as Weber believed, but has in fact usurped it. Technique, in the process, becomes both a means and an end in itself. The technological order therefore is said to close in on itself and becomes a system, a technological system. A brief review of the main theoretical orientation of systems theory will help us understand how Ellul is able to arrive at this conclusion.

The systems approach to social and political analysis builds upon insights from the sciences of physics and biology, the most significant of these being the principle of entropy. This principle describes the propensity of natural processes to move from more ordered to less ordered forms of organization. Thus the natural world is said to 'run down' over time. An explanation of the phenome-non of life therefore necessarily entails an account of the manner in which entropy is arrested, or at least temporarily forestalled. In nature, the combatting of entropy is achieved by means of negative feedback. It is through feedback that an organism is able to adapt to environmental 'noise' (disorder) and hence maintain a homeostatic relationship with it. The maintenance of life, then, is dependent upon the continual flow of messages (information) between a given organism and its environment, and upon the organism's ability to adjust itself positively (negentropically) in response to any increase in the disorder of its environment. Systems theory ties the rationality of an organism to its capacity to adapt positively, in this way, to environmental noise. The more an organism can successfully maintain a homeostatic relationship with its environment, the more 'rational' it is said to be.[15]

The rationality of a system does not have to be set by the indeterminacy of nature's disquiet, however. The science known as cybernetics has as its end the making of the indeterminate more determinate. It does this by solving the problem of control and communication. The solution, it is argued, lies in attaining knowledge of the operation and interrelation of those mechanisms that enable an organism to sustain itself in its environment. The objective of the science of cybernetics is none other than to acquire knowledge of the means to facilitate the maximizing of a system's rationality. Such knowledge then will permit the creation of second-order systems that are more efficient, or rational, than those found in nature itself.

The appropriateness of systems analysis (or the science of cybernetics) as a tool for social understanding rests ultimately on whether or not the contemporary social order exhibits the properties of a system. Ellul certainly thinks it does, for the following reason. The contemporary social order is a system because, like any system, social or otherwise, it comprises an assemblage of parts that, when taken together, form a functional unit. As already noted, Ellul claims that all social orders exhibit a 'collective sociological reality' that transcends the individual. For Ellul, what lends the contemporary social order its distinct sociological reality is technique. Technique, in short, is the organizing principle of the modern social order, that which transforms an assemblage of practices into a coordinated sociological system.

To say that technique is modernity's organizing principle is to say that technique is its end or *telos*. We make the same connection when we equate, for example, the organizing principle of a baseball team – or that which makes the unit a team, in the true sense of the word – with the end of fair play or winning. But the association of technique with *telos* presents us with a difficulty. For technique, by Ellul's own account, is nothing more than 'means and the assemblage of means.'[16] Upon inspection, however, this difficulty reveals itself to be more apparent than real because the ensemble of rational methods and means that constitute technique has, over time, become much more than a mere gathering of methods and means. Ellul departs from the Weberian account of calculative rationality when he claims, borrowing from Engels, it appears, that the quantitative expansion of means-related technologies has reached a point where a qualitative transformation of the phenomenon has occurred, where technique becomes both a means and an end in itself.[17]

It must be remembered at this point that, because Ellul adheres to the view that 'the sociological' is a phenomenon that exists independent of the individual actor, he can conclude that technique, as modernity's prime sociological datum, is likewise an autonomous and determinative force. So if individual decisions are, in a general sense, 'made within the framework' of a sociological reality, as Ellul claims, then in the case of the contemporary social order, individual decisions are made within the framework of technique. Technique, therefore, is not for Ellul a value or end that one can, in Weberian fashion, choose or not choose to adopt, as one would a particular 'lifestyle,' for instance. Rather, technique comprises something akin to modernity's horizon, to the unquestioned thematic backdrop against which all decisions and choices are made. For this reason, technique for Ellul is much more difficult to dislodge than Weber had assumed.[18]

In order to understand more fully why calculative reasoning for Ellul has become an end in itself and determinative, and has not, as Weber intimates, remained at bottom a merely instrumental force, it is necessary that we explore a central aspect of Ellul's philosophical anthropology. Ellul concurs with Weber that the technological phenomenon has the effect, at the most fundamental level, of demythologizing or disenchanting the world. The invasion of technique, he says, 'desacralizes the world ... for technique nothing is sacred, there is no mystery, no taboo.'[19] He goes on to say that people living in this technicized world, who know very well that 'there is nothing spiritual anywhere,'[20] are at the same time psychically unprepared to live in the harsh light of this reality. Ellul asserts, then, that human beings are constituted in such a way as to require a sense of mystery. They need to sense the 'background'[21] that supports the rationally illuminated terrain of nature and self. A disenchanted world frustrates this need by continually illuminating that which, in Ellul's estimation, ought to remain submerged within the depths. Such frustration is bound to persist in a world where the mysterious is taken to be 'merely that which has not yet been technicized.'[22]

Ellul suggests that the tension between man's need for mystery and his inability to satisfy this need in a disenchanted world has been reconciled through the imputation of a sense of the sacred onto the source of demystification, that is, onto disenchanting science itself. In deference to Max Horkheimer and Theodor Adorno, we might add that as a consequence of 'the revenge of the sacred,' technique has taken on the characteristics of that which it has negated.

The Frankfurt School theorists had argued previously in support of the claim that a disenchanted nature avenges itself by seeing to it that its masters suffer a similar fate. As they put it: 'The subjective spirit which cancels the animation of nature can master a despiritualized nature only by imitating its rigidity and despiritualizing itself in turn.'[23] It seems that Ellul believes an alternative form of revenge may be in operation in our technological society. The 'will to mystery,' one might call it, is taken to be such an integral and abiding feature of the human psyche that, in a disenchanted, technological environment, it has no recourse but to mythologize the demythologizer, or technique itself. The end result, Ellul observes, is that technique now is regarded as 'a god which brings salvation.'[24] Technique has become a god in part, Ellul believes, because like every deity, it commands unwavering respect. We respect it for its proven success in providing the means to a commodious existence. We respect it for its promise of even greater freedom from restraint in the future. We even respect technique when the power it unleashes turns back on us, citing our mismanagement of this power as the true source of the problem. All of this proves, Ellul would say, that technique enchants us and holds us in its sway.

We can surmise that technology for Ellul has become a new god in part because Weber's wish to resuscitate an autonomous realm of ends failed to materialize. The growing imbalance between technological and valuative forces that concerned Weber in the early part of this century is no longer an issue for Ellul, since the scales in the latter half of the twentieth century now seemed to have tipped decidedly in favour of the technological. Thus the objective of the contemporary social critic is not, as it was for Weber, to warn us of the impending loss of substantive ends, but to announce the repercussions of that loss.

Weber, let us remember, was extremely sensitive to the modernizing process that saw ends steadily recede as society became increasingly fixated with its new powers of mastery. And, in his own way, he too realizes that the rationalization of the world has deprived human beings of the sense of mystery that seems to be a requirement of psychic health. Weber notes that this lack has been compensated for in modernity through the development of inner- and other-worldly forms of salvation from rationalization. The glorification of the repetitive routines of the everyday (*der Alltag*), the fetishization of 'quantitative bigness,' the growing fascination with eroticism, and the burgeoning of cults seeking 'deeper spirituality,' are just a few of means by which persons have escaped the straitjacket of reason.[25] Although understandable, these attempts at salvation miss the mark, according to Weber. They do so because they fail to address the problem at its root. For Weber, true salvation from modernity's iron cage can be had only by disrupting the hold that instrumental forces have on personal, social, and political practices. This in turn requires a keen sense of the distinction between the realms of means and ends.

Nowhere does Weber express the importance of keeping these two domains distinct as eloquently as in his essay 'Science as a Vocation.' Here he makes it abundantly clear that one of the central problems confronting our disenchanted world is that its inhabitants act as if the tension between means and ends were non-existent. Weber argues that most of us do so when we erroneously believe that modern science – the primary force behind the demagification of the world – is more than merely an instrumental power. We falsely assume that the extent of control science has afforded us is an indication of its capacity to be more than a mere instrument. We presume, in short, that science can tell us something about the meaning of the world in which we live.

This Weber vehemently denies. While science may help us in our bid to master all things by calculation, it cannot, he says, tell us whether 'it ultimately makes any sense to do so.'[26] Thus Weber wanted to impress upon us the problematic nature of science's worth. Granted, it may be 'of value' in that it assists us in our effort to master the world, but use-value is not to be confused with value in the deeper sense of the term. For instance, were Weber alive today, he most assuredly would acknowledge the fact that recent developments in the field of quantum mechanics have helped us understand better the nature of our physical world. However, what he would not assert is that this knowledge brings us any closer to understanding why the world operates as it does. Science, in other words, remains silent on questions of meaning. Weber eloquently summarizes his stand on this matter when he observed, in a now oft-quoted statement, that the 'fate of an epoch that has eaten of the tree of knowledge is that it must know that we cannot learn the *meaning* of the world from the results of its analysis, be it ever so perfect ...' (emphasis in original).[27]

This observation underscores Weber's belief that we have had to strike a Faustian bargain in return for our newfound powers. What we have gained in terms of knowledge of and power over the world, we have lost with respect to its meaning, to our ability to determine rationally its value. This state of affairs Weber stoically accepts. It is the consequence of the 'fate of our times,' as he puts it. Yet this predicament need not lead to despair, in Weber's opinion. What is truly frightening about the new world, in his view, is not its supposed meaninglessness, but its blissful neglect of the question of meaning as witnessed in a culture that tends to measure the value of an end in terms of the end's use-value.

IV

Because, as noted, Weber hypothesizes from within a radically different set of sociological presuppositions than does Ellul, he is in principle more predisposed than Ellul to believing that this cultural disposition can be counteracted. The question that now arises is: To where do we look for meaning in a disenchanted world? By acknowledging that scientific and technical understanding are not privy to matters of ultimate meaning, Weber believed he could clear the path for acts of authentic valuation within the social order. Ideally, if the realms of means and ends could be neatly distinguished in this way, then the means that science at present commands could be made to serve the ends articulated by those persons capable of doing so. Herein, it seems, lies for Weber the only hope for escape from the iron cage.

Given Weber's portrayal of the contemporary world as disenchanted, stripped of intrinsic value, he turns to politics as a principal means of reintroducing meaning to the world. If the world itself, he seems to say, no longer suggests the ends of human existence, then we must look to ourselves for such guidance. The introspection required for the task places it beyond the reach of the means-ends mentality of the bureaucrat, a mentality more properly suited to the business of administration than to politics in the true sense of the term. The bureaucrat, Weber observes, is a mere follower insofar as he executes 'the order of the superior authorities.' His ultimate superior is the political leader, who, unlike the bureaucrat, takes a stand and 'fights' for a cause. The true political leader, then, derives his authority from a passionate commitment to a vision of the political good, rather than by acting in conformity to a pre-existing set of rational rules and expectations.[28]

This means that the political leader is an artist of sorts. He must be able to articulate a vision of the end for politics, and, importantly, command the means needed to realize this vision. To this end, the supreme societal architect, the political leader, utilizes whatever means are available to fashion a world that accords with a valuative vision. In a configuration of this sort, there is a clearly defined hierarchical relationship between the realm of ends, or politics, and the realm of means, as technical modes of action. Here the administrative and technological 'machines' are put to work in the service of the ends of the state as articulated by the political leader. In the final analysis, Weber holds out hope against the irreversibility of the disenchantment process by arguing that the technological order and purposive rational forms of social organization are (as they always have been) value-neutral instruments and thus capable of being employed to realize subjectively held ends, the content of which is immune from the influence of the rationalization process itself.

Contrasting Weber's account of politics against Ellul's is illuminating, for the tension between their respective accounts reveals clearly why Ellul cannot share Weber's guarded optimism about the fate of modernity.

It has been argued here that the true source of Weber's optimism regarding the fate of the iron cage lies in his essentially epistemological conviction that knowing and valuing (or purposive and substantive rationality) are fundamentally distinct operations. Hence, no matter how extensive the kingdom of means becomes, it remains, from the perspective of the individual actor, merely an aggregation of instrumentalities. This is not to say that for Weber the expansion of the kingdom of means is unproblematical. Certainly, as noted, Weber is concerned that this development may lead many to wrongly assume that the ensemble of means is an end in itself. But since Weber takes the individual to be the prime sociological reality, he is not inclined to see the assemblage of calculative technologies in modernity as an autonomous force capable, upon crossing some critical threshold, of transforming itself into the social order's unquestioned *telos*. And because, as noted, the ensemble of means for Weber does not possess a distinct reality of its own, it cannot wield the power to determine the thoughts and actions of individuals. To be sure, the preponderance of purposive rational strategies and modes of action in the modern world conditions the lives of individuals within it. If such were not the case, then Weber would not have found the cage imagery a compelling metaphor for modernity in the first place. However, the fact that Weber looks upon the future as open-ended proves that the loss of freedom experienced by the inhabitants of the iron cage is neither total nor irrevocable. And it is to politics that Weber looks to retrieve a measure of freedom in the world because one can only assume that he saw in politics a power sufficiently extensive to contain and redirect the technological imperative.

Ellul, in contrast, sees in politics just another domain reorganized by technique. The commonly accepted, indeed, Weberian, understanding of the relationship between the 'expert' (or bureaucrat) and the politician (or leader) holds that the expert 'furnish[es] the politician with information and estimates on which he [the politician] can base a decision.'[29] This 'decisionistic' model of political rule, as Jürgen Habermas refers to it, maintains a clear distinction between the role of the value-neutral expert and that of his value-generating superior.[30] What Ellul claims is overlooked in such a relationship, and accounts for its weakness as a model for politics, is that the presentation of alternative plans for action to the politician is not a value-neutral act, at least not within a technological society. From the options presented, one plan will always stand out for selection, and for Ellul that is the plan which holds the most 'value,' the plan that promises to achieve the desired end most efficiently. The politician, therefore, is beholden to the expert not just for technical information on an array of potential means of actions, but for the decision as well, since the information itself reveals the 'one logical and admissible solution.'[31]

This is not the place to enter into a debate on which of the two opposing models of politics more accurately reflects actual political practices in a rationalized world. However, it is clear, from the above description, that Ellul is convinced that politicians are not leaders in the Weberian sense of the term in that they are not shielded from the technological ethos. Politicians, according to this view, are simply high-level managers of the technological system.

We are all, then, captives of the technological system, according to Ellul. The barbarism of reason is nowhere more in evidence than here, where genuine human freedom has been sacrificed on the altar of efficiency, with virtually no hope for its retrieval.[32] In such a world, human action is limited to the performance of those functions that support the system and its needs.[33] But in depicting human beings as mere keepers of the system in this way, Ellul is not implying that all freedom is lost. He does not deny, for example, the tremendous space for lateral movement within the system, a space so intoxicating in its possibilities that it gives the impression of boundlessness. But, of course, freedom of this sort remains constrained within the parameters of technique. Consequently, from the perspective of the system, such freedom is peripheral and serves only to underscore our role as the technology's caretaker.

Interestingly, for systems theorists, the conditional character of human freedom within the technological order indicates a highly rational organizational structure. The proliferation of technique in modernity has resulted in so thorough a mediation of the natural and social environments that its control over these realms is in principle fully established. The social order, therefore, is in possession of the means needed to sustain a homeostatic relationship with its environment: It is truly rational. If, however, the ambit of human freedom were expanded to include non-instrumental (read: inefficient) modes of action and social interaction, then the system's range of control would shrink correspondingly. Disorder would infiltrate the system, thereby reducing its capacity to adapt positively to changes within the environment. For this reason, genuine freedom of action is anathema to the system.

v

We began our investigation by addressing what is, upon reflection, a very curious state of affairs. We wanted to know how an individual who painted such a stark and apparently definitive picture of the modern age, an age whose roots extend back thousands of years, shunned the temptation to predict its likely course into the future. This avoidance, it seemed, required an explanation, for there are many signs in Weber's writing – not the least of which is the imagery of the iron cage – pointing to the conclusion that 'fate' appeared to be on the side of the status quo. Weber certainly did not discount outright such a possibility. As illustrated in the opening quotation, one of the futures he contemplates is the life of 'mechanized petrification,' one of Weber's clearest statements concerning the disenchanted world's potential for self-perpetuation. Yet we know Weber did not stop here. His 'antiprophetic prophecy,' as one commentator refers to it, pits competing futures against each other, leaving uncertainty over the future as the only certainty.[34] It has been argued here that Weber's reluctance to predict is not a reflection of some arbitrary personal preference, but flows out of his epistemological conviction that reasoning and valuing are distinct and incommensurable processes.

Ellul's advantage over Weber is that he lives, as it were, in Weber's 'future.' That is to say, Ellul lives during a time when, out of the indeterminate possibilities that constituted Weber's future, there crystallized a particular actuality. This actuality, Ellul doubtless would argue, proves that Weber seriously underestimated the momentum that the purposive rational instrumentalities of his day carried. In hindsight, we would have to agree.

This much is evident if we take stock of the tremendous growth in the number and reach of means-specific rationalities within society since the beginning of this century. Virtually every aspect of daily existence, be it in the public or private domain, has been transformed of late into an object of rational control and mastery, with the primary 'goal' being to maximize one's ability to reach an intended objective through the learning and application of relevant techniques or strategies. The ubiquity of the term 'skills' in popular culture illustrates well this collective fascination with transforming practices – or customary actions – into sciences. So, for example, we have convinced ourselves of the need to develop 'life skills,' 'learning skills,' and 'parenting skills' in order, one can only guess, to know how to live, learn, and be a good parent.

Other examples of 'means-speak' abound, some of the more prominent being the terms 'program,' 'management,' and 'processing.' Expressions of this sort reinforce what appears to be a general cultural consensus regarding the desirability of living a life that maximizes means. Hence it is no longer sufficient to exercise merely for its own sake, or eat for the love of good food, or play for no particular reason at all. Rather, we exercise, eat, and play knowing that if these activities are not performed in an appropriate manner, then their capacity to serve as means for other ends, such as good health, will remain unfulfilled.

Generally speaking, then, the trajectory of modern culture seems to be moving in the direction of an increased reliance on informational technologies for the express purpose of maximizing means. On the surface, this development appears to vindicate Ellul's claim that technique has taken over 'the whole of civilization.' It appears to vindicate as well his assertion that technique has become modernity's new god. For like God, technique is omnipresent; it reaches into and reworks every facet of social existence. And, like God, technique is omnipotent, in that reordered, rationalized social practices do make use of available means more efficiently than do non-rationalized social practices, often to staggering effect.

There are good reasons to believe, therefore, that the world has become re-enchanted in a specific sense. For the pervasiveness and effectiveness of purposive rationality and purposive rational modes of action have given us the power to create a (hyperreal?) world so rich in possibility and limitless in scope that this power has all but assumed an aura previously reserved for the religious. Certainly Ellul is not alone in making such a claim. The social critic Neil Postman argues precisely the same point in his *Technopoly*, wherein he defines technopoly as 'the deification of technology,' which itself occurs when 'the culture seeks its authorization in technology, finds its satisfaction in technology, and takes its orders from technology.'[35] Ellul himself could not have stated it any better.

Be that as it may, Ellul's assertion that technology has become the secular world's new god in no way conclusively supports his claim that our technological society is in fact a system. That the iron cage persists some seventy years after Weber's death does not prove in itself that new prophets might not still arise in the future, or that old ideals might not someday be reborn. It does not prove decisively that the ensemble of instrumentalities that constitutes the technological order has taken on a life independent of its creators, controlling them as Plato in the *Laws* hypothesized the gods controlled man. However, as stated, the abidingness of the iron cage does indicate that the forces of rationalization are more intractable than Weber assumed. And for this reason alone it is worth remembering that, for all its excesses, Ellul's account of the technological order is a serious attempt to come to terms with this stubborn fact.

NOTES

1 Max Weber, *The Protestant Ethic and the Spirit of Capitalism*, trans. Talcott Parsons (New York: Charles Scribner's Sons 1958), 182.

2 Ibid., 181.

3 Max Weber, 'Science as a Vocation,' in *From Max Weber: Essays in Sociology*, ed. Hans H. Gerth and C. Wright Mills (New York: Oxford University Press 1946), 139.

4 For an excellent analysis of Weber's multiformed notion of rationality, see Rogers Brubaker, *The Limits of Rationality* (London: George Allen & Unwin 1984), especially chaps. 1–3.

5 For a more detailed account of Weber's 'disenchantment thesis,' see Gilbert G. Germain, *A Discourse on Disenchantment: Reflections on Politics and Technology* (Albany, NY: State University of New York Press 1993), especially chap. 2.

6 Max Weber, 'Religious Rejections of the World and Their Directions,' in *From Max Weber*, note 3 above, 331–3.

7 Weber, *Protestant Ethic*, note 1 above, 182.

8 This dissolution of ends begins in earnest with René Descartes. See his remarks on 'practical philosophy' in 'Discourse on the Method of Rightly Conducting the Reason and Seeking Truth in the Field of Science,' in *Descartes: Philosophical Essays*, trans. L.J. Lafleur (New York: The Library of Liberal Arts 1985), part 6, 45.

9 Jacques Ellul, *The Technological Society*, trans. John Wilkinson (New York: Vintage 1964), 74.

10 Ibid., xxv.

11 Max Weber, *Gesammelte Aufsätze zur Wissenschaftslehre* (Tubingen: Mohr 1922), 408. See also Weber's 'The Meaning of "Ethical Neutrality," ' in *The Methodology of the Social Sciences*, ed. Edward A. Shils and Henry A. Finch (Glencoe, IL: The Free Press 1949), 34. There Weber makes the distinction between a subjectively rational action and a 'rationally "correct" action, that is, one which uses the objectively correct means in accord with scientific knowledge.' See also Rogers Brubaker, note 4 above, 53–60.

12 Weber, ' "Objectivity" in Social Science,' in *The Methodology of the Social Sciences*, note 11 above, 72.

13 Jürgen Habermas has much to say, and all of it negative, about Weber's inability to conceive of action other than in terms of the isolated individual. Weber, as he puts it, fails to take into account 'the mechanisms for coordinating action through which interpersonal relationships come about.' See Habermas, *The Theory of Communicative Action*, trans. Thomas McCarthy (Boston: Beacon Press 1981), vol. 1, 173–4.

14 Ellul, *Technological Society*, note 9 above, xxviii–xxix. See also H.T. Wilson's 'The Sociology of Apocalypse: Jacques Ellul's Reformation of Reformation Thought,' *The Human Context* 7 (Autumn 1975), 478.

15 Some of the more illuminating texts on cybernetics include: R.W. Ashby, *An Introduction to Cybernetics* (London: Chapman & Hall 1956); Edgar Morin 'Complexity,' *The International Journal of Social Sciences* 26, no. 4 (1976), 555–81; and Norbert Wiener, *The Human Use of Human Beings* (New York: Avon Books 1950).

16 Ellul, *Technological Society*, note 9 above, 19.

17 Jacques Ellul, *Perspectives on Our Age: Jacques Ellul Speaks on His Life and Work*, trans. Joachim Neugroschel, ed. William H. Vanderburg (Toronto: Canadian Broadcasting Corporation 1981), 50.

18 Martin Heidegger is the most influential exponent of the thesis claiming technology to be a thematizing phenomenon. See Martin Heidegger, *Question Concerning Technology and Other Essays*, trans. William Lovitt (New York: Harper & Row 1977).

19 Ellul, *Technological Society*, note 9 above, 142.

20 Ibid., 144.

21 Ibid., 142.

22 Ibid.

23 Max Horkheimer and Theodor Adorno, *Dialectic of Enlightenment*, trans. John Cumming (New York: Continuum 1988), 57. It is an important component of the revenge-of-nature thesis that man loses more than he gains in exchange for his powers of technical control. As the authors state, what man loses by denying nature in himself is a clear sense of the *telos* of the outward control of nature as well as the *telos* of his own life (p. 54).

24 Ellul, *Technological Society*, note 9 above, 144.

25 See Weber, 'Religious Rejections of the World and Their Directions,' in *From Max Weber*, note 3 above, 346–7; see also Weber, *Protestant Ethic*, note 1 above, 71.

26 Weber, 'Science as a Vocation,' note 3 above, 144. Elsewhere Weber states that 'the question of the appropriateness of the means for achieving a given end is undoubtedly accessible to scientific analysis.' That is all that is amenable to scientific scrutiny, however, according to Weber. Science therefore is a non-valuative instrument, a purely technical means for the attainment of some desired end. See Weber, ' "Objectivity" in Social Science,' note 12 above, 52.

27 Weber, ' "Objectivity" in Social Science,' note 12 above, 57.

28 Weber, 'Politics as a Vocation,' in *From Max Weber*, note 3 above, 78–96.

29  Ellul, *Technological Society*, note 9 above, 258.
30  Jürgen Habermas, *Toward a Rational Society: Student Protest, Science, and Politics*, trans. Jeremy J. Shapiro (Boston: Beacon Press 1970), 63.
31  Ellul, *Technological Society*, note 9 above, 259.
32  I wish to note that my interest in Ellul is limited in this essay to his phenomenological analysis of technique. Excluded from consideration is Ellul's substantive response to the challenge of technique. Although I have argued here that Ellul presents us with a picture of modernity far bleaker than Weber's, this is not to say that Ellul believes all is necessarily lost. It does mean, however, that because our technological society is a system, one must transcend the system in order to find a vantage place from which to launch an assault against it. As some readers are perhaps aware, Ellul looks to 'Christian action' to destroy what he refers to as the 'deified religious character' of technology. See *Perspectives on Our Age*, note 17 above, chap. 4.
33  Ellul, *Technological Society*, note 9 above, xiii.
34  Lawrence A. Scaff, *Fleeing the Iron Cage: Culture, Politics, and Modernity in the Thought of Max Weber* (Berkeley: University of California Press 1989), 230. See also chapter 7 of Scaff's monograph for a well-reasoned commentary on Weber's notion of disenchantment.
35  Neil Postman, *Technopoly: The Surrender of Culture to Technology* (New York: Vintage Books 1993), 71. See also in this regard Albert Borgmann, *Crossing the Postmodern Divide* (Chicago: The University of Chicago Press 1992), especially chap. 4.

# 12

# Max Weber and Post-Positivist Social Theory

## SUSAN HEKMAN

### I. INTRODUCTION

In *Truth and Method* (1975) Gadamer claims that understanding always involves a fusion of horizons: the horizon of the interpreter and the horizon of the text. What this means is that we necessarily understand the work of an author, particularly one removed from us in time, in terms of the questions and concerns of the present. It follows that the interpretation of any thinker will change over time as the problems of his or her interpreters change. This insight is an important preface to a contemporary examination of Weber's social theory and, particularly, his philosophy of social science. The work of Weber, like that of any prominent social theorist, has been subject to interpretations that have varied with the changing trends of social theory. The theme that has dominated social theory in the past several decades has been the critique of positivism, and, thus, it has been the anti-positivist approach that has likewise dominated interpretations of Weber's work. These anti-positivist interpretations of Weber have been generally quite favourable; most have identified him as an ally in their cause. Weber's approach, they claim, embodies many of the themes that have dominated the anti-positivist approach, for example, a distinctive method for the social sciences, an emphasis on the social actor's meaning, and a focus on the interpretation of social reality. Thus Weber has been identified, if not as anti-positivist himself, at least as a precursor of this position.

It is not my intention to claim that there is anything erroneous in this analysis. If Gadamer is correct, we have no choice but to interpret Weber from the perspective of our own theoretical concerns. Thus when the phenomenologists, ethnomethodologists, and ordinary language analysts see a precursor in Weber they are not 'misinterpreting' him; they are simply interpreting his work from the perspective of their horizon. The anti-positivist interpretation of Weber, however, although it has been very influential, is not the only horizon from which his work can be assessed. In the last decade an approach that differs significantly from the anti-positivist schools has been introduced into social theory. Variously termed post-modernism, post-structuralism, or anti-foundationalism, it is an approach that profoundly alters the themes and concerns of social theory. While the anti-positivist critics that preceded the post-moderns were primarily concerned to attack the positivist legacy, their aim was to find a place for the social sciences within the modern episteme, not to challenge the episteme itself. The post-modern approach, however, is much more radical. Post-moderns attack not just the positivist legacy but the Enlightenment project out of which it evolved; they question the very root of the epistemological basis of the modern episteme. Instead of attempting to fit the social sciences into a redefined version of positivist science, the post-moderns, particularly Foucault, argue for the transcendence of the modern episteme altogether. This thesis has a particular relevance for the social sciences. In *The Order of Things* (1971) Foucault argues that, because the modern episteme excludes the social sciences, they must and are reconstructing themselves on a different epistemological plane.

A post-modern reading of Weber produces very different results from that of the anti-positivist readings of his work. While the anti-positivists found an ally in Weber, a thinker who brilliantly restructured the positivist program and revealed its errors with regard to the social sciences, post-modern thinkers see a quite different picture. They see Weber as a theorist who is making a heroic but ultimately doomed effort to restructure the modern episteme to fit the unique needs of the social sciences. Thus post-moderns see Weber as one of the best illustrations of Foucault's point with regard to the social sciences. Weber, like Foucault, perceived that the positivist definition of science excludes the social sciences. But, unlike Foucault, he chose to remain within the epistemological boundaries of the positivist conception of science. His solution to the exclusion of the social sciences was to redefine the positivist program so that it could include these anomolous disciplines. Following the positivists Weber adheres to two of the key dichotomies of the modern episteme: subject/object and fact/value. His adherence to these two dichotomies structures his philosophy of social science as well as his ethics. Finally, a post-modern reading of Weber sees him as a thinker who is directly influenced by Nietzsche, the philosopher who is widely acknowledged to be the father of post-modernism. Like Nietzsche, Weber can be seen as representing the last gasp of the modern episteme and, hence, pointing the way out of it.

What I propose to do in the following is to look at Weber's philosophy of social science from a post-modern perspective. Weber's attempt to redefine the positivist program while remaining within its epistemological space is strikingly evident in his theories of the ideal type, objectivity, and causality. A post-modern critique of these theories provides a different assessment of Weber's program than that provided by previous anti-positivist analyses. It also reveals the connection between Weber's theory of science and his ethics. Because of Weber's adherence to the central dichotomies of Enlightenment thought he has no option but to accept the 'iron cage' of which he writes.

## II. SCIENTIFIC METHOD

Foucault's argument that the modern episteme excludes the human sciences is based on his analysis of the role of 'man' in these sciences. Because 'man' is both subject and object in the human sciences these sciences cannot conform to the positivist/Enlightenment model that was prescribed for all scientific analysis. Foucault claims that no amount of redefinition can succeed in fitting the human sciences into this model, and the many attempts to do so have not been successful. Instead, Foucault looks to those sciences that study human beings without reference to 'man,' sciences that occupy a different epistemological plane. From Foucault's perspective Weber's philosophy of social science represents one of the most comprehensive, although unsuccessful, attempts to do the impossible: create a scientific social science on the positivist model. Because of the difficulties of his task Weber is forced to redefine key terms such as objectivity and causality and, in effect, significantly restructure scientific method. That Weber is undaunted by the magnitude of his task is a tribute to his genius. And, in a limited sense, he is successful. He formulates an anti-positivist approach to the social sciences that explodes some of the positivist myths about social science. His failure lies in the fact that he does not reveal the underlying epistemological flaws of the positivist approach.

## A. The Ideal Type

One of the principal tools that Weber employed to establish the scientific validity of the social sciences was the ideal type. In his definition of the ideal type Weber set out to accomplish two objectives: first, he wanted to establish that the social sciences possessed a conceptual tool that was both uniquely suited to the demands of these disciplines and unquestionably scientific; second, he wanted to establish that although subjective elements are an unavoidable part of the formulation of ideal types, the objective status of these concepts is not in any way diminished by this fact. That Weber's discussion of the ideal type is dense, complicated, and almost tortured is in itself instructive. Given the definition of 'science' to which Weber felt compelled to conform, his task was a formidable one. His central problem was the justification of the presence of subjective elements in a concept that claimed to be objective when, by definition, the objective is that which is free from subjectivity.

The post-modern solution to the dilemma of the subjective/objective as it is encountered in the human sciences is to reject the dichotomy altogether. Post-moderns claim that all knowledge, not just knowledge in the social sciences, is hermeneutic, that is, that it is constituted by the presuppositions (prejudices) that form the basis of all thought. Thus the discovery that knowledge in the social sciences has a 'hermeneutic' element does not detract from its status as knowledge. This move, however, is not an option for Weber. Instead he diligently works to recast the boundaries of the scientific to include his notion of the ideal type. He begins by claiming that the ideal type is neither an individual nor a general concept. In making this statement he is fighting a battle on two fronts. First, he is rejecting the position that the aim of historical research is the reproduction of historical reality. Against this Weber argues that all conceptualization involves abstraction and synthesis. Thus a reproduction of historical reality is neither possible nor desirable. Second, he is arguing against the positivists that the purpose of all scientific investigation must be the formation of general laws. The social sciences, he claims, are concerned with the study of concrete social reality. Since reality cannot be deduced from laws, the formation of general laws cannot be the aim of the social sciences (1949c: 72, 94; 1975: 190; Hekman 1983: 22).

Weber's definition of the ideal type begins with his assertion that the selection of these concepts always involves two steps that are necessarily evaluative. First, the subject matter of the social sciences, social action, is identified by the meaning bestowal of the social actors. It follows that the objects of research in the social sciences are inherently evaluative. Second, the social scientist must select a particular subset of this subject matter for investigation. This choice is unavoidably value-laden; the interest of the social scientist dictates a choice that is subjective in origin. The third step in the process of creating an ideal type, however, is purely logical. The social scientist next selects these subjectively defined elements of social reality and synthesizes them into a conceptual tool: the ideal type. But even in effecting this synthesis the task of the social scientist differs from that of the natural scientist. The synthesis that creates the ideal type rests on the logical compatibility of the elements, not, as in the natural sciences, on their commonality. The concept that results from this process, Weber claims, is the unique tool of the social scientist, objective yet subjectively rooted (1978a: 4; 1949c: 84; Hekman 1983: 29, 60).

Weber's argument for the objectivity of the ideal type entails a significant redefinition of the concept of objectivity as it was formulated by the positivists. In defining the ideal type as an 'objective' concept Weber is challenging the positivist definition of objectivity as totally divorced from the subjective. What is significant about Weber's definition from a post-modern perspective, however, is that he does not challenge the dichotomy itself; he seeks only to redefine it for the purposes of the social sciences. It is also significant that Weber's defence of his concept is consistent with another central aspect of the positivist credo: rigid separation of value judgments and scientific method. Weber is vehement in his claim that although ideal types incorporate subjective elements they do not involve value *judgments*. Ideal types treat the inherently evaluative objects of social-science research as objects; their normative validity is of no concern to the social scientific investigator. Thus although they are constituted subjectively they can be treated objectively because their subjective validity is not relevant to the investigation (1949b: 39–43; 1949c: 60, 98). This argument reveals Weber's strict adherence to the positivist dictum that statements of fact and judgments of value are in radically different spheres and that judgments of value cannot be subject to rational analysis. The sphere of rationality, for both Weber and the positivists, is limited to the realm of facts. Weber's adherence to this dichotomy has a profound effect on both his social-science methodology and his ethics.

In post-modern terminology what Weber is doing with his concept of the ideal type is deconstructing one side of the fundamental subject/object dichotomy. He argues that the *object* of investigation in the social sciences has been erroneously conceived by the positivists and must be redefined. But he neglects to examine the subject side of the dichotomy: the constituting subject. As a consequence his deconstruction is incomplete and the dichotomy itself remains intact. Weber, like the positivists, defines knowledge as the opposition between subject and object. Although he subjects the objects of social scientific research to scrutiny, the knowing subject is still a 'given.' Weber's partial deconstruction of this dichotomy is not completed until the work of Foucault and other post-modern writers. Foucault deconstructs the subject side of the dichotomy by arguing that discourses create subjects as well as objects. His argument not only undercuts the dichotomy itself but, unlike Weber's conception, challenges the positivist/Enlightenment conception of knowledge at its roots.

In defining the ideal type Weber wants to carve out a special place for the social sciences within the definition of 'science' dictated by the modern episteme. His defence of the scientific status of the ideal type is both involved and impassioned. But even in his defence of the scientificity of the ideal type Weber implicitly concedes the inferiority of the scientific status of the social sciences. Another tenet of the positivist definition of science was the superiority of the natural sciences over the social sciences. Despite his defence of the social sciences Weber is willing to accept this tenet of positivist science as well. In the course of his discussion of the ideal type Weber asks whether these concepts indicate the 'adolescence' of the social sciences. He concedes that, to a certain extent, this is the case. Although he denies that the search for general laws is appropriate to the social sciences he is nevertheless conceding here that the natural sciences' search for general laws indicates their superiority to the social sciences. In an argument that sounds somewhat apologetic he declares that 'eternal youth' may be granted to the historical disciplines (1949c: 104). Although the social sciences may be adolescents, this state is one that suits the different tasks that they must perform. Thus without challenging their inferiority vis-à-vis the natural sciences, Weber defines this status as appropriate and legitimate.

## B.   *Objectivity*

Weber's definition of the ideal type is central to his attempt to take on the more comprehensive question of the objectivity of the social sciences. The connection between the two issues is clear in Weber's statement: 'Whoever accepts the proposition that the knowledge of historical reality can and should be a "presuppositionless" copy of "objective" facts will deny the value of the ideal type' (1949c: 92). As in his discussion of the ideal type, Weber's discussion of objectivity represents his attempt to fight a war on two fronts. In the course of his discussion he rejects the claims of both the positivists and the subjectivists that the facts of the social sciences are presuppositionless. The positivists claimed that reality, even social reality, can be deduced from presuppositionless general laws; the subjectivists claimed that immediate experience is 'objective' and 'given.' Against both of these positions Weber developed a concept of objectivity that rests on presuppositions and yet, he claims, is 'objective' and 'scientific' (Hekman 1983: 155).

Weber's argument against the positivists' assertion that social science must seek universal laws is particularly vehement. In this historical sciences, he claims, general laws are devoid of content. It follows that 'an "objective" analysis of cultural events which proceeds according to the thesis that the ideal of science is the reduction of empirical reality to "laws" is meaningless' (1949c: 80). The reason for this, Weber insists, is not that reality is less governed by laws than is the natural world, but, rather, that knowledge of social laws is not equivalent to knowledge of social reality. Weber's argument against the subjectivists, although not as extensive, is equally clear. In his discussion of the ideal type he established that all empirical knowledge is tied to concept formation. It follows that the social sciences cannot rest their knowledge on the self-evidence of inner experience or, for that matter, any other sense of givenness. To equate inner experience with unique empirical certainty, he asserts, is a fundamental error (1975: 185).[1]

Having disposed of his two opponents, Weber is now free to formulate his own conception of the objectivity of the social sciences. Two themes dominate his discussion: the presuppositions of all social inquiry and the role of value judgments. The clearest statement of his position is found in the 'Objectivity' article: 'The "objectivity" of the social sciences depends rather on the fact that the empirical data are always related to those evaluative ideas which alone make them worth knowing and the significance of the empirical data is derived from these evaluative ideas' (1949c: 111). Weber spends a good deal of time discussing what he means by these 'evaluative ideas.' Culture, Weber claims, is a finite segment of the infinite flux of reality; it *becomes* culture for us because we bestow it with meaning and significance. This is the 'transcendental presupposition' of every cultural science; we can have no meaningful knowledge of cultural reality without it (1949c: 81). This inherently subjective selection process that constitutes culture brings order out of the chaos of the infinity of reality (1949c: 78). The point of Weber's discussion of the role of significance in creating the subject matter of the social sciences, however, is not to argue for the subjectivity of these disciplines. On the contrary, he argues that 'it obviously does not follow from this that research in the cultural sciences can only have results that are "subjective" in the sense of *valid* for one person and not for others' (1949c: 84). The significance that creates culture, thus, is not subjective in a solipsistic sense. Rather it is an intersubjective significance that is shared by the members of the culture.

Weber's second theme is one that also dominated his discussion of ideal types: the assertion that evaluative elements can be analysed objectively if value *judgments* are excluded. Weber discusses this issue in the context of whether university professors should introduce value judgments into their teachings. Weber's answer to this question is complex. He begins by asserting that the question itself involves a value judgment and thus cannot be discussed scientifically. He asserts, however, that the question of the freedom of science from value judgments, that is, practical evaluations of the satisfactory or unsatisfactory character of phenomena, has nothing to do with the question of whether they should be used in teaching (1949b: 1). Making a value judgment himself, Weber declares that it is a moral duty of the teacher to distinguish between facts and values even though it is a difficult distinction to make. One of the teacher's primary tasks, he asserts, is to help students make this distinction for themselves (1949b: 2–9).

The theme of Weber's discussion is his often repeated dictum that a science of ethics is impossible (1949b: 13). Following the positivists, Weber asserts that science and ethics are in two distinct spheres. He declares that science can aid in the discussion of value judgments by assessing their internal consistency and analysing their practical implications. He nevertheless maintains that the gap from the 'is' to the 'ought' is unbridgeable (1949b: 14–21; 1975: 117). Objectivity does not involve a compromise among value positions (1949b: 10) nor detachment from the subject matter (Oakes 1977: 8). Rather, it involves the exclusion of subjective, practical evaluations from the analysis of social reality, a reality that, as he has already established, is based on evaluation. What makes such an analysis objective, Weber claims, is rigid adherence to the scientific method, a subject about which he has much to say. Weber's point here is most forcefully established in his well-known discussion of the 'Chinese' in the 'Objectivity' article (1949c: 58–9). Even 'a Chinese,' he asserts, must acknowledge the correctness of a systematically correct proof in the social sciences. This agreement must extend even to the logical analysis of an ideal, the logical consistency of its value axioms and the consequences arising from its implementation. His central claim is that adherence to the scientific method will assure this objectivity even when the data analysed are evaluative.

In this discussion Weber succeeds in 'saving' objectivity from the positivists who wanted to strip it of all evaluative connections and the subjectivists who wanted to strip it of all scientific connections. Weber's argument is that both of his opponents are partially right and partially wrong. The subjectivists are right that the objects of social scientific research differ from those of the natural sciences because they are evaluative. But Weber argues that these value-laden objects are not 'subjective' in a solipsistic sense; they are, rather, intersubjectively valid. Furthermore, the use of these evaluative elements does not involve value judgments, a realm that Weber continues to exclude from the purview of science. The positivists are right in their assertion that all scientific analysis involves abstraction and generalization, but wrong in their assertion that the presence of any evaluative element entails subjectivity. Although Weber accepts the positivists' concept of scientific method, he argues against them that the logical analysis of even a value judgment can be 'objective.'

Weber's success in saving objectivity, however, is achieved at great cost. Weber wants to preserve the purity of science by placing it in an intersubjectively valid realm constituted by scientific method. Furthermore, he wants to make sure that this realm includes the social sciences. But one of the results of his success in establishing this is that he relegates the ethical realm to solipsism. Since it is the ethical that, in a sense, fuels the scientific, gives it motive and purpose, that creates what Weber defines as a dangerous situation. Weber's rigid separation of facts and values, a separation that he accepts, with modifications, from the positivists, creates the disenchanted world, the iron cage, that he will, in other contexts, define as perhaps the greatest danger of the modern world. That Weber is aware of the danger is evident. That he cannot escape it from within the modern episteme is also evident.

It should be noted that Weber's characterization of the plurality of ethical positions as 'dangerous' is a characterization that is a product of his continuing adherence to Enlightenment epistemology. The Enlightenment claimed that ethics is an objective science, that the light of reason could establish rationally correct ethical principles. Weber rejects this claim, but implicitly acknowledges its validity by defining the lack of ethical objectivity as a lamentable, even 'dangerous' situation. The post-moderns, in contrast, accept ethical plurality as a necessary component of the post-modern condition. It is not to be lamented but, on the contrary, embraced.

## C.  Causality

The clearest example of Weber's vision of the ideal of social-science inquiry is found in his discussion of causality. In this discussion the themes of the scientific, the evaluative, and the objective are played out in contexts that are, for Weber at least, relatively clear. That causality is central to Weber's conception of both science and the science of sociology is evidence from his initial definition of sociology in *Economy and Society*: 'Sociology ... is a science concerning itself with the interpretive understanding of social action and thereby with a causal explanation of its course and consequence' (1978a: 4). In his analysis of how causal analysis would be effected in the social sciences Weber is, once again, attempting to carve a middle ground between the positivists and the subjectivists (intuitionists). The positivists wanted to deny the differences between causal analysis in the natural and social sciences and, even worse, claim that causal laws must be the purpose of social-science analysis. The subjectivists or intuitionists wanted to deny the use of causal analysis in the social sciences altogether because it involves abstraction and generalization (Hekman 1979: 67–9). Once more, Weber agrees and disagrees with elements of both of these positions.

Weber dismisses the arguments of the intuitionists quite easily. Attacking the work of both Gottl and Croce, Weber argues that the certainty of immediate experience does not provide the objectivity that the social sciences must seek. He argues that any interpretation of experience, even by the person experiencing it, involves abstraction and generalization; even our own experience must become a conceptual object for us when we reflect on it. On these grounds he rejects the argument that causal analysis is inappropriate in the social sciences as ill-founded (1975: 162–82). The abstraction and generalization that is a necessary part of causal analysis is also a necessary part of reflection on immediate experience.

Weber's argument against the positivists is much more complex. Although he agrees with them that causal analysis is a necessary part of social scientific analysis, he wants to maintain that the form of causal analysis in the social sciences is unique. His central claim is that its uniqueness rests on the role of meaningful interpretation in the social sciences. The fact that the goal of the social sciences is to interpret the meaning of social reality entails that causal analysis is always a means rather than an end in these disciplines. In order to establish these themes, however, Weber is forced to define the precise nature of causal analysis in the social sciences and, even more ambitiously, to redefine the distinction between the natural and the social sciences.

The centrepiece of Weber's definition of causal analysis in the social sciences is an argument about calculability. In an innovative move that is the reverse of his opponents' position Weber argues that human events are actually *more* calculable than events in the natural world. This is the case, he claims, because of the teleological nature of human action. If we know the purpose of someone's action, particularly someone we know, then we can usually predict quite accurately what he or she will do. Such predictions, quite obviously, are impossible in the natural world. Another way of putting this is that rational action is predictable whereas irrational events are not (1975: 193). It follows that '[t]he "calculability" of "natural processes" in the domain of "weather forecasting," for example, is far from being as "certain" as the "calculation" of the conduct of a person with whom we are acquainted' (1975: 121).

This unorthodox reversal of his opponents' position is followed by a careful discussion of both the differences and similarities between causal analysis in the natural and social sciences. The most significant similarity between the two forms of causal analysis is the fact that both employ abstraction and generalization. Weber introduces the notion of 'objective possibility' to describe the process by which causal analysis occurs in a social-science investigation. To establish the causal significance of a historical fact the investigator asks whether the exclusion of this fact would alter the event in any way that is important for our interest (1949a: 176–80). Weber defends this abstraction from the 'real' events by arguing that in order to understand real causal relationships we have to construct unreal ones (1949a: 185). The similarity between the two branches of science, he claims, even extends to an investigation in which the subject is motivation: 'A historical "interpretive" meaning into motives is *causal* explanation in absolutely the same logical sense as the causal interpretation of any concrete natural process. This is because its goal is the discovery of a "*sufficient*" ground (at least as an hypothesis)' (1975: 194)[2]

The differences between the two branches of science with regard to causal analysis, however, are also important for Weber's analysis. The key to these differences is the fact that all causal analysis in the social sciences is guided by *interest*. This fact has several important consequences. First it means that the social scientist is not interested in finding causal laws, but in linking concrete events with concrete causes (1949a: 168). Weber also notes that establishing causal necessity through causal laws is, in any case, the exception rather than the rule, even in the natural sciences (1975: 124, 197). His point here, as in much of his work, is to assuage the inferiority complex of the social sciences by insisting on the validity of their scientific investigations. A second consequence is the fact that, in the social sciences, theory is always involved in the creation of the 'fact' (1949a: 173). It is only because of our historical interest that we are able to select certain facts and subject them to historical analysis (1949a: 169). While insisting that this process of selection is *not* intuition he also claims that intuition guides the significant advances of the natural sciences (1949a: 175–6). Weber offers this summary of his position: 'The question of the special role of the "interpretively" understandable in "history" therefore concerns differences in (1) our causal *interest* and (2) the quality of "self-evidence" pursued in the investigation of concrete causal relations. However, it does *not* concern differences in the concept of causality, the significance of concept formation, or the kind of conceptual apparatus employed' (1975: 186).

The theme of this discussion has a familiar ring. Although Weber insists that the evaluative interest of the investigator is the presupposition of causal analysis, he is once more insistent that value judgments play no role in this analysis. Causal analysis, he insists, cannot provide value judgments (1949a: 123): 'There is simply no bridge which can span the gap from the *exclusively* "empirical" analysis of given reality within the tools of causal explanation to the confirmation or reification of the "validity" of *any* value-judgment' (1975: 117).

It is difficult to find a clearer statement of Weber's adherence to the positivist is/ought dichotomy. What he wants to argue in this context is that the determination of cause is objective even if the interest that motivates the investigation is subjective (1949a: 159). Once more Weber is both agreeing and disagreeing with the positivist position. While rejecting the notion that the facts speak for themselves, and, hence, that causal relations can be grasped without an interest orientation, he wants to retain the fact/value dichotomy to the extent that he claims 'objective' status for the distinctive brand of causal analysis in the social sciences.

## D. Logic and Scientific Method

Weber's attempt to redefine yet remain within the parameters of the positivist/Enlightenment conception of science has, as the above amply demonstrates, forced him into a series of tortuously complicated arguments. Weber was well aware of the difficulty of his arguments and repeatedly apologized for them, defending them only on the grounds of their necessity. The goal of all of these arguments is the same: to establish that the social sciences are unique because of their interest in meaning and significance but that this fact does not relegate them to the realm of subjectivity. Rather, within the parameters established by their subjective presuppositions, the social sciences must and can strive for verifiability through objective, causal analysis (Hekman 1983: 19).

Weber's discussions of the ideal type, objectivity, and causality did not, however, satisfy his demanding sense of the complexity of the problem with which he dealt. Two aspects of that problem still remained to be solved. First, Weber's reflections on causality demanded a new conception of the distinction between the natural and the social sciences. Second, he felt compelled to explore the presuppositions that guide *all* scientific investigations, not just those of the social sciences. He deals with the first problem most extensively in the *Critique of Stammler* (1977). In the course of criticizing Stammler's conception of the difference between the natural and the social sciences Weber argues that the commonly accepted distinction between the two branches of science is ill-conceived. It was Stammler's argument that the natural and the social sciences differ because the objects investigated are different (1977: 95). Stammler also argued that the use of logical analysis separates the natural and the social sciences: investigating empirical reality using abstractions and logical analysis is distinctive of the natural sciences (1977: 96). In a long excursus on these theses Weber shows the absurdity of both of these distinctions and offers an alternative account.

In his argument against Stammler and in other contexts Weber suggests two criteria of distinction between the sciences. First, sciences can be distinguished by those that seek to formulate causal laws and those that investigate individual causal relations (1975: 64–9). This entails the claim that it is method rather than subject matter that distinguishes the two branches of science. His second criterion is the role of subjective interest. The socio-cultural sciences are predicated on the subjective interest of the social-science investigator, an interest that is lacking in the natural sciences (1949a: 160). This subjective interest dictates that all analysis in the socio-cultural sciences is guided by the desire to interpret the meaning and significance of social reality. These factors, Weber claims, define distinctive spheres for the two branches of science. But once more he is careful to argue that although the objects of the social sciences are selected through subjective presuppositions these objects can and must be treated objectively, that is, according to the rules of logic and method that govern both branches of science. But once more he is careful to argue that although the objects of the social sciences are selected through subjective presuppositions these objects can and must be treated objectively, that is, according to the rules of logic and method that govern both branches of science. To establish his point he uses the example of the analysis of the norms that form the basis for legal codes. Although our interest dictates our concern with these norms and the norms themselves are value axioms, they can nevertheless be treated 'objectively' (1977: 122–31).

In another context Weber summarizes his point in a statement that has Foucaultian overtones: 'It is not the "actual" interconnections of "things" but the *conceptual* interconnections of *problems* that define the scope of the various sciences. A new "science" emerges where new problems are pursued by new methods and truths are thereby discovered which open up significant new points of view' (1949c: 68). Although this may sound like an early statement of the discourse theory of truth, such is not, of course, Weber's intent. Weber is interested in challenging the positivists' conception of the division between the natural and social sciences, a division that relegated the social sciences to the realm of subjectivity. Although his second method of distinguishing the two branches does not result in a new division, his first method does not coincide with the accepted division. By Weber's definition 'sciences of concrete reality' included meterology as well as sociology. Although Weber is not satisfied with the positivists' distinction between the two branches of science he is, once more, inclined to redefinition rather than rejection. If, as he asserts, new sciences create new truth, he would nevertheless argue that the truth of a unitary scientific method united these endeavours.

This conclusion informs his treatment of the second issue, the presuppositions that structure the activity of all science, not just that of the social sciences. Here Weber is venturing into dangerous territory. It is one of the fundamental tenets of positivist/Enlightenment thought that scientific knowledge, particularly in the natural sciences, is objective and presuppositionless, free of any taint of subjectivity. Weber challenges this tenet, but he does so in a manner much less radical than that of the post-moderns. His first point is that in order to accept the validity of scientific knowledge one must first accept that such knowledge is valuable. All scientific knowledge, he claims, is anchored in the validity of empirical analysis, a value that cannot itself be established scientifically. Thus from an empirical point of view the value of pure science is problematic; it has the status of a transcendent truth (1975: 114–16). He states 'The *objective* validity of all empirical knowledge rests exclusively upon the ordering of given reality according to categories which are *subjective* in a specific sense, namely, in that they present the *presuppositions* of our knowledge and are based on the presuppositions of the *value* of those *truths* which empirical knowledge alone is able to give us' (1949c: 110).

This seems to be a significant challenge to the positivists' claim of presuppositionlessness. Weber is claiming that a value judgment, the desire to know empirical truth, is the transcendental presupposition of all science. But Weber qualifies his position at the end of this passage, a qualification he specifies in a subsequent passage. Scientific truth, he claims, is unique in its ability to establish truth. Although one could reject the value of scientific truth, if one seeks 'truth' at all, one is forced to employ the scientific method. 'Scientific truth is precisely what is *valid* for all who *seek* truth' (1949c: 84). He concludes: 'Those for whom scientific truth is of no value will seek in vain for some other truth to take the place of science in just those aspects in which it is unique, namely, in the provision of concepts and judgments which are neither empirical reality nor reproductions of it but which facilitate its analytic ordering in a valid manner' (1949c: 110–11).

Weber's argument here is, by post-modern standards, a weak one. He has relativized not the universal truth of scientific method but only the desire to discover empirical truth at all. The post-modern position that each discourse generates its own criteria of truth would have been anathema to Weber. In further discussions of this point, however, he discusses another presupposition of scientific analysis that constitutes a further challenge to the positivist conception. All science, he asserts, must presuppose the validity of the rules of logic and method. He claims that these rules are the 'general foundation of our orientation in the world' and, thus, the least problematic area of science. But he also claims that they cannot be scientifically established (1958: 143); they thus constitute another transcendental truth of scientific analysis. It follows that 'no science is absolutely free of presuppositions and no science can prove its fundamental value to the man who rejects these presuppositions' (1958: 153). It is important to emphasize here, however, that the point of Weber's discussion of the presuppositions of all scientific inquiry is not to relativize such inquiry. Rather it is to attempt to put the natural and social sciences on a more equal footing. His central thesis is that the rules of logic and method form the basis of the social as well as the natural sciences. The method of both branches of science involves a process of concept formation that entails abstraction and logical analysis. As a result the scientific findings in both branches of science are equally valid (1975: 185).

In the 'Objectivity' article Weber states: 'For even the knowledge of the most certain propositions of our theoretical sciences – e.g. the exact natural sciences or mathematics, is, like the cultivation and refinement of the conscience, a product of culture' (1949c: 55). This statement has a distinctly post-modern ring to it. It flies in the face of Enlightenment's claim of knowledge free from the subjectivity of culture. But unlike the post-moderns, Weber does not directly challenge the Enlightenment view of the transcendence of scientific rationalism. He claims that we must presuppose the value of this truth but nonetheless claims that any seeker of truth, presumably all rational human beings who want to understand their world, *must* employ this method. This effectively returns scientific rationalism to its universal status. Although he noted that we must also presuppose the rules of logic and method, he does not seem to take this qualifier very seriously. His discussion of the 'Chinese' in the 'Objectivity' article substantiates this interpretation. His comment that 'even a Chinese' must accept the logic of a scientific proof seems to imply that the Chinese, like us, must presuppose the validity of logic and method. It seems fair to assume that Weber saw this presupposition to be widespread among the major cultures, enjoying nearly universal status.

Whether this constitutes a contradiction in Weber's account is irrelevant. What is relevant is that he saw what was problematic in the definition of science offered by the modern episteme. He saw, as Foucault was to state so clearly half a century later, that it excludes the social sciences from its epistemological plane. But although Weber wanted to rescue the social sciences from the ambiguous status conferred on them by the positivists, he did not attempt to break out of the epistemological plane created by the modern episteme. Rather he attempted to fit the social sciences into that plane. The logical contortions of his philosophy of social science attest to the difficulty of this task. His ultimate failure to achieve his goal thus presages the post-modern's more radical challenge to the modern episteme.

III. ETHICS AND SCIENCE

It is widely acknowledged that one of the principal forerunners of the post-modern movement is Nietzsche. It is thus significant for a post-modern reading of Weber's work that Weber himself was deeply affected by Nietzsche's work. The connection between these two thinkers and their respective relationship to post-modernism is complex. Both Nietzsche and Weber proclaimed what they saw to be the fundamental fact of their world: that the Enlightenment project of creating a rational world through the power of reason had failed and that, as a consequence, the world had been rendered meaningless. Nietzsche framed his proclamation in dramatic terms, claiming that God is dead and formulating a philosophy of nihilism. Weber's proclamation is more subdued. He describes a world in which science and ethics are in two radically different spheres. Since science cannot endow meaning on the world we are forced to do so ourselves, but we can only accomplish this through an act of faith. The rationality that he praises so extravagantly in the scientific sphere is no help here; value choices are inherently individual and subjective. Weber's world, like that of Nietzsche's, is one in which the God of absolute moral standards is dead.[3]

Weber differs from Nietzsche, however, in his belief that one part of the

Enlightenment's project, the establishing of 'objective knowledge,' is worth-while. His sustained effort to define a realm of objectivity for the social sciences is evidence of that belief. It is in the realm of ethics, however, that Weber abandons the Enlightenment program. The Enlightenment envisioned a world in which the light of reason would penetrate the dark recesses of unreason and create a totally rational world. Because Weber refused to allow rationality in the sphere of ethics he saw, not a rational world, but a disenchanted world, an iron cage. For Weber the Enlightenment project had produced a fragmented world in which spheres of rationality could be defined but no overall conception of reason prevailed.[4] The failure of the Enlightenment project had, for Weber, produced an iron cage that could only be escaped through individual commitment.

Post-modernism is also concerned with the failure of the Enlightenment project and its consequences for Western society. While Weber sees the fragmen-tation of Enlightenment rationalism as producing an iron cage, Foucault sees its humanism as inherently repressive. There are striking similarities between Weber's description of the disenchanted world and Foucault's critique of what he calls the carceral society. Weber, like Foucault, is concerned to trace the origins of the particular kind of rationality that is definitive of Western society. Weber's explorations of the process of rationalization in the West, particularly in Western religion, parallel Foucault's analysis of the definition of the modern episteme. Both are concerned with the historical evolution of a pattern of thought and its articulation in a form of life.

Weber's interest in bureaucracy also has parallels to Foucault's work. Weber sees bureaucracy and its attempt to rationalize social life as definitive of the disenchanted world in which we are forced to live. The bureaucratic world is one which is depersonalized and calculable. Bureaucracies can tell us how to achieve our goals most efficiently, but not what those goals should be. Hence it is a kind of institutionalized form of nihilism (Warren 1988: 34). Foucault's analysis of the uniquely repressive features of Western society echoes this analysis, but his examination goes beyond Weber's in attempting to identify the cause of these phenomena. For Foucault it is the subjectivity of the Western humanist tradition that is at fault; subjectivity entails subjectification. Weber, who accepts the constituting subject as a given, cannot make this move. He sees the subjective meaning bestowal of the social actor as the foundation of all significance in the social world. For him subjective meaning bestowal through value choice is the way out of the iron cage, while for Foucault subjectivity has been instrumental in constituting the bars of that cage.

In his critique of Weber's theory of rationality Habermas (1984) faults Weber for abandoning the Enlightenment project of reason. He argues that by restrict-ing rationality to the sphere of science Weber makes it impossible for the

Enlightenment vision to be realized. Against this Habermas argues for an understanding of rationality that extends to the sphere of morality. In other words he tries to complete the Enlightenment project that Weber abandoned by rejecting the positivists' conception of a rationality restricted to the scientific realm. Habermas's solution does not work for Weber because of his continued adherence to the positivists' fact/value dichotomy. But Weber does propose a solution to the nihilistic world he has described. For Weber the meaninglessness of the world constitutes a personal challenge. It is the individual's responsibility to endow the world with meaning through his or her moral choices.

It is at this point that the connection between Weber's belief in value neutrality and his advocacy of an ethics of responsibility becomes evident (Schluchter 1979b: 91). It is precisely the *silence* of science on the question of values that gives Weber his answer to nihilism. Because science cannot tell us what to do individuals are forced to make the choice for themselves and, most importantly, to take responsibility for their choices (1958: 150–2). It is the individual's subjective value choice that bridges the gap between the realm of the is and the ought, a choice forced on us by science itself. This line of argument leads Weber to his famous discussion of the ethic of responsibility as the solution to the problem of meaning in a meaningless world. Particularly in 'Politics as a Vocation' (1978b) Weber emphasizes the necessity of an ethic of responsibility as, if not a solution to the world's meaninglessness, at least the best ethical position that an individual can assume. The fact that the empirical and the evaluative operate in different spheres, combined with the fact that science renders the world meaningless, makes the ethic of responsibility a requirement. It is the only way in which either the scientist or those who value the contribution of empirical analysis can break out of the disenchanted world created by science itself.

Schluchter concludes his analysis of Weber's theory of rationalization with the statement that 'Weber has been called a nihilist, a relativist and a decisionist. He is all of these things if you believe in the existence and discernibility of an objective meaning of the world' (1979a: 58–9). Weber, like the post-moderns, obviously did not believe in an objective meaning of the world. But unlike the post-moderns he was not willing to jettison completely the Enlightenment project that tried to create an objective and rational world. As a result Weber is in an anomalous position with regard to contemporary social theory. On the one hand he is obviously opposed to some of the basic tenets of the positivist orthodoxy that has dominated social-science practice throughout most of this century. Particularly in his philosophy of the social sciences he presents an approach that significantly redefines the positivist program. He redefines objectivity to include subjective elements; he defines the subject matter of the social sciences as constituted by the social actor's bestowal of meaning; he restructures the natural/social science distinction; he claims that both the natural and social sciences can rest on presuppositions that transcend scientific proof. In establishing all of these theses Weber lays the groundwork for anti-positivist schools of social science in the twentieth century. Phenomenology, ethnomethodology, and ordinary language analysis all owe an immense debt to Weber and his 'rebellion' against positivism.

But despite his objections to positivism Weber was, on the other hand, unable to break free from the positivist/Enlightenment epistemology that dominated the thought of his time. He redefined positivist scientific method, he did not transcend it. The limitations of Weber's critique have become particularly apparent in recent years with the advent of post-modernism. Post-modernism, and particularly the work of Foucault, has taught us to question the positivist/ Enlightenment project, to see it as a discourse whose claim of the universality of scientific rationality must be interpreted in terms of its historical generation. It has also taught us to see that discourse as one that excludes the social sciences in a particular way. The subject/object opposition at the root of Enlightenment discourse leaves the social sciences in an untenable position. Because human beings are both subjects and objects in the social sciences the neat opposition between the two that, for the Enlightenment, is definitive of knowledge, is not possible in these disciplines. As a result they are excluded from the modern episteme.

Weber saw the problems imposed by this discourse but, instead of attempting to move beyond it, attempted instead to alter it. Although his attempt is admirable it is also, ultimately, a failure. Foucault is right: Enlightenment discourse creates an epistemology in which the human sciences are untenable. In a sense the contortions that Weber is forced to go through to define his philosophy of the social sciences illustrate Foucault's point better than other, less comprehensive, attempts. Weber's theory created a social science in which objectivity is rooted in subjectivity and presuppositionless science is rooted in transcendental truths. It also creates a meaningless world in which subjective value choices alone provide significance. Both of these formulations are necessary consequences of Weber's adherence to the modern episteme. Like Nietzsche, Weber offers an important critique of that episteme but, finally, fails to transcend it.

NOTES

1 It is interesting to note that the position Weber takes on this issue entails a rejection of the claim to base the objectivity of the social sciences on the certainty of inner experience, a claim that has been influential in certain phenomenological approaches to social theory.

2 One of the interesting aspects of Weber's concept of causality is his argument that causal analysis in the social sciences has much in common with the legal concept of causality (1949a: 168). A legal investigation frequently has to establish the motives of the actors and therefore must assume that these motives constitute publically accessible knowledge. This has important consequences for the discussion of subjective meanings in both ordinary language analysis and phenomenology.

3 For a discussion of Weber's relationship to Nietzsche see Warren (1988) and Eden (1983).

4 See Zygmunt Bauman's *Legislators and Interpreters* (1987) for a discussion of this fragmentation of the Enlightenment project.


REFERENCES

Bauman, Zygmunt. 1987. *Legislators and Interpreters*. Ithaca: Cornell University Press.

Eden, Robert. 1983. *Political Leadership and Nihilism*. Gainesville: University of Florida Press.

Foucault, Michel. 1971. *The Order of Things*. New York: Random House.

Gadamer, Hans-Georg. 1975. *Truth and Method*. New York: Continuum.

Habermas, Jürgen. 1984. *The Theory of Communicative Action*, vol. 1, trans. Thomas McCarthy. Boston: Beacon Press.

Hekman, Susan. 1979. 'Weber's Concept of Causality and the Modern Critique.' *Sociological Inquiry* 49: 67–76.

— 1983. *Weber, the Ideal Type and Contemporary Social Theory*. Notre Dame: Notre Dame University Press.

Oakes, Guy. 1977. Introductory essay. In *Critique of Stammler*, by Max Weber, trans. Guy Oakes. Boston: Free Press, 1–56.

Schluchter, Wolfgang. 1979a. 'The Paradox of Rationalization: On the Relation of Ethics and World.' In *Max Weber's Vision of History*, by Guenther Roth and Wolfgang Schluchter. Berkeley: University of California Press, 11–64.

— 1979b. 'Value-Neutrality and the Ethic of Responsibility.' In *Max Weber's Vision of History*, 65–116.

Warren, Mark. 1988. 'Max Weber's Liberalism for a Nietzschean World.' *American Political Science Review* 82: 31–50.

Weber, Max. 1949a. 'Critical Studies in the Logic of the Cultural Sciences.' In *The

*Methodology of the Social Sciences*, ed. Edward Shils and Henry Finch. Boston: The Free Press, 113–88.

— 1949b. 'The Meaning of "Ethical Neutrality" in Sociology and Economics.' In *The Methodology of the Social Sciences*, 1–47.

— 1949c. ' "Objectivity" in Social Science and Social Policy.' In *The Methodology of the Social Sciences*, 49–112.

— 1958. 'Science as a Vocation.' In *From Max Weber*, ed. H.H. Gerth and C. Wright Mills. New York: Oxford University Press, 129–56.

— 1975. *Roscher and Knies: The Logical Problems of Historical Economics*, trans. Guy Oakes. New York: The Free Press.

— 1977. *Critique of Stammler*, trans. Guy Oakes. Boston: The Free Press.

— 1978a. *Economy and Society*. Berkeley: University of California Press.

— 1978b. 'Politics as a Vocation.' In *Max Weber: Selections in Translation*, ed. W.G. Runciman. Cambridge: Cambridge University Press, 212–25.

# 13

# Max Weber: Legitimation, Method, and the Politics of Theory

## SHELDON S. WOLIN

Max Weber is widely regarded as one of the founders of twentieth-century social science and probably its greatest practitioner. Modern and ancient theorists commonly believed that founding – or giving a form or constitution to collective life – was reckoned to be the most notable action of which political man is capable. It is superior to other types of political acts because it aims to shape the lives of citizens by designing the structure or 'dwelling' which they and their posterity will inhabit. In describing this extraordinary action, political theorists often had recourse to architectural metaphors: the founder 'lays foundations.' No such images were invoked to explain the routine acts that occur in the daily life of a polity. Ordinary action is commonly described as 'doing,' 'effecting,' or 'bringing something about.' If political actors are to bring something about, they presuppose conditions that make possible the action in question and the means for doing it. They also presuppose a context that permits the action to be understood and interpreted. The founder is quintessentially an author of political presuppositions.

By analogy, to found a form of social science entails an act of demarcation that indicates the subject-matter peculiar to the science, the kind of activities that are appropriate (e.g., empirical inquiry), and the norms that are to be invoked in judging the value of the results produced by the activities. These demarcations become presuppositions of subsequent practice. Weber was engaged in founding when he wrote the following:

> The historical and cultural sciences ... teach us how to understand and
> interpret political, artistic, literary, and social phenomena in terms of their

Reprinted with permission of Sage Publications, Inc., from *Political Theory* 9, no. 3 (August 1981), 401–24. © 1981 Sage Publications, Inc.

origins. But they give us no answer to the question, whether the existence of these cultural phenomena have been and are *worth while* ... To take a political stand is one thing, and to analyze political structures and party positions is another.[1]

As this passage indicates, founding attempts to prescribe what shall be considered legitimate activity in a particular field.

But how does the founder acquire his authority to grant or withhold legitimation: who legitimates the legitimator? That question cannot be posed in isolation from the context in which, typically, it arises. The founders of a new science are not in the fortunate position of some of the legendary legislators of antiquity who were able to establish constitutions where none had previously existed. Empty space may be a geographical and even a political reality, but it seems not to be a theoretical possibility. Theories are not like explorations where a flag is planted for the first time. They are, in the revealing language frequently employed, 'attacks' upon another theory. They contest ground that is already held and so they must not only establish their own legitimacy but delegitimate the prevailing theory and its practitioners.

I

Theoretical founding has both a *political* dimension and a *politics*. The former is the constitutive activity of laying down basic and general principles which, when legitimated, become the presuppositions of practice, the ethos of practitioners. This definition is modelled upon the Aristotelian conception of 'the political' (*he politike*) as the 'master science' that legislates for the good of the whole, that is, for the purpose of shaping the whole to the concept of the good relevant to it. Founding is thus *political* theorizing.

The politics of founding, or theory destruction, refers to the critical activity of defeating rival theoretical claims. It is Socrates against Thrasymachus. This politics is conducted by means of strategies (e.g., 'the Socratic method,' Locke's 'clearing Ground a little, and removing some of the Rubbish') and intellectual weapons (various logics, conceptions of 'facts'). The politics of theory was recognized as early as Plato:

> ELEATIC. And when combat takes the form of a conflict of body with body, our natural appropriate name for it will be *force* ...
>
> THEAETETUS. Yes.
>
> ELEATIC. But when it is a conflict of argument with argument, can we call it anything but controversy?[2]

We may call this 'profane politics' in order to distinguish it from a 'higher,' ontological politics. The latter is illustrated by Aristotle's assertion that the theoretical life is 'more than human ... We must not follow those who advise us to have human thoughts, since we are (only) men ... On the contrary, we should try to become immortal.'[3] Ontological politics is preoccupied with gaining access to the highest kind of truth, which is about the nature of ultimate being. The political theorist seeks that truth because he believes that it is the truth about power, the power that holds them together in a perfectly right or just way. The reason why ultimate reality was ultimate was that it contained the solution to the fundamental political riddle, how to combine vast power with perfect right. Holding to this conception of reality, political theorists over many centuries sought to find the way of ordering the life of the collectivity into a right relationship with reality, connecting collective being with ultimate being and thereby assuring that the power and rightness of the one would translate into the safety and well-being of the other. 'For all the laws of men are nourished by one law, the divine law; for it has as much power as it wishes and is sufficient for all and is still left over.'[4] Politics at the ontological level is different from profane politics and more intense. Recall Moses's arguments with Yahweh, Plato's *Phaedrus*, or Augustine's tortuous efforts to find even a small place for the *civitas terrena* in the divine scheme of things. The echoes of ontological politics can still be heard as late as Max Weber's famous essay 'Science as a Vocation':

> So long as life remains immanent and is interpreted in its own terms, it knows only of an unceasing struggle of these gods with one another ... The ultimately possible attitudes toward life are irreconcilable, and hence their struggle can never be brought to a final conclusion. Thus it is necessary to make a decisive choice.[5]

The point of engaging in the politics of theory is to demonstrate the superiority of one set of constitutive principles over another so that in the future these will be recognized as the basis of theoretical inquiry. Thus the founder's *action* prepares the *way* for *inquiry*, that is, for activity which can proceed uninterruptedly because its presuppositions are not in dispute. Inquiry is both a tribute to the triumph of a particular theory and its routinization. Or, to say the same thing differently, inquiry signals that the legitimation struggle is over; it is depoliticized theory. This explains why inquirers are usually quick to deplore as 'political' (or 'ideological') those who challenge the dominant presuppositions and who seek to refound the activity.

As a mode of activity, theorizing has been conceived as a *performance* whose political significance extends beyond the circle of theorists. It is intended as a model for a new form of politics, not only in the manifest sense of presenting a new political vision, but in the exemplary sense of showing how political action should be conducted extramurally. To refer to a previous example, Socrates and Thrasymachus not only represented opposing conceptions of theory, one philosophical and the other rhetorical, and contrasting modes of theoretical action (Socratic *elenchus* or cross-examination versus Thrasymachus's set speeches), but also opposing prescriptions of governance. Socrates not only maintains that the true ruler is one who rules for the betterment of the members of the political community, but in the actual course of the dialogue Socrates can be observed at work improving the mental and moral qualities of the participants, including his opponent Thrasymachus. On the other hand, Thrasymachus both maintains that ruling is and should be in the interest of the stronger and he himself seeks to overpower the listeners by the force of his rhetorical style, to diminish them as tyrants diminish their subjects.

It is within this political conception of theory and of theoretical activity that I want to reconsider Max Weber. The appropriate context for analyzing the political nature of his activity as a founder is provided by the triumph of modern science. Laying the foundations of social science was a possible action only because of the prestige of the natural sciences. Modern science was a new form of theory that rapidly became paradigmatic for all claims to theoretical knowledge. It achieved that position by defeating rival claimants, such as philosophy, theology, and history, and, in the course of more than three centuries of controversy, by delegitimating their respective reality-principles (reason, God, and experience). The spectacular theoretical and practical achievements of science served to obscure the legitimation crisis that was in the making. For centuries science was admired because men thought it provided a true picture of the nature of reality. This had to be so, men reasoned, because of the enormous, godlike power which science was increasingly making accessible to humankind. As long as men continued to believe that science was merely deciphering the laws of nature decreed by a beneficent god, they could preserve sufficient traces of the ancient belief that theoretical knowledge continued to embody the solution to the riddle of power and right. Very few doubted that science had demonstrated its superior ability to generate power. Bacon had compared ancient philosophy to boyish puberty: 'it can talk, but cannot generate.'[6]

This illusion began to dissolve in the nineteenth century. Science appeared to be power without right, an appearance that became all the more unsettling with the realization that science was acknowledging that, by nature, it was incapable of supplying the missing component of rightness, and yet the powers made available by scientific discoveries and technological inventions were increasingly becoming the main influences upon daily life. Equally serious, unlike the discredited forms of theory, such as philosophy, history, and theology, science *qua* science could not even provide a justification of its own activity. This produced a legitimation crisis within theory, or more precisely, within social science. The triumph of modern science had discredited all of the earlier forms of political theory (philosophy, theology, and history) as well as their reality-principles (reason, revelation, and experience). By dint of this discreditation, social science became the natural successor of political theory.

Max Weber was the ideal-type to deal with the developing crisis of the political nature of theory and the politics of theorizing. The title of a book written by his friend Karl Jaspers suggests why: *Max Weber. Politiker. Forscher* (inquirer). *Philosoph.*

Weber was a profoundly political man. At several points in his life he gave serious consideration to abandoning academic life: 'I am born for the pen and the speaker's tribune, not for the academic chair,' he once wrote.[7] He was deeply involved in politics before and during the First World War and in the brief period from the armistice to his death in 1920. Max Weber also wrote a great deal about politics, much of it in newspapers, and his formal sociology was laced with political themes. Yet Weber never set down a coherent political theory comparable to the great theories of the tradition of political theory. That inability may well be the meaning of social science.

Although Weber's formal sociology is not much read outside departments of sociology and his studies of the great religions have been largely superseded, the so-called methodological essays continue to attract attention, especially from philosophers interested in the topic of explanation. Virtually all discussions of Weber's methodology assume that his essays on that subject can be strictly separated from his political writings proper, a distinction that was observed by Weber's German editors who collected his *Politische Schriften* in one volume, his *Aufsätze zur Wissenschaftslehre* in another. Following this principle, two of his best-known essays, 'Politics as a Vocation' and 'Science as a Vocation,' were assigned to different volumes on the assumption, no doubt, that each represented a radically different conception of vocation, one political, the other scientific. I shall suggest, in contrast, that they are companion-pieces, united by common themes, all of them profoundly political. I shall suggest further that methodology, as conceived by Weber, was a type of political theory transferred to the only plane of action available to the theorist at a time when science, bureaucracy, and capitalism had clamped the world with the tightening grid of rationality. Methodology is mind engaged in the legitimation of its own political activity.

## II

In the prefatory note to *Wirtschaft und Gesellschaft*, Weber acknowledged what most readers have keenly felt, that the discussion is 'unavoidably abstract and hence gives the impression of remoteness from reality.' He explained that the 'pedantic' air of the work was due to its objective, to supply a 'more exact terminology' for 'what all empirical sociology really means when it deals with the same problems.'[8] When readers first encounter his famous threefold classification of ideal types of legitimation, for example, they are apt to be puzzled because of the absence of any apparent context. Weber simply stipulates that 'there are three pure types of legitimate domination. The validity of the claims may be based on: ... (1) Rational grounds ... (2) Traditional grounds ... (3) Charismatic grounds ...'[9]

The service being rendered 'empirical sociology' was not as innocent as it was made to appear, either in content or form. The bestowing of names is, as any reader of the Book of Genesis will recall, an act of power, an ordering of the world by specifying the place of things. Establishing the basic terms of sociology is a constitutive act that brings order to a distinct realm, especially if that realm has been disturbed by controversy, by a *Methodenstreit*. Weber's definition of the charismatic grounds of authority become relevant at this point: 'resting on devotion to the exceptional sanctity, heroism or exemplary character of an individual person, and of the normative patterns or order revealed or ordained by him.'[10] In keeping with this note of the extraordinary nature of the pattern represented by basic sociological terms, Weber, in a phrase that echoes temple prophets and early philosophers, remarked that 'the most precise formulation cannot always be reconciled with a form which can readily be popularized. In such cases the latter had to be sanctified.'[11]

The context for reading Weber's abstract terms is political, and for the reading of his methodological essays it is political and theoretical. We can begin to construct the context for his terminology by noting the peculiarities of translation surrounding *Herrschaft*. It is often translated as 'authority,' but it is not an exact equivalent of *die Autorität*; and the meaning of *Herrschaft* is only obfuscated when translated as 'imperative coordination' by Henderson and Parsons.[12] Although *Herrschaft* may refer specifically to the estate of a noble,[13] a reference which was taken up by Weber in his distinctions between patriarchal and patrimonial dominions, *Herrschaft* typically connotes 'mastery' and 'domination.' Thus Weber would write about the 'domination (*Herrschaft*) of man over man.' This means that while in some contexts it may be perfectly appropriate to translate *Herrschaft* as 'authority' or 'imperative control' and to emphasize the element of 'legitimacy,' it is also important to attend to the harsher overtones of *Herrschaft* as domination because these signify its connection to a more universal plane: 'The decisive means for politics is violence ... who lets himself in for politics, that is, for power and force as means, contracts with diabolical powers.'[4] Conflict and struggle were endemic in society as well as between societies. ' "Peace" is nothing more than a change in the form of conflict.'[5] Even when Weber addressed what seemed on its face a purely methodological question, he transformed it into a political engagement, stark, dramatic, and, above all, theological. Thus in the context of 'a non-empirical approach oriented to the interpretation of meaning,' he wrote: 'It is really a question not only of alternatives between values but of an irreconcilable death-struggle like that between "God" and the "Devil." '[6]

Even a casual reader of Weber must be struck by the prominence of 'power-words' in his vocabulary; struggle, competition, violence, domination, *Machstaat*, imperialism. The words indicate the presence of a powerful political sensibility seeking a way to thematize its politicalness but finding itself blocked by a paradox of scientific inquiry. Science stipulates that political expression is prohibited in scientific work, but the stipulation is plainly of a normative status and hence its 'validity' (to use Weber's word) cannot be warranted by scientific procedures and is, therefore, lacking in legitimacy. The same would hold true of all prescriptions for correct scientific procedure. As a consequence, instead of a politics of social scientific theory, there was the possibility of anarchy.

At the same time, the modern theoretical mind had come to regard the political and the scientific as mutually exclusive: the political stood for partisanship, the scientific for objectivity. Since science reigned as the paradigmatic form of theory and the political impulse could not be directly expressed in the form of theory, it had to seek its outlet elsewhere, through the circuitous route of ideal-type constructions and more transparently, as we shall see shortly, in the meta-theoretical form of 'methodology.' This meant, however, that social science *qua* science was unable to externalize a political theory and that Weber's political views, which were strongly held and unhesitatingly expressed publicly, could not be legitimated by his science. Accordingly, in 1917 when he published his remarkable essay on the postwar reconstruction of German political institutions, he felt obliged to preface it with the disclaimer that 'it does not claim the authority of any science.'[7]

Although Weber published his political views, his efforts took the form of occasional pieces. He never created a political theory even though the manifest breakdown of German politics and society cried out for one. His political-theoretical impulse was turned inward upon social science where he replicated the problems, dilemmas, and demands which he perceived in the 'real' political world. For that impulse to be released, Weber had to find a way of modifying the scientific prohibition against the injection of politics into scientific inquiry and locate a domain within science where he could theorize both the profane politics of theory and the ontology of theory. The strategy which he followed required that he attack the positivist ideal of a presuppositionless and hence 'value-free' social science but that, at the same time, he defend the scientific character of social science against subjectivist conceptions of social inquiry that emphasized personal intuitions and moral-political concerns. The positivist position called for the elimination of 'values' from scientific work so that 'objectivity' could be preserved; Weber accepted that formulation as the terrain of controversy and proceeded to invest 'values' with political meaning so that, in the end, values functioned as the symbolic equivalent of politics. At the same time, he adopted from the subjectivist argument its starting-point of the 'subject,' that is, the inquiring self whose passions the positivists had hoped to overcome by the rigors of scientific method. As the price of admitting the morally passionate subject, Weber was willing to concede to the positivists that this would introduce an element of arbitrariness into scientific investigations, but he preferred to gamble that he could revitalize the conception of vocation and make it into a prophylactic that would prevent subjectivity from degenerating into subjectivism.

The initial move that allowed for the political penetration of scientific work was in Weber's definition of social science as one of the 'cultural sciences.' This enabled him to exploit what he saw as the difference between science and culture. The latter was concerned with 'meaning' or 'patterns' rather than with predictions and the closely associated notion of regularities in phenomena.[18] Weberian social science would be devoted to analyzing 'the phenomena of life in terms of their cultural significance.' The social scientist, according to Weber, derives his ideas of what is significant and worthy of investigation from the 'value' element accompanying all human actions and historical events. 'The concept of culture is a *value-concept*.'[19] Significance is grasped as well as expressed by the constructs which Weber designated as 'ideal types.' These are based, he noted, on 'subjective presuppositions' and they are 'formed by the one-sided accentuation of one or more points of view and by the synthesis' of numerous 'concrete individual phenomena.' He likened them to 'a *utopia* which has been arrived at by the analytical accentuation of certain elements of reality' although they 'cannot be found empirically anywhere in reality.'[20]

The subjective element in these one-sided constructs formed part of Weber's conception of human life: 'every single important activity and ultimately life as a whole ... is a series of ultimate decisions through which the soul – as in Plato – chooses its own fate.'[21] That conception, first advanced in the context of a methodological discussion, later reappears to color the whole of Weber's essay on the political 'hero' in Politics as a Vocation.[22] Choice is the essence of true science as it is of true politics: 'The *objective* validity of all empirical knowledge rests exclusively upon the ordering of the given reality according to categories which are *subjective*.'[23] Scientific activity, Weber argued, represents a series of decisions; it is 'always' from 'particular points of view.'[24]

The effect of these formulations is to politicize social science, not in the vulgar sense of corrupting it by ideology, but in an allegorical sense. The highest form of available politics is a politics of the soul. In the passage cited earlier, it is revealing that Weber should have referred to Plato's conception of the soul. Classical political theory was remarkable for its profoundly political conception of the soul. Most readers are familiar with Plato's threefold division of the soul (reason, appetite, and passion) and his comparison of it to the 'three orders' that were to 'hold together' his ideal state.[25] For Weber, the politics of the soul appears in the identical virtues which he ascribed to scientific and political man: 'objectivity' or 'distance,' 'passion,' and 'responsibility' for the consequences of one's choices.

The complexity that the politics of theory took in Weber's case is all the more interesting when we realize that in the early stages of his career, long before he had become embroiled in methodological controversies, he had championed a radically different view of the relation between social science and politics, a view in which the political nature of theoretical activity was frankly espoused. It was set out in the inaugural lecture which he gave at Freiburg in 1895 under the title, 'The Nation State and Political Economy.' The theme of the lecture was political and deliberately provocative. As Weber remarked shortly afterwards, he decided to publish the lecture because of the disagreement it had aroused among his listeners ('nicht die Zustimmung, sondern Widerspruch').[26] Midway through the lecture he announced, 'I am a member of the bourgeois class and feel myself to be such, and I have been educated in its outlook and ideals. But it is precisely the vocation of our science to say what will be heard with displeasure.'[27]

A reader who chances upon the Freiburg lecture and who had associated Weber with a strict view of the fact-value distinction, a rigid commitment to 'ethical neutrality' (*Wertfreiheit*) and 'objectivity,' and disdain for professors who assumed the role of political prophets, would be startled to find Weber declaring roundly that 'the science of political economy is a *political* science' and that it ought to be 'the servant' of politics; that the nation-state is the ultimate value and political economy should be shaped to its needs.[28] In his prescription for the politicalization of this theoretical science, Weber broke with common belief that political economy should be exploited to promote the material happiness of society; and he rejected the sentiment of liberal free traders that economies should serve the cause of international peace by promoting the ideal of free trade and an international division of labour. 'For the dream of peace and humanity's happiness there stands over the portals of the future of human history: *lasciate ogni speranza* (abandon all hope).'[29] The nature and purpose of political economy, he argued, was dictated by 'Machtkämpfe,' the power struggles in a Darwinian world where nations 'were locked in an endless struggle for existence and domination.'[30] 'The economic policy of a German state,' he warned his academic audience, 'like the norm for German economic theoreticians, can only be German.'[31]

The lecture gave not the slightest hint of a possible tension between the conditions needed for scientific inquiry and the requirements of 'die weltliche Machtorganisation der Nation.'[32] Equally notable in the light of Weber's later pessimism, there was no suggestion that political struggle might be meaningless. Rather there was as an air of exaltation at the prospect of participating in 'the eternal struggle for the preservation and improvement of our national type,' as though in serving the *Machstaat* in its quest for 'elbow-room'[33] the political economist placed himself in contact with the most elemental force in the political world, the mustering of national power in the fight for survival.

The explicitly political conception of a social science was, however, abandoned over the next decade. Weber suffered a devastating nervous disorder in 1898 and it was not until 1902 that he began to resume his scholarly activity. Beginning in 1903 and continuing over the next several years, he published a series of essays on the methodology of the social sciences. As we have already noted, in the eyes of later commentators and critics, the essays constitute a self-contained series of texts which can be interpreted independently of Weber's sociological and political writings. They are described as the 'philosophy of social science' which Weber worked out in the context of the famous *Methodenstreit*, initiated in 1883 by Schmoller's attack upon Menger over the fundamental nature of the social sciences.[34]

This is, as I have suggested earlier, a far too restrictive context for interpreting the methodological essays and for grasping the meaning of methodology. That context needs to be enlarged to accommodate its author's political concerns. The expression of these concerns was powerfully evident in Weber's substantive, as opposed to his methodological, writings of the same period. Almost simultaneously with the publication (1903–6) of Weber's first methodological essays, those dealing with Roscher and Knies, Weber published what is perhaps his most famous work, *The Protestant Ethic and the Spirit of Capitalism* (1904–5). So much scholarly ink has been expended on the question of whether and in what sense Weber 'explained' the rise of capitalism that the political importance of the work has been almost totally neglected. Yet it contains the most extensive formulation of Weber's ideal conception of the political actor and the most polemical, for it is directed squarely at Marxism. Weber wanted not only to counter the Marxist explanation of the origins of capitalism, but to celebrate the moral and political superiority of the capitalist hero of the past over the proletarian hero of the present and future. In these respects, the *Protestant Ethic* is a complex work concerned with the historical legitimation of capitalism. It is complex because that work also marks the first sustained discussion of a theme that was to preoccupy Weber for the remainder of his life, the meaninglessness of human existence. This intimation of a post-theological theme has been overlooked in most discussions of Weber's methodology, yet it figures prominently in his later essay on ' "Objectivity" in Social Science.' Meaninglessness was less a concept than a theme. In the *Protestant Ethic* the context for interpreting it was supplied by another crucial theme, 'rationalization.' Rationalization refers to a world shaped by what Weber called 'the special and peculiar rationalism of Western culture.' Rationalization is expressed in the mastery of modern science over nature and of bureaucratic organization over society. It signified the status of human action in a world whose structures encased action in routines and required it to be calculating, instrumentalist, and predictable. Weber attacked that conception of action as its most basic assumption that 'self-interest' is the main motive for action in 'capitalistic culture.'[35] His attack was paradoxical because it was conducted through the figure of a fanatical capitalist who brought an intensity to capital accumulation that would convert it into an epic deed, a spiritual triumph. Puritan zeal would also be brought to bear on human activity and to order it so systematically that it would generate structures of power that would transform the world. The Puritan would be, however, a capitalist without 'purely eudaemonistic self-interest.' He represented, instead, an alternative form of action, the action of a man defined by his 'calling' or vocation, a man who submits to the requirements of a discipline without moderating his passion and who displays 'a certain ascetic tendency' for 'he gets nothing out of his wealth for himself, except the irrational sense of having done his job well.'[36]

The Puritan actor of the *Protestant Ethic* was the prototype for Weber's most famous ideal-types, Political Man and Scientific Man and their respective vocations. His two essays, *Politics as a Vocation* and *Science as a Vocation*, appeared in 1919, during which he was at work preparing a revised version of the *Protestant Ethic*.[37] But the model had not only been developed much earlier, it had exercised a decisive influence upon Weber's conception of scientific activity at the time when he was writing the methodological essays. The exacting, even obsessive, demands which Weber imposed on the social scientist form a counterpart to the Calvinist's adherence to the letter of Scripture and to the rules of piety prescribed by Puritan divines. The Calvinist is, as we have noted, ascetic, but he accumulates material goods with a controlled frenzy. 'The God of Calvinism demanded of his believers not simple good works, but a life of good works combined into a unified system.' The Puritan made no appeal to 'magical sacraments' or confessions; he relied, instead, on 'rational planning' and proceeded 'methodically' to supervise his own conduct and, in the process, to objectify the self.[38] Scientific man is likewise to be a model of rational self-discipline, not only in his scrupulous adherence to scientific protocols, but in controlling his values and biases, and in suppressing the special vice of modern man, his fondness for 'self-expression.' Like the Calvinist, scientific man accumulates, only his activity takes the form of knowledge; yet what he amasses has no more lasting value than other things of the world. Scientific knowledge is always being superseded. Finally, scientific man is also a renunciatory hero. His form of renunciation is dictated by the demands of specialization and require him to abandon the delights of the Renaissance and Goethean ideal of the universal man who seeks to develop as many facets of his personality and as many different fields of knowledge as possible: 'renunciation of the Faustian universality of man ... is a condition of valuable work in the modern world.'[39]

The extent to which Weber shaped his social scientist in the image of the Calvinist went beyond the attempt to emulate the precision of Calvinism. It extended to Calvinist doctrine, which proved to be an extraordinary move for it meant adopting the demands without being able to presuppose a comparable faith. In Weber's portrait, the most striking feature of the Calvinist's furious dedication to ascetic labour is that, during his unending labours, he can never know whether he has been chosen for election and he can never win it by his own efforts, regardless of how strenuously he tries. The dogma of predestination decrees that the Calvinist will labour amidst unrelieved uncertainty. Scientific man is in a comparable predicament. 'Our highest values' are 'a matter of faith.' Although they are crucial in orienting us toward our scientific work, there is no way that we, as scientists, can be assured that these values are 'true.' Knowledge of values, like the knowledge of secret election by God, is inaccessible.[40] Appropriately, when Weber argued this point in the essay on 'objectivity,' he drew upon the oldest theological parallel: 'The fate of an epoch which has eaten of the tree of knowledge is that it must know that we cannot learn the *meaning* of the world from the results of its analysis, be it ever so perfect.'[41] The fundamental premise from which Weber argued for the fact/value distinction, which occupied such an important place in the 'discipline' of Weberian social science, was that values had to be preserved in their unscientific state so that human beings would have to choose.[42] The existence of the fact/value distinction was nothing less than the fundamental article of faith on which rested the entire decisionist framework of Weber's politics of the soul. As long as science could not, in principle, determine choice, men were forced to be free to choose. In that formulation one can see the secular equivalent of the age-old religious controversy over human free will versus divine predestination, only now scientific 'laws' take the place of the providential plan.

Weber laid special emphasis on the transforming effects of Puritan zeal when it was transferred to business activity. It converted money-making into a moral *praxis*, characterized by selflessness and competence. When Weber took the next step of transferring the Calvinist spirit to the domain of social science, he formulated the idea of methodology to serve, not simply as a guide to investigation but as a moral practice and a mode of political action. The Calvinist, Weber wrote, 'strode into the market-place of life, slammed the door of the monastery behind it, and took to penetrate just the daily routine of life, with its methodicalness, to fashion it into a life in the world, but neither of nor for this world.'[43] But as a model for the *bios theoretikos* the Calvinist was worlds removed from the classical idea of theory as contemplative and reflective. 'Scientific work is chained to the course of progress ... this progress goes on *ad infinitum*.'[44]

As Weber sketched the Calvinist, he injected into his portrait the political themes of struggle which had so sharply defined his own view of politics and especially of international politics as evidenced by the Freiburg lecture. The 'heroism' of the Calvinist was displayed in the 'fight' for 'supremacy against a whole world of hostile forces.' In the end he shattered the powers of church, society, and state, ushering in a new era of 'universal history.'[45] 'Bourgeois classes as such have seldom before and never since displayed heroism.'[46]

The bourgeois actor of Weber's epic is a political hero in the classical sense. He is a founder of a new order, the order of capitalism which has transformed the world. He can stand comparison with another hero, the world-conquering proletariat, a comparison that pits a Protestant hero against a classically inspired one. Marx, particularly in his writings of the early 1840s, likened the proletariat to Prometheus, the rebellious god who saved mankind from destruction by bringing it the techniques of material production. While the proletarian hero signifies material and cultural deprivation and hence implies the promise of gratification, the Protestant is a renunciative hero who disdains the material sensuous pleasures eagerly sought by the materially deprived and sensuously starved man of the *Paris Manuscripts*. A major difference between the two epics is that, unlike Marx, Weber knew that he was comparing a portrait of the last hero before the age of rationalization set in and rendered both heroes, Marx's and his own, anachronisms. Henceforth, the possibilities of significant action will be determined and limited by the constraints of rationalization. In the closing pages of the *Protestant Ethic* the fate of action is described in the imagery of the 'iron cage.'

The iron cage is a symbol with many meanings. It symbolizes the transformation of vocation from a religious and moral choice to an economic necessity. It also signifies our helplessness before 'the tremendous cosmos of the modern economic order ... which today determine[s] the lives of all who are born into this mechanism.' And the iron cage stands for the stage of 'victorious capitalism' when the social order no longer needs the spiritual devotion of the ascetic for 'it rests on mechanical foundations.'[47]

The rationalization of existence foreshadowed by the iron cage became a *leitmotif* in all of Weber's subsequent writings. The cage is iron because the main forces of modern life, science, capitalism, and bureaucratic organization are triumphs of rationality and so the mind has no purchase point to attack them. They *are* mind incarnated into legal codes and administrative organizations that promise order, predictable decisions, regularity of procedures, and responsible, objective, and qualified officials; into economies that operate according to principles of calculated advantage, efficiency, and means-ends strategies; and into technologies that promote standardization, mechanical behaviour, and uniform tastes. The advantages of rationalization in terms of power and material satisfaction are so overwhelming that the historical process which has brought that system is 'irreversible.' But, finally, the cage is iron because 'the fulfillment of the calling cannot directly be related to the highest spiritual and cultural values.' Instead of being fired by religious, ethical, and political ideals, action has become simply a response to 'economic compulsion' or to 'purely mundane passions.'[48]

Action without the passions that Weber associated with spiritual and moral ideals was 'meaningless,' a category that became a major one in Weber's thinking henceforth. Meaninglessness was of special concern in the methodological essays because of the central part which modern science had played in destroying the sources of meaning. Capitalism and bureaucratization may have produced the social and political structures of rationalization but the equation of rationalization with meaninglessness was the special responsibility of modern science. Science has attacked religious, moral, and metaphysical beliefs and had insisted that everything could, in principle, be reduced to rational explanation. Such explanations had no need of gods, spirits, revelations, and metaphysical principles. The result was a bare world, denuded and drained of meaning, which science makes no pretense to replenishing. Science deals with fact, material reality, and rational demonstration. It is so helpless to restore what it has destroyed that, *qua* science, it cannot even justify its own value. Its own activity comes perilously close to being the definition of meaninglessness:

'Chained to the course of progress,' its 'fate' is that 'it asks to be "surpassed" and outdated.'[49]

The inherent limitations of science, its inability to make good the deficiencies of the world's meaning, provide the backdrop to the political role of the methodologist. His task is not to undertake scientific investigations or even to instruct his co-workers on how best to conduct research, much less to offer a special field of study. Rather it is to show them that significant action in their chosen realm is possible. It is, therefore, a form of political education in the meaning of vocation. Its politicalness comes from the seriousness, even urgency, of the relationship between vocational action and the world.

In order to bring out the unusual nature of Weberian methodology, a slight excursion is necessary, but it will be one that will reestablish direct contact with our original concern: social science as the post-modern form of political theory. Previously we had noted that Weber frequently asserts that science cannot validate the legitimacy of its own authority. This assertion calls attention to the interesting consideration that Weber never attempted in any systematic fashion to apply his concepts of *legitime Herrschaft* to science, even though the significance of science for the major conceptions of legitimate authority is clear. For example, given Weber's definition of 'traditional authority' as 'resting on an established belief in the sanctity of immemorial traditions and the legitimacy of the status of those exercising authority under them,'[50] it is clear that science, which strives to be 'outdated,' is hostile to that form of authority. Further, *pace* Kuhn, sciences as an institutionalized activity appears to be consistent with the 'rational-legal' type of authority which rests on 'a belief in the "legality" of patterns of normative rules and the right of those elevated to authority under such rules to issue commands.'[51] But the most interesting question concerns the possible relations between science and charisma, the form of authority which appears, on its face, to be the least hospitable to science. Charismatic authority, as we have already noted, rests on 'devotion to the specific sanctity, heroism, or exemplary character of an individual person, and of the normative patterns or order revealed or ordained by him.'[52] Now, although Weber never explicitly connected science and charisma, there is a sufficient number of scattered clues to suggest that the connection was in his mind. Science is charisma 'in a godless and prophetless time' and it is displayed by the person 'with an inward calling' who can endure that 'the world is disenchanted.'[53] It is for the chosen few, 'the affair of an intellectual aristocracy.'[54] It is, above all, charisma because science requires 'inspiration' (*Eingebung*). 'It has nothing to do with any cold calculation.'[55] Weber's discussion of inspiration is compressed but highly suggestive. 'Psychologically,' he declared, inspiration was related to 'frenzy' or 'Plato's "mania" ' – a reference to the discussion of 'divine madness' in the dialogue

*Ion.* 'Whether we have scientific inspiration,' he continued, 'depends upon destinies that are hidden from us, and besides upon "gifts." '[56] 'Gifts' (*Gabe*) clearly refers to a charismatic quality for elsewhere Weber defined charisma as 'the gift of grace,' a phrase which he took the pains to associate with 'the vocabulary of early Christianity.'[57] Although the significance of 'grace' (Gr. *xaris*) was not explicitly connected by Weber to his discussion of science, a brief account of that term should immediately establish its relevance in the highly decisionistic framework of Weberian social science.

In the New Testament, 'grace' refers to the idea of God's redemptive love which is always actively at work to save sinners and maintain them in the right relationship to Him. Grace is God's free gift, and while it is not the result of man having earned it, there is still an element of choice, though an ambiguous one: 'work out your own salvation,' Paul exhorted his followers, 'with fear and trembling; for God is at work in you' (*Phil.* 2:12–13).

From these considerations we can distil three elements in the idea of charisma: a 'gifted' exceptional person of heroic or risk-taking qualities; a normative pattern that he ordains and that gives him authority; and the element of choice, both for the charismatic figure who commits himself to the revelation entrusted to him and for the others who must decide whether to follow him. Throughout, the decisionist element ('work out your own salvation') rests uneasily with a necessitarian one ('God is at work in you'). All of these elements reappear in Weber's methodological discussions.

But what is the meaning of methodology? What is its connection with the disenchanted world and its meaninglessness? How does it compare as a form of action with political theory?

The word 'methodology' did not come into use until the nineteenth century and it was mostly employed in scientific discussions, at least during the first half of the century. Its etymology is revealing. It is derived from two Greek words, *méthodus* and *logos. Méthodus* is itself an interesting compound of *meta* and *hodos. Meta*, which is characteristically used as a prefix, had some meanings that bristle with political overtones. They include: sharing, action in common, pursuit or quest. *Hodos*, on the other hand, means 'way.' It is one of the oldest words in the historical lexicon of Greek philosophy. The pre-Socratics, for example, typically described philosophy as a 'way' to the truth or even as a 'way' to ultimate Being. Ancient philosophy, we should recall, deliberately challenged religion, myth, and tradition; its 'way' often provoked opposition, even danger. Thus Parmenides described his 'way' as 'strife-encompassed.'[58]

*Logos* is probably the richest word in the entire vocabulary of ancient philosophy and theology. It has meant: account, explanation, truth, theory, reason, and, more simply, word. Among several of its usages there is a recurrent element: *logos* as signifying the truth that resides in the deepest layer of Being and that the *logos* has succeeded in embodying. It is represented by a phrase from Parmenides: 'the same thing exists for thinking and for being.'[59]

Methodology might then be rendered as the political action (*meta*) which thought takes on the route (*hodos*) to being (*logos*). Weber referred to it as 'metatheoretical.'[60] The reason for this designation had to do with the political nature of the crisis which gives methodology its *raison d'être*, the kind of crisis experienced by Weber and his contemporaries in the course of the *Methodenstreit* when the nature of the social sciences *qua* science was being contested. Weber took special pains to define the meaning of crisis so that the function of methodology could be made clear. Methodology, he insisted, does not legislate methods; these are 'established and developed' by practising social scientists in the course of dealing with '*substantive problems.*' 'Purely epistemological and methodological reflections have never played the crucial role in such developments.'[61] Crises come about because of the dependence of social scientists upon 'evaluative ideas' which give 'significance' to their work. The 'foundation' for empirical inquiry comes not from empirical data but from 'the meta-empirical validity of ultimate final values in which the meaning of our existence is rooted.' These foundations, however, tend to shift and even crumble because life itself is 'perpetually in flux ... The light which emanates from these highest evaluative ideas falls on an ever changing finite segment of the vast chaotic stream of events which flows away through time.'[62] Meanwhile, researchers gradually lose their immediate awareness of the 'ultimate rootedness' in values of their own research. The result is that research falters. 'The significance of the unreflectively utilized viewpoints becomes uncertain' in the mind of the researcher. 'The road is lost in the twilight.' This crisis creates the opportunity for the type of intervention associated with methodology: 'Science ... prepares to change its standpoint and its analytical apparatus and to view the stream of events from the heights of thought.'[63]

The methodologist seizes the opportunity to show the researcher that science cannot flourish without 'evaluative ideas' for it is these that nourish notions of what is 'significant' and hence worthy of inquiry. 'Significance' becomes the crucial concept in Weber's politics of knowledge. It symbolizes the moment of freedom for the social scientist when he registers his affirmations, when he exchanges the settled routines of inquiry for the risks of action. It is akin to a form of momentary and secular salvation for it creates meaning in an otherwise meaningless world. 'Culture,' Weber declared, 'is a finite segment of the meaningless infinity of the world process, a segment on which *human beings* confer meaning and significance.' Humans impart significance by taking up 'a deliberate posture (*Stellung*) towards the world.'[64]

The politics of mind in its struggles against meaninglessness finds its most powerful expression in Weber's conception of 'ideal types.' These are the most crucial instruments of social scientific inquiry and hence their nature becomes all-important. Ideal types are constructs created by the social scientist to render a particular historical reality intelligible and coherent. They are constructed by abstracting features of a phenomenon (e.g., capitalism or bureaucracy) and reconstructing them to form an internally consistent whole. Ideal types are, Weber emphasized, deliberately constructed to be 'one-sided,' they are meant not only to accentuate the phenomena under study and thereby leave the investigator's mark on a portion of the world, but to accentuate as well the value-orientations of the investigator. Ideal types 'illuminate ... reality' although they cannot 'exhaust its infinite richness': 'They are all attempts ... to bring order into the chaos of those facts which we have drawn into the field circumscribed by our *interest.*'[65] The investigator does not usually face a situation where no prior constructs exist. Rather, he is faced with the challenge of overcoming the constructs of the past. It is not surprising, therefore, to find Weber's description of the use of ideal-types reminiscent of descriptions of the *agon* of classical politics. Inherited constructs are 'in constant tension with the new knowledge which we can and *desire* to wrest from reality. The progress of cultural science occurs through this conflict.'[66]

Weber looked upon the ideal-type as a means of provoking a 'confrontation with empirical reality.'[67] This somewhat curious formulation reflects the larger problem of political action in a world dominated by huge structures. Where theorists of earlier times were haunted by the fragility of order and by the difficulties of maintaining it, post-modern theory appears to suffer from a surfeit of order. Order is the empirical reality of post-modern theory. And ultimately, of course, the heroic meta-theorist will suffer the same fate as the political hero and all charismatics: his *agon* will be routinized. The meta-theorist is replaced by the normal social scientist, the meta-politician by the technician.

The fate of the meta-theorist is not, perhaps, a great loss. He has turned out to be a theorist *manqué*, his methodology a displaced form of political theory confined within the walls of the academy but serving a legitimating function once removed. As practised by Weber, methodology provides a rationale for social science, while social science tacitly bestows the peculiar form of legitimacy that is within its power to grant, the legitimacy of fact. Against the *Herrschaft* of facticity, ideal-type constructions afford only a small purchase-point for criticism. Ideal-types cannot serve as substitutes for a theoretical counterparadigm, an alternative vision to what is too often the case. Weber's own views about bureaucracy confirm that while an ideal-type construction may highlight how bureaucracy trivializes politics and reduces human beings to classifications, the only rational choice is resignation before its massive facticity: 'The needs of mass administration make [bureaucracy] completely indispensable.'[68]

Weber's torment was that while he prophesied 'a polar night of icy darkness and hardness' and a totally bureaucratized condition wherein mankind would be 'as powerless as the fellahs of ancient Egypt,'[69] he could neither turn theory against science – for science *was* theory – nor venture upon the quest for an ontology. His torment was expressed, paradoxically, at the ontological level which science had completely destroyed:

> There are no mysterious incalculable forces ... One can, in principle, master all things by calculation. This means the world is disenchanted ... [In antiquity] everybody sacrificed to the gods of his city, so do we still nowadays, only the bearing of man has been disenchanted and denuded of its mystical but inwardly genuine plasticity. Fate, and certainly not 'science' holds sway over these gods and their struggles. One can only understand what the godhead is for the one order or the other, or better, what godhead is in the one or the other order. With this understanding, however, the matter has reached its limits so far as it can be discussed in a lecture-room and by a professor.[70]

Weber's ontological politics, populated with the furious struggles of gods and demons, and seemingly so incongruous in the thought of a founder of the scientific study of society and politics, issues from the frustration of a consciousness that knows that its deepest values are owed to religion but that its vocational commitments are to the enemy. Science has caused the meaning of the universe to 'die out at its very root.' Science is 'specifically [an] irreligious power.'[71] The tension left Weber ambivalent toward science: 'I personally by my very work ... affirm the value of science ... and I also do so from precisely the standpoint that hates intellectualism as the worst devil.'[72]

The dramatic rendition of this ontological politics where science destroys the possibility of political renewal is in a figure that reappears frequently in Weber's writings, the prophet. The personal significance of the prophet is obscured because, as was his custom, Weber would frequently throw out sarcastic references about professors playing prophet, or about those who 'cannot bear the fate of the times like a man' and for whom 'the arms of the old church are opened widely and compassionately.'[73] But, of course, it was Weber's prophecies that have made his writings enduring; not so much because they see into the future but because they reveal him deeply engaged with the powers that dominate the soul of modern man: bureaucracy, science, violence, and the 'intellectualism' that has destroyed the spiritual resources on which humankind has fed for three thousand years or more. Prophecy, like religion, was a political symbol for Weber, as evidenced by his treatment of the Old Testament prophets. They were, in his eyes, supremely political figures who 'stood in the midst of their people and were concerned with the fate of the political community.'[74] They practised a 'prophetic politics' while exhorting their people in the midst of 'political disaster.'[75] Prophecy, we might say, is closet-theory in the age of science. It achieved pathos in *The Protestant Ethic and the Spirit of Capitalism*, not in the closing pages where Weber pronounced his famous jeremiad about the 'iron cage,' but in the introduction which he wrote shortly before his death. They are powerful pages and can only be described as akin to a secular crucifixion. This was because the book, and the prophecy about the future and the myths of the Protestant hero of the past, was considered to be an invasion of special fields or preserves of scholarly experts, 'trespassing' as Weber called it. Acknowledging that he had violated the scientific division of labour, he was prepared to offer himself up for trial. 'The specialist is entitled to a final judgment' and 'one must take the consequences.' To do otherwise would be to 'degrade' the specialist below the 'seer.' 'Whoever wants a sermon,' Weber wrote contemptuously, 'should go to a conventicle.'[76] He then ends on an equivocal note that gives a glimpse of his own agony: 'It is true that the path of human destiny cannot but appall him who surveys a section of it. But he will do well to keep his small personal commentaries to himself, as one does at the sight of the sea or of majestic mountains, unless he knows himself to be called and gifted to give them expression in artistic or prophetic form.'[77]

The feebleness of Weber's equivocation corresponded to the powerlessness of the prophet in a 'prophetless and godless' world. Meaninglessness was no longer an aesthetic experience of the few, but a contagion. Having undermined religious, moral, and political beliefs, the forces of rationalization had finally exposed the meaning of meaninglessness to be power without right.

NOTES

1 'Science as a Vocation,' *From Max Weber: Essays in Sociology*, trans. H.H. Gerth and C. Wright Mills (New York 1946), 145. Hereafter this volume will be referred to as FMW.

2 *Sophists* 225 A-B, trans. A.E. Taylor (London 1971).

3 *Nicomachean Ethics*, 1177b. 25ff., trans. M. Ostwald (Indianapolis 1962).

4 'Heraclitus,' frag. 253 in G.S. Kirk and J.E. Raven, eds., *The Pre-Socratic Philosophers* (Cambridge 1957), 213.

5 FMW, 152.

6 'The Great Instauration,' Preface in *Selected Writings of Francis Bacon*, ed. H.G. Dick (New York: Modern Library 1955), 429.

7 Wolfgang Mommsen, *Max Weber und die deutsche Politik 1890–1920* (Tübingen 1959), 279. See also the fine study by David Beetham, *Max Weber and the Theory of Modern Politics* (London 1974); and Anthony Giddens, *Politics and Sociology in the Thought of Max Weber* (London 1972).

8 *Economy and Society*, ed. Guenther Roth and Claus Wittich, 3 vols. (New York 1968), vol. I, 3. Hereafter this will be cited as E & S.

9 Ibid., 215.

10 Ibid.

11 Ibid., 3.

12 Max Weber, *The Theory of Social and Economic Organization* (New York 1947), 152 (n. 83).

13 See the comments of the editors, E & S, vol. I, lxxxviii–ix.

14 'Politics as a Vocation,' FMW, 121, 123.

15 Max Weber, *The Methodology of the Social Sciences*, trans. E.A. Shils and H.A. Finch (Glencoe, IL 1949), 27. Hereafter referred to as *Methodology*.

16 Ibid., 17.

17 E & S, vol. 3, 1381.

18 *Methodology*, 74ff.

19 Ibid., 76 (emphasis in original).

20 *Methodology*, 90 (emphasis in original).

21 Ibid., 18.

22 FMW, 128.

23 *Methodology*, 110 (emphasis in original).

24 Ibid., 81.

25 *Republic* 440 B, E, 442 B-D. See also Aristotle, *Nicomachean Ethics* I.2. 1094a27–1094b5.

26 *Gesammelte Politische Schriften*, 2d ed., ed. J. Winckelmann (Tübingen 1958), I. Hereafter referred to as GPS.

27 Ibid., 20.

28 Ibid., 14 (emphasis in original).

29 Ibid., 12.

30 Ibid., 12, 14.

31 GPS, 13.

32 Ibid., 14.

33 'elbow-room in earthly existence will be won only by a hard struggle of man with man.' Ibid., 12.

34 Examples of this genre are: W.G. Runciman, *A Critique of Max Weber's Philosophy of Social Science* (Cambridge 1972); R.S. Rudner, *Philosophy of Social Science* (Englewood Cliffs, NJ 1966), 68ff; Dieter Henrich, *Die Einheit der Wissenschaftslehre* (Tübingen 1952); and the introductory essays of Guy Oakes to his translations of Weber's *Roscher and*

*Knies* (New York 1975) and *Critique of Stammler* (New York 1977).

35  *The Protestant Ethic and the Spirit of Capitalism*, trans. Talcott Parsons (London 1930), 78. Hereafter referred to as PE.

36  PE, 37.

37  See the translator's note, Ibid., ix.

38  Ibid., 117, 153.

39  PE, 180.

40  *Methodology*, 52.

41  Ibid., 57.

42  Ibid., 19.

43  PE, 154.

44  FMW, 137, 138.

45  PE, 56, 63, 13.

46  Ibid., 37.

47  PE, 182–2.

48  PE, 182.

49  FMW, 137, 138.

50  E & S, vol. 1, 215.

51  Ibid. Note the personal remark in 'Science as a Vocation' where Weber notes that in promoting young scholars he followed the practice that 'a scholar promoted by me must legitimize and habilitate himself with *somebody else* at another university.' FMW, 130.

52  E & S, vol. 1, 215.

53  FMW, 148, 153, 155.

54  Ibid., 134.

55  Ibid., 135.

56  Ibid., 136; GAW, 591.

57  Ibid. The scriptural passage that seems closest is Romans 3:24.

58  Fr. 345 in G.S. Kirk and J.E. Raven, eds., *The Pre-Socratic Philosophers* (Cambridge 1957), 271.

59  Fr. 344 in ibid., 269.

60  *Roscher and Knies*, 58.

61  *Methodology*, 116 (emphasis in original).

62  Ibid., 111.

63  Ibid., 112.

64  Ibid., 81 (emphasis in original).

65  Ibid., 105.

66  Ibid.

67  Ibid., 110.

68  E & S, vol. 1, 223.

69  FMW, 128; E & S, vol. 3, 1402.

70  FMW, 139, 148.

71  Ibid., 142.

72  Ibid., 152.

73  Ibid., 155.

74  *Ancient Judaism*, trans. H.H. Gerth and Don Martindale (Glencoe, IL 1952), 299. I have slightly revised the translation.

75  Ibid., 301, 319.

76  *The Protestant Ethic*, 28, 39.

77  Ibid., 29.

# Notes on Contributors

THE EDITORS

**Asher Horowitz** is Associate Professor of Political Science at York University. He is the author of *Rousseau, Nature and History* (Toronto 1987) and with G. Horowitz of *'Everywhere They Are in Chains': Political Thought from Rousseau to Marx* (Nelson 1988).

**Terry Maley** has taught at York University, Trent University, and the Univerity of Waterloo. He is completing a PhD dissertation on Weber's political thought in the Department of Political Science at the University of Toronto and is a contributor to J. Braun, ed., *Psychological Aspects of Modernity* (Praeger 1993), and J. Braun, ed., *Social Pathology in Comparative Perspective: The Nature and Psychology of Civil Society* (Praeger, forthcoming 1995).

THE CONTRIBUTORS

**David Beetham** is Professor of Politics at Leeds University. His most recent books are *Bureaucracy* (Open University Press 1987) and *Legitimacy* (Macmillan Hyman 1989). His *Max Weber and the Theory of Modern Politics* has recently appeared in a second edition (Polity 1985).

**Fred Dallmayr** is Dee Professor of Government at the University of Notre Dame and has published widely on modern political thought. His recent books include *G.W.F. Hegel: Modernity and Politics* (Sage 1993), *The Other Heidegger* (Cornell 1993), and *Life-World, Modernity and Critique: Paths between Heidegger and the Frankfurt School* (Polity Press/Blackwell 1991).

**Gilbert Germain** is Assistant Professor of Political Studies at the University of Prince Edward Island. He is author of *A Discourse on Disenchantment* (SUNY Press 1993).

**Susan Hekman** is Professor of Political Science at the University of Texas at Arlington. She has published extensively on the philosophy of social science and is author of *Hermeneutics and the Sociology of Knowledge* (Polity 1986) and *Weber, the Ideal Type, and Contemporary Social Theory* (Notre Dame 1983) and, most recently, of *Gender and Knowledge: Elements of a Post-Modern Feminism* (Northeastern 1990).

**Alkis Kontos** is Associate Professor of Political Science at the University of Toronto. He has published on modern political thought from Machiavelli and Hobbes to Marcuse, Friedrich Dürenmatt, George Orwell, and Camus. He is editor of *Domination* (Toronto 1970) and *Powers, Possessions and Freedom* (Toronto 1975).

**Christian Lenhardt** is Associate Professor of Political Science and in the Social and Political Thought Program at York University. He is translator of Adorno's *Aesthetic Theory* (RKP 1984) and Habermas's *Moral Consciousness and Communicative Action* (MIT 1991), has published a number of articles on Critical Theory, and is editing a collection of essays on Adorno's aesthetics.

**Ray Morrow** is Associate Professor of Sociology at the University of Alberta and has published widely on critical theory and cultural studies and is the author of *Critical Theory and Methodology* (Sage 1994) and co-author (with C.A. Torres) of *Social Theory and Education* (SUNY, forthcoming 1995).

**Tracy Strong** is Professor of Political Science at the University of California at San Diego and the current editor of *Political Theory*. He has published extensively on modern political thought. Among his books are *Friedrich Nietzsche and the Politics of Transfiguration* (California 1975, 1988), *Towards New Seas: Philosophy, Aesthetics and Politics in Nietzsche* (Chicago 1990), and *Rousseau and the Politics of the Ordinary* (Sage 1994).

**Mark Warren** is Associate Professor of Government at Georgetown University. He has published articles on Nietzsche, Marx, Weber, and democratic theory and is author of *Nietzsche and Political Thought* (MIT 1988).

**Sheldon Wolin** has taught at Cornell University, Princeton University, and the University of California at Berkeley. He is best known for his *Politics and Vision*, was editor of *Democracy*, and has published widely in modern political theory.